David Jennings, Philip Furneaux

Jewish antiquities

David Jennings, Philip Furneaux

Jewish antiquities

ISBN/EAN: 9783337102357

Printed in Europe, USA, Canada, Australia, Japan

Cover: Foto ©Lupo / pixelio.de

More available books at **www.hansebooks.com**

JEWISH ANTIQUITIES:

OR A

Course of LECTURES

On the Three FIRST BOOKS of

GODWIN'S MOSES and AARON.

To which is annexed,

A

DISSERTATION

ON THE

HEBREW LANGUAGE.

By the late Rev. *DAVID JENNINGS*, D.D.

VOL. II.

LONDON:

Printed for J. JOHNSON and B. DAVENPORT, at the Globe in Paternoster-Row.

MDCCLXVI.

THE

CONTENTS

OF THE

SECOND VOLUME.

BOOK II.

Concerning Places.

BOOK III.

Concerning Times.

CHAP.

CONTENTS.

JEWISH

JEWISH ANTIQUITIES:

BOOK the SECOND

Concerning Places.

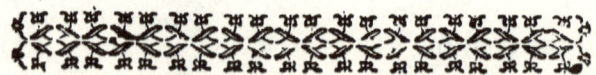

VOL. II.   B

CHAP. I.

Of the tabernacle and temple.

HAVING in the laſt book, given an account of the moſt remarkable civil and eccleſiaſtical perſons, officers and ſects among the Jews, we now proceed to the conſideration of the moſt eminent ſtructures, or places, which were eſteemed ſacred, or held in high veneration amongſt them. On this head, Godwin treats firſt of the tabernacle and temple, though indeed but imperfectly, eſpecially of the former: On the deſcription of whoſe ſtructure and ſumptuous furniture Moſes has beſtowed almoſt as many pages, as he has lines on his account of the creation of the world; no doubt, becauſe the tabernacle was a deſigned emblem of the bleſſings of the new creation, which far excelled thoſe of the old; or, as the apoſtle ſtiles it, was " a figure for the time then preſent (*a*)."

We have an account of three publick tabernacles, before the building of Solomon's temple;

B 2 The

(*a*) Heb. ix. 8, 9.

The firſt which Moſes erected for himſelf, ונטהילו venatah lo (a); and this the ſeptuagint calls την σκηνην αυτε. In this tabernacle he gave audience, heard cauſes, and enquired of God; and perhaps, alſo, the publick offices of reli- ·gious worſhip were performed in it for ſome time, and therefore, Moſes ſtiled it the taber- nacle of the congregation.

The ſecond tabernacle was that which Moſes built for God, by his expreſs command, part- ly to be a palace of his preſence as the king of Iſrael (b), and partly to be the medium of the moſt ſolemn publick worſhip, which the people were to pay to him (c). This tabernacle was erected on the firſt day of the firſt month of the ſecond year of the Iſraelites migration out of Egypt (d).

The third publick tabernacle was that which David erected in his own city, for the reception of the ark, when he received it from the houſe of Obededom (e).

It is the ſecond of theſe tabernacles we are now to treat of, called the tabernacle κατ' εξοχην, by way of diſtinction and eminence. It was a moveable chappel, ſo contrived as to be taken to pieces, and put together, at pleaſure, for the convenience of carrying it from place to place, during the wandering of the Iſraelites in the wilderneſs for forty years.

The learned Spencer * has fetched this taber- nacle, with all its furniture and appurtenances, from Egypt; ſuggeſting, that Moſes projected it after the faſhion of ſome ſuch ſtructure, which

he

_____

(a) Exod. xxxiii. 7.   (b) chap. xl. 34, 35.   (c) ver. 26,—29.   (d) ver. 2, 17.   (e) 2 Sam. vi. 17. 1 Chron. xvi. 1.
    * De legibus Hebr. Differt. 1.

he had obferved in that country, and which was
in ufe among other nations; or at leaft that
God directed it to be made with a view of in-
dulging the Ifraelites in a compliance with their
cuftoms and modes of worfhip, fo far as there
was nothing in them directly finful   And he
quotes both facred and profane writers, to prove
that the heathens had fuch portable temples, in
which they depofited the moft valuable facred
or religious utenfils.   Such a temple or tabernacle we read of in the prophecy of Amos :
" Ye have borne the tabernacle of Moloch and
Chiun, your images, the ftar of your god which
ye made to yourfelves (a)." It is indeed paft
difpute, that the heathens had fuch tabernacles,
as well as many other things, very like thofe
of the Jews, but that they had them before the
Jews, and efpecially that God condefcended fo
far to the humour of the Ifraelites, as to introduce them into his own worfhip, is neither
proved, nor is it probable. It is more likely,
that the heathens took thefe things from the
Jews, who had the whole of their religion immediately from God, than that the Jews, or
rather that God, fhould take them from the
heathens. Befides, this account of the origin
of the jewifh tabernacle and its furniture evidently thwarts the account which the apoftle
gives of the typical defign and ufe of them, in
the ninth chapter of the epiftle to the Hebrews.
And further, fuppofing thofe heathen tabernacles to have been more ancient, than that built
by Mofes by divine direction, yet, fo far from
there being any defign of complying with the
idolatrous heathen, the contrary rather appears,

B 3   in

(a) Amos v. 26.

in that this tabernacle was ordered to be directly the reverſe of theirs, both in its form and ſituation. In its form : for, whereas the heathen
tabernacles were carried about whole upon the
ſhoulders of the prieſts, this was to be taken to
pieces whenever it was to be removed. And as
to the ſituation : whereas it was the general
practice of the heathens to worſhip with their
faces towards the eaſt, God directed his tabernacle to be ſo placed, that the people ſhould
worſhip towards the weſt ; for to that point the
holy of holies ſtood, in which were the more
ſpecial ſymbols of God's preſence, and which
the people were to face as they worſhipped in
the court at the eaſt end of the tabernacle, where
was the altar of their ſacrifices : as will appear
hereafter. This detects a miſtake of Godwin's,
who makes our cathedral churches anſwer to
the jewiſh tabernacle or temple, the ſanctuary
reſembling the body of the church; the ſanctum
ſanctorum the choir ; and the court round a-
bout the tabernacle the church-yard ; it being
evident, that the form of theſe churches, in
which the choir or chancel is placed towards the
eaſt, is directly contrary to the jewiſh tabernacle and temple, and it is borrowed from the
heathens, who placed their ναιος to the eaſt, and
the προναιος to the weſt *. That the heathen
idolaters worſhipped towards the eaſt, appears
from the following paſſage of the prophet Ezekiel, " And he brought me into the inner
court of the Lord's houſe ; and behold at the
door of the temple of the Lord, between the
porch and the altar, were about five and twenty
men with their backs towards the temple of the
Lord,

* Vid. Vitruv. lib. iv. cap. v.

Lord, and their faces towards the east, and they worshipped the sun towards the east (*a*):" And from Virgil, who, giving an account of Æneas's sacrificing before the battle with Turnus, saith,

Illi ad furgentem converfi lumina folem,
Dant fruges manibus falfas, et tempora ferro
Summa notant pecudum, paterifque altaria li-
    bant,   Æneid. xii. l. 172,—174.

And accordingly many heathen temples have been converted into christian churches, without any alteration in the form of the building.

The tabernacle we are now to describe, though otherwife called a tent, becaufe it was a move-able fabric, and becaufe it had no proper roof, but was only covered with curtains or canopies of cloth and fkin, was nevertheless built with extraordinary magnificence, and at a prodigious expence, that it might be in fome meafure fuit-able to the dignity of the king whofe palace it was to be, and to the value of thofe fpiritual and eternal bleffings of which it was alfo de-figned as a type or emblem. The value of the gold and filver only, ufed for the work of that holy place, and of which we have an account in the book of Exodus (*b*), amounted, according to bifhop Cumberland's reduction of jewifh ta-lents and fhekels to englifh coin, to upwards of one hundred eighty two thoufand five hun-dred fixty eight pounds. If we add to this the vaft quantity of brafs, or copper, that was alfo ufed about this fabric, its court and furni-ture; the fhittim wood, of which the boards of the tabernacle, as well as the pillars which fur-
                    B 4   rounded

(*a*) Ezek. viii. 16,   (*b*) Exod. xxxviii. 24, 25.

rounded the court, and other utenſils were made, (which, though we do not know what name the ſame wood bears now, was no doubt the beſt and moſt coſtly that could be got,) as alſo the rich embroidered curtains and canopies that covered the tabernacle, divided the parts of it, and ſurrounded the court;—and if we further add the jewels that were ſet in the high prieſt's ephod and breaſtplate, which are to be conſidered as a part of the furniture of the tabernacle; the value of the whole materials, excluſive of workmanſhip, muſt amount to an immenſe ſum. This ſum was raiſed, partly by voluntary contributions and preſents (a), and partly by a poll tax of half a ſhekel a head for every male Iſraelite above twenty years old (b); which amounted to a hundred talents, and one thouſand ſeven hundred ſeventy five ſhekels, that is, thirty five thouſand three hundred fifty nine pounds, ſeven ſhillings and ſix pence ſterling (c).

We may here remark that this tax of the half ſhekel a man was, in after times, levied yearly for the reparation of the temple, and for defraying the charge of publick ſacrifices, and other neceſſaries of divine ſervice. This, as I have before obſerved *, was probably the tribute, demanded of our Saviour (d); from which, as it was paid to God for the ſervice of his houſe, and the ſupport of his worſhip, Chriſt, as being the Son of God, might, according to the cuſtom of all nations, have pleaded an exemption (e). However, that he might give no offence, he choſe to pay it, though he was obliged

---

(a) Exod. xxv. 2, &c.   (b) ch. xxx. 11,—16.
(c) ch. xxxviii. 25.
* See p. 86. Vol. I.
(d) Matt. xvii. 24.   (e) ver. 25, 26.

obliged to work a miracle to raife fo fmall a fum (a).

Upon this general view of the prodigious expence of building the tabernacle, it may naturally be enquired, whence had the Ifraelites, who had not been come a year from their flavery in Egypt, and from labouring at the brickkilns, riches enough to defray it? To this it may be anfwered †,

1ft. That though the bulk of the people had been reduced to the condition of flaves, yet it may be reafonably fuppofed, that fome, efpecially of the pofterity of Jofeph, had preferved, and, it may be, concealed their wealth, till they had an opportunity of efcaping with it out of Egypt.

2dly. Perhaps the wildernefs, where they now were, might fupply them with fome part of the materials for this building; in particular, the wood. Some tell us of a grove of fhittim trees near mount Sinai, from whence they had their wood, with no other expence, then that of labour.

3dly. Abarbanel conjectures, that the neighbouring nations came and traded with the Ifraelites in the wildernefs, and that God bleffed their commerce to the very extraordinary increafe of their opulence. But the fcriptures give no account of any ftrangers reforting to them at this time, befides Jethro and his family; probably the fate of their egyptian enemies terrified the other neighbouring nations, and made them afraid to come near them.

4thly. The fpoil of the Egyptians, who were drowned in the red fea, and whofe dead bodies were

_____

(a) Matt. xvii. 27.
† Vid. Witfii Mifcell. tom. i. lib. ii. Differt. i. § x.

were providentially caſt upon the ſhore, where
the Iſraelites were, might very conſiderably en-
rich them (a).

5thly, But we are chiefly to account for their
riches by their having brought out of Egypt a
very large quantity of gold and ſilver jewels,
or veſſels, as the word כלי chelè ſignifies, which
were lent, or rather given them, by the Egyptians at their departure. For by the command
of God (b), they " borrowed" or required " of
the Egyptians jewels," or veſſels " of ſilver
and veſſels of gold, and raiment. And the
Lord gave them favour in the ſight of the E-
gyptians, ſo that they lent," or gave " them
ſuch things as they required (c)." The verb
שאל ſhaal, which in Kal our tranſlators have
rendered " borrow," ſignifies more properly,
petere, to require or demand; and in Hiphil,
where they have rendered it " to lend," it denotes, mutuum dare, to give *. This ſenſe of
the verb, in both the conjugations, is warrant-
ed by the following paſſage, " The Lord, ſaith
Hannah in reference to the birth of Samuel,
hath given me my petition, which I aſked of
him, שאלתי, ſhaalti; therefore alſo I have
lent, השאלתיהו hiſhiltihu, given him to the
Lord as long as he liveth. He ſhall be lent,
שאול ſhaul, given to the Lord (d)." Now ſome
of thoſe veſſels, which were given to the Iſraelites, might probably be the ſilver bowls and
chargers and golden ſpoons, which were offered
by the princes for the ſervice of the tabernacle (e). By this means the divine prediction and
promiſe

(a) Exod. xiv. 30.   (b) ch. iii. 21.
(c) ch. xii. 35, 36.
* Vid. Stockii Clav. in verbum.
(d) 1 Sam. i. 27, 28.   (e) Numb. vii.

promife to Abraham was fignally accomplifhed,
" The nation whom thy feed fhall ferve, and
who fhall afflict them four hundred years, will
I judge, and afterwards they fhall come out
with great fubftance (a)."

Having cleared the ground, and provided the
proper funds for building the tabernacle, we
come now to erect the edifice, or rather to take
a view of it, as it was erected by Mofes according to the vifionary model fhewed him in
the mount (b).

The tabernacle was an oblong rectangular
figure, thirty cubits long, ten broad and ten in
height, which reduced to englifh meafure, according to Dr. Cumberland, who fuppofes it
the egyptian cubit, nearly equal to twenty two
inches *, was fifty five feet long, eighteen broad,
and eighteen high.   The two fides and one end
were compofed of broad boards, ftanding upright; each board being about two feet nine
inches broad, faftened at the bottom by two
tenons in each board, fitted into two mortices
in the foundation ; at the top by links or hafps,
and on the fides by five wooden bars, which
run through rings or ftaples in each of the
boards. The thicknefs of thefe boards is not
determined in fcripture. Dr. Lightfoot makes
it to be very great †; he fuppofes about nine
inches, becaufe the middle bar is faid to fhoot
" through the boards from one end to the o-
ther (c);" that is, as he conjectures, through a
hole in the body of the boards. And no doubt
they muft be of a very confiderable thicknefs,
if

(a) Gen. xv. 13, 14.   (b) Exod. xxv. 40.
* Effay on jewifh meafures, chap. 2. p. 56.
† See his Handful of gleanings upon Exodus, §. xxxiv.
(c) Exod. xxxvi. 33.

if they were pierced with a hole big enough to receive a wooden bar which, confidering its length of fifty five feet, could not be flender. But as boards or timbers of fuch a length and breadth, and of fuch a fuppofed thicknefs, would be almoft unmanageably heavy; may we not rather conceive, that the middle bar, fhooting through the boards from end to end, denotes only that it reached the whole length of the tabernacle, whereas the other bars reached but about, or little more than, half way. For though it is faid " the middle bar in the midft of the boards fhall reach from end to end (a),". there was no occafion they fhould all do fo.

Each fide confifted of twenty of thefe boards; and the end, of eight; which comes to about three feet more than the breadth of the tabernacle. Therefore if thefe eight boards ftood together in a right line, the end muft project confiderably on each fide of the building. But, perhaps the two end boards of the eight ftood in an angular pofition to the fides, and the end of the building; for which reafon they are diftinguifhed from the other fix, and called " the two boards of the corners of the tabernacle (b)." Thefe boards and thefe bars were all overlaid with gold; and their rings for the ftaves, and their hafps at top, were all of the fame metal.

The foundation on which they ftood, was alfo very coftly and magnificent. It confifted of folid blocks of filver, two under each board; they were each about fixteen inches long, and of a fuitable breadth and thicknefs; each weighing a talent, or about an hundred weight. Of thefe there were about an hundred in number,

ninety

(a) Exod. xxvi. 28.   (b) ver. 23.

ninety fix of which were laid for the foundation of the walls of the tabernacle, under the forty eight boards ; and the other four were the bafes of the columns that fupported the veil or curtain, which divided the infide of the tabernacle into two rooms (*a*)." From hence fome have derived the ancient fafhion of fetting porphyry columns on bafes of white marble.

The tabernacle, thus fitted and reared, had four different coverings, or curtains, or carpets thrown one over the other, which hung down on the fide near to the filver foundation.

The firft and loweft carpet was made of fine linnen, richly embroidered with figures of cherubim, in fhades of blue, purple and fcarlet. It is reafonable to fuppofe, that the right fide of this carpet was undermoft, and fo it formed a beautiful cieling in the infide of the tabernacle. This carpet confifted of ten breadths, which were joined together with blue loops and clafps of gold.

The next carpet, which lay over the embroidered one, was made of a fort of mohair ; the breadths of thefe were joined together with clafps of brafs.

The third carpet was made of ram's fkin dyed red ; and the uppermoft of all, which was to fence the reft from the weather, was made of tachafh fkins. What beaft this was is not certain ; it appears that fhoe leather was made of its fkin ; for God faith concerning Jerufalem, " I clothed thee with broidered work and fhod thee with badger's (tachafh) fkin (*b*)." It is conceived the latin word taxus, and the german tachs, may come from the hebrew תחש tachafh ;

(*a*) Exod. xxxviii. 27;   (*b*) Ezek. xvi. 10.

tachafh; therefore we tranflate it badger. However the Jews hold this to be a clean beaft,
which the badger is not.

Thus we have feen the outfide of the tabernacle compleat, on the top, the two fides, and
one end, namely, that which was fet towards
the weft, when the tabernacle was reared (*a*).
As for the eaft end, it had no boards; but was
fheltered with a fine embroidered curtain, hung
upon five pillars of fhittim wood overlaid with
gold (*b*). The text does not tell us how low
this curtain hung. Philo makes it to touch the
ground *; but Jofephus will have it to come
only half way down, that fo the people might
have a view of the infide of the tabernacle, and
of what was done there; but then he fays, there
was another curtain over that, which came
down to the ground, and was to preferve it
from the weather, that was drawn afide on the
fabbath and other feftivals ‡. Philo's opinion
is the more likely, fince we find, by the ftory of Zechariah's miniftry (*c*) in the temple,
(which was built after the model of the tabernacle,) that the people who were without, could
not fee into the fanctuary.

The infide of the tabernacle was divided into two rooms, by means of a veil or curtain,
hung upon four pillars mentioned before. This
veil was made of the richeft ftuff, both for matter and workmanfhip, and adorned with cherubim and other ornaments, curioufly embroidered

(*a*) Exod. xxvi. 22.　　　(*b*) ver. 36, 37.
　* Philo Jud. de vitâ Mofis, lib. iii. p. 516. D, E. edit.
Colon. Allobr. 1613.
　‡ Jofeph. Antiq. lib. iii. cap. vi. §. 4. p. 134. edit.
Haverc.
　(*c*) Luke i.

ed upon it. It does not appear, in the scripture
account, at what diftance from either end of
the tabernacle this veil was hung; but it is
reafonably conjectured, that it divided the tabernacle, in the fame proportion in which the
temple, afterwards built according to its model, was divided; that is, two thirds of the
whole length were allotted to the firft room,
and one third to the fecond; fo that the room
beyond the veil, which was called the holy of
holies, was exactly fquare, being ten cubits
each way; and the firft room, called the fanctuary, was twice as long as broad.

Round the tabernacle there was a fpacious
area, or court, of an hundred cubits long and
fifty broad, furrounded with pillars, fet in bafes
of brafs and filletted with filver, at the diftance
of five cubits from one another. So that there
were twenty pillars on each fide, and ten at
each end of the court. Thefe pillars had filver
hooks, on which the hangings were faftened,
that formed the inclofure of the court. Thefe
hangings were of fine twined linnen (a). The
word קְלָעִים kelangnim, which we render hangings, is fuppofed to mean open or net work,
from קלע kalang, fculpfit. Accordingly the
Targum tranflates it grate-work. So that this
inclofure did not wholly conceal the view of
the tabernacle, and of the worfhip performed
in the court, from the people that were without.

The entrance into this court was at the eaft
end, facing the tabernacle; where richer hangings, for the fpace of twenty cubits, were fupported by four of the pillars; and thefe were
not faftened like the reft of the hangings, but
made

(a) Exod. xxvii. 9;

made either to draw or lift up; the text does
not fay which, but the Jews believe the latter.

It is made a queftion, whether there was only one court, or more, furrounding the tabernacle. Mofes mentions but one; yet David
fpeaks of " the courts of the Lord " in the
plural number (a). Which hath led fome people to imagine, there were at leaft two; one
for the Levites, and the other for the people.
But this cannot be inferred with any certainty
from the word being in the plural number,
which is fo often ufed in the hebrew with a fin-
gular fignification, to denote the excellency of
the thing fpoken of. Or otherwife, Mofes's
account of but one court may be reconciled
with David's mentioning more then one; by an
eafy fuppofition, that after the fettlement in
Canaan, when the tabernacle was no longer to
be moved about as formerly, they inclofed it
and its court with a ftrong fence, at fome diftance without the pillars and hangings; which
formed an outward court, befides that in which
the tabernacle ftood.

Though the court furrounded the tabernacle
there is no reafon to fuppofe that the tabernacle
ftood in the centre of it; for there was no occafion for fo large an area at the weft end, as at
the eaft; where the altar of burnt offering ftood,
and feveral other utenfils of the facred fervice.
It is more probable, that the area at this end
was at leaft fifty cubits fquare; and indeed a
lefs fpace than that could hardly fuffice for the
work that was to be done there, and for the
perfons who were immediately to attend the fervice.

Having

(a) Pfal. lxxxiv. 2, 10. lxv. 4. et alibi.

Having defcribed the tabernacle and the court that furrounded it, we proceed now to take a view of the furniture that belonged to both.

The chief things in the court were the altar of burnt offering, and the brazen laver.   The altar of burnt offering, which is defcribed in the beginning of the twenty eighth chapter of Exodus, was placed towards the eaft end of the court, fronting the entrance of the tabernacle ; and we muft fuppofe, at fuch a convenient diftance from it, that the fmoke of the fire which was conftantly burning on the altar, might not fully that beautiful tent, its veil and curtains.

The dimenfions of the altar were five cubits, or about nine▬▬ feet fquare, and three cubits, or about five feet and an half high.   It was made of fhittim wood plated over with brafs, and it had four brafs rings, through which two bars were put, by which it was carried upon the priefts fhoulders.   It is defcribed with horns at the four corners, but what was the fhape and ufe of thefe horns is not now known ; perhaps they were for tying the victims, according to the allufion of the Pfalmift, " Bind the facrifice with cords even to the horns of the altar (*a*)."

The fire was kept upon a fquare grate, fufpended by rings at the corners, and, it may be, by chains in the cavity of the altar.   The fcripture account does not determine the dimenfions of this grate ; but if we fuppofe it to be five feet fquare, which probably was large enough for the ufe it was defigned for ; and if we allow fix inches for the thicknefs of the fides of the altar, there would be a fpace of one foot

(*a*) Pfal. cxviii. 27.

and an half betwixt the grate and the altar on
every fide; which was fufficient to preferve the
wooden fides, (efpecially as they were plated over
with brafs,) from being damaged by the fire on
the grate.

This grate is faid to be put under the compafs of the altar, as we underftand the word
כרכוב carcobh, in the only two places where
it occurs *(a)*. The meaning of it, therefore,
can hardly be conjectured, for want of parallel
places by which to fix it. Mr. Saurin fuppofes the
כרכוב carcobh might be a copper veffel, hung
by rings or chains to the altar over the fire on
the grate, in which the flefh of the victims was
confumed *.

But it is a material objection againft this
conjecture, that there are fome paffages, in
which it is enjoined, that the victims with the
head and the fat fhould be laid upon the wood;
that is, upon the fire, which is on the altar *(b)*.

Others, therefore, conceive the כרכוב carcobh
to be nothing but a kind of cincture to the
grate. Others, again, have imagined it to be
a fort of dome over the fire, contrived to collect the flame, and concenter the heat; fo as
to confume the vapour that would arife from
the flefh in burning, and thereby to prevent
that offenfive fmell which the burning fuch
quantities of flefh and fat muft otherways have
caufed. To ftrengthen this conjecture, the authors of the univerfal hiftory tell us, they have
feen in France a kind of portable hearth, not
unlike a chaffing difh, fo artfully contrived,
that

(a) Exod. xxvii. 5. and xxxviii. 4.
* See Saurin's difcours fur la Pentateuch, difc. liv. or
Chamberlayne's tranfation, p. 458.
(b) Levit. i. 8.

that the fire within (though not very fierce to outward appearance) confumed feathers, brimftone, and other like fetid materials, without caufing the leaft fmell *. Now if fuch a thing is poffible, it is not at all unlikely, there might be fome fuch contrivance in the altar, to prevent any offence from the fmell of the facrifices.

The fire on this altar was looked upon as facred, having firft defcended upon it from heaven (a). It was, therefore, to be kept conftantly burning, and never to go out. b). From hence, probably, the Chaldeans and Perfians borrowed their notion of their facred fire, which they preferved and nourifhed with religious care and attention; a cuftom which afterwards paffed from them to the Greeks and Romans.

The rabbies have recourfe to a miracle, to account for the preferving of the facred fire in their marches in the wildernefs, when the altar was covered with a purple cloth and a covering of badger's fkins (c). But it may be as well accounted for, by fuppofing, that the grate with the fire, was on thefe occafions taken out of the altar, and carried by itfelf.

The other confiderable utenfil in the court of the tabernacle, was the brazen laver, defcribed in the thirtieth chapter of Exodus (d). The place of this laver was betwixt the altar and the eaft end of the tabernacle. Neither the fhape, nor fize of it, is mentioned by Mofes; probably it was confiderably capacious, fince it was

C 2   for

* Univerf. hiftory, Vol. 1. part 2. p. 662. folio edit.
(a) Lev. ix. 24.   (b) chap. vi. 13.   (c) Numb.
iv. 13, 14.   (d) Exod. xxx. 18,—21.

for the ufe of all the priefts to wafh their hands
and feet, before they performed their miniftry.

It is faid, that Mofes " made the laver of
brafs, and the foot of it of brafs, of the looking glaffes of the women, who affembled at the
door of the tabernacle of the congregation (a)."
Such were the ancient mirrours, made of polifhed brafs, or other metal * ; which gave but a
dark or obfcure image, in comparifon of glafs
mirrours. Hence we read of " feeing through
a glafs darkly (b)," or rather " in or by a
glafs," as δι' εσοπτρε fignifies.

As for the cuftom of the women's affembling
at the door of the tabernacle of the congregation, that is, the tabernacle of Mofes, (for it
was before the tabernacle of the Lord was
reared) fome derive it from a cuftom of the
egyptian women, who, (if we may credit Cyril
of Alexandria,) ufed to go to the temple with
looking glaffes in one hand, and a timbrel in
the other †.

The rabbies have reprefented it as very meritorious in thefe jewifh women, devoutly to
facrifice the moft precious ornament of their
toilets to holy ufes (c). Others have fufpected
a graphical error in the word במראת bema-
roth, " of the looking glaffes," namely, that
the prefix ב beth may have flipped into the
text, inftead of כ caph, by reafon of the fimilitude

***

(a) Exod. xxxviii. 8.

* Vid. Ezek. Spanheim. Obferv. in Callimach. hymnum
in Pallad. v. 21. p. 548,—550. edit. Ultraject. 1697.
octav. The targum of Jonathan renders the text laft
quoted, ex æreis fpeculis.

(b) 1 Cor. xiii. 12.

† Vid. Cyril. de Adoratione in fpiritu et virtute, tom. 1.
lib. 2. p. 64.

(c) Vid. Aben-ezra in Exod. xxxviii. 8.

litude of thofe letters; and to ftrengthen this conjecture they obferve, that ב beth is very feldom ufed to exprefs the metal or ftuff of which any thing is made; though fometimes, it muft be owned, it is*; as, on mentioning the brafs which David collected, it is added, wherewith, בה bah, " Solomon made the brazen fea, &c (a)." And it is faid of Afa, that " he carried away the ftones and timber of Ramah, wherewith Baafha was a building, and therewith, בהם baham, built Geba and Mizpah (b)." They fuppofe, however, the true reading of this place was כמראת chemaroth, and if fo, the proper rendering would be " Mofes made the laver of brafs AS or LIKE the looking glaffes of the women," that is, he finely polifhed it.

Having thus taken a view of the two moft confiderable things in the court, let us now enter into the tabernacle; where in the fanctuary, or firft room, we fee the altar of incenfe, the golden candleftick, and the table of fhew bread.

1ft, The altar of incenfe (c) was made of fhittim wood and overlaid with gold. It was one cubit fquare, and two high, with an ornament of gold, in the nature, we may fuppofe, of a carved moulding, round the top of it. The ufe of it was to burn incenfe upon every morning and evening. It was alfo to be fprinkled with the blood of the facrifices, that were offer-

---

* Vid. Noldii Concordant. Particul. in partic. ב, fignif. 14, ex, è, Materiæ. And Aben-ezra vindicates this fenfe of ב in the place before us. Vid. Cartwright. Electa targum. rabbin. in loc.

(a) 1 Chron. xviii. 8.   (b) 2 Chron. xvi. 6.

(c) See the defcription of it in Exod. xxx. 1,—10.

ed for the ſins of ignorance, committed either by particular perſons, or by the people in general (a).

2dly, The golden candleſtick (b) was the richeſt piece of furniture in the tabernacle. It was made of ſolid gold, to the weight of a talent ; and excluſive of the workmanſhip, which was very curious, it was worth, according to Cumberland, upwards of five thouſand, ſeventy ſix pounds. It contained ſeven lights, ſix branching out in three pairs, from the upright ſtem, and one on the top of it. This was a moſt uſeful, as well as moſt ornamental, piece of furniture in a room that had no windows.

3dly, The table of ſhew bread (c) was made of the ſame ſort of wood with the altar of incenſe, and like that overlaid and ornamented with gold. Its dimenſions were two cubits long ; one broad, and one and an half high. It is ſaid to have a golden border, or crown, which may be ſuppoſed to be a kind of rim round it, ſomething like that of our tea-tables. Upon this table were ſet two rows or piles of loaves, or cakes of bread, ſix in a row or pile, which were changed for new ones every ſabbath. The ſtale bread belonged to the prieſts.

This table was alſo furniſhed with golden diſhes, ſpoons and bowls, of the uſe of which we have no certain account. Perhaps they were uſed about the holy oil, which was kept in the tabernacle (d), and very probably upon this table. Perhaps, alſo, this was the place of the book

(a) Exod. xxx. 10. Lev. iv. 3, 7, 13, 18.
(b) Deſcribed Exod. xxv. 31, et ſeq.
(c) Deſcribed Exod. xxv. 23,—30.
(d) See 1 Kings i. 39.

book of the law of the kingdom, which Samuel wrote, and laid up before the Lord (a).

We now go, through the second veil, into the holy of holies; where we are to view the ark of the teſtimony, and its lid or cover, called " the mercy ſeat (b)."

The ark was a cheſt of fine proportion, two cubits and an half long, one and an half broad, and one and an half high. It was made of ſhittim wood, but plated over with gold, both within and without, and richly ornamented with curious workmanſhip. Its chief uſe was to be a repoſitory for the two tables of ſtone, on which were engraven the ten commandments by the finger of God himſelf, and which he gave to Moſes on mount Sinai (c). Theſe are called the tables of teſtimony (d), not only as they were a witneſs and laſting monument of the covenant between God and the people of Iſrael, but as they would in effect teſtify againſt them, if they kept not that covenant. For this end alſo the book of the law, which Moſes wrote, is ordered to be laid in or by the ſide of the ark ; that it " might be there for a witneſs againſt the diſobedient (e)." From theſe tables the ark, in which they were preſerved, is called the ark of the teſtimony (f) ; and the lid of this cheſt, which covered theſe tables of the law, is called " the mercy ſeat," as fitly repreſenting the effect of God's mercy to the tranſgreſſors of his law ; or the covering, (as it were) of their tranſgreſſions. And hence the word ιλαςηριον, by which the ſeptuagint renders

C 4

the

(a) 1 Sam. x. 25.
(b) Both theſe are deſcribed in Exod. xxv. 10,—21.
(c) Exod. xxv. 16.   (d) chap. xxxi. 18,   (e) Deut. xxxi. 26.   (f) Exod. xxx. 6.

the mercy feat, and which is used for it by the
apoſtle, in the epiſtle to the Hebrews (a), is
likewiſe given to Chriſt in the epiſtle to the Romans (b); inaſmuch as, by his death, he hath
ſo covered the tranſgreſſions of his people, that
they ſhall not be puniſhed for them.

The upper face of the mercy feat was a-
dorned with two figures of cherubim, either
in chaſed work, as ſome think, or in ſtatuary,
as it is more commonly underſtood, and as
ſeems moſt agreeable to the deſcription of them
in the book of Exodus (c).

We have no ſufficient light in ſcripture abſo-
lutely to determine the form, the poſture, or
the ſize of theſe cherubim.

As to their ſize, indeed, ſince they are deſcribed as having wings, and their wings are
ſaid, when ſtretched forth on high, to cover
the mercy feat, of which we know the dimenſions, upon the reaſonable ſuppoſition that their
wings were in a juſt proportion to their bodies, we may form ſome idea of their bigneſs.

As to their poſture, their faces are ſaid " to
be towards one another and towards the mercy
feat; " which probably means that they ſtood
in an erect poſture on the mercy feat, with their
faces towards each other, and both of them
with their heads ſomewhat inclined, as looking
down upon, contemplating and admiring the
myſteries typified by the ark and mercy feat on
which they ſtood. This may give occaſion to
the alluſion of St. Peter, when ſpeaking of the
myſte-

(a) Heb. ix. 5.
(b) Rom. iii. 25. where our tranſlators render it, propi-
tiation.
(c) Exod. xxv. 18,—20.

myfteries of redemption he fays " which things the angels defire to look into (a)."

But we are at the greateft lofs of all to determine the true fhape and form of thefe cherubim. Some, upon obferving that the verb כרב charabh, in the fyriac language, fometimes means, fimulavit, conceive the noun כרוב cherubh, fignifies no more than an image, figure, or reprefentation of any thing. Aben Ezra is of this opinion *. Jofephus fays, they were flying animals, like none of thofe which are feen by men, but fuch as Mofes faw about the throne of God †. In another place he fays, " As for the cherubim, nobody can tell or conceive what they were like ‡." However, the generality of interpreters both ancient and modern, fuppofe them to be of a human fhape, only with the addition of wings §. The reafon of which fuppofition is perhaps, chiefly, becaufe Mofes defcribes them as having faces; though that will by no means prove the point, becaufe faces are attributed to beafts as well as to men. It is certain, that what Ezekiel, in one place, reprefents as the face of an ox, in another he reprefents as the face of a cherub (b). From whence others have conceived the cherubim to be rather of the fhape of flying oxen; and it is alledged in favour of this opinion,

that

(a) 1 Pet. i. 12.

* See the reafons on which Aben-ezra grounds his opinion in Chriftoph. Cartwright. electa targum. rabbin. in Exod. xxv. 18.

† Antiq. lib. iii. cap. vi. §. 5. p. 135, 136. edit. Havercamp.

‡ Antiq. lib. viii. cap. iii. §. 3. p. 424. edit. Haverc.

§ That this was the opinion of feveral rabbies, fee in Cartwright ubi fupra.

(b) Ezek. i. 10. compared with chap. x. 14, 15.

that the far more common meaning of the verb
כרב charabh, in the Arabic, Syriac and Chaldee, being to plow, the natural meaning of
כרוב cherubh is a creature ufed in plowing,
which in the eaftern countries was generally the
ox *.   This feems to have been the ancient
opinion, which tradition had handed down,
concerning the fhape of the cherubim with the
flaming fword, that guarded the tree of life (a).
And Ovid's fable concerning Jafon's golden
fleece being guarded by brazen-footed bulls,
which breathed out fire, was, perhaps, grounded upon it.

Ecce adamanteis Vulcanum naribus efflant
Æripides tauri.
                    Metamorph. lib. vii. l. 104.

We obferve further, that as Ezekiel defcribes
the face of a cherub and the face of an ox as
the fame, fo St. John, in his defcription of the
four ζωα or living creatures, which he faw in
his vifion, and which feem in all refpects to
anfwer to the four living creatures in Ezekiel's
vifion, calls that the calf, which Ezekiel calls
the ox or cherub (b).   From hence we may
give a probable account of the ftrangeft part
of the ftory of Jeroboam's idolatry, his fetting
up the two golden calves for objects of worfhip in Dan and Bethel (c).   I call it the
ftrangeft part, becaufe it appears wonderful,
not only that Jeroboam himfelf fhould be fo
ftupid as to fet up calves for gods, but that the
                                        bulk

---

* Bochart. Hierozoic. part. i. lib. ii. cap. xxxv. oper.
tom. 2. p. 358. edit. 1712.
  (a) Gen. iii. 24.   (b) Rev. iv. 7.
  (c) 1 Kings xii. 28, 29.

bulk of the nation fhould fo readily fall into
fuch fenfelefs idolatry : but it relieves our conceptions, if we confider thefe calves as nothing
but cherubim, the very fame fort of figures
that were placed in the temple by God's own
appointment; fo that Jeroboam not only fet
up the worfhip of the fame God, and in the
fame modes and forms that were practifed at
Jerufalem, but the fame fymbols of the divine
prefence, to which the people had been accuf-
tomed. It is therefore no wonder they fo generally fell in with him in fome little alterations, particularly as to the place of their moft
folemn publick worfhip; efpecially if we attend to the plaufible things he might alledge
on this head: namely, that it was an ufual
practice of the holy patriarchs to build altars,
and to worfhip God, wherever they came and
made any ftay.   Abraham facrificed in She-
chem, and at Bethel, in the plain of Mamre;
and at Beerfheba.   The ark and the tabernacle
were many years at Shiloh, and there the people facrificed.   It was from thence moved to
Kirjath-jearim, and after that to feveral other
places; in all which facrifices were offered to
God with acceptance.   At length David, and
then Solomon his fon, having chofen to fix
their court at Jerufalem, and to have the temple near to the royal palace, it was built in that
city.   However, the whole land is holy; and
they fhould not be fo fuperftitious, as to imagine the prefence of God is limited to one place
more than another; but wherever his pure worfhip is performed, he would meet his people,
and blefs them.   Or if it fhould be alledged,
that Solomon had built the temple at Jerufalem
by the exprefs appointment of God, might
not

not Jeroboam reply, that Solomon had so defiled that city by his lewdness and his idola-
tries, that it was now become an impure place;
and any other therefore might surely be as proper for the most solemn worship, especially Bethel, the house of God, the place where he
had anciently chose to dwell * ? Thus might
Jeroboam vindicate his conduct, perhaps as
well as any will worshipper could ever do.
Nevertheless, as he went contrary to a divine
institution, his cherubim are contemptuously
called calves, and he is frequently branded,
as that great sinner who made Israel to sin;
which should be a caution to us by no means
to depart from, but to keep close to, divine
institutions in all matters of religious worship †.

To

* The greatest part of the speech which I have put into
the mouth of Jeroboam is taken from Josephus, who seems
to have supposed, that the sin of this prince was not wor-
shipping another God; but, for political reasons, worship-
ping the true God in a manner contrary to his institution. Joseph. Antiq. lib. viii. cap. viii. p. 445. edit. Havercamp.

† Concerning the figure of the cherubim, and the sin
of Jeroboam, in erecting such in Dan and Bethel, in imitation of those at Jerusalem, see Moncæus de Vitulo aureo, cap. iv,—ix. apud Criticos sacros, tom. ix. p. 4429
et seq. In cap. x, et seq. he answers the objections to his
opinion. A short abstract of what he offers on the subject,
may be seen in Pool's synopsis on 1 Kings xii. 29. It is
remarkable that the author, who was a papist, takes occasion from this sin of Jeroboam, to harangue the protestants, and the king of Great Britain in particular, on the
heinous guilt of schism. There would have been more
propriety in his addressing the church of Rome, and her
infallible head, the Pope, on the guilt of abrogating, or
dispensing with divine institutions.——Consult likewise on
this subject Bochart. Hierozoic. part. i. lib. ii. cap. xxxv.
oper. tom. 2. p. 354,—360.

To return to the cherubim. Clemens of Alexandria seems to have been of opinion, that the egyptian sphynx, and other hieroglyphical beasts, were borrowed from these cherubim and those in Ezekiel's vision *. Hence it appears that he did not take them to be, entirely at least, of a human form and shape †.

It was betwixt these two cherubim over the mercy seat, that the Schechinah, or miraculous light, used to appear, as the visible token of the special presence of God ‡. From whence he

---

* Strom. lib. v. apud oper. p. 566, 567. edit. Paris. 1641.

† On this head consult Dr. Watts on the figure of a cherub, in his remnants of time improved, in his works, vol. 4. and Witsii Ægyptiaca, lib. ii. cap. xiii.

‡ This Schechinah, or visible glory of Jehovah after it had conducted the Israelites through the wilderness, (see vol. 1. p. 23.) had its more stated residence in the tabernacle, and the temple. For a further account of this miraculous phænomenon, consult part ii. chap. ii. of Mr. Lowman's rational of the hebrew ritual. There are some remarkable things in Lord Barrington's dissertation on God's visible presence, at the end of the second edit. of his essay, and in p. 39, of his essay, note 12. where he hath endeavoured to trace this divine appearance from the creation till a little after the flood, and from the giving of the law to the destruction of the first temple. Toland's attempt to prove that this apprehended miraculous appearance had nothing miraculous in it, but was only a kind of beacon made use of by the Israelites for their direction in their journey, (see his " Hodegus, or pillar of cloud and fire not miraculous," in his piece, called Tetradymus,) was answered in a pamphlet, called " Hodegus confuted, or a plain demonstration, that the pillar of cloud and fire, that guided the Israelites in the wilderness, was not a fire of human preparation, but the most miraculous presence of God ;" published 1721. 8vo. And likewise in " A Discourse upon the pillar of cloud and fire, &c." inserted in the Bibliotheca literaria, 1723. Numb. v. p. 1. and following. The sentiments of the jewish writers upon this subject may be seen in Buxtorf. exercitat. de arcâ fœderis.

he is faid to " dwell between the cherubim(a)," and " to fit betwixt the cherubim (b)." In confequence of which the people are called up-on to worfhip at his footftool (c); that is, the ark and the mercy feat.

We have before obferved, that the two ta-bles of the law, which God gave to Mofes, were depofited in the ark under the mercy feat; and with them were laid up, it fhould feem in the fame cheft, the golden pot that had manna, and Aaron's rod that budded. For the author of the epiftle to the Hebrews, fpeaking of the tabernacle, σκηνη η λεγομενη αγια αγιων, which is called the holieft of all, which had the golden cenfer, and the ark, την κιβωτον, of the cove-nant, adds, wherein εν η, was the pot, that had manna, and Aaron's rod that budded, and the tables of the covenant (d). But how to recon-cile this paffage, if we underftand it to affert, that the pot of manna, and Aaron's rod were laid up in the ark, with the affertion in the firft book of kings, that there was nothing in the ark fave the two tables of ftone which Mo-fes put there at Horeb (e), is fomewhat diffi-cult. Some fay, the apoftle fpeaks of the ark as it was in the time of Mofes; the text in kings, as it was in Solomon's time, when up-on fome occafion or other the pot of manna and Aaron's rod had been taken out of it. But this is hardly probable. Therefore εν η, in which, muft either fignify, " near to which;" in which fenfe the particle εν is fometimes ufed*: or rather, I apprehend, εν η, in which, refers, not to κιβωτον, the

(a) Pfal. lxxx. 1.   (b) Pfal. xcix. 1.   (c) ver. 5.
(d) Heb. ix. 3, 4.   (e) 1 Kings viii. 9.
* See Whitby in loc.

the ark, immediately preceding, but to the remote antecedent, σκηνη η λεγομενη αγια αγιων the second tabernacle or holy of holies; and is parallel to the expreſſion, which juſt before occurs, σκηνη γαρ κατεσκευαϑη η πρωτη, "there was a firſt tabernacle made, wherein, εν η, was the candleſtick, and the table, &c."

That the tabernacle and all its furniture were typical and emblematical of ſpiritual bleſſings *, we are aſſured by the apoſtle (a). But for the particular meaning of theſe ſeveral myſteries we refer to Witſius's diſſertation de tabernaculi myſteriis, in the firſt volume of his miſcellanea †.

Of the temple.

Having taken a ſurvey of the tabernacle, we proceed to the temple at Jeruſalem, which was built much after the model of the former edifice, but every way in a more magnificent and expenſive manner.

According to the opinion of ſome perſons, there were three different temples; the firſt built by David and Solomon; the ſecond, by Zerubbabel and Joſhua the high prieſt; and the third by Herod, a little before the birth of Chriſt. The Jews acknowledge only two ‡; for they do not allow the third to be a new temple, but only the ſecond rebuilt. And this beſt agrees
with

---

* Vid. Deyling. obſerv. ſacr. part. i. obſer. xvii. p. 69.

(a) Heb. ix. 9. x. 1. et alibi.

† On this ſubjeƈt conſult Buxtorf's exercitat. de arca fœderis. And with reſpeƈt to the tabernacle, as well as all its furhiture, read Joſeph. Antiq. lib. iii. cap. vi.

‡ Vid. Reland. antiq. hebr. part. i. cap. vi. §. ii. p. 59, edit. 1717. and the paſſages of the talmud there quoted.

with the prophecy of Haggai (a), that " the glory of this latter house, namely, Zerubbabel's temple, should be greater than that of the former ;" which undoubtedly was said in reference to the Meſſiah's honouring it with his perſonal preſence and miniſtry.

The firſt temple was built by David and Solomon. David provided materials for it before his death, and Solomon raiſed the edifice. It ſtood on mount Zion (b), which was the general name of a range of hills in that neighbourhood. The name of that particular hill, on which the temple ſtood, was Moriah (c). The Jews will have it to be the very ſpot, on which Abraham went about to ſacrifice Iſaac ; and where Adam paid his firſt devotions after his creation, and ſacrificed after his fall. This hill had been purchaſed by David of Araunah, or Ornan, king of the Jebuſites (d).

It is remarkable, that though in the ſecond book of Samuel, we have an account that " David purchaſed the threſhing floor of Ornan, with the oxen, for fifty ſhekels of ſilver (e) ;" in the firſt book of Chronicles it is ſaid, " he gave to Ornan for the place, ſix hundred ſhekels of gold (f)." To ſolve this difficulty, ſome learned men, obſerving that the words כסף kaſſaph and זהב zahab which we render ſilver and gold in theſe two paſſages, are both uſed, ſometimes, for money in general, imagine that the former ſum was fifty ſhekels of gold, and the latter ſix hundred ſhekels

of

(a) Hag. ii. 9.   (b) Pſal. cxxxii. 13, 14.
(c) 2 Chron. iii. 1.
(d) 2 Sam. xxiv. 23. where the literal verſion is, " All this did Araunah the king give unto the king."
(e) 2 Sam. xxiv. 24.   (f) 1 Chron. xxi. 25.

of filver; and if fo, both amount to much the fame value, about five hundred forty feven pounds. But it feems an eafier and more natural fuppofition; that the former fum was for the floor, oxen and wooden inftruments only, and the latter was afterwards paid for the whole hill, whereon David chofe to build the temple *.

The expence of erecting this magnificent ftructure was prodigious; and indeed, according to the common acceptation of the fcripture account, next to incredible; the gold and filver only, which was provided for that purpofe, amounting to upwards of eight thoufand millions fterling (a); which, fays Dr. Prideaux, was fufficient to have built the whole temple with folid filver †; and greatly exceeds all the treafures of all the monarchs in chriftendom.

But it may be obferved that the number of thefe talents, by which the gold and filver is computed, is mentioned only in the book of chronicles, which was undoubtedly written after the return from the babylonifh captivity, as appears from its mentioning Cyrus's decree for the building the temple (b), and from its

Vol. II.   D   carry-

---

* Capel in his Critica Sacra, lib. i. cap. x. §. x. p. 37. fuppofes, that thefe different numbers are owing to the blunder of fome tranfcriber, and are therefore moft eafily reconciled by admitting a various lection. And many of this learned man's conjectures, to his immortal honour, are confirmed by the hebrew manufcripts, as Dr. Kennicott hath had occafion to obferve; and perhaps this may appear in various other inftances, when that gentleman hath finifhed his great work of the collation, in which he is now engaged.

(a) 1 Chron. xxii. 14.   xxix. 4, 6, 7.

† Prideaux's connect. part 1. book 1. vol. 1. p. 7, 8. note (q).

(b) 2 Chron. xxxvi. 22, 23.

carrying the genealogy beyond Zerubbabel, who was one of the chiefs that returned from Babylon (*a*); and it is not therefore improbable, that at the time of writing this book the Jews might compute by the babylonish talent, which was little more than half the mosaic talent, or perhaps by the syriac talent, which was but one fifth of the babylonish; and thus the whole mass of gold and silver would be reduced to a comparatively moderate quantity, and yet be abundantly sufficient to build a most magnificent temple.

The plan, and the whole model of this structure was laid by the same divine architect, as that of the tabernacle, namely, God himself (*b*). We may reasonably therefore conclude, it was the compleatest building that was ever erected; and it is no improbable conjecture of those who are for deriving all the grecian orders, and just ornaments in architecture from this temple.

It was built, as was said before, much in the same form with the tabernacle, only every way of larger dimensions. It was surrounded, except the front, or east end, with three stories of chambers, each five cubits square, which reached to half the height of the temple; and the front was graced with a magnificent portico, which rose to the height of an hundred and twenty cubits. So that the shape of the whole was not unlike some churches we have seen, which have a lofty tower in the front, and a lower isle running along each side of the building.

The utensils for sacred service were the same as in the tabernacle; only several of them, as

the

(*a*) 1 Chron. iii. 19.　　- (*b*) chap. xxviii. 11, 12.

the altar, candleſtick, &c. were larger, in proportion to the more ſpacious edifice to which
they belonged. This firſt temple was at length
plundered by Nebuchadnezzar king of Babylon
of all its rich furniture, and the building itſelf
deſtroyed, after it had ſtood, according to Joſephus, four hundred and ſeventy years ſix
months and ten days from its dedication *.
Though other chronologers, as particularly
Calviſius and Scaliger, reduce the number of
years to four hundred twenty ſeven or eight;
and Uſher to four hundred twenty four, three
months and eight days †.

The ſecond temple was built by the Jews upon their return from the babyloniſh captivity,
under the influence and direction of Zerubbabel
their governor, and of Joſhua the high prieſt,
with the leave and by the encouragement of
Cyrus the perſian emperor, to whom Judæa
was now become a tributary kingdom. This
is that Cyrus, of whom Iſaiah had prophecied
by name two hundred years before he was born,
and had predicted his encouraging the rebuilding Jeruſalem and the temple (a). It is probable, that Daniel had ſhewed Cyrus this prophecy, and that Cyrus refers to it in his procla-
mation for rebuilding the temple: " The Lord
God, ſaith he, hath given me all the kingdoms
of the earth, and charged me to build him a
houſe in Jeruſalem (b)." He alſo reſtored the
ſacred utenſils, which Nebuchadnezzar had put
in the temples of his God; and not only gave
leave to the Jews to rebuild their temple, but

     encou-

---

* Antiq. lib. x. cap. viii. §. 5. p. 528. edit. Haverc.
† Uſſer. Annal. A. M. 3416. p. 71. and Scaliger. de
emend. temp. p. 400. edit. Colon. Allobr. 1629.
     (a) Iſai. xliv. 28. xlv. 1.   (b) Ezra i. 2.

encouraged his own people to affift them with
prefents, for carrying on the work (*a*). Upon
which the foundation of a new building was
laid with great rejoicing of the people ; only
fome old men who remembered the glory of
Solomon's temple, and had no expectation that
this, which was erecting by a few poor ex-
iles, juft returned to their own country, could
ever equal that in magnificence, wept with a
loud voice, while others were fhouting with
joy (*b*). However, the work, which was thus
chearfully begun, went on but flowly, partly
for want of zeal for God's honour and worfhip,
for which they were reproved by the prophets
Haggai and Zechariah ; and partly alfo, through
the envy and malice of their neighbours, the
Samaritans, who by their ill offices at court prevailed with the emperor to put a ftop to the
work (*c*). At length, after an intermiffion of
about thirteen years, it was vigoroufly reaffum-
ed under the encouragement of the emperor
Darius, and compleatly finifhed in the fixth
year of his reign (*d*). Upon which the new
remple was dedicated with great folemnity and
much rejoicing (*e*).

That there was really a very confiderable
difference and difparity betwixt the old, and
this new temple, is very certain, not only from
the old men's lamentation before mentioned,
but from the following paffage of the prophet
Haggai, " Who is left amongft you, that faw
this houfe in its firft glory ? And how do you
fee it now ? Is it not in your eyes in comparifon
of

(*a*) Ezra i. 4.   (*b*) chap. iii. 12, 13.
(*c*) chap. iv. 23, 24.   (*d*) chap. vi. 15.
(*e*) ver. 16, 17.

of it, as nothing (*a*)?" And also from the promise which God gave them, in order to comfort them on this occasion, that he would raise the glory of this latter temple above that of the former, by the presence of the Messiah in it (*b*).

The Jews tell us, the second temple wanted five remarkable things, which were the chief glory of the first temple:—the ark and mercy-seat:—the divine presence, or visible glory in the holy of holies, which they call the Shechinah:—the holy fire on the altar, which had been first kindled from heaven:—the urim and thummim:—and, the spirit of prophecy.

This temple was plundered and wretchedly profaned by Antiochus Epiphanes, who not only rifled it of all its riches, but caused it to be polluted by sacrificing swines flesh upon the altar. He also caused the publick worship in it to cease *.

It was afterward purified, and the divine worship restored, by Judas Maccabeus; on which occasion the temple, or at least the altar, was dedicated anew; and an annual festival was instituted in commemoration of this happy event. This is the feast of dedication, which we read of in the gospel of St. John (*c*), and which is said to be in winter; and could not therefore be kept in remembrance of the dedication of the temple of Solomon; for that was in the seventh month, which is just after harvest (*d*): nor of Zerubbabel's temple, which was dedicated in the month Adar, in the spring.

D 3

It

(*a*) Haggai ii. 3.　　(*b*) ver. 9.
* Joseph. Antiq. lib. xii. cap. v. §. 4. p. 609. edit. Haverc. and 1 Maccab. i. 20,—24. 45,—47.
(*c*) John x. 22.　　(*d*) 1 Kings viii. 2.

It muft, therefore, be the feftival, which was
inftituted, by Judas Maccabeus on his having
purified the temple and altar from the pollution
of Antiochus. This feaft was celebrated for
eight days fucceffively, from the twenty fifth
day of the month Cafleu, anfwering to our december (a). And it is alfo mentioned by Jofephus, as a feftival to, which great regard was
paid in his time *... This feftival is ftill obferved by the Jews; yet not as a time of rejoicing,
but of mourning, on account of the deftruction
of their temple, and the calamities which have
befallen their nation. :

When this fecond temple was grown old, and
out of repair, having ftood five hundred years,
king, Herod, in order to ingratiate himfelf with
the Jews, and, to perpetuate his own memory,
offered to rebuild it : Which brings us ..

Thirdly, to Herod's temple; which was a
far more magnificent ftructure than Zerubbabel's, and came much nearer to the glory of
Solomon's. Tacitus, the roman hiftorian, calls
it "Immenfæ opulentiæ templum," a temple
of immenfe opulence †. Jofephus fays it was
the moft aftonifhing ftructure he had ever feen
or heard of, as well on account of its architecture as its magnitude, and likewife the richnefs
and magnificence of its various parts, and the
fame, and reputation of its facred appurtenances §. As for rabbi Jehuda, the compiler
of the talmud, and other more modern writers,
who have given us defcriptions of this temple,

(a) 1 Maccab. iv. 59.
* Antiq. lib. xii. cap. vii. §. 7. p. 617. edit. Haverc.
† Tacit. hiftor. lib. v. §. viii. p. 202. edit. Glafg. 1743.
§ Jofeph. de bell. judaic. lib. vi. cap. iv. §. 8. p. 386.
edit. Haverc.

ple, which none of them had ever feen; we can have little dependence on their accounts; efpecially as they differ, fo much from one another, each having in a manner erected a feparate edifice; to which one cannot help fufpecting that the ftrength of imagination has fometimes contributed more largely, than the knowledge of hiftory. But Jofephus was himfelf a prieft in the temple he defcribes, and wrote foon after its deftruction, when if he had given a falfe, or remarkably inaccurate account, he might have been contradicted by numbers, who had viewed it as well as himfelf. For that reafon, he is to be credited beyond any of the reft *; though one cannot avoid fufpecting, that even in his defcription, there is fome panegyrick exceeding the bounds of truth, intermixed with faithful and exact narrative; for inftance, when he tells us of fome ftones in the building, forty five cubits long, five high, and fix broad. That there were, indeed, fome extraordinary large ftones may be collected from the following paffage of the evangelift Mark, "And as he went out of the temple, one of his difciples faith unto him, mafter, fee what manner of ftones, and what buildings are here! (a)" And in Luke they are ftiled "goodly ftones (b)." But I apprehend, it would puzzle all the mathematicians of the prefent age, to contrive machines by which ftones of fuch prodigious weight and fize, as thofe mentioned by Jofephus, could be raifed and managed. We are to confider, he wrote before the invention of printing, when books

D 4   could

---

* See his defcription of the temple, de bell. judaic. lib. v. cap. v. p. 331 et feq.

(a) Mark xiii. 1.   (b) Luke xxi. 5.

could not be foon and eafily publifhed and
difperfed into many hands, as they now are.
It is poffible, therefore, a vain defire of ex-
alting, the glory of his nation, might prevail
with him, in fome cafes, above a ftrict regard
to truth, when it was probable none who were
able to contradict him, might ever fee his book;
or if they fhould, and were of his own nation,
they would not be inclined to do it *.

Hitherto we have only confidered the temple
itfelf, which confifted of the portico, the fanctuary, and the holy of holies. But this was
only a fmall part of the facred building on the
top of mount Moriah; for the temple was furrounded with fpacious courts, making a fquare
of half a mile in circumference.

- The firft court, which encompaffed the temple and the other courts, was called the court
of the Gentiles; becaufe Gentiles were allowed
to come into it, but no further. It was inclofed with a wall, twenty cubits high, on the
top of which were chambers or galleries, fupported by the wall on the outer fide, and by
rows of columns on the infide; as the fides of
the Royal Exchange, or the piazzas in Covent
Garden are. Thefe piazzas of the temple are
called ςοαι by Jofephus, and in the new teftament; which we tranflate porches, though not
very properly, for the englifh word porch, con-
veys a very different idea from the greek word
ςοα, which is better rendered, piazza. That

on

* There is, however, a furprifing account in Mr. Maun-
drel's travels, p. 138. edit. 1749. Oxon. of the fize of
fome ftones, which he faith he faw himfelf in a wall which
encompaffed the temple of Balbec; one ftone was twenty
one, and two others, each twenty yards long, four yards
deep, and as many broad And the authors of the univerfal hiftory quote De La Roque, a french author, as
giving the fame account.

on the eaſt ſide was called Solomon's piazza (*a*), becauſe it ſtood upon a vaſt terraſs which he built up from the valley beneath, four hundred cubits high, in order to enlarge the area on the top of the mountain, and make it equal to the plan of his intended building. As this terraſs was the only work of Solomon's remaining in Herod's temple, the piazza, that ſtood upon it, ſtill retained the name of the former prince.

Of the ſame kind with theſe piazzas were doubtleſs the five ςϛαι, which ſurrounded the pool of Betheſda (*b*). The pool was probably a pentagon, and the piazzas round it were de-ſigned to ſhelter from the weather the multitude of diſeaſed perſons, who lay waiting for a cure by the miraculous virtue of thoſe waters.

Within this outward great court was a leſs court, of an oblong rectangular figure, near to the weſt end of which the temple ſtood. In-to this court none but Iſraelites might enter. It was alſo ſurrounded with a wall, and adorn-ed with piazzas, in the manner of the great court. The rabbies ſpeak of two walls, and a ſpace betwixt them of ten cubits broad, which they call the חיל chel, that parted the court of the Iſraelites from the court of the Gentiles. This is what they underſtand by the word חיל in the lamentations of Jeremiah (*c*) : " He made the chel and the wall to lament ; they lan-guiſhed together *." But however that be, the wall that divided betwixt the court of the Gen-tiles

(*a*) See John x. 23. Acts iii. 11.
(*b*) John v. 2.   (*c*) Lament. ii. 8.
* Vid. Maimon. de ædificio templi, cap. vii. §. iii. p. 39. Crenii faſciculi ſexti. There is, however, a miſtake in the tranſlation ; inſtead of being altitudine, in height ten cubits, it ſhould be latitudine, in breadth. Vid. Miſhn. tit. Mid-doth. cap. 2. §. 3. L'Empereur. not. 3. in loc. tom. 5. p. 326. Surenhuſ.

tiles and the court of the Ifraelites, is evidently
alluded to in the following paffage of St. Paul,
" But now in Chrift Jefus, ye who fometime
were afar off are made nigh by the blood of
Chrift : for he is our peace, who hath made
both one, and hath broken down the middle
wall of partition between us (a) : " which expreffes the union of the Jews and Gentiles in
one Church by Jefus Chrift.

In the outer court was probably kept the
market of beafts for facrifice, which is mentioned by St. John (b) ; and there likewife were
the money changers, which he alfo fpeaks of,
who for a fmall gratuity furnifhed people, in
exchange for other coin, with half fhekels, for
payment of the annual tribute which every Ifraelite was to give into the facred treafury.

The court of the Ifraelites was divided into
two parts. The firft, entering at the eaft end,
was called the court of the women, becaufe
they were allowed to come no nearer the temple than that court. Of this indeed we have
no account in fcripture, except it be the fame
that was called, in Jehofhaphat's time, the new
court (c). There feem to have been but two
courts originally belonging to Solomon's temple ; one called " the court of the priefts ;"
the other, " the great court (d) ;" and we read
that " Manaffeh built altars for all the hofts of
heaven, in the two courts of the houfe of the
Lord (e)." In the great, or outward court,
devout Gentiles were allowed to pay their devotion to the God of Ifrael ; and in the court of
the priefts, or the inner court, the priefts and
other

(a) Eph. ii. 13, 14.   (b) John ii. 14.
(c) 2 Chron. xx. 5.   (d) 2 Chron. iv. 9.
(e) 2 Chron. xxxiii. 5.

other Ifraelites worfhipped. And as in thofe times there feems to have been no other diftinction of courts but thefe two, the fetting the women at a greater diftance from the temple, and from the fpecial tokens of God's prefence, than the men, muft have been the contrivance of fome later ages, without any divine inftitution, that we find, to fupport it.

In this court of the women there was placed one cheft, or more, the Jews fay eleven, for receiving the voluntary contributions of the people towards defraying the charges of public worfhip : fuch as providing the publick facrifices ; wood for the altar, falt and other neceffaries. That part of the area where thefe chefts were placed, was the γαζοφυλακιον, or treafury, mentioned by St. Mark (a). And perhaps the whole court, or at leaft the piazza on one fide and the chambers over it, in which the facred ftores were kept, was from hence called by the fame name ; as the following paffage of St. John feems to imply, " Thefe words fpake Jefus in the treafury, as he taught in the temple (b)."

From the court of the women, which was on higher ground than the court of the Gentiles; they afcended by fifteen fteps into the inner court, in which the temple and altar ftood. Into this court, not only the priefts, but all male Ifraelites might enter. Neverthelefs, in this court there was a diftinction made in Herod's temple, of which we read nothing in Solomon's, betwixt the court of the priefts, and that of the people. The court of the priefts was nothing but an inclofure of a rail or wall of one cubit high, round about the altar, at a con-

(a) Mark xii. 41.   (b) John viii. 20.

convenient diftance from it, to which the people were to bring their offerings and facrifices;
but none befide the priefts were allowed to come
within that enclofure.

From hence probably the papifts have taken
the hint of railing in their altars.

Herod began to build the temple about fixteen years before the birth of Chrift, and fo
far compleated it in nine years and an half,
that it was fit for divine fervice. In all which
time, the Jews fay, it never rained in the day
time, but only in the night, that the facred
building might not be retarded. However, the
outbuildings of the courts were not finifhed till
feveral years after our Saviour's death; fo that
when he was about thirty years old, the temple
had been forty fix in building: which is the
meaning of this paffage in the evangelift John,
" Forty and fix years was, *ωκοδομηθη*, which
fhould rather be rendered, hath been, this temple in building (*a*)."

The external glory of this latter temple confifted not only in the opulence and magnificence
of the building, but in the rich gifts, *αναθηματα*,
with which it was adorned, and which excited
the admiration of thofe who beheld them (*b*).
The hanging up of *αναθηματα*, or confecrated
gifts, was common in moft of the ancient temples; as we find it particularly was in the temple at Jerufalem; where, among the reft, was
a golden table given by Pompey, and feveral
golden vines of exquifite workmanfhip, and of
an immenfe fize, with clufters, faith Jofephus,
ανδρομηκεις, as tall as a man *.

This

(*a*) John ii. 20.   (*b*) Luke xxi. 5.
  * Jofeph. de bell, judaic. lib. v. cap. v, §. 4. p. 333.
edit. Haverc.

This magnificent temple was at length through the righteous judgment of God on that wicked and abandoned nation, who had literally turned it into a den of thieves, utterly deftroyed by the Romans, on the fame month, and on the fame day of the month, on which Solomon's temple was deftroyed by the Babylonians.

On this fubject may be confulted Lightfoot's defcription of the temple, and Capel's Templi Hierofolymitani triplex delineatio ex Villalpando, Jofepho, Maimonide et Talmude, prefixed to Walton's Polyglot.

CHAP. II.

Of the synagogues, schools and houses of prayer.

THE term synagogue, primarily signifying an assembly, came, like the word
church, to be applied to places in which any
assemblies, especially those for the worship of
God, met, or were convened. The Jews use
it in the primary sense, when they speak of the
great synagogue; meaning the court of seventy
elders, which they pretend to have been instituted originally by Moses, and the members of
which they afterwards increased to one hundred
and twenty.

We are now to treat of synagogues, chiefly,
in the latter sense; namely, as denoting places
of worship. And thus they were a kind of
chapels of ease to the temple, and originally intended for the convenience of such, as lived too
remote statedly to attend the publick worship
there. But in the latter ages of the jewish
state, synagogues were multiplied far beyond
what such convenience required. If we may
believe the rabbies, there were no less than
four

four hundred and eighty, or according to others four hundred and sixty *, of them in Jerusalem, where the temple stood. So great a number indeed exceeds all reasonable belief. Nevertheless it is easy to imagine, that as the erecting synagogues came to be considered as a very meritorious work of piety (a), the number might soon be encreased, by the superstition of religious zealots, beyond all necessity or convenience.

The almost profound silence of the old testament concerning synagogues hath induced several learned men to conclude, that they had a very late original. Mr. Basnage supposes them to be coeval with the traditions in the time of the asmonean princes, but a few ages before Christ. Dr. Prideaux does not admit, there were any synagogues before the babylonish captivity †. Vitringa is of the same opinion, and hath said a great deal in support of it ‡. In favour of which sentiment Reland also quotes some passages from the rabbies §. But I cannot think their arguments are conclusive. For in the seventy fourth psalm, which seems to have been written on occasion of the babylonish captivity, there is mention made of their enemies having burnt or destroyed " all the synagogues

---

* Gemar. Hierosol. tit. Megill. cap. iii. fol. 73. col. 4. and tit. Cethuboth. cap. xiii. fol. 35. col. 3. Vid. Selden. prolegom. in librum de successionibus in bona defunctorum. p. xv, xvi. apud Opera, vol. ii. tom. 1. Or Lightfoot. Centur. chorograph. Matt. xxvi.

(a) See Luke vii. 4, 5.

† Connect. vol. 2. p. 534,—536.

‡ Vitring. de synag. vet. lib. i. part. ii. cap. ix,—xii.

§ Reland. Antiq. sacr. part. i. cap. x. §. iii. p. 128, 129. edit. 3. 1717.

nagogues of God in the land," כל־מוערי־אל
בארץ col-mongnadhè-èl baarets(a): In which
paffage not only מוערי mongnathè, from יער
jangnadh, convenire fecit ad locum tempufque
ftatutum, feems to be properly tranflated fynagogues, where the people were ftatedly to meet
for divine worfhip; but the words כל col and
בארץ baarets, all the fynagogues of God in
the land, being added, prevent our underftanding this expreffion, as fome do, only of the temple, and the holy places belonging to it at Jerufalem. Vitringa feems fenfible of the force
of this argument, and endeavours therefore to
fhow, that the phrafe may either mean all the
places throughout the land, where God had
occafionally met his people in old time, and
which on that account were had in peculiar veneration; or at leaft, the fchools and academies
of the prophets. An interpretation, which
feems not very natural; and indeed this learned
author himfelf was fo doubtful of it, that he
adds, Difcerning perfons will not imagine, that
this one paffage, which is of an uncertain fenfe,
is fufficient to counterbalance the arguments I
have produced, to prove that fynagogues were
of a later original.

Again, I obferve that St. James fpeaks of
Mofes being read in the fynagogues " of old
time (b)." And indeed it can hardly be imagined, that the bulk of a nation which was the
only vifible church of God in the world, fhould
in their pureft times, in the days of Jofhua,
Samuel, and David, feldom or never pay him
any publick worfhip: and this muft have been
the cafe, if they had no other places for it, befides

(a) Pfal. lxxiv. 8.   (b) Acts xv. 21.

fides the tabernacle; and on this fuppofition
likewife the fabbath could not be kept according to the law, which required a holy convocation מקרא־קדש mikra-kodheih, on, or for,
that day, in, or among, all their dwellings, or
throughout the whole land (*a*). The word
מקרא mikra, which we render a convocation,
feems more naturally to import a place of publick worfhip in which the people affembled,
than the affembly itfelf. As in the following
paffage of Ifaiah, "And the Lord will create
upon every dwelling place of mount Zion, and
upon her affemblies מקראיה mikrajeha, a cloud
and fmoke by day, and the fhining of a flaming
fire by night (*b*)." In which there is a manifeft
allufion to the tabernacle, whereon the cloud
and pillar of fire refted in the wildernefs (*c*).
And what then could thefe מקראי קדש mikrè
kodhefh be, but fynagogues, or edifices for publick worfhip * ?

However, the difpute, perhaps, may be com-
promifed, if we allow that the cuftom of erecting thofe forts of chapels, in later ages called
fynagogues, and appropriated to publick worfhip alone, firft began after the return from the
captivity; and that in former times, from their
firft fettlement in the land of Canaan, the people ufed to meet either in the open air, or in
dwelling houfes, particularly in the houfes of
the prophets, (as feems to be intimated in the
hufband of the Shunamite enquiring of her,
when fhe was going to Elifha's houfe on occa-

(*a*) Lev. xxiii. 3.   (*b*) Ifai. iv. 5.   (*c*) Exod.
xl. 38.
* See on this fubject Leydecker, de Republ. Hebr. lib.
viii. cap. v, §. ii.

fion of the death of her fon, " Wherefore wilt
thou go to him to day ? It is neither new moon
nor fabbath (a) : ") or in any other place or
building convenient for the purpofe.

But though we cannot help concluding, they
had extempore fynagogues, if we may fo flile
them, without which religious affemblies could
not be ordinarily held, from their firft fettlement in Canaan ; neverthelefs, it muft be acknowledged, thefe affemblies were fometimes
neglected, and in a manner laid afide, for years
together ; which made it neceffary for Jehofa-
phat to fend Levites, a fort of itinerant preachers,
with a book of the law with them, throughout
the cities of Judah (b). And from the long
difufe of reading it in fuch publick affemblies
the knowledge of the law was at a very low
ebb in Jofiah's time ; which may be fuppofed,
in part, to have occafioned the pleafure and
furprize of the king and of Hilkiah the high-
prieft, when the book, or autograph of the law,
which had been long neglected and loft, was
found, as they were repairing the temple (c).

In the fixth chapter of the Acts of the Apoftles there is mention made of the fynagogue
of the libertines (d) ; concerning whom there
are different opinions, two of which bid faireft
for the truth. The firft is that of Grotius and
Vitringa *, that they were italian jews or profelytes. The ancient Romans diftinguifhed betwixt libertus and libertinus. Libertus was one
who had been a flave, and obtained his freedom ;

(a) 2 Kings iv. 23.　　　　(b) 2 Chron. xvii. 9.
(c) 2 Kings xxii. 8.　　　　(d) Acts vi. 9.
　　* Grot. in loc. Vitring. de Synag. vetere, lib. i. part. i,
cap. 14 p. 254, 255.

dom *; libertinus was the fon of a libertus †.
But this diftinction in after ages was not ftrictly
obferved; and libertinus alfo came to be ufed
for one not born, but made free, in oppofition
to ingenuus, or one born free ‡. Whether the
libertini mentioned in this paffage of the acts,
were gentiles, who had become profelytes to
judaifm, or native Jews, who having been made
flaves to the Romans were afterwards fet at liberty §, and in remembrance of their captivity
called themfelves libertini, and formed a fyna-

E 2   gogue

* Cives Romani funt Liberti, qui vindicta, cénfu aut
teftamento, nullo jure impediente manumiffi funt. Ulpian.
tit. 1. §. 6.

† This appears from the following paffage of Suetonius
concerning Claudius, who he fays, was ignarus temporibus
Appii et deinceps aliquamdiu Libertinos dictos, non ipfos,
qui manumitterentur, fed ingenuos ex his procreatos. In
vitâ Claudii, cap. xxiv. §. 4. p. 78. Pitifci.

‡ Quintilian. de inftitutione oratoriâ, lib. v. cap. x. p.
246. edit. Gibfon. 1693. Qui fervus eft, fi manumittatur
fit Libertinus.—Juftinian. Inftitut. lib. i. tit. v. Libertini
funt, qui ex juftâ fervitute manumiffi funt. Tit. iv. Ingenuus eft is, qui ftatim ut natus eft, liber eft; five ex duobus ingenuis matrimonio editus eft, five ex libertinis duobus,
five ex altero libertino, et altero ingenuo.

§ Of thefe there were great numbers at Rome. Tacitus
informs us (Annal. lib. ii. cap. lxxxv.) that four thoufand
Libertini, of the jewifh fuperftition as he ftiles it, were
banifhed at one time, by order of Tiberius, into Sardinia;
and the reft commanded to quit Italy, if they did not ab-
jure, by a certain day. See alfo Suetonius in vitâ Tiberii,
cap. xxxvi. Jofephus (Antiq. lib. xviii. cap. iii. §. 5. edit.
Haverc.) mentions the fame fact. And Philo (legat. ad
Caium, p. 785. C. edit. Colon. 1613.) fpeaks of a good
part of the city beyond the Tiber, as inhabited by Jews,
who were moftly Libertini, having been brought to Rome
as captives and flaves, but being made free by their mafters, were permitted to live according to their own rites
and cuftoms.

gogue by themfelves, is differently conjectured by the learned *.

It is probable, the Jews of Cyrenia, Alexandria, &c. built fynagogues at Jerufalem at their own charge, for the ufe of their brethren, who came from thofe countries ; as the Danes, Swedes, &c. build churches for the ufe of their own countrymen in London ; and that the italian Jews did the fame ; and becaufe the greateft number of them were libertini, their fynagogue was therefore called the fynagogue of the libertines.

The other opinion, which is hinted by Oecumenius on the Acts †, and mentioned by Dr. Lardner, as more lately advanced by Mr. Daniel Gerdes ‡, profeffor of divinity in the univerfity of Groningen ; is this, that the libertines are fo called from a city or country called Libertus or Libertina in Africa, about Carthage. Suidas in his lexicon, on the word λιβερτινος, fays it was ονομα εθνες, nomen gentis. And the Gloffa interlinearis, of which Nicolas de Lyra made great ufe in his notes, hath, over the word Libertini, è regione, denoting that they were fo ftiled from a country.

In the acts of the famous conference with the Donatifts at Carthage anno 411. there is mentioned one Victor, bifhop of the church of Libertina ; and in the acts of the Lateran council, which was held in 649. there is mention of Januarius gratia Dei epifcopus fanctæ ecclefiæ Libertinenfis ; and therefore Fabricius, in his geographical index of chriftian bifhopricks, has placed

---

* Vid. Selden. de jure nat. et gent. lib. ii. cap. v. oper. vol. 1. tom. 1. p. 200, 201. et Alting. de profelytis.

† In loc. tom. 1. p. 57.

‡ Vid. ejus Exercit. Academ. lib. iii. Amftel. 1728. 4to.

placed Libertina in what was called Africa pro-
pria, or the proconfular province of Africa.
Now as all the other people of the feveral fynagogues, mentioned in this paffage of the Acts,
are denominated from the places from whence
they came; it is probable, that the Libertines
were fo too; and as the Cyrenians and Alexan-
drians, who came from Africa, are placed next
to the Libertines in that catalogue, it is probable they alfo belonged to the fame country.
So that, upon the whole, there is little reafon
to doubt of the Libertines being fo called from
the place from whence they came *; and the
order of the names in the catalogue might lead
us to think, that they were further off from Jerufalem than Alexandria and Cyrenia, which
will carry us to the proconfular province in
Africa about Carthage †·

When Godwin mentions it as a jewifh tradition, that wherefoever there were ten men of
Ifrael, there ought to be a fynagogue built; he
is fomewhat miftaken in the meaning of the
tradition, which was, that a fynagogue ought to
be built where there were ten בטלנים batlanim,
that is, men of leifure, who could take care of
the affairs of the fynagogue, and give themfelves to the ftudy of the law. So faith Lightfoot, underftanding it to be a general name for
the elders or officers of the fynagogue‡. However,

---

* It is furprizing that this opinion fhould be rejected by
Mr. Selden, fince he hath not only mentioned it, but quoted on the occafion the paffages here produced out of Suidas, the Gloffa interlinearis, and the Acts of the confer-
rence at Carthage. De jure nat. et gent. ubi fupra.

† See Dr. Lardner's Cafe of the Demoniacs, p. 152,
—156.

‡ Vid. Lightfoot. hor. hebraic. in Matt. iv. 23.

ever, others are of a different opinion; particularly Rhenferdius, who hath wrote a large differtation, chiefly againft Lightfoot, in order to prove that they were perfons, who at a ftated falary were obliged to attend the fervice of the fynagogue at proper hours, that whoever came might find a fufficient number to make a lawful congregation, which the Jews imagine muft confift, at leaft, of ten*.

In the fynagogue, faith Godwin, the fcribes ordinarily taught; but not only they; for Chrift himfelf alfo taught in them. It is queried by what right Chrift and his apoftles, who had no publick character among the Jews, taught in their fynagogues? In anfwer to which Dr. Lightfoot obferves, that though this liberty was allowed to no illiterate perfon or mechanick, but only to the learned; they neverthelefs granted it to prophets, and workers of miracles, and fuch as fet up for heads and leaders of new fects †; I fuppofe, in order that they might inform themfelves of their dogmata, and not condemn them unheard and unknown. And under all thefe characters, Chrift and his apoftles were admitted to this priviledge.

He that gave liberty to preach was termed Ἀρχισυναγωγος. Which word is fometimes ufed in a larger fenfe, for any one of the officers, who had power in the affairs of the fynagogue.

Thus

---

* Vid. Rhenferdii Differtationes philolog. de decem Otiofis Synagogæ. Franekeræ, 1686. 4to. Vitring. de Decem-viris Otiofis, Franek. 1687, in defence of what he had advanced in his Archifynagog. Franeker. 1685. cap. ii, iii. et eundem de Synagog. vetere, lib. ii. cap. vi, vii, viii. where he fhews at large the grounds of Lightfoot's opinion, more fully than he had done himfelf, but leaves the difpute undetermined.

† Lightfoot. hor. hebr. in Matt. iv. 23. ad finem.

Thus in the thirteenth chapter of the Acts (a)
we read of the Αρχισυναγωγοι, rulers of one fynagogue.   Sometimes it is ufed, in a ftricter
fenfe, for the prefident or chief of thofe officers.
As in the following paffage of St. Luke, "And
the ruler of the fynagogue, Αρχισυναγωγος, anfwered with indignation, becaufe that Jefus had
healed on the fabbath day (b)."   And perhaps
in thefe paffages of the Acts, "And Crifpus,
the chief ruler of the fynagogue, Αρχισυναγωγος,
believed on the Lord with all his houfe (c)."
Again, "All the Greeks took Softhenes, the
chief ruler of the fynagogue, Αρχισυναγωγος, and
beat him before the judgment-feat (d)."

Next to the Αρχισυναγωγος, was an officer,
whofe province it was to offer up publick prayer
to God for the whole congregation, and who on
that account was called שליח צבור Sheliach
Zibbor, the angel of the church *, becaufe as
their meffenger, he fpoke to God for them.
Hence the paftors of the feven churches of Afia,
in the book of the revelation, are called by a
name borrowed from the fynagogue, "Angels
of the churches."   Dr. Lightfoot makes this
officer to be the fame with the Υπηρετης †, mentioned in the fourth chapter of St. Luke, and
by our tranflators rendered "minifter (e)."   He
alfo confounds it with the חזן chazan ‡, as
Vitringa did when he wrote his Archifynago-
                                E 4   gus,

<hr/>

(a) Acts xiii. 15.   (b) Luke xiii. 14.   (c) Acts
xviii. 8.   (d) ver. 17.
  * Mifh. rofh hafshanah, cap. 4. §. 9.   Maimon. et
Bartenor. in loc. tom. 2. p. 353. edit. Surenhus. et Vitring. de Synag. vetere, lib. 3. part. 2. cap. i. p. 889,—
895. et cap. ii. p. 905, et feq.
  † See his Harmony on Luke iv. 20.
  (e) Luke iv. 20.
  ‡ See his Harmony on Luke iv. 15. §. iv.

gus *, but on maturer confideration he afterwards altered his opinion.

The Chazan, I apprehend, was, generally at
leaft, a different officer from the Sheliach Zibbor, and inferior to him.   Some underftand the
word Chazan to anfwer to the greek διακονος † ;
but according to the account the rabbies give
of his office ‡ , it fhould anfwer to the englifh.
word fexton ; for he was the fervant of the fynagogue, as Dr. Doddridge on the forecited
paffage of St. Luke tranflates the word υπηρετης,
feeming to underftand it, as moft interpreters
do, of the Chazan.

The worfhip performed in the fynagogue
confifted of three parts, reading the fcriptures,
prayer, and preaching.

The fcriptures they read, were the whole law
of Mofes, and portions out of the prophets,
and hagiographa.

The law was divided into fifty three, according to the Maforets, or according to others, fifty
four פרשות parafhoth or fections. For the
jewifh year confifted of twelve lunar months,
alternately of twenty nine or thirty days, that
is, of fifty weeks and four days.   The Jews,
therefore, in their divifion of the law into Parafhoth or fections, had a refpect to their intercalary year, which was every fecond or third,
and confifted of thirteen months ; fo that the
whole law was read over this year, alloting one
Parafhah, or fection to every fabbath.   And in
com-

* Archifynag. p. 58, et feq.
† Vitring. de Synag. vetere, lib. 3. part. 2. cap. iv.
p. 914, et feq.
‡ Vid. Mifhn. Sotah, cap. 7. §. 7. Bartenor. et Wagen-
feil. in loc. tom. 3. p. 266. edit. Surenhus. Vitring. de
Synag. vetere, ubi fupra. cap. ii. p. 895. et feq.

common years they reduced the fifty three or fifty four sections to the number of the fifty sabbaths, by reading two shorter ones together, as often as there was occasion. They began the course of reading the first sabbath after the feast of tabernacles; or rather, indeed, on the sabbath day before that, when they finished the last course of reading, they also made a beginning of the new course *; that so, as the rabbies say, the devil might not accuse them to God of being weary of reading his law †.

The portions selected out of the prophets are called הפטרות haphtaroth The tradition ‡ is, that when Antiochus Epiphanes forbad them reading the law in their synagogues, they picked out portions of the prophets, somewhat answering in sense to those of the law §, and read them on the same days when the others should have been read ‖.

The

---

* See Vitringa de Synag. vetere, lib. iii. part. 2. cap. viii. p. 964, et seq. Leusden. Philolog. hebræ. differt. iv.

† Leusden. ubi supra, §. xx.

‡ Elias Levita in Thisbi ad rad. פטר. See the passage quoted by Vitringa de Synag. vetere, lib. iii. part 2. cap. xi. p. 1006. This tradition of the origin of reading the haphtaroth, is very improbable, as Vitringa shews, p. 1007, 1008.

§ That the passages of the prophets were to be similar to those of the law, we are informed by Maimonides, de precibus, cap. xiii. §. iii. See Vitring. p. 985, 986.

‖ See a table of the Parashoth and Haphtaroth in Maimon. de ordine precum. in de Voisin. Observat. ad Raymundi Martini Pugionem fidei, proœm. p. 80, et seq. p. 108, et seq. or at the end of Athias's Hebrew Bible.

It is debated among learned men, whether the greek version of the septuagint was anciently used in the synagogues of those Jews, who were not well versed in the hebrew; or whether the original alone was read to them, and then interpreted. We have already declared our opinion that the Hellenists mentioned in the Acts were Jews, who used the greek version in sacris, or in their synagogues.

The second part of the synagogue service was prayer. For the performance of which, saith Dr. Prideaux, they had liturgies, in which are all the prescribed forms of the synagogue worship. The most solemn part of these prayers are eighteen collects, which, according to the rabbies, were composed and instituted by Ezra, in order that the Jews, whose language after the captivity was corrupted with many barbarous terms, borrowed from other languages, might be able to perform their devotions in the pure language of their own country. This is the account which Maimonides gives out of the Gemara, of the origin of the jewish liturgies *. And the eighteen collects, in particular, are mentioned in the Mishna †. However some better evidence than that of the talmudical rabbies is requisite in order to prove their liturgies to be of so high an antiquity; especially when some of their prayers, as Dr. Prideaux acknowledges, seem to have been composed after the destruction of Jerusalem, and to have reference to it ‡, It is evident they were

gogues. See on the other side of the question Vitringa, (de Synag. vetere, lib. iii. part. 2. cap. 7. p. 950,—958.) who hath laboured to prove, against Scaliger (animadverf. ad Eusebii Chronicon, p. 134.) and Walton (prolegom. ix. §. 14. p. 60.) that no greek version was ever used in any jewish synagogues. In support of the opinion we have espoused, besides Scaliger and Walton, see in particular, Hody de Bibliorum textibus, lib. iii. part. 1. cap. 1. p. 224,—233.

* Maimon. de precibus et benedict. facerdot. cap. i. §. i,--ix. ex Gem. tit. Barachoth, fol. xxxiii. col. 1. et Megill. fol. xviii. col. 2. See Vitringa, lib. 1. part. 2. cap. 12. p. 414,—416.

† Mishn. tit. Barachoth, cap. 4. §. 3. p. 14. edit. Surenhus.

‡ Connect. part 1. book vi. vol. 2. p. 538. note d. edit. 10. 1729.

were composed, when there was no temple, nor
sacrifices; since the seventeenth collect prays,
that God would restore his worship to the inner
part of his house, and make haste with fer-
vour and love to accept the burnt sacrifices of
Israel, &c *. They could not, therefore, be
the composition of Ezra, who did not receive
his commission from Artaxerxes to go to Judea,
till more than fifty years after the second temple
was built, and its worship restored. However,
Dr. Prideaux not doubting but they were used,
at least most of them, in our Saviour's time;
and consequently, that he joined in them †,
whenever he went into the synagogues, as he
did every sabbath day (a); infers from hence
two things, as he saith, for the consideration of
dissenters.

1st, " That

---

* Prideaux, ubi supra, p. 541, 542. The fifth, tenth,
eleventh, and fourteenth collects have the same allusion
and reference as the seventeenth. See the original prayers
in Maimonides de Ordine precum, or in Vitringa, (de Synag. vetere, lib. iii. part. 2. cap. xiv. p. 1033,—1038.)
who observes, that the Talmudists will have the seventeenth collect, which prays for the restoration of the temple worship, (reduc ministerium Leviticum in Adytum Domus tuæ, as he translates it) to have been usually recited
by the king in the temple at the feast of tabernacles;
which is such an absurdity, that it confutes itself, and
shows how little the jewish traditions concerning the antiquity and use of their liturgies are to be depended upon.

† Supposing these forms were used in our Saviour's
time, it will not follow, that he joined in them, or worshipped God by them, because he frequently attended the
jewish synagogues; which he might do for other reasons.
And indeed many of them, as the author of the letter to
Dr. Prideaux in the Occasional paper (vol. 3. numb. 3.
p. 14,—17.) justly observes and shews, were such as he
cannot be supposed to have joined in, not being consistent
with his character and circumstances.

(a) Luke iv, 16.

1st, " That our Saviour difliked not fet forms of prayer in publick worship."

2dly, " That he was content to join with the publick in the meaneft forms (for fuch he allows thefe jewifh forms to be) rather than feparate from it." " And this, fays he, may fatisfy our diffenters, that neither our uſing fet forms of prayer in our publick worſhip, nor the uſing of ſuch forms as they think not ſufficiently edifying, can be objection ſufficient to juſtify them in their refufal to join with us in the uſe of them *."

As both thefe inferences are built upon the fuppofition, that forms of prayer were uſed in the jewifh church in our Saviour's time, if that cannot be fatisfactorily proved, they ftand upon a very precarious foundation. And though the doctor is pleafed to fay, there is no doubt of it, yet, unlefs he could produce fome better and earlier evidence than the talmudical rabbies, I think there is great reafon to withold our affent. If they were in uſe fo early as the jewifh writers pretend, it is ftrange there ſhould be no hint of it in the Old Teftament, and in the Apochrypha; and if they came into uſe in or before our Saviour's time, fome intimation of it might naturally have been expected in the New Teftament. Nor is the total filence of Jofephus and Philo, and all other writers, previous to the talmudical rabbies, eafy to be accounted for on fuppofition that fuch liturgical forms were then in uſe.

How-

---

* The fame argument is uſed by Dr. Whitby on Luke iv. 16. by Archbiſhop Tillotfon, Serm. 135. vol. 3. p. 227. fol. by Dr. Bennet, in his brief hiſtory of forms of prayer, chap. 1, 2, and 3. and by feveral others.

However granting they were then ufed, and that our Saviour ordinarily attended the jewifh publick worfhip, at that time very corrupt and loaded with ceremonies of mere human invention; it may neverthelefs be doubted how far his example in this cafe will oblige us to join with a national church in any forms of worfhip, which we apprehend to be corrupted from the divine inftitution: For

1ft. Though our bleffed Saviour for wife reafons was prefent at the corrupt worfhip of the jewifh church, he frequently remonftrated againft their corruptions. The argument, therefore, drawn from hence, for our complying with human inventions and corruptions in the worfhip of God feems not quite remote from that which Cardinal Bellarmine ufes for the worfhip of angels; " St. John fell down before an angel, in order to worfhip him; and why are we blamed for doing what St. John did?" To which Archbifhop Tillotfon properly replies, becaufe St. John was reproved by the angel for doing what he did. In like manner when we are afked, why we cannot comply with corrupt forms and human inventions, as Chrift did? We may reply, becaufe he remonftrated againft fuch corrupt forms and human inventions, and reproved the Jews for them. Indeed if this argument proves any thing, it proves too much; it proves that we muft not only comply with corrupt modes and forms in divine worfhip, but that we muft at the fame time continue to bear our teftimony againft fuch corruptions; and this, we apprehend, would not only be difagreeable to our chriftian brethren, with whom we differ, but would ordinarily be the caufe of more uncharitable contentions, and

give

give a more mortal wound to the peace of the church, for the fake of preferving which the example of Chrift is fo ftrongly urged upon us, than a quiet and peaceable feparation. Not to add,

2dly. That if we are under an obligation, from the example of Chrift, to comply with the eftablifhed worfhip in any nation, I apprehend, we muft be under the like obligation to comply with it in every nation, to be epifcopalians, or prefbyterians, papifts, or proteftants, according to the law and conftitution of the country in which we refide.

3dly. Though our Saviour for a time complied with the corrupt worfhip of the jewifh church, he neverthelefs afterwards diffented, and fet up another church and another form in oppofition to theirs ; injoining on his difciples a nonconformity to the rites of the jewifh church, and a ftrict and clofe adherence to him as their lawgiver, and to his inftitutions as their rule, and not to fuffer themfelves to be again entangled with the yoke of carnal and ceremonial ordinances, but to ftand faft in the liberty wherewith Chrift hath made them free ; to own and fubmit to his authority alone as obligatory on confcience, and to oppofe every ufurpation on his fovereignty, and every invafion of the rights of his fubjects. Which leads me to obferve,

4thly, That the argument is built on this miftaken principle, that the church of England is a national eftablifhed church, on the fame, or as good, authority as the jewifh church was. That indeed was a divine eftablifhment ; and all perfons born in the land of Ifrael, and of jewifh parents being confidered as members of

it,

it, were therefore bound to conform to its rites,
and worſhip, at leaſt ſo far as they were conſo-
nant to the divine inſtitution.   But is there a
divine eſtabliſhment of any national church under the goſpel diſpenſation ? If the New Teſtament gives us no other idea of the churches of
Chriſt, but their being voluntary ſocieties, unit-
ing, under the laws of Chriſt, for publick worſhip, and other purpoſes of religion ; then is
no man born a member . of any church, but
every one is at liberty to join himſelf to that,
whoſe conſtitution and worſhip appear to him
moſt agreeable to the rule of ſcripture, and moſt
for his own edification.   And ſince the unity
which the goſpel recommends, does not conſiſt
in the uniformity of rites and modes of worſhip, but in harmony of affection, and in the
mutual love of all chriſtians ; it follows, that
the peace of the church is not broken by quiet
and conſcientious nonconformiſts, but by thoſe
who are bitter and violent againſt their fellow
chriſtians for not approving thoſe human forms
of which they are fond and tenacious *.

The third part of their ſynagogue ſervice was
expounding the ſcriptures, and preaching to the
people.   The poſture, in which this was performed, whether in the ſynagogue, or other
places (a), was ſitting.   Accordingly, when our
Saviour

---

* See Mr. Robinſon's Review of the caſe of liturgies, in
anſwer to Dr. Bennet, chap. iii. p. 49, et ſeq. and the
letter to Dr. Prideaux in the Occaſional Paper, vol. 3.
Numb. iii.

If any are deſirous of being acquainted with the jewiſh
forms, and with their manner of diſcharging the duty of
publick prayer, as deſcribed by the rabbies, they may have
ample ſatisfaction in Vitringa de Synag. vetere, lib. iii.
part. 2. cap. xiii,—xviii. or in Buxtorf. de Synag. ju-
daicâ.

(a) See Matt. v. 1. and Luke v. 3.

Saviour had read the הפטרות haphteroth in the
fynagogue at Nazareth, of which he was a
member, having been brought up in that city; and then inſtead of retiring to his place,
fat down in the deſk or pulpit, it is ſaid, " the
eyes of all that were preſent were faſtened upon him," as they perceived by his poſture that
he was going to preach to them (*a*). And
when Paul and Barnabas went into the ſynagogue at Antioch, and ſat down, thereby in-
timating their deſire to ſpeak to the people, if
they might be permitted; the rulers of the ſynagogue ſent to them, and gave them leave (*b*).

The ſynagogues were uſed, not only for divine ſervice, but for holding courts of juſtice,
eſpecially upon eccleſiaſtical affairs. And as
among us, leſſer puniſhments are often inflicted
in the court, as ſoon as judgment is given;
for inſtance, burning in the hand; ſo among
the Jews, the puniſhment of beating or whip-
ping was often inflicted in the ſynagogue, while
the court was ſitting (*c*).

To this uſe of the ſynagogues for holding ju-
diciary courts, Dr. Whitby thinks, St. James
refers, when he ſays, " If there come into
your aſſembly, εἰς την συναγωγην υμων, a man
with a gold ring, in goodly apparel, and there
come in alſo a poor man, in vile rayment;
and ye have reſpect to him that weareth the
gay cloathing, and ſay unto him, Sit thou here
in a good place; and ſay to the poor, Stand
thou there, or ſit here under my footſtool; are
ye not partial in yourſelves, and are become
judges of evil thoughts," or judges who think
and

(*a*) Luke iv. 20.   (*b*) Acts xiii. 14, 15.
(*c*) See Matt. x. 17. Luke xii. 11. Acts xxii. 19.

and reafon ill (*a*)? That the apoftle here fpeaks
of confiftories for civil judicature, is argued,
1ft. From the ufe of the word συναγωγη, which
never fignifies in the New Teftament an affembly of chriftian worfhippers. 2dly. From the
word προσωπολημψια being ufed to exprefs the
partiality here cenfured, in the claufe immediately preceding: " My brethren, have not
the faith of our Lord Jefus Chrift, the Lord of
glory, with refpect of perfons, εν ταις προσωπο-
λημψιαις (*b*)." Now this term is moft commonly,
if not always, ufed for a partial refpect of perfons in judgment; like the inftance here mentioned, favouring a rich man's caufe before a
poor man's. 3dly. The phrafe " Sit thou under my footftool (*c*)," moft naturally refers to
courts of juftice; where the judge is commonly exalted upon a higher feat than the reft of
the affembly; but it cannot be well applied to
affemblies of worfhippers. 4thly, The Apoftle's accufing them, on account of this conduct towards the poor, with being partial
judges (*d*); and reminding them, that the
rich were the perfons, who " drew them before the judgment-feats (*e*)," feems very natural, if we underftand him in the preceding
paffage, as difcourfing concerning courts of judicature. 5thly, The Apoftle fays, fuch a refpect of perfons, as he here fpeaks of, is contrary to the law, and thofe who are guilty of
it, are " convinced of the law as tranfgref-
fors (*f*)." Now there was no divine law againft
diftinction of places in worfhipping affemblies,
into thofe which were more or lefs honourable;

VOL. II. F this

this muſt therefore, no doubt, refer to the law of partiality in judgment, "Ye ſhall do no unrighteouſneſs in judgment; thou ſhalt not reſpect the perſon of the poor, nor honour the perſon of the mighty (a)." The talmudiſts ſay*, it was a rule, that when "a poor man and a rich man pleaded together in judgment, the rich ſhould not be bid to ſit down, and the poor to ſtand; but either both ſhall ſit, or both ſhall ſtand." To this rule, or cuſtom the Apoſtle ſeems to refer, when he inſinuates a charge againſt them, of ſaying to the rich man, "Sit thou here in a good place, and to the poor, Stand thou there (b)."

So that, upon the whole, by the ſynagogue is not here meant, as is commonly underſtood, the church aſſembly for worſhip, but a court of judicature, in which men are too apt to favour the cauſe of the rich againſt the poor.

With reſpect to the ſchools amongſt the Jews, it ſhould be obſerved, that beſides the common ſchools, in which children were taught to read the law, they had alſo academies, in which their doctors gave comments on the law, and taught the traditions to their pupils. Of this ſort were the two famous ſchools of Hillel and Sammai, and the ſchool of Gamaliel, who was Paul's tutor (c). In theſe ſeminaries the tutor's chair is ſaid to have been ſo much raiſed above the level of the floor, on which the pupils ſat, that his feet were even with their heads. Hence St. Paul ſays, that "he was brought up

(a) Lev. xix. 15. See alſo Deut. i. 17.

* Vid. Hottinger. de juris Hebræor. legibus, leg. ccxlii. p. 364. edit. Tigur. 1655.

(b) James ii. 3. (c) Acts xxii. 3.

up at the feet of Gamaliel." Thefe academies
were commonly furnifhed with feveral tutors,
of whom one was prefident, and from whom
the fchool was denominated. They were called בית־רבנין beth-rabbonin, whereas the inferior fchools were called בית־רבן beth-rabban,
as having only one mafter.

The doctors in thefe academies not only read
lectures to their pupils, but held difputations or
conferences, at which other perfons might be
prefent, and propofe queftions to them. It was
perhaps in one of thofe fchools, which were
kept in fome apartment in the courts of the
temple, that Mary found her young fon Jefus,
" fitting in the midft of the doctors, both
hearing and afking them queftions (*a*)." Or
it might be even in the fanhedrim, which, Dr.
Lightfoot fays, was the great fchool of the nation, as well as the great judicatory *.

In order to prove that thefe fchools were different from the fynagogues, Godwin obferves,
that Paul, having difputed for the fpace of
three months in the fynagogue, " becaufe divers
believed not, but fpake evil of that way, then
departed from them, and feparated his difciples, difputing daily in the fchool of one Tyrannus (*b*)." This argument is grounded on a
fuppofition, that this fchool of Tyrannus was
a jewifh academy; which is very unlikely, confidering it was at Ephefus. Befides, it does not
feem probable, that on account of the Jews
oppofing and blafpheming the gofpel, St. Paul
fhould merely retire from a jewifh fynagogue

to

(*a*) Luke ii. 46.
* Lightfoot. Harmony on John iii. 10.
(*b*) Acts xix. 8,—10.

to a jewifh fchool. Was he likely to meet
with lefs oppofition amongft the fame people
by teaching in a different place? The truth
feems to be, that he departed from the Jews,
as being under obftinate and invincible preju-
dices, and taught among the Gentiles, in the
fchool of one Tyrannus; and that for the fpace
of two years: fo that all the inhabitants of
Afia heard the word of the Lord, Greeks as
well as Jews. Some take Tyrannus to be the
proper name of a gentile philofopher, who favoured St. Paul, and lent him his fchool to
preach and difpute in; others, to be a title or
name of place or office, Ἰυραννος fignifying, in
the greek language, a king or prince; and accordingly the chaldee paraphrafe, which often
borrows words both from the greek and latin,
renders the hebrew word סרני zarnè, which
we tranflate lords in the books of Joſhua and
Judges (a), by טורני turnè. Thus Phavorinus
interprets Ἰυραννος by αρχων πωλεως: It may therefore, in this place fignify a magiftrate; which
interpretation feems to be favoured by the addition of τινος. Neverthelefs it muft be owned,
τις is fometimes joined with a proper name; as
τινα Σιμωνα (b), and Τερτυλλα τινος (c). However, if by τυραννε.τινος we underftand a certain
magiftrate of Ephefus, σχολη may fignify his
hall or gallery, in which people ufed to meet
for difcourfe: a fenfe, in which the word is
very commonly ufed both by the Greeks and
Latins. Others, again, take σχολη here to fignify a γυμνασιον, in which wreftlers and other
combatants in the publick games exercifed
them-

(a) Joſh. xiii. 3.　Judg. xvi. 5, 8.
(b) Mark xv. 21.　(c) Acts xxiv. 1.

themſelves; and which perhaps had been built
at the expence of one Tyrannus, and therefore
bore his name *.

With reſpect to their oratories or προσευχαι,
it is a queſtion among the learned, whether they
were different from their ſchools or ſynagogues.
It is ſaid, that our Saviour " went up into a
mount to pray, and continued all night" εν τη
προσευχη τε Θεε, which can hardly bear the ſenſe
our tranſlators have put upon it, " in prayer
to God (a)." Beza indeed renders it, " per-
noctavit illic, orans Deum ;" but acknowledges
he is forced to depart from the Greek, " ut
planius loqueretur." But Dr. Whitby infers
from the uſe of parallel phraſes, ſuch as " the
mount of God," " the bread of God," " the
altar of God," " the lamp of God," which are
all of them things conſecrated or appropriated
to the ſervice of God, that προσευχη τε Θεε might
in like manner ſignify " an oratory of God,"
or a place that was devoted to his ſervice, eſpecially for prayer. In the ſame ſenſe he underſtands the word in the paſſage of the Acts,
wherein we are informed, that Paul and his
companions, on the ſabbath day, went out of
the city by a river ſide, ε ενομιζετο προσευχη ειναι,
which we render, " where prayer was wont to
be made." But the Syriac renders it, quoniam
illic videbatur Domus precationis; becauſe there
was perceived to be an houſe of prayer; and
the Arabic, ad locum quendam qui putabatur
eſſe Locus orationis, to a certain place, which
was ſuppoſed to be a place of prayer: ε ενομιζετο,

* Vid. Stephani Theſaurus in verb. Schol.
(a) Luke vi. 12.

where there was taken, or famed to be *, or
where according to received cuſtom there was †,
or where there was allowed by law ‡, a proſeu-
cha, or oratory, and where therefore they expected to meet an aſſembly of people. Mr.
Mede obſerves, that it ſhould have been ε ενομιζετο προσευχη γινεϑαι, not ειναι, to expreſs where
prayer was wont to be made. And De Dieu
ſeems to be of the ſame opinion.

That the Jews had houſes, or places for
prayer, called προσευχαι, appears from a variety
of paſſages in Philo §; and particularly in his
oration againſt Flaccus, he complains, that
their προσευχαι were pulled down, and there was
no place left in which they might worſhip God,
and pray for Cæſar ‖: And Joſephus, in his
life, mentions the proſeuchæ more than once,
and ſpeaks of the people's being gathered εις την
προσευχην **. To the ſame purpoſe is the following paſſage of Juvenal, if he be rightly underſtood by Godwin, Vitringa ††, and others,
                                        Ede

* Mede's Diatrib. Diſc. xviii. p. 67. of his works. And
De Dieu, Animadverſ. in Acta xvi. 13.
† Elſner. Obſerv. Sacr. in loc. where he oppoſes Bos,
who (in his Exercitat. philolog. in loc.) had endeavoured
to ſhow, that ενομιζετο was redundant, and that the paſſage
ought to be tranſlated ſimply, "where there was a Pro-
ſeucha."
‡ Lardner's Credibil. part 1. vol. 1. book 1. cap. iii.
§. iii. p. 239. edit. 3. p. 1741. Eraſmus Schmidius (in
loc.) ſupports this ſenſe of ενομιζετο by ſome paſſages in
Ariſtophanes. Conſult Scapula and Conſtantine in verb.
§ Vid. in Flaccum, et Legat. ad Caium. paſſim.
‖ Phil. in Flacc. apud Opera, p. 752. F. edit. Colon.
Allobr. 1613.
** Joſeph. in Vit. §. 54, et 56. p. 27. tom. 2. edit.
Haverc.
†† Vitring. de Synag. vetere, lib. 1 part. 1. cap. 4.
p. 119.

Ede ubi conſiſtas; in quâ te quæro Proſeuchâ?
*Sat. 3. l. 296.

F 4 Among

* The late learned Mr. Samuel Jones of Tewkeſbury, in
his MS lectures on Godwin hath the following note on
this paſſage of Juvenal:

Autor noſter et etiam Vitringa aliique poetam his verbis
Synagogam Judæorum innuiſſe putant. Sed aliter mihi videtur. Nam in hoc loco de Judæis nil habet; inducit verò Umbritium, Romanum quidem, non Judæum, de con-
tumeliis, quibus pauperes afficiebant ebrii petulanteſque ju-
venes, conquerentem; et referentem verba talium juvenum
rogantium pauperem quendam, à quo conches et porra
mendicaſſet, et quo in loco ad medicandum ſtare aſſuetus
erat. Quinetiam haud veriſimile eſt Romanos mendicandi
causâ ſynagogas frequentâſſe, quum ipſi tunc temporis pau-
perrimi habebantur et mendici, ut ex hoc ipſo aliiſque con-
ſtat poetis. Inſuper quum poeta dicit; in quâ te quæro
Proſeuchâ? innuit, quod plurimæ erant tunc temporis Ro-
mæ Proſeuchæ. Non autem veriſimile eſt plurimas ibi
fuiſſe ſynagogas, quia Judæi tunc temporis pauperes erant
et exoſi et ſæpe ab Imperatoribus longè ab urbe diſcedere
juſſi.

Turnebus, ut hanc quæ autoris eſt ſententiam probet,
citat locum Cleomedis. Extat ille locus, lib. ii. p. 204.
Κυκλικῆς Θεωρίας μετεώρων, ubi Epicurum in ſuâ, de quâ glo-
riabatur, locutione vocibus corruptis, ridiculis et abſur-
dis uſum fuiſſe dicit; quarum quaſdam perſtringit, quaſi
ἀπο μεσης της προσευχης και των επ᾽ αυτης προςαιτουντων Ιουδαικα
τινα και παρακεχαραγμενα και κατα πολυ των εγπιτιο ταπεινο-
τερα. Sed de Synagogis Judæorum non videtur loqui.
Tempore enim Epicuri, nempe circa Ptolomæi Philadelphi
ætatem, lingua græca in ſynagogis, dum precabantur, uſos
fuiſſe Judæos, haud veriſimile eſt; et ſi uſi fuiſſent, an eas
Epicurus, homo gentilis et irreligioſus, frequentaret, ut
inde verba depromeret? et ſi ita feciſſet, an neceſſe eſſet
eæ voces eſſent corruptæ et humiles? Porro, quod non de
ſynagogis, ſed de locis ubi mendicantes ſtabant, egit,
conſtare mihi videtur ex voce προςαιτουντων, quæ non in ſynagogis precantibus, optimè verò alibi mendicantibus, con-
venit. Nec quicquam eſt hoc in loco, quod cujuſquam in
animum ſuſpicionem induceret, Cleomedem de Judæis e-
giſſe, niſi ſola vox Ιουδαικα. Sed ut ea vox hìc videtur ab-
ſurda,

Among thoſe who make the Synagogues and
Proſeuchæ to be different places, are the learned Mr. Joſeph Mede *, and Dr. Prideaux †;
and they think the difference conſiſts, partly,
in the form of the edifice; a ſynagogue, they
ſay, being ædificium tectum, like our houſes,
or churches; and a proſeuchæ being only en-
compaſſed with a wall, or ſome other mound
or encloſure, and open at the top, like our
courts ‡. They make them to differ in ſituation, ſynagogues being in towns and cities;
proſeuchæ in the fields, and frequently by the
river ſide §. Dr. Prideaux mentions another
diſ-

ſurda, et à contextu aliena, ita nullus dubito, quin corrup-
ta eſt. In verſione de Judæis ne verbum quidem; Ιsδαικα
autem redditur "vulgaria;" verſionis igitur autor non legit Ιsδαικα, ſed Ιδιωτικα; aut talem aliquam vocem. Eodem
modo ex Ιδιων, Act. xxiv. 23. aliqui conflaverunt Ιsδαιων,
ut in quibuſdam editionibus extat, et ad locum notat Eraſmus.—Προσιυχη ideo apud proſanos hoſce autores erat locus
publicus, in quo pauperes ſtipem petebant.

  * Ubi ſupra, p. 65, et ſeq.
  † Connect. part. i. book vi. vol. 2. p. 556, et ſeq.
edit. 10.
  ‡ See the account which Epiphanius gives of the jewiſh
Proſeuchæ, Hæres. lib. iii. tom. ii. hæres. lxxx. §. 1 Oper.
vol. 1. p. 1067, 1068. edit. Petav.
  § See a decree of the people of Halicarnaſſus, in favour
of the Jews, (Joſeph. Antiq. lib. xiv. cap. x. §. 23. p. 712.
edit Haverc.) in which are the following words,—διδοχται
ημιν Ιsδαιων τας βsλομιsας—τας πρcσιυχας ποιιsαι πρcς τη θα-
λασcη κατα το πατριον ιθος. The cuſtom of building Proſeuchæ by the water-ſide ſeems to have been derived from
another cuſtom of the Jews, namely, their waſhing before
prayer. (vid. Elſner. Obſerv. ſacr. in Act. xvi. 13.) though
De Dieu ſuppoſes it to be derived from the example of
Iſaac. There is a remarkable paſſage in Philo, which
ſhows how fond the Jews were of praying by the ſides of
rivers, or on the ſea-ſhore, Phil. in Flacc. p. 760. D, E.
edit. Colon. Allobr. 1613. See alſo de vit. Moſis, lib. 2.
p. 510. F. and Tertullian (ad nationes, lib. 1. cap. 13.
Oper. p. 50. edit. Rigalt.) among ſeveral jewiſh rites mentions Orationes litorales.

diftinction, in refpect to the fervice performed
in them ; in fynagogues, he faith, the prayers
were offered up in publick forms in common
for the whole congregation ; but in the profeuchæ they prayed, as in the temple, every one
apart for himfelf.   And thus our Saviour prayed in the profeucha into which he entered.

Yet after all, the proof in favour of this notion is not fo ftrong, but that it ftill remains a
queftion with fome, whether the fynagogues
and the profeuchæ were any thing more than
two different names for the fame place ; the
one taken from the peoples affembling in them,
the other from the fervice to which they were
more immediately appropriated ; namely, prayer.   Neverthelefs the name profeuchæ will not
prove, that they were appropriated only to
prayer, and therefore were different from fynagogues, in which the fcriptures were alfo read and expounded; fince the temple, in
which facrifices were offered, and all the parts
of divine fervice were performed, is called
οικος προσευχης, an houfe of prayer (*a*).   And
we find St. Paul preaching in the profeucha
at Philippi, in the forecited paffage of the
Acts (*b*)   Dr. Prideaux acknowledges, that
in our Saviour's time fynagogues were called
by the fame name with the profeuchæ ; and
fo both Jofephus * and Philo † feem to ufe the
word.

(*a*) Matt. xxi. 13.   (*b*) Acts xvi. 13.
* See the paffages before quoted from the life of Jofephus, where the Profeucha in which the people affembled
in a great multitude, feems to have been the great fynagogue at Tiberias.
† Philo fpeaks of many Profeuchæ in the city of Alexandria : πολλαι δε (προσιυκαι fc.) ιισι καθ ικαςον τμημα της
πολιως. (Legat. ad Caium, p. 782. F.) and of one in particular,

word *. Mr. Mede lays great ſtreſs upon that paſſage in the book of Joſhua, wherein he is ſaid "to
ſet up a pillar under an oak that was by the ſanctuary of the Lord (a);" to prove, that there were
proſeuchæ, even in Joſhua's time, diſtinct from
the tabernacle; arguing, that becauſe the law
expreſsly forbad planting trees near to God's
altar (b), therefore this ſanctuary of the Lord,
by the oak could not be the tabernacle, which
had the altar by it, but was one of the proſeuchæ, which were very often incloſed with trees †.
But Biſhop Patrick obſerves, that though it
was ſinful to plant trees near to God's altar, it
was not ſo to ſet up the ſanctuary under or near
the trees which had been planted before, eſpecially when it was done only for a ſhort time.
And he further remarks, that the words, " by,"
or, as it may be rendered, in " the ſanctuary of
the Lord," do not neceſſarily refer to the oak,
but may be connected with " the book of the
law of God," mentioned in the former clauſe:
" Joſhua wrote theſe words in the book of the
law of God, (and took a great ſtone, and ſet
it up under an oak) that was by, or in, the
ſanctuary of the Lord:" that is, he wrote theſe
words in the book of the law of God, that was
in the ſanctuary of the Lord; the intermediate
words

---

ticular, which he ſtiles μεγιςη και περισημοτατη, (p. 783. A.)
and it was, no doubt, that very celebrated and magnificent ſynagogue, of which the Jeruſalem Talmud gives a
very pompous deſcription. Vid. Vitring. lib. 1. part. 1.
cap. 14. p. 256.

* Vid. Vitring. de Synag. vetere, lib. 1. part. 1. cap. 4.
p. 119,—129. et Witſii Meletem. de vit. Pauli, ſect. v. iv.
p. 70, 71.

(a) Joſh. xxiv. 26.   (b) Deut. xvi. 21.

† Philo legat. ad Caium, p. 782. F. ταἱ μεν (προσευχαὶ)
επιφροτομησαν.

words being inſerted in a parentheſis.   There is
a ſimilar inſtance of a remote connection in the
following paſſage of the book of Geneſis, " And
Lot lifted up his eyes, and beheld all the plain
of Jordan, that it was well watered every where,
before the Lord deſtroyed Sodom and Gomor-
rah, even as the garden of the Lord, like the
land of Egypt, as thou comeſt unto Zoar (a):"
where the connection is, he " beheld all the
plain of Jordan, as thou comeſt unto Zoar, that
it was well watered every where, &c."

(a) Gen. xiii. 10.

CHAP. III.

Of the gates of Jerusalem and of the temple.

JERUSALEM, saith Godwin, had nine gates; or rather, according to the authors of the universal history, ten; five from west to east by south, and five from west to east by north.

By south	By north
1. Dung-gate,	1. Valley-gate,
2. Fountain-gate,	2. Gate of Ephraim,
3. Water-gate,	3. Old-gate,
4. Horse-gate,	4. Fish-gate,
5. Prison-gate, or Miphkadh.	5. Sheep gate.

This account is very little, if any thing, different from the plan of the city prefixed to the Polyglot. But Hottinger in his notes on Godwin *, hath given a very different description of the situation of these gates, which he endeavours to trace by the account of the order in which they were erected after the captivity, in the book of Nehemiah. Where the sheep-gate is mentioned first, which he places on the west side

* Thomæ Godwini Moses et Aaron &c. illustrati, emendati et præcipuis thematibus aucti, studio Joh. Henr. Hottingeri. p. 392 et seq. edit. 2. Francof. ad Mænum 1716.

fide of the city, and towards the fouth ; principally for thefe two reafons, becaufe he fuppofes it was the fame with the gate which Jofephus calls πυλη εσσηνων, that is, not the gate of
the Effenes, it being improbable, that a gate of
the city, which muft of courfe be common to
all forts of perfons, fhould be called by the
name of a particular fect; but the word Jofephus ufes, is, he imagines, only the hebrew
word הצאן hatfan, ovis, with a greek termi-
nation; and if fo, πυλη εσσηνων which Jofephus
faith was on the weft fide of the city, literally
fignifies the fheep-gate.   Another reafon for
his affigning it this fituation is, that the fifh-
gate, which is next mentioned in Nehemiah,
is placed by moft on the weft, with great probability, faith Hottinger, becaufe large quantities of fifh were brought into the city from that
quarter; and becaufe this fituation feems to be
affigned it in the following paffage of the fecond
book of chronicles: " Now Manaffeh built a
wall without the city of David, on the weft fide
of Gihon, in the valley, even to the entering
in at the fifh-gate."   Thus beginning at the
fouth-weft, he proceeds to the weft, and fo by
the north, quite round the city; affigning the
feveral gates their fituation according to the order in which they are mentioned in the facred
hiftory.

Spanheim places the fheep-gate on the eaft *,
Lightfoot on the fouth†; and in this and feveral
other refpects, the topography of Jerufalem is
a matter of great uncertainty.

Godwin informs us, that near the fheep-gate
was fituated the pool of Bethefda; επι τη προβα-
τικη,

---

* Spanheim. Hierofol. veteris topograph. defcrip. p. 50.
Oper. Geograph. &c. Lugd. Bat. 1701.
† Lightfoot's Harmony on John v. 2.

πικη, faith the evangelift John, where our tranflators take the word αγορα to be underftood;
and accordingly. have rendered it, " by the
fheep-market;" others with Godwin fupply the
noun πυλη, and render it " the fheep-gate;"
which is the more probable fenfe, referring to
the gate mentioned under this name by Nehemiah. And if this gate was fituated near the
temple, as is moft commonly fuppofed, perhaps it was fo called, becaufe the fheep and o-
ther cattle for facrifice, were ufually drove in
through it.

This pool of Bethefda demands our particular attention, on account of the miraculous
cures, which are afcribed to it in the gofpel of
St. John (a). It is there called Κολυμβηθρα : a
word, which though it be rendered pifcina by
Beza and the Vulgate, yet does not properly
fignify a fifh-pond, but rather a bath or pool
for fwimming, from κολυμβαω, nato. The Syriac
therefore renders it, according to the Polyglot
tranflation, locus baptifterii. Its proper name
in the hebrew or fyriac language, was Bethefda;
which Bochart *, Gomarus and fome others derive from בית beth domus vel locus, and אשד
afhadh effudit. So that according to this etymology, Βηθεσδα eft locus effufionis; that is,
as they conceive, either a refervoir for rain
water, or a kind of cefs-pool, that received the
wafte water which run from the temple. Wa-
genfeil † produces a paffage from the talmud
concerning a fmall ftream iffuing from the fanctuary, and proceeding to the gate of the city
of David, by which time it was become fo confiderable, that perfons in particular cafes, efpecially

(a) John v. 2,—4.
* Bochart. Geograph. lib. i. cap. xxxiv. oper. tom. 1.
p. 614. edit. Lugd. Bat. 1707.
† Sotah, cap. 1 §. xlvii. annot. 4. p. 508.

cially women, ufed to bathe in it.   And as he
fuppofes the water daily ufed in the temple fervice, in wafhing the hands and feet of the
priefts, the victims, veffels, &c. was fomewhere
or other collected into a refervoir ; if that was
called the pool of Bethefda, he profeffes he
fhould incline to explain the word by effufionis
domus.   But on the whole, he declares himfelf
uncertain.

Others, with greater probability, derive the
word from בית beth domus, and the fyriac
חשדא chefdo, gratia vel mifericordia; and fo
the name fignifies the houfe or place of mercy,
becaufe of the miraculous healing virtue, with
which God mercifully endowed the water of
that pool ; and this is indeed the moft extraordinary thing to be obferved concerning it.

The Evangelift fays, that " an angel went
down at a certain feafon into the pool, and troubled the water ; whofoever then, firft after the
troubling the water, ftepped in, was made
whole of whatever difeafe he had ;" and therefore there lay at this pool, in the five porticos
that furrounded it (of which we have already
taken fome notice) " a multitude of impotent
folks, as blind, halt, withered, waiting for the
moving of the water."   Now it is difputed,
whether the virtue of thefe waters, and the
cures performed by them, were miraculous or
natural ?   Dr. Hammond contends for the latter, and imagines that the healing virtue of this
bath was owing to the warm entrails of the victims being wafhed in it : that the angel who is
faid to come and trouble the water, was only a
meffenger fent by the high prieft to ftir up the
bath, in order to mix the congealed blood and
other groffer particles that were funk to the
bottom,

bottom, with the water; that fo they might infufe their virtue into it more ftrongly. By κατα καιρον, which we render " at a certain fea- fon" he underftands at a fet time, that is, at one of the great feafts, when a vaft multitude of facrifices were killed and offered, and by that means the waters of this pool were impreg- nated with more healing virtue than they would have at other times. But this fenfe of the paf- fage, in which Dr. Hammond thinks himfelf countenanced by the authority of Theophylact*; appears improbable from almoft all the circum- ftances of the ftory †. As

1ft, From the healing virtue of this water extending to the cure of all manner of difeafes. For it is faid, " he that ftepped in was made whole of whatever difeafe he had." Dr. Ham- mond indeed fuppofes, that " whatever difeafe he

---

* An attentive reader of Theophylact's commentary in loc. will eafily perceive that Dr. Hammond hath miftaken his meaning; for Theophylact never intended to affert, that thefe miraculous cures were owing to the wafhing the entrails of the beafts flain for facrifice in the waters of this pool, which thereby acquired, in a natural way, a fanitive virtue. All he faith, is, that by this wafhing the water was fanctified, and become thereby the more fit (for what ? for healing difeafes by any natural quality hereby impart- ed to it ? no; but) for receiving δυναμιν θειοτεραν a divine power by the operation of the angel, who came to it not as to common water, but as to chofen water, υδατι ως εκλικτω, and wrought the miracle, θαυματεργειν. He fays exprefsly, that the water did not heal by any virtue in itfelf, other- wife thefe cures would have been conftant and perpetual; but folely through the energy ενεργεια of the angel, who imparted to it its healing virtue.

† See alfo an attempt to account for the virtue of thefe waters in a fimilar manner from natural caufes, in a tract publifhed by Bartholine a learned foreign phyfician, enti- tled, Paralytici Novi Teftamenti medico et philologico commentario illuftrati; and republifhed in Crenius's Fafci- culus quintus. Vid. p. 313,—333. and p. 390,—411.

he had," refers only to the three forts of di-
feafed perfons beforementioned, namely, " the
blind, lame and withered." But that will not
remove the objection, fince no fuch healing virtue could ever be communicated to any other
water by the fame means, by wafhing the warm
entrails of beafts in it, fo as to render it effectual for the cure of all thefe difeafes, or indeed
of any one of them.

2dly, It is highly improbable, that the troubling or ftirring up the water fhould increafe
its healing virtue; but rather, the ftirring up
the blood and fœces, that were funk to the
bottom, muft make the bath fo foul and fetid,
that it would be more likely to poifon than cure.

3dly, No good reafon can be given on this
fuppofition, why thefe medicinal waters fhould
not have cured many perfons as well as one
only, the firft that ftepped in. The doctor is
indeed aware of this objection, and endeavours
to evade it, by fuppofing the bath might be fo
fmall, that it would hold but one at a time;
and by the time one was cured, the healing
particles were fubfided, and therefore it could
not heal another. But then, why could it not
be ftirred up a fecond time, and a third, and as
many as there were perfons to be cured? However,

4thly, The whole foundation of this fuppofition appears to be a miftake; namely, that the
entrails of the victims were wafhed in this pool
out of the temple; for Dr. Lightfoot fhows that
it was done in the temple, in the wafhing room
as it was called, appointed for that purpofe *.

_____

* See Dr. Lightfoot's Defcription of the temple, chap.
31. And he fuppofes, (Hor. Heb. Joh. v. 2.) that the
pool

And indeed, if this pool was near the sheep-gate, and if we suppose Hottinger's, or even Lightfoot's account of the situation of that gate to be true, it was then at too great a distance from the temple, to be used as a washing-place for the entrails of the beasts slain for sacrifice.

Upon the whole therefore, there is reason to conclude, that the healing virtue of this pool was miraculous; that the angel was a heavenly angel, and that the design and use of his coming was either to work the miracle, as God's instrument, by the use of the water; or at least, by troubling the water, and giving it some unusual motion, to give notice to those who were waiting for a cure, when they might seek it.

It is further enquired, when this miraculous pool first received its healing virtue? I take the most probable opinion to be, that it was about the time of, or not long before, our Saviour's coming; and very likely the chief intent of the miracle might be, to give notice, by an illustrious type, of the speedy accomplishment of Zechariah's prophecy, " In that day there shall be a fountain opened to the house of David, and to the inhabitants of Jerusalem, for sin and for uncleanness (a)." Thus the fountain of the blood of Christ to take away all sin, was afresh typified by the miraculous virtue, which God put into this pool to heal all manner of diseases. And as the fountain of Christ's blood was to be opened at the passover, at which feast he was crucified, so Dr. Lightfoot imagines

gines

of Bethesda was a bath, κολυμβηθρα, in which those who were unclean purified themselves.

(a) Zech. xiii. 1.

gines, that the miraculous cure was effected by this pool at that feaft only *.

It may feem a little ftrange, that there is no mention made of this miracle, either by Jofe-phus, or the writers of the talmud; who on all other occafions are ready enough to celebrate the miracles which God wrought for, and which did honour to their nation. But fuppofing, which is highly probable, that the miraculous virtue was firft imparted to this pool about the time of our Saviour's coming, and that it ceafed at his death; whereby it plainly appeared that this miracle was wrought in honour of Chrift; we need not wonder, that Jofephus paffes it over in filence; fince he could not relate it without reviving a teftimony to Chrift, greatly to the difcredit of his own nation, who rejected and crucified him. And as it is not recorded by Jofephus, it is not unlikely, that the memory of it was loft among the Jews at the time when the talmud was written, which was not till feveral hundred years afterward †.

Concerning the gates of the temple Godwin obferves, that there were two of principal note, both built by Solomon; the one for thofe that were new-married, the other for mourners and excommunicated perfons. The mourners, he faith, were diftinguifhed from the excommunicated by having their lips covered with a fkirt of their garment; none entered that gate with

G 2 their

* Horæ hebraic. Joh. v. 4.
† There are two very learned differtations on this fub-ject in the fecond volume of the Thefaurus novus theolo-gico philologicus; one by Joan. Conrad. Hottingerus de pifcinâ Bethefda; the other by David Ebersbach, de Mira-culo pifcinæ Bethefdæ. The laft contains a full reply both to Bartholine and Hammond. See alfo Witfii Mifcell. tom. 2. Exercitat. xi. §. liv,—lx. p. 314,—320.

their lips uncovered, but such as were excommunicated.   The Mishna saith, " All that enter according to the custom of the temple, go
in on the right hand way, go round and go out
on the left hand way ; except a person, cui ac-
cidit aliquid, who is rendered unclean by a particular circumstance, who goes round and en-
ters on the left.   And being asked why he does
so ; if he answers, because I mourn, they reply,
he who inhabits this house comfort thee.   If
he answer, because I am excommunicated, the
reply is, according to R. Jose, he who inhabits
this house, put it into thy heart, to hearken to
the words of thy companions, or brethren, that
they may receive thee *."   It appears from
hence, (at least according to the opinion of the
mishnical rabbies,) that excommunicated persons were not excluded from the temple ; though
they were from the synagogue, as we learn from
several passages in the evangelist John (a), where
such persons are said to be αποσυναγωγοι, excluded from the synagogue.   Not that we are to
infer from this, that the Jews accounted their
synagogues more holy than the temple ; but it
shows what was, and should be, the true intent
of excommunication, namely, the shaming and
humbling an offender, in order to bring him to
repentance ; on which account he was excluded
the society of his neighbours in the synagogue :
but not his eternal destruction, by driving him
from the presence of God in the temple, and
depriving him of the use of the most solemn
ordinances, and the most effectual means of
grace

---

* Mish. tit. Middoth. cap. 2. §. 2. et Maimon. in loc.
tom. 5. p. 334, 335. edit. Surenhus. Lightf. Hor. hebr.
1 Cor. v. 5.

(a) John ix. 22. xii. 42. xvi. 2.

grace and falvation.　The temple was the common place of worfhip for Ifraelites; by allowing him to come thither they fignified, that they did not exclude him from the common privilege of an Ifraelite, though they would not receive him into their familiarity and friendfhip.　How much heavier is the yoke of Antichrift than the jewifh yoke of bondage! How much more cruel is the excommunication of popery, which deprives perfons of all their liberties and privileges, of their goods and lives, and configns over their fouls to be tormented in hell for ever! How infinitely more cruel, I fay, is this modern excommunication, than even that of the wicked and barbarous Jews, who crucified the Lord of glory!

C H A P. IV.

Of their groves, and high places.

WE have several times had occasion to observe, that in order the more effectually to guard the Israelites from idolatry, the blessed God in instituting the rites of his own worship, went directly counter to the practice of the idolatrous nations. Thus, because they worshipped in groves *, he expresly forbad " the planting a grove of trees near his altar (a)" Nor would he suffer his people to offer their sacrifices on the tops of hills and moun-

---

* Hæc (nemora sc.) suere numinum templa, priscoque ritu simplicia rura Deo præcellentem arborem dicant. Nec magis auro fulgentia atque ebore simulacra quam lucos et ipsa silentia adoramus. Plin. nat. hist. lib. xii. cap. 1. p. 4. tom. 3. edit. Harduin. 1685. See also Lucian. de Sacrif. tom. 1. p. 355. C, D. edit. Salmur. 1619. These groves Plutarch calls αλση Στων, the groves of the gods, which he saith Numa frequented, and thereby gave occasion to the story of his commerce with the goddess Egeria. Plutarc. in Numa, p. 61. F. oper. tom. 1. edit. Francof. 1620. They are expresly injoined by the laws of the twelve tables, as a part of the publick religion, Lucos in agris habento. Vid. Duodecim Tabular. Fragm. tit. Ubi colendi. ad calcemCod. Justiniani p. 751. apud Corp. Juris Civil. edit. Lipf. 1720.

(a) Deut. xvi. 21. See Spencer's learned dissertation on this and the following verse, de Leg. Hebræor. lib. ii. cap. xxvii, xxviii.

mountains, as the heathens did *; but ordered that they fhould be brought to one altar in the place which he appointed (a). And as for the groves, which the Canaanites had planted, and the idols and altars which they had erected on the tops of high mountains and hills for the worfhip of their Gods, the Ifraelites are commanded utterly to deftroy them (b).

The groves and high places do not feem to have been different, but the fame places, or groves planted on the tops of hills, probably round an open area, in which the idolatrous worfhip was performed; as may be inferred from the following words of the prophet Hofea, " they facrifice upon the tops of mountains, and burn incenfe upon the hills, under oaks and poplars and elms (c)." The ufe of groves for religious worfhip is generally fuppofed to have been as ancient as the patriarchal ages; for we are informed that " Abraham planted a grove in Beerfheba, and called there on the name of the Lord (d)." However, it is not exprefsly faid, nor can it by this paffage be proved, that he planted the grove for any religious purpofe; it might only be defigned to

G 4   fhade

---

* Sophocles introduces Hercules asking Hyllus, whether he knew mount Œta, which was facred to Jupiter? Yes, faith he, for I have often facrificed upon the top of it. Trachin. v. 1207, 1208. tom. 2. p. 325. edit. Glafg. 1745. And Strabo faith of the Perfians, αγαλματα και βωμυς υκ ιδρυονται, θυυσι δε εν υψηλω τοπω τον υρανον ηγεμενοι Δια. Geograph. lib. xv. p. 732. C. edit. Cafaub. 1620. See alfo Herodot. Clio, cap. cxxxi. p. 55. §. 131. edit. Gronov. Xenophon. Cyr. lib. viii. p. 500. edit. 3. Hutchinf. And Appian (de bello Mithrad. p. 361, 362. §. 215. edit. Tollii, Amftel. 1670.) faith, that Mithridates facrificed to Jupiter according to the cuftom of his country, επι ορυς υψηλυ, upon a high mountain.

(a) Deut. xii. 13, 14.   (b) ver. 2, 3.   (c) Hof. iv. 13.
(d) Gen. xxi. 33.

fhade his tent. And this circumftance perhaps
is recorded to intimate his rural way of living,
as well as his religious charaƈter ; that he dwelt
in a tent under the fhade of a grove, or tree,
as the word אשל efhel, may more properly be
tranflated ; and in this humble habitation led a
very pious and devout life.

The reafon and origin of planting facred
groves is varioufly conjeƈtured ; fome imagining, it was only hereby intended to render the
fervice more agreeable to the worfhippers, by
the pleafantnefs of the fhade * ; whereas others
fuppofe it was to invite the prefence of the
gods. The one or the other of thefe reafons
feems to be intimated in the forecited paffage of
Hofea, " they burn incenfe under oaks, and
poplars and elms, becaufe the fhade thereof is
good (a)." Others conceive their worfhip was
performed in the midft of groves, becaufe the
gloom of fuch a place is apt to ftrike a religious awe upon the mind † ; or elfe, becaufe
                                            fuch

---

* This feems, according to Virgil, to have been the
reafon of Dido's building the temple of Juno in a delight-
ful grove,

Lucus in urbe fuit mediâ, lætiffimus umbrâ :
Hic templum Junoni ingens Sidonia Dido
Condebat.   Æneid. lib. i. v. 445.

(a) Hof. iv. 13.
† Si tibi occurrit, faith Seneca, (Epift. xli.) vetuftis ar-
boribus, et folitam altitudinem egreffis frequens lucus, et
confpeƈtum cœli denfitate ramorum aliorum alios protegen-
tium fubmovens : illa proceritas fylvæ, et fecretum loci et
admiratio umbræ, in aperto tam denfæ atque continuæ, fi-
dem tibi numinis facit. Et fiquis fpecus faxis penitus ex-
efis montem fufpenderit, non manufaƈtus, fed naturalibus
caufis in tantam laxitatem excavatus : animum tuum qua-
dam religionis fufpicione percutiet. See alfo a remarkable paffage in Virgil, Æneid. viii. v. 347, et feq.

fuch dark concealments fuited the lewd myfteries of their idolatrous worfhip *.

I have met with another conjecture, which
feems as probable as any; that this practice
began with the worfhip of demons or departed
fouls.   It was an ancient cuftom to bury the
dead under trees, or in woods.   "Deborah
was buried under an oak, near Bethel (a);" and
the bones of Saul and Jonathan under a tree at
Jabefh (b).   Now an imagination prevailing a-
mong the heathen, that the fouls of the deceaf-
ed hover about their graves, or at leaft delight
to vifit their dead bodies ; the idolaters, who
paid divine honours to the fouls of their departed heroes, erected images and altars for
their worfhip in the fame groves where they
were buried † ; and from thence it grew into
a cuftom afterwards to plant groves, and build
temples, near the tombs of departed heroes (c),
                                        and

* For proof of the lewdnefs and obfcenity of many of
the religious rites of the heathen, vid. Herodot. Euterp. cap.
64. p. 112, 113. edit. Gronov. et Clio. §. 199. p. 80. Dio-
dor. Sicul. lib. 4. init. Valer. Maxim. lib. ii. cap. vi. §. 15.
p. 185. 186. edit. Thyfii, Ludg. Bat. 1655. Juvenal. Sat.
ix. v. 24. and what Eufebius faith of a grove on mount
Libanus, dedicated to Venus, in his life of Conftantine,
lib. iii. cap. 55.   Compare 1 Kings xiv. 23, 24.
   (a) Gen. xxxv. 8.   (b) 1 Sam. xxxi. 13.
   † Plato, after having declared his approbation of the
fentiment of Hefiod, that when any of the golden age
died, they became demons, and the authors of great good
to mankind ; and after having afferted that all who died
bravely in war, were entitled to be ranked in the fame
clafs ; reckons among the honours they deferved, their fepulchres being efteemed and worfhipped as the repofitories
of demons.—ως δαιμονας ατω δεραπευσομεν τι και προσκυνησο-
μεν αιτων τας δηκας. De Republ. lib. v. p. 662. D, E. edit.
Ficin. Francofurt. 1602.
   (c) 2 Kings xxiii. 15, 16.   See Arrian's defcription of
the tomb of Cyrus, de Expedit. Alexandr. lib. vi. p. 435.
edit. Blancard. Amftel. 1678.

and to furround their temples and altars with
groves and trees * ; and thefe facred groves being conftantly furnifhed with the images of the
heroes or gods that were worfhipped in them,
a grove and an idol came to be ufed as convert-
ible terms (a).

We have before obferved, that thefe facred
groves were ufually planted on the tops of hills
or mountains ; from whence they are called in
fcripture, במות bamoth, or " high places."
Perhaps fuch an exalted fituation was chofen by
idolaters, in refpect to their chief god, the fun,
whom they worfhipped, together with their inferior deities, on the tops of hills and mountains, that they might approach as near to him
as they could †. It is no improbable conjecture concerning the Egyptian pyramids, that
they were intended as altars to the fun, as well
as very likely for fepulchral monuments, like
thefe ancient groves. Accordingly they are all
flat at the top, to ferve the purpofes of an altar. It is faid, that altars to the fun, of the
fame form though not fo large as the pyramids,
were found among the american idolaters ‡.

There might be another reafon for planting
the facred groves on the tops of hills and
mountains ; namely, for the fake of retirement from noife and difturbance in their acts
of

---

* On account of the cuftom of planting trees near temples, " the poets, as Strabo informs us, ftiled all their
temples groves, even thofe which had no plantations around
them." Geograph. lib. ix. p. 412. D. edit. Cafaub. 1620.

(a) 2 Kings xxiii. 6.

† Tacitus fpeaks of fome places, which were thought
maximè cœlo propinquare, precefque mortalium à Deo
nufquam proprius audiri. Annal. lib. xiii. §, lvii. p. 281.
edit. Glafg. 1743.

‡ See Young's Hiftorical Differtation on Idolatrous corruptions in religion, vol. 1. p. 222,—228.

of worſhip *. And on this account, probably,
the worſhippers of the true God had alſo their
proſeuchæ, or places of retirement for worſhip,
generally on hills or high places. Accordingly
we read, that Chriſt " went up into a mountain apart to pray (a)." And at his transfigura-
tion, he retired with three of his " diſciples to
the top of a high mountain apart (b)." I ſee no
reaſon therefore to conclude, that thoſe high
places, of which we read in the Old Teſtament,
where holy men and worſhippers of the true
God paid their devotion, were the ſacred groves
of the idolaters ; but rather they were jewiſh
proſeuchæ, or ſynagogues. Such were the high
places by the city where Samuel lived, and
where he ſacrificed with the people (c) ; and
upon the hill of Gath, where was either a ſchool
of the prophets, or they had been thither to
pay their devotion, when Saul met them (d).
And of the ſame ſort was the great high place
at Gibeon, where Solomon ſacrificed, and where
God appeared to him in a dream (e).

The grand difficulty on this head is how to
reconcile their ſacrificing in other places beſide
the national altar, as Gideon did at Ophrah (f),
Manoah in the country of Dan (g), Samuel at
Mizpah (h), and at Bethlehem (i), David in the
threſhing floor of Ornan (k), and Elijah on
mount Carmel (l) ; with the law in the book of
Deuteronomy, " Take heed to thyſelf, that
                                                    thou

---

* Lucos et ipſa ſilentia adoramus, ſaith Pliny in a paſſage before-cited.
    (a) Matt. xiv. 23.   (b) Matt. xvii. 1.   (c) 1 Sam.
ix. 12,—14.   (d) See 1 Sam. x. 5,—13.   (e) 1 Kings
iii. 4, 5.   (f) Judg. vi. 24.   (g) Judg. xiii. 16,—20.
(h) 1 Sam. vii. 10.   (i) chap. xvi. 5.   (k) 1 Chron.
xxi. 22.   (l) 1 Kings xviii. 30, et ſeq.

thou offer not thy burnt-offerings in every place
that thou feeft.   But in the place, which the
Lord thy God fhall choofe, there thou fhalt offer thy burnt-offerings, and there thou fhalt do
all that I command thee (*a*)."

The beft folution, I apprehend, is, that it
was done by fpecial divine direction and command, God having an undoubted right to fu-
perfede his own pofitive laws, when, and in
what cafes he pleafes; and as this is exprefsly
afferted to have been done in David's cafe beforementioned (*b*), it may the more reafonably
be fuppofed in all the reft.

This may intimate to us the true folution
of another difficulty, how to reconcile the law
which prefcribes an altar " of earth only to be
made in all places where God fhould record his
name (*c*)," with the order, which Mofes received
to make a brazen altar in the court of the tabernacle.

Some have fuppofed, that the brazen altar
was filled with earth and ftones, and fo was an
altar of earth, though cafed with brafs.   But
the real folution I take to be this : " In all
places where I record my name," means, in
whatever particular place befide the national
altar, I fhall caufe my name to be recorded,
by commanding my fervants to facrifice unto
me, there thou fhalt make an altar of earth.

The reafon of God's appointing fuch plain
and inartificial altars on thefe fpecial occafions,
was in all likelihood to prevent that fuperftitious veneration, which the people would probably have entertained for them, as having a
more than ordinary fanctity in them, if they
had

(*a*) Deut. xii. 13, 14.   (*b*) 1 Chron. xxi. 18.
(*c*) Exod. xx. 24.

had been more expensive and durable ; whereas being raised just to serve a present exigence, and presently pulled down, or falling of themselves, they could not administer any temptation to superstition or idolatry.

But to return : Though some places were called by the name of high places, which had never been polluted with heathen idolatry, and in which God was acceptably worshipped ; nevertheless, all which had been actually so defiled, the Israelites are commanded utterly to destroy ; insomuch that it is left upon record, as a stain and blemish upon the character of some of the more pious kings of Judah, that they did not destroy them, but suffered the people who were very prone to idolatry, to sacrifice in them. Which is the case of Asa (*a*), Jehoshaphat (*b*), and several others.

(*a*) 1 Kings xv. 14.   (*b*) chap. xxii. 43.

C H A P.

CHAP. V.

Of the cities of refuge.

THE latin word afylum, ufed for a fanctuary or place of refuge, has fo near an
affinity with the hebrew word אשל efhel, a tree
or grove, as to make it probable, that the facred groves which we fpoke of in the laft chapter, were the antient places of refuge, and that
the Romans derived the ufe of them from the
eaftern nations. So we find in Virgil, that the
afyla were groves * :

Hinc lucum ingentem quem Romulus acer
        afylum
Rettulit.   Æneid. viii. l. 342.

And

* Mr. Jones fuppofes, that the reafon why thefe groves
were confidered as places of refuge was the opinion which
prevailed, that the demons to whom they were dedicated,
afforded their affiftance to thofe who fled to them for pio-
tection. Afylorum origo mihi deducenda videtur ex anti-
quorum erga mortuos reverentia, et opinione eorum poten-
tiæ opem ferendi fupplicibus.—Illi, qui à potentioribus
metuebant. ad fepulcra virorum eximiorum confugiebant.
Vid. Senecam in Troad, Act. 3.—Ita Plutarchus Thefei
                                        fepul-

And God's altar appears to have been the afylum of the Jews, before the cities of refuge
were appointed (*a*).   Some perfons have imagined that all the cities of the Levites, in number forty two, were afyla.   But that appears to
be a miftake; for in the book of Numbers (*b*),
among the cities that were given to the Levites,
only fix are mentioned, as appointed to be cities
of refuge.

Thefe afyla were not only intended for Jews,
but for Gentiles, or for ftrangers, who dwelt
among them (*c*).

They were not defigned as fanctuaries for
wilful murderers and all kinds of atrocious vil-
lains among the Jews, as they were among the
Greeks and Romans *, and now are in roman
catholic

---

fepulcrum fuiffe afylum dicit, in vitâ Thefei, fub fin.   He
obferves, that God never appointed his altar for an afylum;
neverthelefs, it was fo confidered before the giving of the
law in Exodus concerning the cities of refuge.   On which
account he imagines, that the origin of afyla was not a
divine inftitution; but that God, by his appointment of cities of refuge, perhaps intended to check and reftrain the
fuperftitious and idolatrous ufe of groves and altars for this
purpofe.   Annot. MS. in Godwini Mof. et Aaron.

(*a*) Exod. xxi. 14.   (*b*) Numb. xxxv. 6.   (*c*) ver. 15.
* Privilegia afylorum, inquit Jonefius, fumma erant;
certa enim in illis fupplicibus falus, nec ullus inde fub
quovis prætextu ad pœnam extrahendus, διδωχασι γαρ δε
αδιαν ενταυθα ικετευσι. Paufan. lib. 2. p. 108. l. 45. edit.
Xyland. Hanov. 1613. nec de eo qui in afylum confuge-
rat, judicium inftituebant, nec examinabant, an talis vitæ dignus erat, an non.   Eum verò Diis relinquendum
cenfebant.   Ita Leotycidam, quamvis proditionis reum,
nunquam extrahere conati funt Lacedæmonii.   Paufan.
lib. 3. p. 171. l. 44, et feq.   Ita Livius, lib. 44. cap.
29.   Sanctitas templi infulæque inviolatos præftabat
omnes.   Et idem de cujuflibet generis maleficis, quinetiam
obæratis, teftatur Tacitus, Annal. lib. 3. cap. 60. Verum
eft quod aliqui aliquando hæc violârunt privilegia; fed ii
habe-

catholic countries*; but merely for securing
those who had been guilty of involuntary ho-
micide (a) from the effects of private revenge,
until they were cleared by a legal process. And
it is observable, that the Israelites are commanded to " prepare the way," that is, to make
the road good, " that every slayer may flee thither" without impediment, and with all expedition (b). And as Godwin observes, the rabbies inform us, among other circumstances,
that at every cross-road was set up an inscrip-
tion, Asylum, Asylum. Upon which Hottinger remarks, that it was probably in allusion to
this custom, that John the Baptist is described
as " the voice of one crying in the wilderness,
prepare ye the way of the Lord, make his paths
straight (c)." He was the Messiah's forerunner,
and in that character was to remove the obsta-
cles to men's flying to him as their asylum, and
obtaining σωτηριον τε Θεε, the salvation of God.

For any thing further on this subject we refer
to Godwin's Moses and Aaron, especially with
Hottinger's notes.

habebantur hominum scelestissimi, nec à pœnâ ab homini-
bus erant liberi, nisi nimia eos tuebatur potentia. Vid.
Thucyd. lib. i. §. 126. p. 69, 70. et §. 134. p. 174, 175.
edit. Hudson. Saltem vero violatorum horum privilegio-
rum acerrimi vindices habebantur Dii. Vid. Juitin. lib. 8.
cap. 1, 2. Pausan. lib. 1. p. 36. l. 20. et seq. et lib. 7.
p. 445. l. 50, et seq. p. 447. l. 37. edit. Xyland. Hanov.
1613.

* Middleton's Letter from Rome, p. 156,—158 of his
miscellan. works, vol. 5, octav.

(a) Deut. xix. 4,—10.   (b) ver. 3.   (c) Luke iii.
4,—6.

JEWISH ANTIQUITIES:

BOOK the THIRD

Concerning Times.

CHAP. I.

Of days, hours, weeks and years.

THE Hebrews, in common with other nations, diftinguifhed their days into natural, confifting of twenty four hours; and artificial, that is, from fun-rife to fun-fet.

Concerning the natural day, it is enquired, when it began and ended.

Godwin conceives the ancient Jews had two different beginnings of the natural day; one of the facred or feftival day, which was in the evening; the other of the civil or working day, which was in the morning. That the facred day began in the evening, is certain from the following paffage of Leviticus: "From even unto even fhall ye celebrate your fabbaths (a);" and alfo from the following words in the book of Exodus, "In the firft month, on the fourteenth day of the month at even, ye fhall eat

H 2
un-

unleavened bread, untill the one and twentieth
day of the month at even (a)." Neverthelefs,
the paffage which our author alledges out of the
evangelift Matthew, " In the end of the fabbath, as it began to dawn towards the firft day
of the week (b) ;" does not fo certainly prove
that the civil, natural day began in the morning. For, " the firft day of the week" may
there be underftood of the artificial day ; as
indeed the word επιφωσκουση * feems to imply.
In like manner, though we begin the natural
day at midnight, yet we fpeak of the day breaking or dawning a little before fun-rife. That
the Jews began the day, not at evening, but at
midnight, or in the morning, at the time of
their migration out of Egypt, appears from
hence, that the fifteenth day of the month, in
which they departed from Egypt, is faid to be
the morrow after the paffover, which was kept
on the fourteenth day in the evening (c). But
neither will this prove, that they reckoned the
beginning of their civil, and facred day, from
a different epocha. It is more probable, that,
before their departure out of Egypt, they began
all their days, both civil and facred, with the
fun's rifing, as the ancient Babylonians, Perfians, Syrians, and moft of the eaftern nations
did †. And, at the time of their migration,
God ordered them to change the beginning,
not only of the year and of the week, but likewife of the day, from the morning to the evening, in oppofition to the cuftoms of the idolatrous

---

(a) Exod. xii. 18.   (b) Matt. xxviii. 1.
* See on this word Dr. Macknight's Commentary in
loc.
(c) Numb. xxxiii. 3. compared with Exod. xii. 6.
† Petav. de doctrinâ temperum, lib. vii. p. 609.

trous nations, who, in honour to their chief God, the fun, began their day at his rifing.

Cocceius, who fuppofes, that only the facred day began in the evening, finds out this myftery in it; that God appointed the fabbath of the jewifh church to begin with the night, in order to fignify the darknefs of that difpenfation, compared with the fubfequent one of the Gofpel; the light of divine knowledge being in thofe times like that of the moon and ftars in the night, but under the chriftian difpenfation, like that of the fun in the day *.

It has been commonly fuppofed, that the epocha, or beginning, of the natural day was originally in the evening; " the evening and the morning, faith Mofes, in the book of Genefis, were the firft day (*a*)." And if fo, we are to conclude, that the idolaters had changed the beginning of the day to the morning, in honour of the fun; and that God reftored it, by the law which he gave to the Jews, to its original epocha. But learned men are not agreed about the meaning of this paffage, and the reafon of Mofes's fetting the evening before the morning. Le Clerc † begins the firft day from the creation of the chaos, and by the evening he underftands all the time it remained in darknefs, before the production of light. But this opinion does not well agree with the import of the hebrew word עֶרֶב gnerebh, the evening, from עָרַב gnarabh, mifcuit; which therefore denotes twilight, in which there is a kind of mixture of light and darknefs; rather

    than

---

* Vid. Cocceii Comment. in Lev. xxiii. §. 18. oper. tom. 1. p. 173.

(*a*) Gen. i. 5.   † In loc.

than total darkneſs, ſuch as there was before
light was produced.

Others think it more natural, to date the beginning of time, and the ſucceſſion of day and
night, from the firſt production of light. But
as for the reaſon of Moſes's ſetting the evening
before the morning, the moſt probable opinions
are thoſe of Cocceius and Lyra. Cocceius underſtands the words in the following manner,
that the light moved away from the place or
hemiſphere, on which it firſt appeared, and
was ſucceeded by darkneſs ; and when it returned to enlighten the ſame hemiſphere again,
the firſt day was compleated *. So that, according to him, the evening ſignifies the light
moving away, which it began to do from its
firſt appearance.

The other opinion is, that the two parts of
the natural day, namely, the artificial day and
artificial night, are denominated from the terms
which compleat them, from the evening which
is the end of the day, and from the morning
which is the end of the night ; and ſo the evening and the morning make up one natural day ;
namely from morning to morning †.

But whatever were the reaſons of Moſes's
ſetting the evening before the morning, or the
night before the day, his expreſſion has plainly
been followed by other writers, and in other languages. Hence days are expreſſed in the book
of Daniel, by ערב־בקר gnerebh-boker, evening and morning (a). Hence alſo is the uſe of
the greek word νυχθημερον (b). And may we
not obſerve ſome faint traces of the ſame original

---

* Vid. Cocceii Cur. prior. in Gen. i. 5.
† Vid. Lyr. apud Poli Synops. in loc.
(a) Dan. viii. 14.   (b) 2 Cor. xi. 25.

ginal in the englifh language, in our computing
time by nights rather than by days; as, in the
words fe'n-night, fortnight, &c.

With refpect to the artificial day and night,
I obferve, that the Hebrews divided the night
into four watches, as appears from St. Matthew,
who fpeaks of the fourth watch of the night (*a*);
and from St. Mark, who ftiles thefe watches,
the even, midnight, cockcrowing, and the
morning (*b*).   Neverthelefs it fhould feem, that
they anciently divided the night into an odd
number of watches, probably into three ; fince
we read in the book of Judges, of "the middle watch (*c*)."

It is probable, thefe watches had their rife,
and their name, from the watchmen, who kept
guard at the gates of the city and of the temple by night, and who relieved one another by
turns.   And if anciently there were but three
watches, then each watched four hours ; and
more, in the winter, when the nights are above
twelve long.   But that being found too te-
dious and tirefome, the number of watches was
afterwards increafed to four.   We, therefore,
never read of the middle watch in the new
teftament.

The day was divided into hours ; which are
reckoned to be of two forts, lefs and greater.
The leffer hours were twelve, as appears from
the following queftion in the evangelift John,
" Are there not twelve hours in the day (*d*)?"
Each of thefe was a twelfth part of the artificial day.   Herodotus obferves, that the Greeks
learned

(*a*) Matt. xiv. 25.   (*b*) Mark xiii. 35.   (*c*) Judg.
vii. 19.   (*d*) John xi. 9.

learned from the Egyptians, among other things, the method of dividing the day into twelve parts. But whether the Hebrews derived it from the Egyptians, or the Egyptians from the Hebrews, cannot now be known. Nor does it appear how ancient this division of the day into hours, among the Hebrews, was. The first hint in scripture, which seems to imply such a division, is a passage in the second book of Kings (a), where we read of the shadow's going back twenty degrees on the sun-dial of Ahaz. But the history gives us no intimation, what those degrees were, or what portion of time was marked by them.

The mention of this dial suggests a question which has occasioned much dispute among the learned : Whether the miracle of the shadow's going back was wrought upon the sun, or only upon the dial ? Vatablus, Montanus, and several moderns observe, that there is not a word said of the sun's going back, but only of the shadow upon the dial ; which might be effected by the divine power, perhaps by the ministry of angels, obstructing or refracting the rays of the sun, or altering the position of the dial, so as to make the shadow retire without changing the motion of the sun itself. The Jews in general are of the contrary opinion, with which archbishop Usher agrees; who says, that the sun and all the heavenly bodies went back, and as much was detracted from the next night, as was added to this day *.

The arguments on this side of the question are

1st, The

1ft, The words of Ifaiah (a), that " the fun returned ten degrees." But this may poffibly be meant only of its fhadow, efpecially in fo poetical a writer as Ifaiah.

2dly, That the miracle was obferved at Babylon, from whence Meradach-Baladan fent to enquire about it (b). Which could not have been the cafe, unlefs it had been wrought on the fun itfelf, and not merely on the dial of Ahaz. To this it is anfwered, that it does not appear the miracle was obferved at Babylon; rather the contrary. For it is faid, " The princes of Babylon fent to enquire of the wonder that was done in the land;" not as a thing they themfelves had feen in their own country, which muft have been the cafe, if the miracle had been wrought on the fun; but which they had heard reported as done in the land of Ifrael *.

To return to our fubject; the firft mention we have of hours in the Old Teftament is in the book of Daniel, particularly in the fourth chapter; where Daniel, upon hearing Nebuchadnezzar's dream, is faid to have been aftonifhed for one hour (c), שעה fhangnah. But that word is of too general a fignification, to prove that hours, in the modern fenfe of the term, were then in ufe; it feems rather to import any portion of time; and perhaps, in the decree of Nebuchadnezzar, that all who refufed to worfhip his image fhould be caft into the fiery furnace, it might as well be rendered that minute or moment, as " the fame hour (d)." And

in

(a) Ifai. xxxviii. 8. (b) 2 Chron. xxxii. 31.
* Voffius de Origine et Progreffu Idololatriæ, lib. ii. cap. ix. p. 179. Amftel. 1668.
(c) Dan. iv. 19. (d) Dan. iii. 15.

in the prefent cafe, it is not very likely, that
a poor jewifh flave, as Daniel was, fhould ftand
as one ftupid, a whole hour, in the prefence of
fo great a monarch as Nebuchadnezzar. On
the whole, I do not find that the antiquity of
the jewifh hours can be traced and afcertained,
by any thing that is faid in the Old Teftament.

Befides the twelve lefler hours, (which, as
they are fuppofed to be equal divifions of the
artificial day, muft be of different lengths at
different times of the year, and which are the
fame that we now call jewifh hours;) Godwin,
with many others, fpeaks of the greater hours;
which are faid to be four, each containing three
of the lefler hours; the firft beginning at fun-
rife, (and not at fix o'clock, as Godwin erro-
neoufly fays,) and holding till about nine. The
fecond ended at noon, the third in the middle
of the afternoon, and the fourth at fun-fet.
However, this divifion of the day into greater
hours, is not fufficiently fupported by the paffages of fcripture, which Godwin quotes in
proof of it. And feveral learned men, very
fkilful in thefe matters, have doubted, whether
any fuch hours were in ufe among the Jews.

Mayer * thinks he has proved, that the greater hours were in ufe in the days of Nehemiah,
from the following paffage, "they read in the
book of the law one fourth part of the day,
and another fourth part they confeffed and worfhipped the Lord their God (a)." This, however, will prove no more, than that they had
fkill enough, in thofe times, to divide the day,
                                          upon

Johannis Mayeri Tractat. de temporibus et feftis diebus Hebræor. part. 1. cap. x. §. xiv,—xvii. p. 68,—70.
edit. 2. Amftel. 1724.
(a) Nehem. ix. 3.

upon occasion, into four parts; but that these divisions were called the greater hours, or that this was a stated division of the day, does not appear.

Since then the use of the greater hours is so uncertain, even in our Saviour's time, we must not rely on them, as Godwin does, for reconciling the different accounts of the evangelists concerning the time of our Lord's crucifixion. St. Mark says it was at the third hour (a); whereas, according to St. John (b), it was about the sixth hour, when he was arraigned before Pilate. Some endeavour to remove this difficulty by the supposition that St. John's gospel was written after the destruction of Jerusalem *, and that he therefore uses the computation of the Romans, who began the natural day, as we do, from twelve o'clock at night; accordingly the sixth hour, when Pilate condemned Christ to be crucified, was six in the morning: But St. Mark uses the jewish computation, according to which the third hour answers to our nine in the morning, at which time Christ was nailed to the cross.

This is an ingenious way of reconciling the two evangelists; and provided it could be made appear, that St. John uses the roman computation in any other part of his history, we should readily acquiesce in it. But, I apprehend, the contrary is very probable from the following passage in the fourth chapter (c), " Jesus there-

fore

(a). See Mark xv. 25. (b) John xix. 14.

* That St. John's gospel was written, not after, but before the destruction of Jerusalem, see proved by Dr. Lardner, in his Supplement to the Second part of his Credibility, vol. 1. chap. ix. §. 9, 10. p. 391,—445.

(c) John iv. 6,—8.

fore being wearied with his journey, fat thus
on the well, and it was about the fixth hour."
" There cometh a woman of Samaria to draw
water; Jefus faith unto her, Give me to drink.
For his difciples were gone away into the city
to buy meat." Now it is not fo probable, that
the difciples fhould be gone to procure provifions for their refrefhment on their journey at
fix in the morning, as at twelve at noon; much
lefs is it likely, that Chrift was wearied with his
journey at fo early an hour; and if St. John
ufes the jewifh computation in this part of his
hiftory, it is hardly confiftent with the character
of a good hiftorian to ufe the roman in another
part of it; at leaft, without giving notice of
the change. Perhaps therefore an eafier way
of folving this difficulty is to admit the reading
of the Cambridge manufcript, which has τριτη,
the third, inftead of εκτη, the fixth hour, in the
preceding paffage. And this reading is confirmed by Nonnus's paraphrafe *, and by Peter
of Alexandria, or whoever was the author of
the fragment prefixed to the Chronicon Pafchale †; who exprefsly afferts, that it was τριτη
in the original copy ‡, which, he faith, was at
that time preferved with great care in the church
of Ephefus ‖.

                                 Before

---

* See the paffage in Dr. Lardner's Credibility, part 2.
chap. 128. vol. 11. p. 63.

   † Confult Cave, Hift. literar. ad init. §. 4.

   ‡ Chronicon Pafchale, in Præf. auctoris de pafchate,
p. 5. edit. Du Frefne, Paris 1688.

   ‖ See this matter difcuffed by Dr. Whitby in his Annotations on Mark xv. 25. and by Pfaffius in his Differtatio
critica de genuinis librorum Novi Teftamenti lectionibus,
cap. viii. p. 154,—162. edit. Amftel. 1709. who particularly confiders what Mill hath advanced againft this reading on Mark xv. 25. and John xix. 14.

Before we quit the subject of the jewish hours, it is proper to take notice of the hours of prayer, which we find mentioned in scripture. Peter and John, it is said in the Acts, " went up into the temple at the hour of prayer, being the ninth hour (*a*)." This indeed refers to the publick prayers, offered up in the temple at the time of the evening sacrifice. But the Jews had also stated hours for private prayer, at least when they did not attend those which were publick. It was Daniel's custom to pray three times a day, which he would not omit, though he was liable, on that account, to be cast into the den of lions (*b*). The same was the practice of David, " Evening and morning," saith he, " and at noon will I pray (*c*)." From whence we learn not only how frequently, but at what times of the day that duty was commonly performed. It is generally supposed, that the morning and evening prayers were at the time of offering the morning and evening sacrifice, that is, at the third and ninth hour. And the noon prayer was at the sixth hour, or twelve o'clock. For it is said, that " Peter went up on the house-top to pray, about the sixth hour (*d*)." Though Ludovicus Capellus makes the morning and the noon prayer to correspond to the morning and evening sacrifices. According to him, the morning prayer was performed any time betwixt sun-rise and the fourth hour; the noon prayer, betwixt the sixth hour and sun-set; and evening prayer, any time betwixt sun-set and

. break

(*a*) Acts iii. 1.

(*b*) Dan. vi. 10,—12.

(*c*) Psal. lv. 17.

(*d*) Acts x. 9.

break of day *. We find in scripture, no expres institution of the stated hours of prayer. The Jews say, they received them from the Patriarchs; the first hour, from Abraham; the second, from Isaac; and the third, from Jacob †.

From hence, the papists have borrowed their canonical hours; as they call certain prayers, which are to be repeated at certain times of the day, namely, matins, lauds, vespers, and complins. Cardinal Baronius fancies they were instituted by the apostles; of which he imagines, that Peter and John going into the temple at the hour of prayer, being the ninth hour, is proof sufficient. Indeed, if we reject this evidence, there is none to be produced, of their being instituted earlier than the ninth century, in a capitular ‡ of Hatto, or Hetto, bishop of Basil, directed to his curates, injoining that none of them be absent at the canonical hours ‖.

From the Jews the Mohammedans have borrowed their hours of prayer, enlarging the number of them from three to five; which all Mussulmans are bound to observe; the first in the morning before sun-rise; the second when noon is past, and the sun begins to decline from the meridian; the third in the afternoon, before sun-set; the fourth in the evening after sun-set,

and

---

* Ludov. Capell. in Act. iii. 1. apud Crit. Sacr. See also Mishn. tit. Berachoth, cap. 4. Bartenor. et Maimon. in loc. et annot. Guisii et Surenhus. tom. 1 p. 13, 14. edit. Surenhus.

† Vid. Drusii Præter. in Act. iii. 1. sive apud Critic. Sacros.

‡ A capitular is an act passed in a chapter, that is, in an assembly held by religious or military orders, for deliberating on their affairs, and regulating their discipline.

‖ Du Pin's Ecclef. Hist. cent. ix. vol. 7. p. 142.

and before the day be fhut in; the fifth after
the day is fhut in, and before the firft watch of
the night*. To thefe fome of their devotees
add two more, the firft an hour and an half
after the day is fhut in, the other at midnight;
but thefe are looked upon as voluntary fervices,
practifed in imitation of Mohammed's example,
but not enjoined by his law †.

We now proceed to confider the jewifh weeks;
which, Godwin obferves, were of two forts;
the one ordinary, confifting of feven days; the
other extraordinary or prophetical, confifting of
feven years.

As for the ordinary week of feven days, it is
a divifion of time, which appears to have been
obferved by all nations, probably from the beginning of the world ‡. It was firft made by
God himfelf, who, after he had created the
world in fix days, " refted on the feventh, and
blefied the feventh day, and fanctified it (a)."
From whence every feventh day has been ever
held facred.

To prove that this diftinction of time prevailed in the firft ages of the world, fome alledge the following paffage of the book of Genefis, " In the end of the days, מקץ ימים
mikkèts jamim, Cain and Abel brought their
offering to the Lord (b):" that is, fay they, at
the end of the week, or on the fabbath-day;
for according to the learned Gataker, there was
                                    then

* See Sale's Preliminary difcourfe to his tranflation of
the Koran, Sect. iv. p. 107, 109. edit. 1734.
† De Dieu, Animadverfiones in Act. iii. 1.
‡ See Grotius de Veritate Chriftianæ Religionis, lib. 1.
§. 15. p. 45, 46. notis Clerici, Glafg. 1745. Selden. de
Jure nat. et gent. lib. iii. cap. xvi,—xix.
(a) Gen. ii. 2, 3.   (b) Gen. iv. 3.

then no other diftinction of days but into
weeks *. We may however obferve, with defe-
rence to fo great an authority, that it is not impoffible, nor improbable, that by this time they
might have learned to diftinguifh time, by the
changes of the moon, into months ; and by the
courfe of the fun, and the revolutions of the
feafons, into years. It is very evident, that the
phrafe מקץ ימים mikkèts jamim does not always import the end of a week, from the ufe
of it in the fecond book of Samuel (*a*); where
it is faid, that " at the end of the days, Abfa-
lom polled his head, becaufe his hair was heavy
on him; and he weighed it at two hundred
fhekels." It cannot be imagined, his hair
fhould grow fo heavy, as to need polling every
week. Probably in this place, the phrafe means,
as we render it, " at every year's end." In the
fame fenfe the learned Ainfworth underftands
it in the paffage in Genefis which we are now
confidering : " At the end of the year," when
the fruits of the earth were ripe, " Cain brought
of the fruits of the ground an offering unto the
Lord." So God afterwards appointed " a feaft
of ingathering," to be obferved by the Jews in
the end of the year, when they had gathered in
their labours out of the field (*b*)." The fame
cuftom prevailed among the Gentiles, who at
the end of the year, when they gathered in
their fruits, offered folemn facrifices, with
thanks to God for his bleffings. Ariftotle
fays †, that the ancient facrifices and affemblies
were after the gathering in of the fruits, being
defign-

---

* Vid. Poli Synopf. in Gen. iv. 3.
(*a*) 2 Sam. xiv. 26.   (*b*) Exod. xxiii. 16.
† Ariftot. Ethic. lib. viii.

defigned for an oblation of the firft fruits unto God. Again, days are put for years in the twenty fifth chapter of Leviticus (a) : " within a year fhall he redeem it :" in the hebrew ימים jamim, which yet is immediately explained to fignify a whole year. It is therefore probable, that it was at the end of the year, Cain brought of his ripe fruits an offering unto the Lord.

Neverthelefs, though the evidence of this paffage, in favour of the antiquity of diftinguifhing time by weeks, fail us, we have other fufficient proofs of its being ufed in very early ages. It appears, that Noah divided his days by fevens, in fending the dove out of the ark (b) ; and that the fame divifion was ufed in Jacob's time ; for in the hiftory of his marriage with Leah and Rachel, we meet with this expreffion, " Laban faid, fulfill her week, שבע fhebhuang, and we will give thee this alfo for the fervice which thou fhalt ferve with me yet feven other years (c)." That the word שבע fhebhuang, here fignifies a week of days, is plain from its being exprefsly diftinguifhed from feven years ; and alfo becaufe it was the cuftom in ancient times to keep marriage feafts for feven days. It is faid of Samfon's wife, that " fhe wept before him the feven days, while their marriage feaft lafted ;" in order to obtain from him the interpretation of a riddle, for explaining which " within the feven days of the feaft," he had offered a reward to his guefts (d).

As for the extraordinary or prophetical weeks, they confifted of feven years each. And it is not unlikely, that this fort of computation by

VOL. II.   I   weeks

(a) Lev. xxv. 29.   (b) Gen. viii. 10,—13.   (c) Gen. xxix. 27.   (d) Judg. xiv. 12, 17.

weeks of years, which is ufed in the prophetick writings, owed its origin to the expreffions in which Mofes records the inftitution of the year of jubilee: " Thou fhalt number feven fabbaths of years unto thee, feven times feven years, and the fpace of the feven fabbaths of years fhall be unto thee forty and nine years; then fhalt thou caufe the trumpet of the jubilee to found,—and ye fhall hallow the fiftieth year (*a*)." Accordingly a day is put for a year in Ezekiel, where three hundred and ninety days means as many years, and forty days forty years: " I have appointed thee, faith the Lord, each day for a year (*b*)." In the fame fenfe feven days, or a week, is in the prophetick ftile feven years. Of this fort are the feventy weeks in the ninth chapter of Daniel's prophecy (*c*), which appears from hence, that having occafion immediately after this prophecy, to mention weeks in the ordinary acceptation of the word, he exprefsly calls them, by way of diftinction from the weeks he had been before fpeaking of, " weeks of days (*d*);" for fo is the expreffion in the original, which we render, " three full weeks *." Befides, it is certain, that fo many great events, as are predicted to come to pafs in the fpace of feventy weeks, could not be crouded into feventy weeks of days, which is lefs than one year and an half. The feventy prophetical weeks, therefore, amount to four hundred and ninety years.

Months,

(*a*) Lev. xxv. 8,—19.   (*b*) Ezek. iv. 5, 6.   (*c*) Dan. ix. 24.   (*d*) Dan. x. 1, 2, 3.

* Mayer. de temporibus et feftis Hebræor. part. 1. cap. x. §. v. p. 65. edit. Amftel. 1724. Marfhall's Chronological treatife on the feventy weeks of Daniel, p. 8, 9. Lond. 1724.

Months, with the Hebrews, take their name from the moon; the word חדש chodhesh, being used by them to signify both a new moon, and a month; becaufe their months began with a new moon. And therefore they confifted of twenty nine or thirty days; for fince the fynodical lunar month is nearly twenty nine days and an half, they made their months to confift of twenty nine and thirty days alternately; fo that what one month wanted of being equal to the fynodical courfe of the moon, was made up in the next; and by this means their months were made to keep even pace, pretty nearly, with the lunations. Thus was the jewifh calendar regulated by the law of Mofes, which appointed the day of the new-moon, or rather perhaps the firft day of its appearance, to be a folemn feftival, and the beginning of a month. But it fhould feem, that at the time of the deluge they were not come to this regulation; but then the years confifted of twelve months, and each month of thirty days. That the year confifted of twelve months, may be inferred from the time that Noah lived in the ark, namely, a year and ten days; for the flood began on the feventeenth day of the fecond month of the fix hundredth year of Noah's life (a), and on the twenty feventh of the fecond month, in the fix hundred and firft year of his life, was the earth dried (b). Now if the month confifted of thirty

I 2   days,

(a) See Gen. vii. 11.

(b) Gen. viii. 13, 14. In the thirteenth verfe it is faid, that " in the fix hundred and firft year, the firft day of the month, the waters were dried from the earth, and Noah removed the covering of the ark, and looked, and behold the face of the ground was dry." This muft be underftood of the waters being fo far dried from off the face of the

earth,

days, as we fhall prefently fhew that it did; and
if the year then in ufe was nearly either lunar
or folar, there muft have been twelve months
in the year; for thirty multiplied by twelve is
three hundred and fixty, that is, fix days more
than the lunar year, and five lefs than the folar.
Perhaps the form of the year then ufed was the
fame afterwards ufed by the Egyptians, confifting of twelve months and five days.

That the month, in Noah's time, confifted
of thirty days, is made out thus. It is faid in
the account of the deluge, that in the fecond
month, the feventeeth day of the month, the
fountains of the great deep were broken up(a);"
and afterwards it is faid " the ark refted in the
feventh month, on the feventeenth day of the
month, upon the mountains of Ararat(b)."
From the beginning of the flood, therefore, to
the time of the ark's refting, was juft five
months.   Now the waters are faid to have prevailed upon the earth one hundred and fifty
days (c), that is, till the time of the ark's refting; and one hundred and fifty divided by five,
the number of the months, gives juft thirty
days for each month.

From this account of the antediluvian months
and years, we may infer the abfurdity of the
fuppofition, which Varro and others have made,
in order to take off the wonder of men's living
fo long before the flood, as the fcripture hiftory relates; namely, that their ages are to be
                                        com-

---

earth, that they no longer flood on the ground; neverthelefs the earth was not fufficiently hardened to be fit for
habitation till near two months after, when on the twenty
feventh day of the fecond month Noah left the ark.

(a) Gen. vii. 11.   (b) Gen. viii. 4.   (c) Gen. vii.
24. viii. 3, 4.

computed, not by folar years, but by months;
whereas it plainly appears, that they computed
by months and years before the flood, as we
now do, and that their years were nearly equal
to ours; and it cannot be thought fo good an
hiftorian as Mofes, would ufe the word years
for months only, in fome part of his antidelu-
vian hiftory, and for twelve months in other
parts of it. Befides, this way of computing
will reduce the lives of the ancient patriarchs
to a fhorter period than ours. Peleg, who is
faid to have lived two hundred and thirty nine
years (a), will be found in reality to have lived
only about twenty years; and Serug, who is
faid to have lived two hundred and thirty
years (b), muft have lived but a little more than
nineteen; and both of them muft have begot
children before they were three years old, inftead of thirty, according to the fcripture account.

Godwin is undoubtedly miftaken, when he
faith, that " the Jews, before their captivity,
counted their months without any names, according to their number, as the firft, the fecond month, &c." For we meet with the
names of months in the fcripture hiftory, long
before that period; as the month Abib (a), the
month Zif (b), the month Bul (c), and the
month Ethanim (d).

We proceed now to confider the jewifh year,
which was partly lunar and wandring, and partly folar and fixed. It confifted fometimes of
twelve, and fometimes of thirteen fynodical
months; ordinarily it confifted of twelve fyno-
I 3   dical

(a) Exod. xiii. 4.   (b) 1 Kings vi. 1, 37.   (c) ver.
38.   (d) 1 Kings viii. 2.

dical months, amounting to three hundred and
fifty four days. As the years of this form fall
eleven days short of the solar year, had they
used them constantly, their months and festivals would have wandered in thirty two years
through all the seasons. But since the rites they
were to perform at some of their festivals had
a necessary connection with a particular season
of the year; as the offering the first fruits of
the wheat harvest at the feast of pentecost,
which must necessarily be kept in the sum-
mer, and their dwelling in booths at the feast
of tabernacles, which would have been highly inconvenient in winter; it was necessary, by
some means to reduce the lunar years to the solar, that their months, and consequently their
festivals, might always fall at the same season.
This therefore they did by adding a whole
month to the year, as often as it was needful,
commonly once in three, and sometimes once
in two years. This intercalary month was added at the end of the year, after the month
Adar, and was therefore called ואדר veadar, or
a second Adar *.

The year was also distinguished into the civil
and sacred year; each of which had a different
beginning. The civil begun with the equinoctial new moon in autumn; the sacred or eccle-
siastical, with the equinoctial new moon in
spring. The civil, according to which all political matters were regulated, was the more ancient, and was perhaps the same with the patriarchal year, which we gave an account of before, and which is supposed to have originally
com-

---

* Maimon. de Consecratione Calendarum, cap. iv. §. 1.
p. 356. ad calcem tractatus de sacrificiis, edit. et vers. De
Veil, Lond. 1683.

commenced at the creation. Hence, since this
year began in autumn, some have thought it
probable the world was created at that season,
or in its autumnal state, with respect to that
hemisphere in which Adam was placed *. But
the premises, from which this inference is drawn,
are somewhat uncertain, namely, that the ancient year was a fixed solar year, always beginning at the same season ; whereas we have before shewn, that the patriarchal year consisted
of twelve months of thirty days each, which
fell about five days short of the true solar year.
Unless, therefore, we suppose, as some have
done †, that they added five days to their last
month, according to the form of the Annus
Nabonassarius, or the Egyptian year ‡ ; which
five days were called ημεραι επαγομεναι : this year
must have been wandering, and the beginning
of it have run through all the seasons. Nay,
even supposing the addition of the ημεραι επαγομεναι, yet the neglect of five hours forty nine
minutes, by which the egyptian year fell short
of the true solar year, would make the beginning of it wander through all the seasons in
about fourteen hundred years ; so that, though
it happened to begin at the autumnal equinox
at the time when Moses regulated the jewish
calendar, it might have begun originally at another

I 4

● * Vid. Meyer. de temporibus et festis Hebræor. part. 1.
cap. 1. p. 4,—17. Amstel. 1724. et Fred. Spanhemii Chronol. Sacr. part. 1. cap. 1. Talmud. tit. Rosh hashanah,
cap. 1. Abarbanel de principio anni et consecratione novi-
lunii, ad calcem lib. Cozri, p. 443,—445. edit. Buxtorf.
1660.
     † Vid. Spanhem. Chronol. Sacr. part. 1. cap. iii. p. 8.
oper. Geograph. Chronolog. &c. Lugd. Bat. 1701.
     ‡ See Strauchius's Chronology, by Sault, book iv. chap.
xviii. p. 261. Lond. 1722.

other feafon. However, it is thought, that
the feaft of ingathering of the harveft, which
muft certainly be at autumn, being faid to be
" in the end of the year (a)," favours the opinion that the ancient year began at that feafon.
Therefore, though fome have fuppofed, that
the world was created in fpring *, the more
commonly received opinion is, that it was
created in autumn. In fupport of which fome
alledge the following paffage in the firft chapter of Genefis, " The earth brought forth
grafs, the herb yielding feed, and the fruit
tree yielding fruit after his kind, whofe feed is
in itfelf (b) ;" which, they fay, muft be in autumn, when the fruits are ripe.

As for the jewifh facred, or ecclefiaftical year,
it began with the month Nifan, the feventh of
the civil year, about the vernal equinox (c).
By this year the order of all their religious ceremonies was regulated ; fo that the paffover,
which was kept in the middle of the firft month
of this year, was as it were the mother of all
the other feftivals.

While the Jews continued in the land of Canaan, the beginnings of their months and years
were not fettled by any aftronomical rules or
calculations, but by the phafis or actual appearance of the new moon. When they faw the
new moon, they began the month. Perfons
were therefore appointed to watch on the tops
of the mountains for the firft appearance of the
moon after the change. As foon as they faw
it,

(a) Exod. xxlii. 16.   xxxiv. 22.
* Jacobi Capelli Obferv. in Gen. i. 14. p. 583. edit. unà
cum Lud. Capell. Comment. et not. critic. in Vet. Teft.
Amftel. 1689.
(b) Gen. i. 11.   (c) Exod. xii. 2, et feq.

it, they informed the fanhedrim, and publick
notice was given by lighting beacons throughout the land; though after they had been often
deceived by the Samaritans, who kindled falfe
fires, they ufed, fay the mifhnical rabbies, to
proclaim its appearance by fending meffengers.
Yet as they had no months longer than thirty
days, if they did not fee the new moon the
night following the thirtieth day, they concluded the appearance was obftructed by the clouds,
and without watching any longer, made the
next day the firft day of the following month *.
But after the jews became difperfed through all
nations, where they had no opportunity of being informed of the firft appearance of the new
moon, as they formerly had, they were forced
to make ufe of aftronomical calculations and
cycles for fixing the beginning of their months
and years †.   The firft cycle they made ufe of
for this purpofe was of eighty four years.   But
that being difcovered to be faulty, they came
afterwards into the ufe of Meto's cycle of nineteen years, which was eftablifhed by the authority of Rabbi Hillel Hannafi, or prince of the
fanhedrim, about the year of Chrift 360. This
they ftill ufe, and fay, it is to be obferved till
the coming of the Meffiah.   In the compafs of
this cycle there are twelve common years, confifting of twelve months, and feven intercalary
years, confifting of thirteen months ‡.
   We find the Jews and their anceftors computing their years from different eras, in different

---

* Vid. Mifh. tit. Rofh. hafhanah, cap. 2. §. 1,—7. Maimon. de Confecratione Calendarum, cap. iii. §. v,—viii.
p. 352.
   † Maimon. de Confecratione Calendarum, cap. v. §. 1,
—iii. p. 362.
   ‡ See Prideaux's Connect. part 1. preface.

ent parts of the Old Teſtament; as from the
birth of the patriarchs; for inſtance, of Noah(a);
afterwards from their exit out of Egypt(b); then
from the building of Solomon's temple (c), and
from the reigns of the kings of Judah and Iſrael. In later times the babyloniſh captivity
furniſhed them with a new epocha, from whence
they computed their years (d). But ſince the
times of the talmudical rabbies, they have con-
ſtantly uſed the era of the creation, which according to their computation *, in this preſent
year of the chriſtian era 1762, is A. M. 5522.
They uſually in writing contract this by omit-
ting the thouſands, writing only תקבב, 522†. If
to the jewiſh year, thus expreſſed, you add 1240
it gives the year of the chriſtian era, as 522 with
the addition of 1240 makes 1762 ‡.

If it be enquired, why God appointed a new
beginning of the year to the Iſraelites at the
time of their deliverance out of Egypt; the
anſwer may, perhaps, be

1ſt. The more effectually to diſtinguiſh and
ſeparate his own people from the idolatrous nations, and detach them from their cuſtoms; to
which end the beginning their days, their weeks,
their months, and their years at a different time
from

(a) Gen. vii. 11.   viii. 13.   (b) Numb. xxxiii. 38.
1 Kings vi. 1.   (c) 2 Chron. viii. 1.   (d) Ezek.
xxxiii. 21. xl. 1.

* The Jews reckon only 3760 years from the creation to
the birth of Chriſt. See Scalig. de emendat. tempor. lib.
vii. p. 628. and Strauchius's Chronol. by Sault, book iv.
chap. ii. p. 168,—171.

† This is called the computus minor; when the thouſands are expreſſed at length, it is called computus ma-
jor.

‡ Reland. Antiq. Heb. part iv. cap. 1. §. viii. p. 428,
429. edit. 3.

from thofe of the idolaters, was undoubtedly fubfervient.

2dly, Becaufe the month, in which they were delivered out of Egypt, and in which fuch a furprizing feries of miracles was wrought in their favour, might be well accounted a fort of menfis natalis of that nation, in which God as it were revived them from a ftate of death, and took them under his future fpecial protection and providence; on which account, to fet a particular mark upon that month, and to perpetuate the memory of fo great a mercy, he ordered, that it fhould ftand at the head of the months, and be reckoned the firft of the year.

CHAP.

CHAP. II.

Of their feasts.

"AS, among the Jews, their ordinary meals, saith Godwin, were not many in a day, so neither were they costly ; and therefore they were called ארחת aruchoth, which properly signifieth such fare as travellers use on their journies ; whereas the extraordinary and more liberal kind of entertainment was commonly called משתה mishteh." There is no doubt, but the word ארחה aruchah, as it comes from the root ארח arach, iter fecit, properly and primarility signifies provisions on a journey, or such a meal as was common with travellers, which can hardly be supposed to have been either elegant or plentiful in those countries where there were no inns or houses of entertainment on the road, and where travellers used to carry their provisions with them ; and though, as Godwin observes, the word is used for a mean and scanty meal in the book of Proverbs (a), where ארחת ירק aruchath jarak, a dinner of herbs, stands in opposition to a stalled or fatted ox ;

(a) Prov. xv. 17.

ox: neverthelefs, as the whole life of man is
reprefented as a pilgrimage or journey, the word
ארהה aruchah, in an allufive fenfe, is ufed for
a meal in general, whether fumptuous or mean,
whether plentiful or fparing.   In the book of
Jeremiah (a) it is ufed for the daily provifion,
which the king of Babylon alloted to Jehoia-
kim king of Judah, after he had brought him-
out 'of prifon, and fet his throne above the
thrones of all the kings that were with him in
Babylon, and admitted him to eat bread con-
tinually before him (b); and no doubt the provifions of his table were plentiful and elegant.

The word משתה mifhteh, from שתה fha-
thah, bibit, anfwers to the greek συμποσιεν, and
primarily fignifies compotatio; or perhaps as
we call it, a drinking bout.   And as delicious
liquors were always fuppofed to make a confiderable part of an elegant entertainment, the
word משתה mifhteh, is ufed, by a fynecdoche,
for a feaft in general; fuch as Abraham made
at the weaning of Ifaac (c); Pharoah on his
birth-day (d); Samfon at his wedding (e); and
Ifaac for Abimelech and his friends, who, it is
exprefsly faid, eat as well as drank (f).   " A
feaft of fat things" is called משתה mifhteh, as
well as " a feaft of wine (g)."   And as the
Hebrews fometimes denominated their feafts
from drinking, fo likewife from eating: " Jacob offered facrifice on the mount, and called
his brethren to eat bread, &c (h)."   Belfhazzar
made a great feaft, לחם lechem (i), which primarily fignifies bread.   At other times it was
deno-

(a) Jer. lii. 34.   (b) ver. 31,—33.   (c) Gen.
xxi. 8.   (d) Gen. xl. 20.   (e) Judg. xiv. 10.
(f) Gen. xxvi. 30.   (g) Ifai. xxv. 6.   (h) Gen.
xxxi. 54.   (i) Dan. v. 1. See alfo Ecclef. x. 19.

denominated from both: " Come, eat of my
bread, and drink of the wine which I have
mingled (a)."

It is Godwin's opinion, that the agapæ, or
love feafts, of the primitive chriftians, were derived from the חגים chiggim, or feafts upon
the facrifices, at which the Jews entertained
their friends and fed the poor (b).

There were alfo feafts of much the fame kind,
in ufe among the Greeks and Romans. The
former were wont to offer certain facrificcs to
their gods, which were afterwards given to the
poor. They had likewife publick feafts for certain diftricts, fuppofe for a town or city, towards which all, who could afford it, contributed, in proportion to their different abilities,
and all partook of it in common. Of this fort
were the Συσσιτια of the Cretans ; and the Φιδιτια
of the Lacedemonians, inftituted by Lycur-
gus, and fo called, παρα της φιλιας, (the λ being
changed into δ according to their ufual orthography,) as denoting that love and friendfhip
which they were intended to promote among
neighbours and fellow-citizens *.

The Romans likewife had a feaft of the fame
kind, called chariftia ; which was a meeting
only of thofe who were akin to each other ;
and the defign of it was, that if any quarrel
or mifunderftanding had happened among any
of them, they might there be reconciled †. To
this Ovid alludes in the fecond book of his fafti,

Prox-

(a) Prov. ix. 5. See alfo Ecclef. ix. 7. (b) Deut.
xii. 18. xxvi. 12.

* Vid. Cragium de Republ. Lacedæm. lib. i. cap. ix.
apud Gronov. Thefaur. Græc. Antiq. vol. 5. p. 2541. et
Stuckii Antiquitat. convivial. lib. 1. cap. 31.

† Valer. Maxim. lib. ii. cap. i. §. 8. p. 136. edit. Thyfii, Lugd. Bat. 1655.

Proxima cognati dixere chariftia chari,
Et venit ad focios turba propinqua deos.

v. 617.

In imitation either of thefe jewifh or gentile
love feafts, or probably of both, the primitive
chriftians, in each particular church, had likewife their love-feafts, which were fupplied by
the contribution of the members, according to
their feveral abilities, and partaken of by all
in common. And whether they were converts
from among the Jews or Gentiles, they retained their old cuftom with very little alteration,
and as their αγαπαι had been commonly annexed to their facrifices, fo they were now annexed
to the commemoration of the facrifice of Chrift
at the Lord's fupper; and were therefore held
on the Lord's day, before or after the celebration of that ordinance. It fhould feem at Co-
rinth, in the apoftle's days, they were ordinarily held before; for when the Corinthians are
blamed for unworthily receiving the Lord's
fupper, it is partly charged upon this, that
fome of them came drunk to that ordinance,
having indulged to excefs at the preceding love-
feaft: " Every one taketh before, προλαμβανει,
his own fupper, and one is hungry and another
is drunken (a)." This fhows, faith Dr. Whitby, that this banquet, namely, the love-feaft,
was celebrated before the Lord's fupper. But
Chryfoftom gives an account of it, as being in
his time, kept after it *.

It

(a) 1 Cor. xi. 21. See Whitby in loc.
* Vid. Suiceri Thefaur. in verb. αγαπη. This opinion
is maintained by Mr. Hallet in his Notes and Difcourfes,
Vol. 3. Difc. vi. and by Dr. Chandler in his Account of
the

It is commonly ſuppoſed, that when St. Jude mentions certain perſons, who were ſpots in the feaſts of charity, *ιν ταις αγαπαις*(*a*), he means, in the chriſtian love-feaſts; though Dr. Lightfoot and Dr. Whitby apprehend the reference in this paſſage is rather to a cuſtom of the Jews, who on the evening of their ſabbath had their *κυιωρια*, or communion, when the inhabitants of the ſame city met in a common place to eat together *. However that be, all antiquity bears teſtimony to the reality of the chriſtian *αγαπαι*, or love-feaſts. Indeed Suicer conceives they are referred to in the following paſſage of the Acts, " They," that is, the apoſtles, " continuing daily with one accord in the temple, and breaking bread from houſe to houſe, did eat their meat with gladneſs and ſingleneſs of heart (*b*)." And when it is ſaid, that " the twelve called the multitude of the diſciples unto them, and ſaid, It is not reaſon that we ſhould leave the word of God, and ſerve tables (*c*)," he ſuppoſes the tables mean theſe love-feaſts; which expreſſion, I think, primarily refers to the tables of the poor of the church, or to the making a proper proviſion for them; as appears from its having been mentioned as the ground of complaint of " the Grecians againſt the Hebrews, that their widows were neglected in the daily miniſtration (*d*)." To the love-feaſts he likewiſe refers the following

the Conference in Nicholas-Lane Feb. 13, 1734-5. between two romiſh prieſts and ſome proteſtant divines, p. 55,—62.

  (*a*) Jude, ver. 12.

  * Whitby in loc. and Lightfoot, Horæ Hebraic. 1 Cor. x. 16.

  (*b*) Acts ii. 46.   (*c*) Acts vi. 2.   (*d*) ver. 1.

ing paffage concerning St. Paul, " When he had broken bread and eaten and talked a long while even till break of day, he departed (a)." But this may very naturally and properly be underftood of the Lord's fupper. Indeed how far St. Paul might join in thefe love-feafts with other chriftians, before they were abufed, does not appear. But when he blamed the fcandalous irregularities of the Corinthians, in their participation of the Lord's fupper; which were very much occafioned by their preceding love-feafts, and in order to bring them back to its original fimplicity and purity, gives them a very particular account of the primitive inftitution (b), in which there is not one word of thefe agapæ ; he evidently condemns the addition they had made to this ordinance, which had occafioned fo much fin, and fo many diforders and confufions.

However the agapæ were not wholly laid afide till fome ages after. For they are mentioned by Ignatius *, by Clemens of Alexandria †, by Tertullian ‡, and even by St. Jerom § and St. Auftin ‖ in the fourth century, as practifed in their times.

Dr. Lightfoot hath a peculiar notion concerning thefe chriftian agapæ, that they were a fort of hofpitals for the entertainment of ftrangers, in imitation of thofe which the Jews

---

(a) Acts xx. 11.   (b) 1 Cor. xi 23, et feq.
* Epift. ad Smyrn. §. 8. apud Coteler. Patres Apoftol. p. 37. vol. 2. edit. Clerici 2. 1724.
† Pædag. lib. ii. p. 141. B. et Strom. lib. iii. p. 430. C, D. edit. Paris. 1641.
‡ Apolog. cap. xxxix. p 32. edit. Rigalt. Paris 1675.
§ Ad Euftoc. de Cuftod. Virgin. Epift. xxii. p. 286. D. Paris. 1579.
‖ Contra Fauftum Manich. lib. xx. cap. xx.

had, adjoining to their ſynagogues. And Gaius, who is called "the hoſt of the whole church (a)," he ſuppoſes to have been the maſter of ſuch an hoſpital; and that Phœbe, who is called the διακονος of the church at Cenchrea (b), and thoſe other women, who in the epiſtle to the Philippians, are ſaid to labour in the goſpel (c), were ſervants attending theſe hoſpitals. Neverthelefs he does not call in queſtion the ancient uſe of love-feaſts together with the euchariſt : to doubt of that, he ſays, would be to contradict all antiquity. But he ſeems to queſtion, whether they were ſo ancient as the days of the apoſtles *. However, notwithſtanding all the doctor has ſaid, on the authority of the rabbies, of theſe jewiſh hoſpitals, which he ſuppoſes the chriſtians to have imitated in their agapæ, it may reaſonably be doubted, whether they had ordinarily ſuch hoſpitals adjoining to their churches ſo early as the days of the apoſtles ; for as yet they had hardly any churches or buildings appropriated to chriſtian worſhip, but were forced to meet in private houſes, and often ſecretly, to avoid the rage and violence of their perſecutors. Nor can I think it ſo probable, that the Corinthians, who were for the moſt part gentile converts, ſhould borrow the inſtitution of ſuch hoſpitals from the Jews, as that they ſhould follow their former cuſtom, and that of their anceſtors, in annexing love-feaſts to their ſacrifices, and ſo adopt them into chriſtian worſhip.

Godwin hath diſcourſed pretty largely on the ceremonies uſed by the Jews at their feaſts.

And

(a) Rom. xvi. 23.   (b) Rom. xvi. 1.   (c) Phil. iv. 3.
* See Hor. Hebraic. 1 Cor. xi. 21.

And under the head of falutation, as one of
their preparatory ceremonies, he occafionally
mentions the prophet Elifha's order to his fervant Gehazi, " If thou meet with any man,
falute him not; and if any man falute thee,
anfwer him not again (a)." It is enquired,
whether this is to be taken for a general prohibition of all ceremonies betokening civil refpect, according to the ufage of the modern
quakers; or only as an injunction peculiar to
the prefent occafion? I apprehend, there is no
reafon to take it for a general prohibition, fince
in the fcripture hiftory, we find fuch ceremonies of civil refpect practifed by good men,
without any cenfure paffed upon them; as by
Mofes to his father in law (b); by Abraham
to the three angels, whom he took for three
men (c); and afterwards to the children of
Heth (d). Befides, when our Saviour fent forth
the twelve apoftles to preach, he enjoined them
to pay to all perfons and families, where they
came, the ufual tokens of civility and refpect:
" When ye come into a houfe falute it (e)."
The reafon then of Elifha's forbidding his fervant either to give, or return, a falutation to
any man, was probably either on account of
the expedition which the prophet fuppofed his
journey to the Shunamite required, (for perhaps
he did not underftand her child was quite dead,
when he ordered Gehazi to go and lay his ftaff
on it;) or elfe, it might be to keep the child's
death, out of tendernefs, a fecret to the father,
till he was raifed to life again; and if the fer-

K 2   vant

(a) 2 Kings iv. 29.   (b) Exod. xviii. 7.
(c) Gen. xviii. 2.   (d) Gen. xxiii. 7.
(e) Matt. x. 12.

vant fo much as fpoke to any perfon on the
road, he might imprudently divulge it.

This may enable us to account for a prohibition of the fame kind, given by Chrift to the
feventy difciples, when he fent them " two and
two before his face, to every city and place,
whither he himfelf would come (*a*)." " Carry, faith he, neither purfe, nor fcrip, nor fhoes,
and falute no man by the way." We may,
with equal reafon fuppofe, that our Lord intended to forbid his difciples and minifters, the
ufe of fhoes and purfes, as the cuftomary tokens
of civil refpect. His defign was only to prohibit them while they were employed on that
particular meffage. It is further enquired, why
he forbad it at this time ? Dr. Lightfoot, from
the rabbies, obferves, that it was the cuftom of
the Jews, during the days of their mourning,
not to falute any one. He conceives, therefore,
that our Saviour would have his difciples appear like mourners; partly, as reprefenting himfelf, who was a man of forrow, that fo from
thefe meffengers the people might guefs, in
fome meafure, what fort of perfon he was who
fent them; partly, as they were to fummon
the people to attend upon Chrift, in order to
be healed, both of their fpiritual and their bodily difeafes; and it was, therefore, fit their
behaviour fhould be mournful and folemn, in
token of their fellow-feeling with the afflicted
and miferable *.

But the teftimony of the rabbies is too weak a
foundation to fupport this interpretation. The
cuftom mentioned might have prevailed in their
times,

(*a*) Luke x. 1, 4.
* Lightfoot, Hor. Heb. Luc. x. 4.

times, without being near fo ancient as our Saviour's.   It may alfo be objected, that our
bleffed Lord was fo far from defiring his difciples fhould appear as mourners, that he reprefents this to be unfuitable to their condition,
while he, the bridegrom was with them (*a*).

Perhaps, therefore, the prohibition of falut-
ing any man by the way, may be taken in a
more general fenfe, as a caution againft trifling
away their time in compliment and ceremony.
Or if we underftand it more literally, it might
be defigned to make the difciples appear as men
in hafte, and fully occupied, whofe minds were
intent on the difpatch of the moft important
bufinefs; to awaken the people's attention to
their meffage, and at the fame time, like the
fymbolical actions of the prophets, to repre-
fent in a fenfible manner, the main drift and
tenor of it, namely, that finners fhould make
all poffible fpeed to fly from the wrath to come,
and lay hold on eternal life, and for that end
fhould apply to Chrift in earneft and without
delay.

The fecond preparatory ceremony, mentioned by Godwin, is wafhing the feet of the guefts.
However, it does not appear in the inftitution
of any of the jewifh feafts, nor by any fcripture examples, that this was ever ufed, except
when perfons had defiled their feet by travelling.
And indeed, if it had been a conftant cuftom,
I can hardly think, that Simon the pharifee,
who civilly invited our Lord to an entertainment at his houfe, would have omitted it (*b*).

The inftance produced, namely, our Saviour's
wafhing his difciples feet (*c*), is quite befide the

K 3   pur-

(*a*) Matt. ix. 15.   (*b*) Luke vii. 44.   (*c*) John xiii. 5.

purpofe ; fince that was plainly an extraordinary cafe, performed, not out of refpect to any
cuftom, but with a particular intent of inftructing them in the duties of humility and conde-
fcending benevolence (a). Befides, this was not
done before they began fupper, but in fome interval of the meal, as appears from its being
faid of our Lord, that " he rofe from fupper,
and laid afide his garments, and took a towel
and girded himfelf (b)." We conclude from
hence, that the difciples had not wafhed their
feet before fupper ; for it is highly improbable,
that Chrift fhould chufe to fet them an example
of mutual condefcention and benevolence, by
an action, which, if they had been wafhed before, was altogether needlefs *.

It is Godwin's apprehenfion, that the fix water pots of ftone, mentioned on occafion of the
marriage at Cana in Galilee (c), and faid to be
" after the manner of the purifying of the
Jews," were defigned for thefe complimental
wafhings. But as the word καθαρισμος is commonly, if not always ufed, for the purifying or
wafhing the whole body ; as for the purifying
of a woman after child-birth (d), and of a leper
after his cure (e); in both which cafes the law
prefcribed that the body fhould be wafhed or
bathed all over ; fome have thought it more
probable, that thefe water pots were fuch as
were ufed for that purpofe. And if we confider,

(a) John xiii. 13,—15.   (b) ver. 4.

* That wafhing the feet was not an ufual preparatory
ceremony, is fhewn at large by Buxtorf, in his Differtationes philologico-theolog. Differt. vi. de Cænæ Domin.
primæ ritibus et formâ, §. xxx. p. 302,—306. Bafil.
1662.

(c) John ii. 6.   (d) Luke ii. 22.   (e) Luke
v. 14. Mark i. 44.

der, how many legal pollutions, unavoidably
and frequently contracted, required this larger
purification, especially among the women, it is
likely, that all persons, who could provide con-
veniencies for it, would keep sufficient quantities of water in their houses ready for such oc-
casions. According to this opinion, these water pots must have been large vessels. How
large, is not certain. The text fays, they
" contained two or three μετρηται apiece ;" a
word, which though it properly fignifies a meafure in the general, was yet, doubtlefs, in common ufe for fome particular meafure; otherwife, this account of the contents of these water pots would be altogether indeterminate, and
convey no idea at all. It is probable, therefore,
that as the word rod, in englifh, which primarily fignifies a ftick to meafure with, of any
length, is yet appropriated to that particular
meafure of length which is moft ufed in meafuring lands, namely, five yards and an half,
fo the word μετρητη was particularly appropriated to that meafure of capacity, which was
moft ufed by the Jews in meafuring liquids, and
that was the בת bath. This is ftill more probable, becaufe the feptuagint renders the word, bath,
by μετρητη, in the fourth chapter of the fecond
book of Chronicles (a). Now the bath, according to Dr. Cumberland, contains feven gal-
lons and a quarter. Each water pot, therefore,
may be fuppofed to contain about twenty gal-
lons, and all of them when filled to the brim,
as they were when our Saviour turned the water
into wine, about an hundred and twenty *.

K 4   As

(a) 2 Chron. iv. 5.
* See on this fubject a differtation of Hoftus, in the Cri-
tici Sacri, vol. ix.

As to the deſign of this miracle, we are not to ſuppoſe that Chriſt produced ſo great a quantity of wine, merely, or chiefly for the uſe of the gueſts at that entertainment. Beſides the grand purpoſe of diſplaying his divine power, he might hereby intend to make a handſome preſent to the new married couple, as ſuch a quantity of excellent wine undoubtedly was, in grateful return for their favour in inviting him and his diſciples to the marriage feaſt.

As to the third preparatory ceremony, pouring out oil, I can find no ſufficient evidence of this being in common uſe. The woman's anointing our Saviour's head with ointment, which St. Luke mentions (a), and to which Godwin refers, was without doubt an extraordinary caſe.

As to the ברכה barachah, or benediction of the bread and wine, from whence many others ſuppoſe, as well as Godwin, that our Saviour borrowed the rites which he uſed in the celebration of his ſupper; the authority of the rabbinical writers, who mention this barachah, is too precarious, to furniſh a certain concluſion, that it was in uſe among the Jews in our Saviour's time. The correſpondence betwixt the ſacramental rites, and thoſe of the jewiſh barachah, as practiſed in the days of the talmudical rabbies, may be ſeen at large in Buxtorf on this ſubject *.

The laſt thing which Godwin mentions as remarkable in the feaſts of the Jews, was their table geſture †. And this was reclining on
couches

(a) Luke vii. 37, 38.

   * Buxtorf. Differtationes philolog. theolog. differt. vi. de Cænæ Domin. primæ ritibus et formâ.

   † Vid. Buxtorf. ubi ſupra, §. xxxii,—xl. p. 306,—309. et Lightſoot, Horæ Hebr. in Matt. xxvi. 20.

couches after the manner of the Romans *, the upper part of the body refting upon the left elbow, and the lower lying at length upon the couch. When two or three reclined on the fame couch, fome fay the worthieft or moft honourable perfon lay firft, Lightfoot fays in the middle †. The next in dignity lay with his head reclining on the breaft or bofom of the firft ; as John is faid to have done on the bofom of Jefus at fupper (*a*). And hence is borrowed the phrafe of Abraham's bofom, as denoting the ftate of celeftial happinefs (*b*). Abraham being efteemed the moft honourable perfon, and the father of the jewifh nation, to be in his bofom fignifies in allufion to the order in which guefts were placed at an entertainment, the higheft ftate of felicity next to that of Abraham himfelf.

* Plutarchi fympos. lib. v. problem. vi. p. 769, 780. edit. Francofurt. 1620. See the Accubitus of the Romans defcribed, with a delineation from fome antique marbles, by Hieron. Mercurialis, de Arte Gymnaft. lib. 1. cap. xi. Amftel. 1672.

† Horæ hebr. Joh. xiii. 23.

(*a*) John xiii. 23.   (*b*) Luke xvi. 22.

CHAP. III.

Of the SABBATH.

THE word fabbath, from שבת fhabath, quievit, is ufed in fcripture, in a limited fenfe, for the feventh day of the week, which by the jewifh law was peculiarly confecrated to the fervice of God; and in a more extenfive fenfe, for other holy days, as for the annual faft or day of atonement on the tenth of the month tizri (a); and, in the new teftament, the word σαββατον is fometimes ufed for a week: "I faft twice in a week," " Νησευω δις τε σαββα-τε (b)," and " μια σαββατων" fignifies the firft day of the week (c). But commonly the word fabbath is peculiarly appropriated to the feventh day.

In the fixth chapter of St. Luke, we read of the σαββατον δευτεροπρωτον (d), the explaining of which has given the critics and commentators not a little trouble. Some alledge there were two fabbaths in the year, each of them called the firft, in refpect to the two different beginnings of the year, the civil and the facred.

That

(a) Lev. xxiii. 32. (b) Luke xviii. 12. (c) Matt. xxviii. 1. (d) Luke vi. 1.

That the Jews had fome peculiar regard to the firft fabbath in the year, appears from a paffage in Clemens Alexandrinus ; " εαν μη σεληνη φανη, σαββατον εκ αγυσι το λεγομενον, πρωτον *. Nifi luna appareat, fabbatum non celebrant quod primum dicitur, &c. Now as their year had two different beginnings, one with the month tizri in autumn, the other with the month nifan in fpring, there were confequently two firft fabbaths ; of which this, according to the computation of the civil year, was the fecond, and is therefore called δευτεροπρωτον, or the fecond-firft fabbath.

Grotius, whofe opinion is followed by Dr. Hammond, conceives, that when any of the folemn yearly feafts fell on the fabbath day, that fabbath had a fpecial refpect paid to it, and was called μεγα or (which Dr. Hammond faith is the fame thing) σαββατον πρωτον. Now of thefe prime or firft fabbaths there were three in the year, at the paffover, at pentecoft, and at the feaft of tabernacles. The firft of them, that is, when the firft day of the paffover fell on the fabbath day, was called πρωτοπρωτον σαββατον, or the firft prime fabbath. The fecond, that is, when the day of pentecoft fell on the fabbath, was called δευτεροπρωτον, which, he apprehends, was the fabbath here intended †. But as neither Grotius nor Hammond have produced any paffage, in which either the word πρωτοπρωτον or τριτοπρωτον occurs, this interpretation remains doubtful and uncertain. Sir Ifaac Newton imagines this σαββατον δευτεροπρωτον was the fecond great day of the feaft of the paffover : as we call eafter day high eafter, and its octave low eafter,

---

* Strom. lib. vi. p. 636. A. edit. Paris. 1741.
† Grotii et Hammondi Annot. in loc.

easter, or low sunday, so it seems, St. Luke
stiles the feast on the seventh day of the unleavened bread, the second of the two prime sabbaths *. To this sense Dr. Doddridge objects,
that though the seventh day of unleavened bread
was to be an holy convocation, yet the law expressly allowed the Jews to dress victuals on
it (*a*); and therefore the pharisees could have
had no pretence for charging Christ's disciples
with breaking the sabbath by their plucking
and rubbing the ear of corn on that day, as
they did (*b*).

Theophylact †, who is followed by J. Scaliger ‡, Lightfoot §, and Whitby, makes the
σαββατον δευτεροπρωτον to be the first of the seven
sabbaths betwixt the passover and pentecost, or
the first sabbath after the second day of unleavened bread, from whence the fifty days to
pentecost were computed (*c*). There want only
instances of the word δευτεροδευτερον being used
for the second, and δευτεροτριτον for the third of
these sabbaths, to confirm this sense beyond dispute. However, though it be not quite free
from uncertainty, it seems to stand as fair in
point of probability as any of them ‖. Thus
much for the word sabbath : we proceed to treat
of the thing.

It hath been controverted both among Jews
and christians, whether the sabbath was first
insti-

---

* Sir Isaac Newton's Observations on the prophecies of
Daniel and the Revelation, p. 154.
(*a*) Exod. xii. 16.   (*b*) Luke vi. 2.
† Comment. in loc.
‡ Scalig. de emendat. temp. lib. vi. p. 557. edit. Colon.
Allobr. 1629.
§ Lightfoot, Horæ hebraic. in loc. et in Matt. xii. 1.
(*c*) Lev. xxiii. 15, 16.
‖ See Whitby and Doddridge in loc.

inftituted immediately after the creation, and given to Adam and Eve in paradife? or, whether the account, of God's blefling the feventh day and fanctifying it, which Mofes mentions in connection with God's refting on the feventh day when the work of creation was finifhed (*a*), is to be underftood proleptically, of his appointing that day to be obferved as a fabbath, not at that time, but by the Ifraelites many ages afterwards.

Limborch*, Le Clerc†, and fome other learned men are of the latter opinion. But furely it is more natural to underftand this paffage as relating to the time in which it is placed in the feries of the hiftory, that is, to the firft ages of the world, previous to the fall. The chief reafon for underftanding it proleptically is, that there is no mention of the fabbath afterwards, in the facred hiftory, till the time of Mofes; that is, for about two thoufand five hundred years. However, the fame argument will hardly be admitted in the cafe of circumcifion, of which there is no exprefs mention in fcripture, or however no inftance recorded of the obfervation of it, from the fettlement of the If- raelites in Canaan, to the circumcifion of Chrift. Neverthelefs, as this rite was the fign of the covenant with Abraham and his pofterity, and the characteriftic of the peculiar people of God, its being conftantly obferved, cannot reafonably be called in queftion; efpecially as the heathen are called " the uncircumcifed " in contradif- tinction to the Ifraelites, which implies, that it was practifed conftantly by the latter. The fi- lence of hiftory with refpect to the continuance
of

(*a*) Gen. ii. 3.   * Limborc. Theolog. Chriftian. lib. v. cap. xxviii. §. vii,—ix. p. 478, 479. edit. Amftel. 1715.
† Clerici Annot. in Gen. ii. 3.

of a rite or cuftom, well known to have been
inftituted or adopted, is no argument againft
fuch continuance; provided the reafon on which
the inftitution was originally grounded, remains
the fame. It can by no means be concluded,
that becaufe there is no exprefs mention of the
obfervation of a fabbath in the patriarchal hiftory, therefore no fabbath was obferved in thofe
times. On the contrary; that the fabbath was
inftituted at the time, to which Mofes's relation
of the inftition of it refers, and was in confequence hereof obferved by the patriarchs, is at
leaft probable, from their diftinguifhing time
by weeks of feven days (a); for which it is not
eafy to account on any other fuppofition, than
of fome pofitive divine appointment, there being no ground in nature for fuch a divifion *.
The changes and quarters of the moon would
not occafion it to be adopted, a lunar month
being more than four times feven days, by
above a day and an half.

It is a further confirmation of this argument,
that all heathen nations, many of whom cannot
be fuppofed to have had any knowledge of the
law or hiftory of Mofes, divided their time in
the fame manner as the patriarchs and the Jews
did, by weeks of feven days. And it appears
by their moft ancient writers, Homer and Hefiod in particular, that they accounted one day
of the feven more facred than the reft. Hefiod
ftiles the feventh day the illuftrious light of the
fun :

Εβδοματη δ' αυθις λαμπρον φαος .11ερ.1019.

Homer

(a) Gen. viii. 10,—12. xxix. 27.
   * See a remarkable paffage, to this purpofe, of Johannes
Philoponus in Witfh·Ægypt. lib. iii. cap. ix. §.ii. p. 241,242.

Homer faith,

Εβδοματη δ' ηπειτα κατηλυθεν ιερον ημαρ :

then came the feventh day, which is facred or holy *.

Now can we fuppofe, they fhould all agree in this divifion of time, unlefs from a divine inftitution imparted to our firft parents, from whom it was derived by tradition to their pofterity.

Some have apprehended, as we have already obferved, that " the end of the days," when Cain and Abel are faid to have " brought their offerings to the Lord (a)," means the end or laft day of the week, that is, the fabbath-day. But fhould this expreffion be thought to fignify more probably the end of the year, when the fruits of the earth were ripe ; it is not however unlikely that the day, when " the fons of God" are faid in the book of Job to come to " prefent themfelves before the Lord (b)," was the fabbath, when pious perfons (ftiled in Genefis " the fons of God (c),") affembled for publick worfhip.

It is further obferved by Dr. Kennicott, that when the fabbath is firft mentioned in the time of Mofes, namely in the fixteenth chapter of the book of Exodus, it is not fpoken of as a novel inftitution, but as one with which the people were well acquainted: " To morrow, faith he, is the holy fabbath to the Lord:" and then he informs them, not of their general duty at fuch a feafon, of which they were perfectly apprized, but only how they fhould act on that day

* See Clemens Alexandrinus, Strom. lib. v. p. 600. edit. Paris. 1641. et Selden. de Jure nat. et gent. lib. iii. cap. xvi.
  (a) Gen. iv. 3.   (b) Job i. 6.   (c) Gen. vi. 2.

day with refpect to the manna, which was not to fall on the feventh, as it had done on the fix preceding days*.

Indeed it cannot be fuppofed that God left the world deftitute of fo falutary an inftitution; and confequently that no fabbath was obferved, for fo many ages as intervened between Adam and Mofes. The obfervation of a fabbath, of fome particular feafon for reft and devotion, is primarily a moral law, or law of nature; certain intervals of refpite from bufinefs and labour being neceffary for the prefervation both of our intellectual and corporeal frame; and it being highly reafonable, that thofe, who are wholly dependent on God, from whom they receive many publick as well as private bleffings, fhould prefent him not only private, but publick and focial worfhip; which cannot be done unlefs certain days or times are appointed, when they may affemble for that purpofe.

And for this end the bleffed God hath been pleafed to eftablifh a due proportion of time, namely, one day in feven. " God bleffed the feventh day, it is faid, and fanctified it, becaufe that in it he had refted from all his work, which God created and made." He fanctified it, that is, he feparated and diftinguifhed it from the days of the week, fetting it apart for the purpofes of a fabbath; agreeable to the primary meaning of the verb קדש kadhafh, feparavit or confecravit. What is meant by his " bleffing the day," may be underftood by the oppofite phrafe, " curfing a day." Both Job (a) and Jeremiah (b) in the warmth and bitternefs of their fpirits " curfed the day of their birth," that

---

* Kennicott's two Differtations on the tree of life, and oblations of Cain and Abel, differt. 2. p. 141. Oxford 1747.
(a) Job iii. 1, &c.   (b) Jer. xx. 14.

that is, wifhed no favourable or agreeable event
might happen on that day, that it might not
be a time of rejoicing, but of mourning: " Let
the day be darknefs; let a cloud dwell upon it;
let no joyful voice come therein (*a*)." The
Greeks had their *αποφραδες* *, and the Romans
their dies infaufti, that is, certain days, which
had been diftinguifhed by fome great calamity;
on which, therefore, they did not indulge themfelves in any mirth or pleafure, and expected
no good event to happen to them. Tacitus relates, that the fenate, to flatter Nero, decreed,
ut dies natalis Agrippinæ inter nefaftos effet †.
To blefs a day on the contrary, is to wifh that
it may prove happy, and to devote it to joy
and pleafure. And by God's blefling the feventh
day, we are naturally to underftand his appointing it to be a facred feftival, a day not only of
reft, but delight, as the fabbath is called by the
prophet Ifaiah (*b*); and perhaps it might have
a further refpect to fome happy event, which
was afterwards to happen on this day of the
week, I mean the refurrection of Chrift. For
if, as we fhall prefently make appear to be probable, the jewifh fabbath was appointed to be
kept the day before the patriarchal fabbath, then
the firft day of the week, or the chriftian fabbath, is the feventh day, computed from the
beginning of time, and the fame with the fabbath inftituted, and obferved by the patriarchs,
in commemoration of the work of creation.

Thus much with refpect to the patriarchal
fabbath: As to the jewifh we fhall confider

* Lucian. Pfeudologifta feu *περι της Αποφραδος*, præfertim
ab init. cum not. Cognati in loc. Etiam Lexico. Conftantini
in voc. *Αποφραδες ημεραι.*   (*a*) Job iii. 4, 5, 7.
† Annal. lib. xiv. §. xii. p. 289. edit. Glafg. 1743.
(*b*) Ifai. lviii. 13.

1ft, The inftitution of it:

2dly, The duties that belonged to it: And

3dly, The defign and end of it.

1ft, As to the inftitution of the jewifh fabbath: The firft account we have of it is in the fixteenth chapter of the book of Exodus, where the day that God appointed to be kept by the Jews for their fabbath, was marked out by its not raining manna, which it had done for fix days before (a). The obfervation of a fabbath was probably not wholly new to the Jews; it is not likely they had entirely omitted this weekly day of reft and devotion. Neverthelefs the manner of keeping the fabbath by a total ceffation from labour, and the particular day on which it was to be kept by the Jews, feems to have been a new inftitution; otherwife, as to the day, there would have been no occafion for its being fo particularly marked out by Mofes, as the reafon of there being a double quantity of manna on the fixth day (b), for it muft have immediately occurred to the people, that it was intended for their provifion on the fabbath, if the next day had been the fabbath in courfe. And the expreffion which Mofes ufeth is remarkable, " See, or take notice, for that the Lord hath given you the fabbath, (as if this day were then firft appointed to them,) therefore he giveth you on the fixth day the bread of two days (c)." And it feems to have been too trivial a circumftance to be recorded in the facred hiftory, that the people " refted on the feventh day (d)," if this had been merely what they and their fathers had always done.

It

(a) Exod. xvi. 23,—26.   (b) See verfes 23, 25.
(c) ver. 29.   (d) ver. 30.

It moreover appears, that that day week, before the day, which was thus marked out for
a fabbath by its not raining manna, was not
obferved as a fabbath.   On the fifteenth day of
the fecond month they journeyed from Elim,
and came at night into the wildernefs of Sin (a);
where, on their murmuring for want of provifions, the Lord that night fent them quails; and
the next morning, which was the fixteenth day,
it rained manna, and fo for fix days fucceffively; on the feventh, which was the twenty-fecond, it rained none, and that day they were
commanded to keep for their fabbath; and if
this had been the fabbath in courfe, according
to the paradifaical computation, the fifteenth
muft have been fo too, and would have been
doubtlefs kept as a fabbath, and not have been
any part of it fpent in marching from Elim to
Sin.

Again, that the jewifh fabbath was on a different day from the paradifaical is probable,
from its being appointed as a fign between God
and the people of Ifrael, by obferving which
they were to know or acknowledge Jehovah as
their God (b).   Agreeable to which is the opinion of the jewifh doctors, that the fabbath
was given to Ifraelites, and none elfe were bound
to obferve it.   But how could it be a fign between God and the people of Ifrael, more than
any other people, if it had been merely the old
paradifaical fabbath, which had been given to
all mankind?

The jewifh fabbath being declared to be inftituted as a memorial of their deliverance out
of the land of Egypt, and this being fuper-
L 2   added

_____

(a) ver. 1.   (b) Exod. xxxi. 13, 17. Ezek. xx. 20.

added to the reafon for keeping the ancient paradifaical fabbath, makes it highly probable it
was appointed to be on a different day ; otherwife how could it be a memorial of a new event,
or with what propriety could it be faid, as it is,
that becaufe God " had brought them out of
the land of Egypt, therefore he commanded
them to keep the fabbath day (a) ? " Some
learned men have endeavoured to compute that
the jewifh fabbath was appointed on the fame
day of the week, on which they left Egypt ;
or rather, on which their deliverance was compleated by the overthrow of Pharoah in the
red-fea ; but whether that computation can be
clearly made out, or not, this new reafon affigned for keeping the fabbath, makes it very
likely that it was fo.

To the foregoing arguments it is replied,

1ft, That the Ifraelites had probably loft the
ancient fabbath during their flavery in Egypt,
if not before * ; for that it cannot be thought
their egyptian tafk-mafters would fuffer them to
reft from their labours one day in every week ;
and that therefore the fabbath having been laid
afide or forgot, the inftitution of the jewifh
fabbath, was only, by a new order, reviving
the ancient fabbath.

But to this it may be anfwered, That if the
Ifraelites had forgot the original fabbath, God
certainly had not ; and it is very improbable he
would have commanded them to travel from
Elim to Sin on the day he had confecrated to
facred reft, before he had either repealed the
law of the fabbath, or declared his will that any
alteration fhould be made in it.   For the children

(a) Compare Exod. xx. 11. and Deut. v. 15.
* This was the opinion of Philo, de vitâ Mofis, p. 491. E.
edit. Colon. Allobr. 1613.

dren of Ifrael never journeyed, but at the command of God (a).

Again, it is not probable, the Egyptians would be fo blind to their own intereft, as by fubjecting the Ifraelites to exceffive and inceffant labour, to wear out and deftroy their conftitutions *. It is more likely, they allowed them a weekly day of reft, as is allowed by their mafters to the negroes in the Weft-Indies, more for the fake of their health, than out of any regard to religion.

But if there is reafon to believe, that the Egyptians themfelves obferved the ancient paradifaical fabbath, it is ftill more probable they would allow the Ifraelites to do the fame; and as the Egyptians and other heathens received the law of the fabbath by tradition from Noah and Adam, it is reafonable to fuppofe they kept the day of the week originally appointed; for what fhould alter it as long as men meafured their time by a regular fucceffion of weeks, but a new divine inftitution?

It is a very probable conjecture, that the day which the heathens in general confecrated to the worfhip and honour of their chief god the fun, which according to our computation was the firft day of the week, was the ancient paradifaical fabbath. What, but the tradition of a divine inftitution, fhould induce them to confecrate that day to their principal deity, and to efteem it more facred than any other?

The reafon perhaps for God's changing the day might be to take off the Ifraelites more effectually from concurring with the Gentiles in their idolatrous worfhip of the fun. For the

L 3   fame

ſame reaſon, as the heathens begun their ſabbath, and other days, from the ſun-riſing, the
Iſraelites are ordered to begin their ſabbath from
the ſun-ſetting (*a*) : " from evening to evening
ſhall ye celebrate your ſabbath."   As the worſhippers of the ſun adored towards the eaſt, the
point of the ſun's riſing, God ordered the moſt
holy place, in which were the ſacred ſymbols of
his preſence in the tabernacle and temple, and
towards which the people were to worſhip, to
be placed to the weſt.

2dly, It is objeſted, that the paradiſaical ſabbath was appointed to be kept on the ſeventh
day; and ſo, in the fourth commandment, was
the jewiſh; and they are ſuppoſed, therefore,
to have been kept on the ſame day. But this
conſequence will not follow from the premiſes.
It is by no means certain, that the ſeventh day
of the jewiſh week coincided with the ſeventh
of the paradiſaical. For upon their migration
out of Egypt, God appointed the Iſraelites a
quite new computation of time. The beginning of the year was changed from the month
Tizri to the oppoſite month Abib (*b*); and the
beginning of the day from the morning to the
evening; for whereas the fifteenth day of the
month, on which they departed from Egypt,
was reckoned to be the morrow after the evening in which they eat the paſſover, that is, on
the fourteenth day (*c*), they were, for the time
to come, to compute their days, at leaſt their
ſabbaths, from evening to evening; by this
means the fifteenth day was changed into the
fourteenth, and the ſeventh into the ſixth; and
the

the change of the ſabbath made a change likewiſe of the beginning of the week, it always
beginning the next day after the ſabbath, which
was ſtill the ſeventh day of the week, or the ſeventh in reſpect of the preceding ſix of labour,
though not the ſeventh from the beginning of
time.

We may further obſerve, that the law of the
ſabbath is limitted, not only to the people of
Iſrael, but to the duration of their ſtate and po-
lity. " Thy children ſhall obſerve the ſabbath
throughout their generations (a):" that is, as
long as their political conſtitution ſhould en-
dure, to the days of the Meſſiah; ſo long the
ſabbath was to be kept for a " perpetual covenant" without interruption, and was to be a
" ſign between God and the children of Iſrael
for ever (b)," or while they were his peculiar
people, and only viſible church in the world.
In the ſame ſenſe the prieſthood of Aaron and
his ſons is called an everlaſting prieſthood (c);
and God promiſed that he would give to the
ſeed of Abraham all the land of Canaan for an
everlaſting poſſeſſion (d).

This law or inſtitution of the ſabbath was
inforced by the threatening of capital puniſhment to ſuch as violated it : " Every one that
defileth it ſhall ſurely be put to death; and whoever doth any work thereon, that ſoul ſhall ſurely be cut off from among his people (e)." Theſe
two clauſes of the threatening are generally underſtood in the following manner : the firſt, as
referring to any open violation of the ſabbath;
which was to be puniſhed by the magiſtrate

L 4 with

<hr />

(a) Exod. xxxi. 16.   (b) ver. 17.   (c) Exod.
xl. 15.   (d) Gen. xvii. 8.   (e) Exod. xxxi. 14.

with death, but it was not yet declared by what
kind of death. Accordingly a perfon being
afterwards convicted of this crime, he was put
in ward, " becaufe it was not declared what
fhould be done to him (a)." And God being
afrefh confulted on this occafion, it was now
determined the execution for this offence fhould
be by ftoning (b). The fecond claufe of the
threatening, " that foul fhall be cut off from
among his people," is commonly fuppofed to
relate to fecret violations of the fabbath, of
which there being no witneffes, they could not
be punifhed by the magiftrate ; and therefore
they fhould be punifhed by the immediate hand
of God. The fame phrafe is ufed concerning
the punifhment of inceftuous and unlawful con-
junctions, which are generally practifed fecret-
ly, and therefore can be punifhed by none but
God (c).

Thus much for the inftitution of the jewifh
fabbath. We now proceed

2dly, To confider the duties that belonged
to it ; which are to remember to keep it holy,
to abftain from all work and worldly bufinefs
on that day, and to fanctify it.

The firft duty of the fabbath is to remember
to keep it holy (d) ; which may import two
things.

1ft. The commemoration of bleffings formerly received. And

2dly. Preparing themfelves for the due obfervance of it.

1ft. The word " remember" hath naturally
a retrofpect to thofe former bleffings, which
they were particularly to recollect and commemorate

(a) Numb. xv. 34.   (b) ver. 35.   (c) See Lev.
xviii. 29.   (d) Exod. xx. 8.

morate on the fabbath. And they were chiefly
two, God's creating the world, and his delivering their nation from bondage in Egypt. The
firſt was a bleſſing common to the Jews and the
reſt of mankind; and is accordingly aſſigned as
the reaſon of God's appointing a fabbath to be
kept by Adam and all his poſterity (*a*). This
reaſon, therefore, for the obſervation of the
fabbath was not peculiar to the Jews, but common to them and all others, on whatever day it
was kept. But beſides this reaſon mentioned
in the book of Exodus, on occaſion of the inſtitution of the jewiſh fabbath (*b*), there was a
further reaſon aſſigned in the book of Deuteronomy (*c*) which was peculiar to themſelves;
namely, their deliverance from their bondage
in the land of Egypt.

2dly. To " remember the fabbath, to keep
it holy," may further imply, that they ſhould
not forget to prepare themſelves beforehand for
the right obſervance of it. The fabbath began
at ſix, the preparation at three o'clock in the
afternoon, and then they got every thing in rea-
dineſs, for which they had occaſion, and the
procuring or providing which was prohibited
on the fabbath, or inconſiſtent with the ſtrictneſs which the law required on that holy day.
The whole preceding day, according to Godwin, was a kind of preparation, which, ſaith
he, will appear by the particulars then forbidden: Firſt, on this day they might go no more
than three parſas; ten of which a man might
go in an ordinary day: Secondly, judges might
not ſit in judgment upon life and death: Thirdly, all forts of artificers were forbidden to work,
three only excepted, ſhoemakers, taylors, and
                                        ſcribes

(*a*) Gen. ii. 3.   (*b*) Exod. xx. 11.   (*c*) Deut. v. 15.

ſcribes, who were allowed to employ themſelves
during half the time alloted for preparation,
the two former in repairing apparel, the laſt in
getting ready to expound the law *.

It was uſual to give notice of the approach
of the ſabbath, by blowing the trumpet from
ſome high place †. Rhenferd concludes that the
מוסך השבת muſſak haſſabath, or, as our verſion renders it, the covert for the ſabbath,
which king Ahaz took away from the temple (*a*), was ſome kind of watch tower, from
the top of which the prieſts uſed to proclaim
in this manner the approach of the ſabbath ‡.
But it may as well ſignify a canopy, under
which the king uſed to ſit in the court or porch
of the temple on the ſabbath-day; which Ahaz
probably took away, to expreſs his contempt
of the ſabbath, and his not intending to come
to the temple any more.

The ſecond duty of the ſabbath was to abſtain from all manner of work or buſineſs;
from the labour of their trades and callings (*b*),
buying and ſelling (*c*), carrying burthens (*d*),
and travelling. The law injoins, that " no
man ſhould go out of his place on the ſabbath-
day (*e*);" which could not be meant to confine
them to their houſes, ſince the ſabbath was to
be celebrated by a holy convocation (*f*), or by
the peoples aſſembling for publick worſhip. It
can only therefore be underſtood as forbidding
them to travel any further than was neceſſary
for that purpoſe; how far that might be, the
law

---

* Concerning the preparation for the ſabbath, ſee Bux-
torfii Synag. judaic. cap. xv.   † Maimon. in tract.
Sabbath, cap. 5. §. 18, 19. Leuſden. Philolog. hebræo-
mixt. Diſſert. xxxvi. ſub fin.   (*a*) 2 Kings xvi. 18.

‡ Vid. Rhenferd. opus philolog. diſſert. xviii.

(*b*) Exod. xxxi. 15.   (*c*) Nehem. x. 31.   (*d*) Jer.
xvii. 21.   (*e*) Exod. xvi. 29.   (*f*) Lev. xxiii. 3.

law does not determine ; but leaves it to every
one's difcretion, according as the fynagogue or
place of worfhip, when the Jews came to be
fettled in Canaan, might be nearer or more remote.   But the rabbies, the expounders of the
law, have fixed it at two thoufand cubits*, or
about two thirds of an englifh mile.   This they
ground, partly, on Jofhua's appointing the fpace
of two thoufand cubits between the ark and the
people, when they marched into Canaan (a) ;
and partly, on two thoufand cubits being affigned for the fuburbs of the cities of the Levites : all around them (b) ; beyond which, fay
they, it was not lawful for them to travel on
the fabbath-day.   The chaldee paraphrafe †
fays, "Naomi faid unto Ruth, we are commanded to keep the fabbath and good days,
and not to go about two thoufand cubits."   The
fame meafure is affigned in the babylonifh tal-
mud‡.   This, in all probability, was the diftance
of mount Olivet from Jerufalem, it being faid (d)
to be a fabbath-day's journey §.

    Again, the Jews were forbid " doing and
finding their own pleafure on the fabbath ;"
which, I conceive, is to be underftood of re-
creations and diverfions ; and " fpeaking their
own words," that is, talking about worldly matters, making bargains, &c. (e)

They

---

* Vid. Meyer. de temporibus et feftis diebus Hebræor.
part. ii. cap. ix. §. xxxix, xl. p. 188, 190.   Hottinger.
Juris Hebræor. leges, leg. xxiv. p. 32.—34.   Lightfoot,
Horæ Hebraic. in Luc. xxiv. 50. et Act. x. 12.

    (a) Jofh. iii. 4.   (b) Numb. xxxv. 5.   † On Ruth i. 16.
    ‡ Cod. Gnerubin, fol. 48. 1. et fol. 51. 1. Vid. Meyer.
Hottinger. et Lightfoot ubi fupra.   (d) Acts i. 12.
    (e) Ifa. lviii. 13.   § See Voightii Differt de viâ Sab-
bathi, et Waltheri Differt. de itinere Sabbathi, in Act. i. 12.
pud Thefaur. theolog. philolog. tom. 2. p. 417, et feq. p.
423, et feq. Amftel. 1702.

They were likewise forbid kindling fires in their habitations on the sabbath-day (a). This law it is supposed was not intended to prohibit their having fires on the sabbath, to keep them warm in cold weather, but only to dress their meat, or for any other work. They were to dress their victuals for the sabbath the day before, that no servile labour, or as little as possible, might be done on the day itself, and that their servants might rest as well as themselves (b). Nay, the sabbatical rest was ordered to extend even to the beasts of labour; they were not to be set to work on that day (c), The ancient doctors inculcated the rest of the sabbath with a very superstitious rigour, forbidding even all acts of self-defence on that day, though assaulted by their enemies. Upon this principle a thousand Jews suffered themselves to be slain on the sabbath, not making the least resistance, in the beginning of the maccabean wars (d). Upon which Matathias and his followers, reflecting, that if they went on to act upon this principle, they must all be destroyed in like manner, decreed, upon a full debate of the matter, that for the future, if they were assaulted on the sabbath, they should defend themselves, and it was lawful for them so to do (e). However, though they would defend themselves against a direct attack, they would do nothing to hinder the enemies works : which Pompey observing, as he was besieging Jerusalem in favour of Hyrcanus against his brother Aristobulus, ordered that no assault should be made on the

---

(a) Exod. xxxv. 3.   (b) Exod. xvi 23.   (c) Exod. xx. 10.   (d) 1 Mac. ii. 31,—38. Joseph. lib. xii. cap. vi. §. 2. p. 612. edit. Haverc.   (e) ver. 39,—41. Joseph. ubi supra, et §. 3.

the fabbath, but that the day fhould be employed by his army in carrying on their works, fuch as filling up the ditches with which the temple 'was fortified, placing their battering engines, &c. by which means he took the city, and brought the Jews under fubjection to the Romans, who at length took away both their place and nation *. Thus their traditionary precepts, by which, in many cafes, they made void the law of God, proved in the end to be one means of their utter deftruction.

Neverthelefs, the modern or rabbinical doctors have regarded the reft of the fabbath, if poffible, more fuperftitioufly ftill : they advance thirty-nine negative precepts concerning things not to be done on that day, befides many others which are appendages to them. Two of thefe may ferve as a fpecimen of the whole : grafs might not be walked upon, leaft it fhould be bruifed, which is a fort of threfhing ; and a flea muft not be caught, while it hops about, becaufe that is a kind of hunting. They acquaint us alfo with many pofitive precepts, which run much in the fame ftrain; that they fhould put on clean linnen, wear better cloaths than on any other day, eat once in fix hours, &c †. But the true key for underftanding the law of God concerning the fabbatical reft was given us by our Saviour, when he faid, " The fabbath was made for man, and not man for the fabbath (a) ;" it was intended for his benefit,

---

* Jofeph. Antiq. lib. xiv. cap. iv. §. 2,—4. p. 689. See the ftory in Prideaux's Connect. part ii. book vi. fub. anno 63. vol. 4. p. 620, 621.

† Munfter. in Exod. xx. 2. Mifhn. tom 2. tit. Sabbath. Maimon. tract. Sabbath, paffim. Leufden. Philolog. hebræomixt. Differt. xxxiv, xxxv. de Sabbatho, præfertim. §. vi. p. 235. edit. 2. and Buxtorf. de Synag. judaic. cap. xv. p. 322. cap. xvi. p. 351,—364. edit. Bafil. 1661. (a) Mark ii 27.

fit, for his reft and religious improvement, and
not as a yoke of bondage, reftraining him from
works of neceffity or mercy. And this leads
to the confideration of

The third duty of the fabbath, which is to
" fanctify it (a)." It is enquired, what this
means? Some would have it to import no more
than abftaining from work and labour. Le
Clerc contends for this opinion, and alledges in
fupport of it the following paffage of Jeremiah,
" Neither carry forth a burden out of your
houfes on the fabbath-day, neither do ye any
work, but hallow ye the fabbath-day, as I commanded your fathers (b)." Doing no work on
the fabbath, and hallowing or fanctifying it are
plainly ufed as expreffions of the fame import.
As for what is called in Leviticus " the holy
convocation to be kept on the fabbath (c)," he
fuppofes it means what the Greeks call πανηγυρις,
an affembly for feafting and pleafure*. Vitringa efpoufes the fame fentiment †. The jewifh
doctors are of a contrary opinion ; they make
the fanctification of the fabbath to confift, not
merely in reft and idlenefs, but in meditation on
the wonderful works of God, in the ftudy of
the law, and in inftructing thofe who are under
them ‡. They tell us further, that the ninety-
fecond pfalm was compofed by Adam for the
devo-

'a) Deut. v. 12.   (b) Jer. xvii. 22, 24.   (c) Levit.
xxiii. 3.

* Clerici Comment. in Exod. xx. 8.

† De Synag. vetere, lib. i. part. ii. cap. ii. efpecially
p. 289,—294. Spencer maintains the fame opinion, de
Legibus Hebræor. lib. i. cap. v. §. viii,—x. vol. i. p. 67,
—88. edit. Cantab. 1727.

‡ Vid. Meyer. de temporibus et feftis, part. ii. cap. ix.
§. ix. et feq. p. 197, &c. Chriftoph. Cartwright. Electa
targum. rabbin. in Exod. xx. 8.

devotion of this day *.   We fhall not infift on
the laft particular; in other refpects their opinion feems to be agreeable to fcripture and the
reafon of things, becaufe,

1ft, The word fanctify, applied either to perfons or things, ufually imports not only the
feparation of them from common ufe, but the
dedication of them to the more immediate fervice of God.   To fanctify the fabbath therefore,
according to the true import of the word, is
not only to refrain from common bufinefs, but
to fpend the day in the peculiar fervice of God,
or in religious exercifes and acts of devotion.

2dly, Double facrifices being appointed to
be offered on the fabbath (a), is an intimation
that it was intended to be a day of extraordinary devotion.

3dly, The מקראי קדש mikre kodhefh, or
holy convocations to be held on the fabbath (b),
are moft naturally to be underftood of affemblies for religious worfhip; as in the following
paffage of Ifaiah, "The Lord will create upon every dwelling-place of mount Zion, and
upon her affemblies, מראי קדש mikre kodhefh,
a cloud and fmoke by day, and the fhining of
a flaming fire by night (c).

4thly, That fuch religious affemblies were
anciently held on the fabbath is argued from the
Shunamite's hufband enquiring of her why fhe
wanted to go to the prophet's houfe when it was
neither new moon nor fabbath (d)? Which feems
to imply, that it was cuftomary to go to his
houfe on fabbath-days, and it may reafonably be
fup-

---

* See the title of this pfalm in the Chaldee Paraphrafe.
(a) Numb. xxviii. 9, 10.   (b) Lev. xxiii. 3.
(c) Ifai. iv. 5.   See above. p. 49.   (d) 2 Kings
iv. 23.

fuppofed to be for the fake of religious worfhip performed there, when probably the prophet preached for the inftruction of the people.

This may likewife be inferred with great probability from the following paffage of the Acts, " Mofes of old time *, hath in every city them that preach him, being read in the fynagogues every fabbath-day (a)."

5thly, We may argue with Manaffeh Ben-Ifrael, that as idlenefs is ufually productive of a great deal of evil, if the inftitution of the fabbath had been merely to render people idle one day in the week, it would have been very hurtful inftead of beneficial †.

Upon the whole we conclude, that the fabbath was to be fanctified by acts of devotion, and efpecially by meeting together in folemn affemblies for public worfhip. Of this opinion is Jofephus, who mentions it as an excellent inftitution of Mofes, that, not thinking it fufficient for the Ifraelites to hear the law once or twice or oftener, he commanded them every week, to lay afide all worldly bufinefs, and to affemble in publick to hear the law read and expounded ‡. Philo faith much the fame thing §.

3dly, In the laft place, we are to confider the ends for which the fabbath was inftituted, which were partly political, and partly religious.
1ft, There

* Τὴσὴν ἀρχαίαν, from ancient generations or the firft ages, Vid. Marckii Syllog. differtat. philolog. theolog. Exercitat. xvi. §. vii. p. 454, 455. Rotterod. 1721.

(a) Acts xv. 21.

† Manaff. Conciliat. in Exod. Quæft. 35. See the paffage at large in Cartwright, ubi fupra.

‡ Jofeph. contra Appion. lib. ii. §. 17. p. 483. See alfo Antiq. lib. xvi. cap. ii. §. 4. p. 788. edit. Haverc.

§ Philo in Vit. Mofis lib. iii. p. 529, 530. edit. Colon. Allobr. 1613.

1ft, There is a political end affigned for this inftitution; namely, that the beafts of burden, as well as fervants and other labouring people might be refrefhed by refting one day in feven, which would be a means of recruiting their vigour and preferving their health : " That thine ox and thine afs may reft, and the fon of thy handmaid and the ftranger may be refrefhed(a)." Some of the jewifh doctors, by the fervants that were to reft on the fabbath-day, underftand only fuch as were circumcifed. Uncircumcifed flaves, they fay, might work on the fabbath, as an Ifraelite might on any other day *. Whereas the weekly reft, extending to the labouring beaft, furely much more included all labouring fervants, of whatever religious denomination. By the way, this may fuggeft a good reafon, why the civil magiftrate, whofe province is not religion, but merely the civil weal, fhould neverthelefs maintain the obfervation of the fabbath, becaufe a weekly day of reft is evidently conducive to the civil and national welfare.

2dly, The religious reafon for this inftitution was twofold; partly, to keep up a thankful remembrance of bleffings already received; and partly, to be a means of their obtaining and enjoying future and heavenly bleffings.

The bleffings already received, of which the fabbath was inftituted to be a memorial, were chiefly two, their creation, and their deliverance from bondage in Egypt.

1ft, It was appointed to be kept in memory of God's creating the world, which is the rea-

(a) Exod. xxiii. 12.
* Maimon. de Sabbato, cap. xx. §. 14. See Ainfworth on Exod. xx. 10.

fon afligned for the firft inftitution (a), becaufe " on the feventh day God ended his work, which he had made," or as the word ויכל vaichal, fhould rather be rendered, " he had ended his work," for he did not work on the feventh day ; it follows, " he refted on the feventh day from all his works which he had made, and bleffed the feventh day, and fanctified it, becaufe that in it he had refted from all his work." This, however, is not to be underftood of his ceafing from any further operation and action, the contrary to which our Saviour afferts, " My father worketh hitherto, and I work (b)," that is, in preferving, ordering, and governing the world. It is therefore commonly underftood to mean, that he ceafed from creating any new forts or fpecies of creatures, fo that his power has ever fince been exerted only in continuing and increafing the feveral fpecies which he formed on the firft fix days. And certain it is, no inftance can be given of any new fort or fpecies having been fince brought into being. Though various kinds of mules have been produced by creatures of different fpecies, both in the animal and vegetable world, yet fuch are not to be reckoned diftinct fpecies, fince none of them ever propagate their kind.

As for God's refting, we are not to underftand it as oppofed to toil or wearinefs ; for " the creator of the ends of the earth fainteth not, neither is weary (c)." But it merely imports his ceafing to work as he had done for the preceding fix days. Thus the word שבת fhabath, is ufed for the manna's ceafing to fall,

(a) Gen. ii. 2, 3.   (b) John v. 17.   (c) Ifa. xl. 28.

fall (a), and for the Ifraelites ceafing to be a nation (b). Neverthelefs, it may probably import likewife, the complacency or delight which he took in the works he had made, which were " all very good ;" fince in the twentieth chapter of Exodus, God's refting on the feventh day is expreffed by the verb נוח nuach (c); the fame word which is' ufed for his acceptance of Noah's facrifice : " The Lord fmelt a favour of reft," or as we render it, " a fweet favour (d)," importing that his thankfulnefs and devotion, expreffed by his facrifice, were as grateful to God as fweet odours are to us. To preferve therefore, a remembrance of his creating the world in fix days, and his refting from his work on the feventh, God inftituted a weekly fabbath, commanding men to work fix days, and to lay afide all their worldly employments on the feventh.   And no doubt the right remembrance of God's creating power, wifdom and goodnefs, muft include adoration, thankfulnefs and praife to the great creator.

2dly, The other bleffing, which the Jews in particular were to commemorate, was their deliverance out of the egyptian bondage ; which is mentioned as the fpecial reafon of their being commanded to keep the fabbath (e). The learned Mr. Mede endeavours to prove the feventh day of the jewifh week, which was appointed for the fabbath, to be the day on which God overthrew Pharaoh in the Red Sea, and thereby compleated the deliverance of his people from the egyptian fervitude.   And whereas a feventh day had before been kept in memory

M 2   of

(a) Jofh. v. 12.   (b) Jerem. xxxi. 36.   (c) Exod,. xx. 11.   (d) Gen. viii. 21.   (e) Deut. v. 15.

of the creation (but to what day of the jewiſh week that anſwered we cannot certainly ſay,) now God commanded them to obſerve for the future this day of their deliverance, which was the ſeventh day of their week, in commemoration of his having given them reſt from their hard labour and ſervitude in Egypt *. And both theſe reaſons for their obſerving the ſabbath, implied their obligation to obſerve it with devotion, gratitude and praiſe.

The other religious end of the ſabbath was to be a means of their obtaining and enjoying future and heavenly bleſſings. This is a principal deſign of all acts of devotion and worſhip; ſuch as we have already ſhewn ought to accompany the obſervance of the ſabbath. The Jews accounted this holy day to be a type of the heavenly reſt. On this notion the apoſtle evidently grounds his diſcourſe in the fourth chapter of the epiſtle to the Hebrews (a). Origen makes the ſabbath an emblem of that reſt we ſhall enjoy when we have done our work, ſo as to have left nothing undone which was our incumbent duty †. In the ſame manner the jewiſh doctors ſpeak of the ſabbath. It was a common proverb among them ‡, "Non datum eſt ſabbatum, niſi ut eſſet typus futuri ſeculi." Remarkable to the ſame purpoſe are the words of Abarbanel § : Sabbata dixit in plurali numero, quandoquidem præceptum de ſabbato non ſolum deſignat fundamentalem illum articulum

---

* Mede's Diatrib. on Ezek. xx. 10.

(a) Heb. iv. 1,—11.

† Origen. contra Celſum, lib. vi. p. 317. edit. Spencer. Cantab. 1677.

‡ Vid. Buxtorf. Florileg. hebr. p. 299.

§ On Exod. xxxi. 13.

culum de creatione mundi, verum etiam, mundum ſpiritualem, in quo erit vera quies, et vera poſſeſſio. Illic vera ceſſatio erit, ab omnibus operibus et rebus corporeis. Habemus ergo duo ſabbata, unum corporale, in memoriam creationis, alterum ſpirituale, in memoriam immortalitatis animæ et oblectationis poſt mortem. The Jews, therefore, by no means count the ſabbath a burden, but a great bleſſing; they have it in high veneration, and affect to call it their ſpouſe *. Leo of Modena tells us that ſo far are the modern Jews from being inclined to ſhorten the ſabbath, that they make it laſt as long as poſſible, prolonging their hymns and prayers not only out of devotion to God, but charity to the ſouls of the damned, it being a received opinion among them, that they ſuffer no torments on the ſabbath †.

* Selden. de Jure nat. et gent. lib. iii. cap. x. oper. vol. 1. p. 326, 327. Buxtorf. Synag. judaic. cap xv. p. 299, 300. edit. Baſil. 1661.

† On the ſubject of the ſabbath conſult Selden. de Jure nat. et gent. lib. iii. cap. viii. et ſeq. Capelli Diſputatio de ſabbatho, apud Comment. et not. critic. in Vet. Teſt. p. 263, et ſeq. Amſtel. 1689. Spencer. de Leg. Hebr. lib. 1. cap. v. ſect. vii, et ſeq.

CHAP.

CHAP. IV.

Of the paſſover and feaſt of un- leavened bread.

THE jewiſh feſtivals were either weekly, as the fabbath ; monthly, as the new moons ; or annual, as the paſſover, the pente-coſt, the feaſt of ingathering or of tabernacles, and the feaſt of trumpets ; to which we may add, the annual faſt, or day of expiation. Be-fides theſe, there were others that returned once in a certain number of years ; as the fabbatical year, and the jubilee.

Of the anniverſary feaſts the three former were the moſt confiderable, the paſſover, the pentecoſt, and the feaſt of tabernacles. At each of theſe all the males were to appear before the Lord at the national altar (a). The defign of this was, partly to unite the Jews among them-felves, and to promote mutual love and friend-ſhip throughout the nation, by means of the whole body of them meeting together ſo often : to which the Pfalmiſt ſeems to refer, when he faith,

(a) Exod. xxiii. 14, 17. xxxiv. 22, 23. Deut. xvi. 16.

faith, " Jerufalem is builded as a city that is
compact together: whither the tribes go up,
the tribes of the Lord, unto the teftimony of
Ifrael, to give thanks unto the name of the
Lord (a)." And it was, partly, that as one
church, they might make one congregation and
join in folemn worfhip together ; for I apprehend the fcripture idea of one particular church,
is only one worfhipping affembly. And it was
further, by fo large an appearance and concourfe of people, to grace thefe facred feftivals,
and add greater folemnity to the worfhip; and
partly, likewife, for the better fupport of the
fervice and minifters of the fanctuary ; for none
were to appear before the Lord empty, each
perfon was to bring fome gift or prefent with
him, according to his ability, and as God had
bleffed him (b). Further, as the jewifh fanctuary and fervice contained in them a fhadow of
good things to come, and were typical of the
gofpel-church, this prefcribed concourfe from
all parts of the country to the fanctuary might
be intended to typify the gathering of the people to Chrift, and into his church, from all
parts of the world under the chriftian difpenfation. Hence the apoftle in allufion to thefe general affemblies of the Ifraelites on the three
grand-feafts, faith, " We are come to the general affembly and church of the firft-born (c)."

The law required only the males to appear
before the Lord on thefe folemn occafions. But,
though the women were exempted from a neceffity of attending, yet they were not excluded
if they pleafed to do it, and could with conve-

M 4

nience ;

(a) Pfal. cxxii. 3, 4.   (b) Deut. xvi. 16, 17.
(c) Heb. xii. 23.

nience; as appears from the cafe of Hannah, who ufed to go with her hufband yearly to wor-fhip and facrifice to the Lord of Hofts in Shi-loh (a): and from the cafe of the Virgin Mary, who went with her hufband Jofeph every year at the feaft of the paffover to Jerufalem (b). Mr. Mede affigns three reafons for the women's being exempted from the duty of attending the feafts:

1ft, The weaknefs and infirmity of the fex, they not being able without much trouble and danger to undertake fo long a journey from the remote parts of the country.

2dly, The hazard of their chaftity in fo vaft a concourfe of people.

3dly, The care of their young children, and other houfhold affairs, which muft have been wholly abandoned, if they, as well as the men, had been abfent from their houfes fo long at the fame time *.

To thefe reafons probably another and more confiderable may be added, namely the legal uncleaneffes to which they would be liable in fo long a journey.

Though the law required all the males to appear before the Lord, in the place he fhould choofe at thefe three feafts; no doubt it was to be underftood with fome reftriction, it not be-ing likely that young children or decrepid old men could give their attendance †. Mr. Mede ‡ conceives, the law is to be underftood of all
　　　　　　　　　　　　　　　　　　　males

(a) 1 Sam. i. 3, 7.　　　(b) Luke ii. 41.

* Mede's Diatrib. Difcourfe xlvii. on Deut. xvi. 16. Works, p. 261.

† Thefe, among others, are exprefsly excepted, Mifhn. tit. Chagigah, cap. 1. §. 1. tom. 2. p. 413. edit. Surenhus. See alfo the Gemara in loc.

‡ Mede, ubi fupra.

males within the age of service, from twenty
to fifty years old ; for at fifty all were emeriti,
even the priests and levites serve not after that
age ; but as to the age at which persons entered
on service, that was different ; the priests might
not serve before thirty, nor the levites before
twenty-five ; but the laity were capable of employment at twenty ; as appears from a passage
in Numbers, where God commands Moses " to
take the sum of all the congregation of the
children of Israel, from twenty years old and upwards, all that were able to go forth to war (a)."
But if, according to the rabbies, children came
under the obligation of the law, when they were
twelve years old, this perhaps was the age of
their attendance at these festivals. Which opinion is somewhat countenanced by the history
of Jesus going with his parents to Jerusalem at
the passover, when he was twelve years old (b).
But I take the more probable opinion to be,
that all the males meant all that were capable
of taking the journey *, and of attending the
feast ; which some were able to do sooner and
some later in life ; and therefore by the law no
age was fixed, but it was left to be determined
by every one's prudence and religious zeal ;
only none might absent themselves without sufficient reason.

There are yet two difficulties, which have
been started concerning this law.   One is, how
Jerusalem could contain such multitudes as
flocked from all parts of Judea to these so-
lemnities.   The other is, how the Israelites
could

(a) Numb. i. 3.   (b) Luke ii. 42. Lightfoot. Hor.
hebraic. in loc.
   * Vid. Mishn. ubi supra.

could leave their towns and villages deftitute of men, without the greateft danger of being invaded and plundered by their neighbouring enemies.

As to the former queftion, it may as well be afked, how it is poffible for Bath and Tunbridge to contain fuch multitudes as flock to them in their feafons. For, as at thofe places there are great numbers of lodging houfes, much larger than are requifite for the accommodation of the families ·that conftantly inhabit them ; fo it was doubtlefs at Jerufalem, to which there were every year three ftated feafons of concourfe from all parts of the country. It is probable, that moft families let lodgings at thofe times. The man, at whofe houfe our Saviour eat his laft paffover with his difciples, had a " gueft chamber," or a room which he fpared on thefe occafions (*a*). Or if this be not fufficient to remove the difficulty, it is an eafy fuppofition that many might be entertained in tents erected on thefe occafions ; as the mohammedan pilgrims are at Mecca, to which many thoufands refort at a certain time of the year.

As to the other difficulty concerning the danger of leaving their towns and villages without any men to guard them, we need not have recourfe to the conjecture advanced by fome, that this obligation on all the males was only during their abode in the wildernefs, when their nearnefs to the tabernacle eafily admitted of their attendance. If that had been the cafe, Jeroboam need not have fet up the golden calves at Dan and Bethel, to deliver the ten tribes from going up to Jerufalem to worfhip (*b*).

                                   Befide,

(*a*) Luke xxii. 11.   (*b*) 1 Kings xii. 27, 28.

Beside, there are sufficient instances in the jewish history, to shew that this practice was continued till after our Saviour's time. Thus we are informed in the Acts, that there were multitudes of Jews, out of every nation under heaven, come to Jerusalem at the feast of pentecost (*a*). Κατοικωντες, which our version renders " dwelling" at Jerusalem, should, in this place be rendered " abiding," that is, during the time of the festival: Κατοικησις is used by St. Mark for a place of transient abode, and not a fixed and settled habitation (*b*).

Nor need we suppose with others, that they only sent a certain proportion of men, as one in ten or twelve, to Jerusalem, to be as it were the representatives, and offer the gifts, of the rest, while they kept the feasts in their own towns. Nor need we, again, suppose with others, that since there was a divine permission granted to those, who were unable to celebrate the passover in the first month, to do it in the second (*c*) ; the same indulgence might probably extend to the other festivals ; and so one half of the males might stay at home and guard the country and their houses, while the other half went to the sanctuary ; and those who thus remained behind might celebrate the festival in the next month.

We need, I say, none of these suppositions and conjectures, since God himself had expressly undertaken to guard their habitations and substance, by his special providence, while the men were absent to celebrate the sacred festivals: " Neither shall any man desire thy land,"

it

(*a*) Acts ii. 5.　　(*b*) Mark v. 3.　　(*c*) Numb. ix. 10, 11.

it is ſaid, " when thou ſhalt go up to appear
before the Lord thy God thrice in the year (a)."
This is, by the way, a very remarkable inſtance
of the ſovereign and abſolute power, which God
exerciſes over the hearts and ſpirits of men.
Accordingly we find not in the whole ſcripture
hiſtory, that any ſuch evil ever befell the Iſraelites on theſe occaſions; inſomuch that though
in many other caſes they were backward in believing God's promiſes; yet at theſe ſeaſons they
would leave their habitations and families without the leaſt apprehenſion of danger.

Having thus conſidered a circumſtance, which
was common to the three grand anniverſary feaſts,
we are now to treat of the firſt of them, namely,
the paſſover.

Of the inſtitution of this feſtival we have an account in the twelfth chapter of the book of Exodus.
It is called in the hebrew פסחא paſcha, from פסח
paſach, tranſiit. In the greek it is called πασχα,
but not from the verb πασχω, patior, to ſuffer,
on account of Chriſt's having ſuffered at the
time of this feaſt, according to the illiterate ſuppoſition of Chryſoſtom, Irenæus and Tertullian. Chryſoſtom ſaith, Πασχα λεγεται, οτι τοτε
επαθεν ο Χριϛος υπερ ημων: Paſcha dicitur, quia
Chriſtus illo tempore pro nobis paſſus eſt *.
Irenæus ſaith, A Moyſe oſtenditur Filius Dei,
cujus et diem paſſionis non ignoravit, ſed figu-
ratim pronunciavit, eum paſcha nominans †.
Tertullian, Hanc ſolemnitatem——præcanebat
(ſc. Moyſes) et adjecit, Paſcha eſſe Domini, id
                                              eſt,

(a) Exod. xxxiv. 24.
* Homil. v. in 1 Tim.
† Iren. adverſus hær. lib. iv. cap. xxiii. p. 309 edit.
Grabii, Oxon. 1702.

eſt, paſſionem Chriſti *.   But the greek word
πασχα is derived from the chaldee כפסחא paſ-
cha†, which anſwers to the hebrew פסח peſach;
and the feſtival was ſo called, not from its being prophetical or typical of Chriſt's ſufferings,
but from God's paſſing over, and leaving in
ſafety the houſes of the Iſraelites, on the door-
poſts of which the blood of the ſacrificed lamb
was ſprinkled, when he ſlew the firſt born in
all the houſes of the Egyptians.   This etymology of the name is expreſsly given in the book
of Exodus, " It is the ſacrifice of the Lord's
paſſover," אשר פסח aſher paſach, who paſſed
by, or leaped over, the houſes of the Iſraelites (a).   So that our engliſh word paſſover
well expreſſes the true import of the original
פסח peſach or כפסחא paſcha.

Concerning the paſſover we ſhall conſider,

1ſt. The time when it was to be kept.

2dly, The rites with which it was to be celebrated.

3dly, The ſignification of theſe rites.

1ſt. The time, when this feaſt was to be celebrated, is very particularly expreſſed in Leviticus, " In the fourteenth day of the firſt
month, at even, is the Lord's paſſover (b):"
Wherein is remarked the month, the day, and
the time of the day.

1ſt. The month.   It is called the firſt month,
that is, of the eccleſiaſtical year, which commenced

---

* Tertullian adverſus Judæos, cap. x. ſub fin. p. 197.
A. edit. Rigalt. Paris. 1675.

† Philo in vitâ Moſis, lib. iii. p. 531. A. edit. Colon.
Allobr. 1613. το χαλδαιςι λεγομενον πασχα.   In his treatiſe
de Decalogo he ſaith, ην (ſc. εορτην) Εβραιοι πατριω γλωττη
πασχα προσαγορευουσιν. p. 591. C.

(a) Exod. xii. 27.   (b) Lev xxiii. 5.

menced with the Iſraelites flight out of Egypt (*a*).
This month had two names Abib (*b*), and Niſan (*c*). It is called Abib, that is, the earing
month, or the month of new corn ; for Abib
ſignifies a green or new ear of corn, ſuch as
was grown to maturity, but not dried or fit for
grinding. In the ſecond chapter of Leviticus
the offering of the firſt fruits is called Abib,
and it is ordered to be dried by the fire, in order to its being beaten or ground into flour (*d*);
and in the ninth chapter of Exodus, the barley
is ſaid to be ſmitten with hail, becauſe it was
Abib (*e*), that is, in the ear. Hence the ſeptuagint tranſlates Abib, wherever it is uſed for
the name of a month, μηνα των νεων, underſtanding, no doubt, καρπων. So the vulgate alſo renders it, menſis novarum frugum.

The other name, Niſan, is derived by ſome
from נוס nus, fugere ; and ſo it ſignifies the
month of flight, namely, of the Iſraelites out
of Egypt. Others derive it from נס nes, vexillum, or נסס naſas, vexillum tulit ; and ſo it ſignifies the month of war, when campaigns uſually began. Perhaps " the time when kings
go forth to battle," a phraſe uſed in the ſecond
book of Samuel (*f*), may only be a periphra-
ſis for the month Niſan. Thus the Romans
called this month Martius, quaſi menſis Marti
ſacer : the Bithynians ſtiled the two firſt ſpring-
months ϛρατειος and αρειος, from Απις Mars, the
god of war*. But there are others, who derive it
from the arabic and ſyriac word נוס nus, contur-
batus eſt, becauſe it is uſually a ſtormy month.

Second-

(*a*) Exod. xii. 2.   (*b*) Exod. xiii. 4.   (*c*) Nehem.
ii. 1. Eſth. iii. 7.   (*d*) Lev. ii. 14. eng. 13. heb.   (*e*) Exod.
ix. 31.   (*f*) 2 Sam. xi. 1.   * Bochart. Hieroz. lib. ii.
ſap. i. oper. tom. 2. p. 557, 558. edit. Lugd. Bat. 1712.

Secondly, As to the day of the month, when this feaſt was to begin, it was ordered to be on the fourteenth at even, at which time the paſchal lamb was to be killed and eaten, and from thence the feaſt was to be kept ſeven days, till the twenty firſt (a). Sacrifices, peculiar to this feſtival, were to be offered on each of the ſeven days; but the firſt and laſt, namely, the fifteenth and the twenty-firſt, were to be ſanctified above all the reſt, as ſabbaths, by abſtaining from all ſervile labour and holding a holy convocation (b); eſpecially the ſeventh, or laſt day, was called חג ליהוה chag Laiovah, " a feaſt unto the Lord," κατ' ἐξοχην (c), and עצרת ליהוה gnatſereth Laiovah, which we render " a ſolemn aſſembly (d);" but עצרת gnatſereth, from עצר gnatſar, clauſit vel cohibuit, rather ſignifies a reſtraint from all worldly buſineſs and ſervile labour.

The reaſon of the firſt and ſeventh day being thus peculiarly conſecrated above the reſt, is by Bochart ſuppoſed to be, becauſe the firſt was the day of the Iſraelites eſcape out of Egypt, and the ſeventh that on which Pharaoh and his army were deſtroyed in the red ſea*. But the ſpecial holineſs of the firſt and the laſt day being a circumſtance common to the feaſt of tabernacles, as well as the paſſover (e), for this reaſon others think it was intended to ſignify in general, that we ſhould perſevere in the diligent proſecution of the buſineſs of religion to the end of our lives, and inſtead of growing more remiſs,

(a) Exod. xii. 6, 8, 15. Lev. xxiii. 5, 6.   (b) Exod. xii. 16. Lev. xxiii. 7, 8.   (c) Exod. xiii. 6.   (d) Deut. xvi. 8.

* Hierozoic. ubi ſupra, p. 602.

(e) Lev. xxiii. 39. John vii. 37.

remiſs, ſhould be the more active and vigorous, the nearer we arrive to the period of our race, to our heavenly reſt and reward : agreeable to the exhortation of St. Peter, " Wherefore ſee-ing ye look for ſuch things, be diligent that ye may be found of him in peace, without ſpot and blameleſs (a) :" and of the author of the epiſtle to the Hebrews, " Exhorting one ano-ther ſo much the more, as ye ſee the day ap-proaching (b)."

Although the whole time of the continuance of this feaſt is in a more lax ſenſe ſtiled the paſſover (c) ; yet, ſtrictly ſpeaking, the paſſover was kept only on the evening of the fourteenth day of the month, and the enſuing ſeven days were the feaſt of unleavened bread ; ſo called, becauſe during their continuance the Jews were to eat unleavened bread, and to have no other in their houſes. This diſtinction between the paſſover and the feaſt of unleavened bread, is made in the ſecond book of Chronicles, " The children of Iſrael kept the paſſover, and the feaſt of unleavened bread ſeven days (d) :" and in the book of Ezra, " The children of the captivity kept the paſſover upon the fourteenth day of the firſt month, and kept the feaſt of unleavened bread ſeven days with joy (e)."

It is an enquiry, which hath occaſioned no little debate, whether Chriſt kept his laſt paſſ-over at the ſame time with the reſt of the Jews, or one day ſooner ? Several conſiderable criticks*

are

(a) 2 Pet. iii. 14. (b) Heb. x. 25. (c) John xviii. 39. Luke xxii. 1. (d) 2 Chron. xxxv. 17. (e) Ezra vi. 19, 22.

* Vid. Grotii Annot. in Matt. xxvi. 18. Scaliger. de Emend. tempor. lib. vi. p. 567, et ſeq. edit. Colon. Allob. 1629. Caſaubon. Exercitat. in Baronii Annales, exerc. xvi. §. xii,

are of opinion, that, for ſpecial reaſons, he kept
it the day before the ſtated and uſual time. This
ſentiment they ground on ſeveral paſſages of
ſcripture ; particularly on the account in the
thirteenth chapter of St. John (a), of the ſupper which Chriſt eat with his diſciples, which,
if it be, as there is good reaſon to believe it
was, the laſt ſupper he eat with them, that is,
the paſſover-ſupper, it is expreſsly ſaid to be
Vol. II.		N		before

§. xii,—xxi. p. 405,—439. edit. Genev. 1655. Cud-
worth's True notion of the Lord's ſupper, chap. iii. Sauber-
tus de ultimo Chriſti Paſchate, cap. 1. §. 8,—12. apud The-
ſaurum theolog. philolog. vol. 2. p. 195, 199. It is remarkable, that theſe eminent criticks, who all agree that Chriſt
eat the paſſover on a different day from the Jews, are divided in their opinions concerning the method of account-
ing for it.	Grotius diſtinguiſhes between the paſchal ſa-
crifice, and a ſupper commemorative of the paſſover, and
ſuppoſes our Saviour celebrated the latter only, before the
time preſcribed by the law for the paſchal ſacrifice, which
he foreſaw his death would prevent his obſerving.	Scali-
ger and Caſaubon apprehend that Chriſt eat the paſchal ſacrifice on the day preſcribed by the law, but not when the
Jews did, they having deferred it, according to their ſuppoſed
cuſtom when it fell the day before the ſabbath, that there
might not be two ſabbaths together.	Cudworth oppoſes
the notions both of Grotius and Scaliger, and makes the
ground of this difference of the days to be that our Saviour
and his apoſtles, and divers others of the moſt religious
Jews, regulated the time of their obſervation of the paſſover by computing from the true phaſis of the moon, and
not by the decree of the ſenate.	The opinion of Grotius
concerning the ground of this difference of the days, is
juſtly exploded likewiſe by Leidekker de Republ. Hebræor.
lib. ix. cap. iv. p. 551, 552. though he ſtrenuouſly main-
tains that the days were different.	Leylingius in confor-
mity with the opinion of ſeveral other learned men, ſuppoſes, that Chriſt did not celebrate the paſſover at all, but
only his own ſupper, (Obſervationes Sacræ, vol. 1. Obſerv.
lii. §. xiv,—xix.) but he is confuted by Harenberg. in his
Diſſert. on John xviii. 28. §. xxvi. et ſeq. publiſhed in the
Theſaurus Novus theologico-philolog.

	(a) John xiii. 1, 29.

before the feaft of the paffover (*a*), that is, before the ufual time of keeping it. Again, the
difciples imagined their Lord had ordered Judas " to buy thofe things they had need of
againft the feaft (*b*);" which feems to imply, that
although for particular reafons he eat the pafchal lamb that evening, neverthelefs the time
of the feaft was not yet arrived.

Another paffage alledged in fupport of this
opinion, is in the eighteenth chapter of St. John,
where we are informed, that on the day of our
Saviour's crucifixion, which was the day after
he had eat the paffover, the Jews " would not
go into the judgment hall, left they fhould be
defiled; but that they might eat the paffover (*c*):"
which implies, it is faid, that they had not yet
eat it.

Again, in the nineteenth chapter the fame
day, that is, the day of our Lord's crucifixion,
is faid to be the " preparation of the paffover (*d*); " and therefore it is alledged, the paffover could not yet be eaten.

Dr. Whitby argues on the oppofite fide of
the queftion in the following manner *.

1ft, In the twenty fixth chapter of St. Matthew it is faid, that on " the firft day of unleavened bread the difciples prepared the paffover (*e*); " and in the evening Chrift eat it
with them; and in St. Mark it is obferved,
that this " was the day on which they, that is,
the Jews, killed the paffover (*f*)."

2dly, Chrift

(*a*) John xiii. 1.   (*b*) ver. 29.   (*c*) John xviii. 28.
(*d*) John xix. 14.
    * See his differtation on this fubject, in an Appendix to
the fourteenth chapter of St. Mark.
    (*e*) Matt. xxvi. 17.   (*f*) Mark xiv. 12.

2dly, Chriſt ſays to his diſciples, "Ye know that after two days is the feaſt of the paſſover (a)." Now the feaſt of the paſſover and of unleavened bread, is one and the ſame, or at the ſame time (b). Since, therefore, as hath been juſt ſhewn, Chriſt did not eat the paſſover till the firſt day of unleavened bread, it follows that he did not eat it till after thoſe two days, that is, at the time when the diſciples knew it was to be eaten according to the law.

3dly, The day following our Saviour's eating the paſſover was a feaſt day; for Barabbas, it is ſaid, was releaſed at the feaſt (c). Now the firſt day of the feaſt of unleavened bread, in which a holy convocation was held, was the day after eating the paſſover (d).

4thly, As Chriſt was "made under the law," which continued in full force till after his reſurrection, he could not have kept the paſſover the day before the law preſcribed it, without juſt cenſure, nor before the reſt of the Jews obſerved it, according to their interpretation of the law, without their cenſure, which he does not appear to have incurred; nor can it be imagined his diſciples would have come to him with that queſtion, "Where wilt thou that we prepare to eat the paſſover," before the time which the law appointed, or which was uſual, for eating it.

5thly, The paſchal lamb could not be ſlain but "in the place which God had choſen, to put his name there (e);" that is, in the tabernacle or temple. Now it cannot be ſuppoſed,

　that

(a) Matt. xxvi. 2.　(b) Mark xiv. 1.　Luke xxii. 1.
(c) Mat xxvii. 15, 26.　Mark xv. 6, 15.　(d) Lev. xxiii. 4,
et ſeq.　(e) Deut. xvi. 6.

that the prieſts would have killed the paſchal lamb for Jeſus, or ſuffered it to have been killed in the temple, before the day which the law preſcribed, namely, the fourteenth day of the month Niſan, when they killed it for all the people ; or before the day, which was obſerved according to their rules of interpreting the law.

Theſe reaſons ſeem to me to prove unanſwerably, that Chriſt eat the paſſover at the uſual time, when the reſt of the Jews did. Let us then enquire, how the paſſages alledged to the contrary, are to be underſtood.

1ſt. Biſhop Kidder *, and the doctors Lightfoot † and Whitby ‡ are of opinion that the ſupper ſpoken of in the thirteenth chapter of St. John, was not the paſſover, but another ſupper at Bethany ſome nights before ; but the contrary is proved by Dr. Doddridge and Dr. Guyſe §. As for the phraſe, " Before the feaſt of the paſſover (a)," it need only be underſtood to mean before the feaſt begun, or before they ſat down to ſupper ; and δειπνυ γενομενυ, which in our verſion is, " Supper being ended (b)," may be better rendered, " Supper being come:" Πρωιας γενομενης ſignifies " when morning was come (c) :" ημερας γενομενης " when day was come (d) :" σιγης γενομενης, " when ſilence was made (e)."

As to Judas's buying things againſt the feaſt, it is eaſy to be underſtood of the ſacrifices, and whatever they would need to celebrate the enſuing feſtival, or the feaſt of unleavened bread.

2dly, The

---

* Demonſt. of the Meſſiah, chap. 3. p. 60, 61.
† Horæ hebr. Matt. xxvi. 6.
‡ Ubi ſupra.
§ See Doddridge and Guyſe in ver. 1.
(a) ver. 1.   (b) ver. 2.   (c) John xxi. 4.
(d) Acts xii. 18. xvi. 35.   (e) Acts xxi. 40.

2dly, The paſſage in the eighteenth chapter of St. John, relating to the ſolicitude which the Jews expreſſed, not to be defiled on the day of our Lord's crucifixion, in order that they might eat the paſſover (a), may be underſtood of the ſacrifices, which were offered on the feaſt of unleavened bread, otherwiſe called the paſſover.

3dly, As for the παρασκευη τε πασχα, or preparation of the paſſover, ſpoken of in the nineteenth chapter of St. John (b), as being the day of our Lord's crucifixion, it ſignifies the preparation for the paſchal ſabbath, or the ſabbath which fell in the paſchal week, and was obſerved with ſome peculiar ſolemnity; for it was eſteemed to be, as it is expreſsly ſtiled (c), " an high day, " or the great day of the feaſt *.

Thirdly, As to the time of the day, when the paſſover was to be killed and eaten, it was בין הערבים bein hangnarbaim, " betwixt the two evenings (d);" which means the after part of the day, as appears from the uſe of the ſame phraſe in the twenty eighth chapter of the book of Numbers, where it ſtands oppoſed to the

N 3   morn-

<hr />

(a) John xviii. 28.   (b) John xix. 14.   (c) ver. 31.
* Among thoſe who maintain that our Saviour kept the paſſover at the ſame time with the Jews, ſee Bochart. Hieroz. lib. ii. cap. l. oper. tom. 2. p. 560,—571. edit. 4. Lugd. Bat. 1712. Baſnage in his hiſtory of the Jews, lib. v. cap. x. §. xliv. p. 437. Friſchmuthi Diſſertat. in Matt. xxvi. 2. apud Theſaur. Theolog. philolog. tom. 2. p. 189. Harenbergi Diſſertat. in Joh. xviii. 28. apud Theſaur. Nov. theolog. philolog. tom. 2. p. 538. Reland. Antiq. pars iv. cap. iii. §. ix. ad ult. p. 467,—472. edit. 3. 1717. Bynæus, de Morte Chriſti, lib. 1. cap. 1. §. 19, —32. p. 24,—65. edit. Amſtel. 1691. hath repreſented the arguments on both ſides. See alſo Witſii Meletem. Diſſert. xi. and Leuſden. Philolog. hebræo-mixt. Diſſert. xxxviii. de Paſchate. Quæſt. v.   (d) Exod. xii, 6.

morning: " One lamb ſhalt thou offer in the
morning, and the other lamb ſhalt thou offer
at evening (a)." But what part or hour of the
afternoon is intended by it, is diſputed betwixt
the rabbiniſts and the karraites.

The rabbiniſts underſtand by the firſt of the
two evenings, the time of the ſun's beginning
to decline from his meridian altitude, which
they fix at half an hour after twelve; by the
other, the time of his ſetting. In the ſame
manner the ancient Grecians diſtinguiſhed betwixt the two evenings, as we learn from a note
of Euſtatius on the ſeventeenth book of the
Odyſſey; who ſaith, that according to the an-
cients, there are two evenings; one, which they
called the latter evening, at the cloſe of the
day; the other, the former evening, which
commences preſently after noon *. Theſe were
the two evenings more generally underſtood by
the Jews in the time of Joſephus; for he ſays,
they killed the paſchal lamb from the ninth
hour to the eleventh, that is, from our three
to five o'clock in the afternoon †.

The karraites underſtand the firſt of the two
evenings to commence from ſun ſet; before
which, according to them, the paſſover was
not to be killed and eaten; and the latter, from
the beginning of dark night; ſo that, in their
opinion, " betwixt the two evenings" means
in the twilight. Their notion, at leaſt as to the
time of eating the paſſover, ſeems to be countenanced by the letter of the law in Deuteronomy;

(a) Numb. xxviii. 4.
* Vid. Bochart. Hierozoic. part. 1. lib. ii. cap. 1. oper.
tom. 2. p. 559. edit. 1712.
† De Bello judaic. lib. vi. cap. ix. §. 3. p. 399. edit.
Haverc.

my : " Thou ſhalt ſacrifice the paſſover at even‑
ing, at the going down of the ſun (a)." And
in the book of Joſhua it is ſaid, that " the
children of Iſrael encamped in Gilgal, and kept
the paſſover on the fourteenth day of the month
at even (b)." Nevertheleſs, the duration of the
twilight at the equinoctial ſeaſons, at one of
which the paſſover was kept, being ſhorter than
at any other time of the year, would hardly af‑
ford time ſufficient, eſpecially in that climate,
for killing, roaſting and eating the lamb. It
is therefore probable, either that by " ſacri‑
ficing and keeping the paſſover" in the forecited
text in Deuteronomy, is meant merely the eat‑
ing of it; or that by " evening and the going
down of the ſun," is denoted the whole time of
its declining from the meridian altitude till ſun‑
ſet*.

Thus much for the time of this feaſt.

2dly, Concerning the rites with which it was
to be celebrated, we are to obſerve,

1ſt, The matter of the paſchal feaſt; which
was to be " a lamb without blemiſh, a male
of the firſt year from the ſheep or from the
goats (c)." The hebrew word שׂה ſeh, which
we render lamb, ſignifies the young either of
the ſheep or of the goats; which we have no
engliſh word, as I remember, to anſwer. The
שׂה ſeh, of the paſſover might be, what we
call, either a lamb or a kid. But as lambs
were preferable, being the better food, Theo‑

N 4   doret

(a) Deut. xvi. 6.   (b) Joſh. v. 10.
* On this controverſy ſee Martinii Etymologicum, Bux‑
torfii Lexic. Biblic. et Bocharti Hierozoic. part. 1. lib. ii.
cap. 50. p. 558,—560.
(c) Exod. xii. 5.

doret * hath probably given the juſt ſenſe of this law, " he that has a lamb, let him offer it; but if not, let him offer a kid †." Though our Saviour, therefore, is ſo often called a lamb, in reference to this ancient type of him, yet he is never called a kid.

The paſchal lamb muſt be a male ; which is accounted preferable to a female (a). Therefore, though the peace offerings, which were eaten by the people, might be either male or female (b); yet the burnt offerings, which were wholly offered to God or conſumed upon his altar, and which were therefore the more perfeᴄt ſacrifices, muſt be all males (c).

Perhaps in this circumſtance, as in many others, Jehovah deſigned to oppoſe the rites of the jewiſh worſhip to the cuſtoms of the idolatrous Gentiles, who eſteemed ſacrifices of the female kind to be the moſt valuable, and the moſt acceptable to their gods : " In omnibus ſacris fœminei generis plus valent victimæ," ſays Servius in his notes on Virgil ‡. We are informed, indeed, by Herodotus, that it was the cuſtom of the Egyptians to offer only males §, which Bochart ſuppoſes they borrowed from the Jews ‖.

Again,

---

* Theodorit. Quæſtion. in Exod. Quæſt. xxiv. oper. tom. 1. p. 90. B. edit. Paris. 1642.
† Vid. Miſhn. tit. Cherithoth, cap. vi. §. 9. cum. not. Bartenor. tom. 5. p. 265.
(a) Mal. i. 14.   (b) Levit. iii. 6.   (c) Levit. i. 3, 10.
‡ Serv. in Æneid. viii. v. 641. Other proofs may be ſeen in Bochart. Hieroz. part. i. lib. ii. cap. xxxiii. oper. tom. 2. p. 322.
§ Herodot. Euterp. cap. 41. p. 104. edit. Gronov.
‖ Ubi ſupra, p. 321. et cap. l. p. 584.

Again, the paſchal lamb muſt ·be בֶּן־שָׁנָה ben-ſhanah, " the ſon of a year;" by which ſome underſtand a lamb of the laſt year, which, conſidering the uſual yeaning time, muſt be upward of a year old at the ſeaſon of the paſſover. But as a lamb, grown to that degree of maturity, was rather too large to be conveniently roaſted whole, and eaten up at one family meal, as the paſchal lamb was to be; the opinion of the jewiſh doctors is, in this inſtance, more probable, that it was to be a lamb of the preſent year, or of the laſt yeaning time *, which ordinarily preceded the paſſover by a month or two. This well agrees with the uſe of the hebrew phraſe, " The ſon of ſo many years;" which ordinarily ſignifies the year current; as appears from the ſeventh chapter of Geneſis, wherein it is ſaid, " that Noah was ſix hundred years old " בֶּן־שֵׁשׁ מֵאוֹת ben ſheſh meoth, the ſon of ſix hundred years, when the flood of waters was upon the earth (a); and preſently afterwards, this is ſaid to be in the " ſix hundredth year of Noah's life (b)." Thus the prieſts and levites were to enter on their miniſtry " at thirty years old (c);" but that is properly to be underſtood of the year current, or when they had entered on the thirtieth year. So Chriſt entered on his publick miniſtry, ωσει ετων τριακοντα αρχομενος, when he began to be about thirty years of age (d).

The age then of the paſchal lamb is thus determined by the rabbies; it muſt not be leſs than eight days, and yet under a year old: not

leſs

* Vid. Cartwright. Electa targumico-rabbin. in Exod. xii. 5.

(a) Gen. vii. 6.   (b) ver. 11.   (c) Numb. iv. 3.   (d) Luke iii. 23.

leſs than eight days, for ſo is the law concerning firſtlings and burnt-offerings, that they were
to be ſeven days with the dam, and from the
eighth they might be accepted in ſacrifices (*a*).
Which law the jewiſh doctors extend, and perhaps not without reaſon, to the paſchal ſacrifice ; and Maimonides ſays, " if the lamb was
older than the year only an hour, it was not
permitted as an oblation *.

Once more, As to the qualities of the paſchal lamb, " it muſt be without blemiſh."
The rabbies reckon up fifty blemiſhes, which
diſqualified beaſts for ſacrifices ; as five in the
ear, three in the eyelid, eight in the eye, &c †.
but what thoſe blemiſhes were, which diſquali-
fy according to the law of God, ſufficiently
appears in the twenty ſecond chapter of Leviticus : the beaſts that were blind, or broken, or
maimed, or that had a wen, or the ſcurvy or
ſcab, or any part ſuperfluous or defective, or
that was bruiſed, or cruſhed, or broken, or cut ;
theſe were not to be offered in ſacrifice (*b*).

We muſt not paſs over a conjecture of ſome
perſons concerning the reaſon of God's commanding the Iſraelites to eat a male lamb, or
young ram with ſo much ſolemnity about the
vernal equinox ; namely, that it was in oppoſition to the idolatry of the Egyptians, who at
this ſeaſon, of the ſun's entering into the ſign
Aries, paid ſome ſolemn worſhip to the creature by whoſe name that ſign was diſtinguiſhed.
           The

(*a*) Exod. xxii. 30.   Lev. xxii. 27.

 * Maimon. de ratione ſacrificiorum faciendorum, cap.
1. §. 12, 13. apud Crenii Faſcicul. Sext. p. 288.

 † Maimon. de ratione adeundi templi, cap. vii. apud
Crenii Faſcic. Sext. p. 208, et ſeq.

 (*b*) Lev. xxii. 20,—24.

The author of the Chronicon Orientale, as quoted by Patrick *, faith, that the day on which the ſun entered Aries was moſt ſolemn among the Egyptians; and R. Abraham Seba obſerves, that this feaſt of the Egyptians being at its heighth on the fourteenth day, God ordered the killing and eating of a lamb at that time † ; in contempt, it ſhould ſeem, of their worſhip of Aries, and as a ſenſible evidence, that he could be no God whom the Iſraelites eat ‡. Rabbi Levi Ben Gerſhom faith, God intended by this to expel from the minds of the Iſraelites the bad opinions of the Egyptians. This, however, Dr. Patrick looks upon to be mere conjecture §. The

2d. Thing we obſerve in the paſchal rites is the taking the lamb from the flock four days before it was killed (a). For which the rabbies aſſign the following reaſons :—that the providing it might not, through a hurry of buſineſs, eſpecially at the time of their departure from Egypt, be neglected till it was too late : —that by having it ſo long with them before it was killed, they might have the better opportunity of obſerving, whether there were any blemiſhes in it :—and by having it before their eyes ſo conſiderable a time, might be more effectually reminded of the mercy of their deliverance

---

* Patrick on Exod. xii. 3.

† Tzeror. Hammor. fol. 70. col. 4. See the paſſage in Spencer de Legibus Hebræor. lib. ii. cap. iv. Sect. 1. vol. 1. p. 296. edit. Cantab. 1727.

‡ Cæſo ariete, ſays Tacitus, velut in contumeliam Hammonis. Hiſtor. lib. v. cap. iv. p. 200. edit. Glaſg. 1743. See alſo Targum Jonathan on Exod. viii. 22. in Walton's Polyglot, tom. 4.

§ Patrick, ubi ſupra.

(a) Exod. xii. 3.

liverance out of Egypt:—and likewise to prepare themselves for so great a solemnity as the
approaching feast. On these accounts, some of
the rabbies inform us, it was customary to have
the lamb tied these four days to their bed-posts;
a rite which they make to be necessary and es-
sential to the passover in all ages *.

Others conceive, with an equal degree of
probability, that this was one of those circumstances of the first passover, which were not
designed to be continued and practised afterwards; of which sort we shall observe several
others. It was highly proper the providing the
lamb before their departure out of Egypt should
not be left to the very day of their departure,
when they must unavoidably be in some hurry
and confusion : a reason, however, which would
not take place in after-times. Besides, those who
came annually out of all parts of the country
to keep the passover at Jerusalem, could not
well observe it, unless they came at least four
days beforehand. It is indeed related in the
eleventh chapter of St. John (a), " that many
went out of the country to Jerusalem before the
passover;" but the reason assigned is, that it
was " to purify themselves." Nothing is said
of their providing lambs beforehand. It moreover appears, that on the former part of that
very day on which the passover was to be killed
and eaten, Christ and his disciples had not so
much as provided a place where they should eat
it : for " The disciples said unto him, Where
wilt

---

* Targum Jonathan et R. Solomon in loc. Vid. Cartwright. Electa Targumico-rabbin. in Exod. xii. 3.
(a) John xi. 55.

wilt thou, that we go and prepare, that thou mayeſt eat the paſſover (a)" Whereas, if they had provided the lamb four days before, they would in all probability have kept it at the houſe where they intended to eat it; and there would have been then no room for this queſtion. It is more likely they went and bought one in the market, kept on the preparation of the paſſover for that purpoſe, as well as to furniſh the other ſacrifices that were to be offered on the enſuing feſtival: which market ſome had profanely brought into the very court of the temple (b). Again, if the lamb, the principal thing, had been provided, it is not ſo probable, the diſciples ſhould have ſuppoſed, as we know they did, that Chriſt by his ſpeech to Judas, " What thou doeſt, do quickly," meant, that he ſhould " buy thoſe things which they had need of againſt the feaſt (c)."

3dly, Next followed the killing of the paſchal lamb; which at the firſt paſſover in Egypt, as there was no national altar, was performed in private houſes. But after their ſettlement in Canaan, it was ordered to be done in " the place, which the Lord ſhould chuſe to place his name there (d)." By the name of God in this paſſage is denoted God himſelf: to " call upon his name" is to call upon him. And by placing his name there, is meant fixing in that place the ſpecial tokens of his preſence, as the ark with the mercy ſeat, and the cloud of glory over it. This place ſeems at firſt to have been Miſpah, afterwards Shiloh; and when that was deſtroyed, the ark was removed to

several

(a) Mark xiv. 12.　　(b) John ii. 13, 14.　　(c) John xiij. 27, 29.　　(d) Deut. xvi. 2.

feveral places, till at laft it was fixed at Jerufalem.

It is obfervable, that though there is frequent
mention in the law of Mofes of fome place
which God would chufe to fix his name there,
it is no where declared where that place fhould
be: For this Maimonides * affigns feveral reafons; the beft and moft probable is, leaft every
tribe fhould defire to have that place to their
lot, and thus ftrife and contention fhould arife
among them. But when the place was afterwards fixed by a new revelation, there the national altar was to be erected, and thither all
their facrifices were ordinarily to be brought
and offered. The law to which we before referred, concerning their " facrificing the paffover unto the Lord their God, of the flock
and of the herd, in the place which the Lord
fhould choofe to place his name there (a),"
chiefly refpects the facrifices that were to be
offered on the feven days of the feaft of unleavened bread, which feaft, we have obferved
before, was fometimes called the paffover; as
appears, in that the facrifice of the paffover is
faid to be of the flock and of the herd; whereas the paffover, properly fo called, was of the
flock only. This law, neverthelefs, included
the pafchal lamb, and was fo underftood by
the ancient Jews, as is evident from the account
of the folemn paffover kept in the reign of king
Jofiah (b); when " the priefts and the levites
ftood in the holy place, and they flew the paffover, and the priefts fprinkled the blood, and
the

---

* Maimon. Moreh Nebhoc. part. iii. cap. xlv. p. 475.
edit. et verf. Buxtorf. Bafil. 1629.
(a) Deut. xvi. 2.   (b) 2 Chron. xxxv. 5, 6, 10, 11.

the levites flayed it." They, who killed the
paſſover, are diſtinguiſhed from the prieſts who
ſprinkled the blood ; for a common Iſraelite
might kill the paſchal lamb according to the law
in Exodus *(a)*, " the whole aſſembly of the congregation of Iſrael ſhall kill it." Accordingly
in the paſſover, which was kept in Hezekiah's
reign, the ſervice of killing the paſſover fell
upon the levites, only for thoſe of the congregation that were not clean *(b)* ; otherwiſe, every
Iſraelite was to kill his own paſchal lamb. Nor
was this a circumſtance peculiar to the paſs-
over ; in all other ſacrifices, even in burnt-offerings, which were reckoned the moſt ſolemn
and ſacred of all others, every man might kill
his own ſacrifice. The proper duty of the
prieſts was only to ſprinkle the blood, and offer it on the altar after it was ſlain *(c)*. The
argument, therefore, as formerly hinted, which
ſome have alledged againſt the prieſthood of
Chriſt, and the ſacrifice of his death, that then,
as prieſt, he muſt have killed himſelf, is futile
and groundleſs, becauſe it did not properly belong to the prieſts to kill the ſacrifices. We
proceed to the

4th Article of the paſchal rites, the ſprinkling of the blood ; in order to which it muſt
be received in a baſon : " Ye ſhall take a bunch
of hyſſop and dip it in the baſon," בסף be-
ſaph *(d)*. Both the ſeptuagint and the vulgate
ſeem to have miſtaken the meaning of this word,
taking it to ſignify the door, or the threſhold
of the houſe, where ſome ſuppoſe the lamb was
killed. The ſeptuagint renders it παρα την θυραν,
the

(a) Exod. xii. 6.   (b) 2 Chron. xxx. 17.
(c) Lev. i. 2,—5.   (d) Exod. xii. 22.

the vulgate, in limine ; whereas סִפִּים ſippim
and סִפּוֹת ſippoth, which are plurals of סַף ſaph,
are mentioned among the veſſels of the ſanctuary in the firſt book of Kings and in Jeremiah (a). This blood was to be ſprinkled with
a bunch of hyſſop upon the lintel, and the two
ſide poſts of the doors of their houſes, as a
ſignal to the deſtroying angel to paſs over thoſe
that were thus marked when he went forth to
ſmite the firſt-born in all the other houſes in
Egypt (b). The blood was to be ſprinkled only on the lintel and the ſide poſts, nor on the
threſhold, that it might not be trod on, but
that a proper reverence might be preſerv'd for
it as ſacred and typical. It cannot be ſuppoſed,
either that this blood had any natural virtue in
it, to preſerve the family upon whoſe houſe it
was ſprinkled from the plague, or that God or
his angel needed ſuch a ſignal to diſtinguiſh betwixt Egyptians and Iſraelites. The uſe of it
could only be as a ſenſible token of the divine
promiſe of protection and ſafety to the Iſraelites,
deſigned to aſſiſt and encourage their faith.
With the like view God made the rainbow a token or ſign of his covenant and promiſe to
Noah, that he would never again bring a deluge on the earth (c). No doubt the blood of
the paſchal lamb, ſprinkled on their houſes,
was intended, likewiſe, to be a typical ſign of
protection from the vengeance of God through
the blood of Chriſt, which is therefore called
" the blood of ſprinkling (d)." In both re-
ſpects it is ſaid that Moſes " through faith kept
the

(a) 1 Kings vii. 50.   Jerem. lii. 19.

(b) Exod. xii. 13,—23.

(c) Gen. ix. 10,—15.

(d) Heb. xii. 24.

the paſſover and the ſprinkling of blood (a) ;" through faith in God's promiſe of a preſent temporal protection, and through faith in the blood of Chriſt, as typified by this blood, for ſpiritual and eternal Salvation.

The Egyptians, who were, in many caſes, unacquainted with the original of their own rites, had among them, many ages afterwards, according to Epiphanius, a very ſenſible memorial of the preſervation of the Iſraelites, by this red mark being fixed on their houſes ; for at the vernal equinox, which was the time of the paſſover, they uſed to mark their ſheep, their trees and the like εκ μιλτιως, with red oker, or ſomewhat of that kind, which they ſuppoſed would preſerve them *.

The circumſtance of ſprinkling blood upon the door poſts was plainly peculiar to the firſt paſſover ; for we find in after ages, when the paſchal lamb was killed in the court of the tabernacle or temple, the blood of it was ſprinkled on the altar like the blood of the other ſacrifices (b).

5thly, The paſchal lamb was to be roaſted whole : " Eat it not raw, nor ſodden at all with water, but roaſt with fire his head, with his legs, and with the purtenance thereof (c)." The prohibition of eating it raw ; for which there might ſeem to be little occaſion ſince mankind have generally abhorred ſuch food, is underſtood by ſome to have been given in oppoſition to the barbarous cuſtoms of the Heathens, who in their feaſts of Bacchus, which, according to Herodotus † and Plutarch ‡, had their

(a) Heb. xi. 28. * Epiphan. adverſus Hæres. hæres. xviii. Nazaræor §. iii. p. 39. edit. Petav.
(b) 2 Chron. xxxv. 11. (c) Exod. xii. 9.
† Herodot. Enterp. cap. 49. p. 107, 108. edit. Gronov.
‡ Plutarch. de Iſide et Oſiride, oper. tom. 2. p. 355, 356, 362. B, &c. edit. Francfort. 1620.

original in Egypt, used to tear the members of living creatures to pieces, and eat them raw. It is therefore observable, that the syriac version renders the clause " Eat not of it raw, eat not of it while it is alive *."

Bochart, after R. Solomon and Aben-Ezra, derives the hebrew word נא na, which we render raw, from the Arabic נא naa or ני ni, semicoctus, half dressed †.

The paschal lamb was to be roasted; which, besides its typical meaning, to be hereafter considered, might be ordered as a matter of convenience at the first passover, in order that their boiling vessels might be packed up, ready for their march out of Egypt, while the lamb was roasting.

It must be " roasted whole, with its legs and appurtenances." By the appurtenances we are not to understand the guts, but the heart, lights, liver, and whatever other parts of the inwards are fit for food. This injunction might perhaps be designedly opposed to the superstition of the Gentiles, who used to rake into the entrails of their sacrifices, and collect auguries from them; and it might be partly intended for expedition in the celebration of the first passover.

6thly, The first passover was to be eaten standing, in the posture of travellers, who had no time to lose; and with unleavened bread and bitter herbs, and no bone of it was to be broken (a). The posture of travellers was enjoined them, both to enliven their faith in the promise of their now speedy deliverance from Egypt;

---

* Spencer. de Leg. Hebr. lib. ii. cap. iv. Sect. ii. p. 300,—305.

† Hierozoic. lib. ii. cap. ʟ. oper. tom. 2. p. 595.

(a) Exod. xii. 8, 11, 46.

Egypt; and alſo, that they might be ready to begin their march preſently after ſupper. They were ordered, therefore, to eat it with their loins girded; for as they were accuſtomed to wear long and looſe garments, ſuch as are generally uſed by the eaſtern nations to this day, it was neceſſary to tye them up with a girdle about their loins, when they either travelled or betook themſelves to any laborious employment. Thus, when Eliſha ſent his ſervant Gehazi on a meſſage in haſte, he bad him " gird up his loins (a);" and when our Saviour ſet about waſhing his diſciples feet, " he took a towel and girded himſelf (b)."

They were to eat the paſſover " with ſhoes on their feet." For in thoſe hot countries they ordinarily wore ſandals, which were a ſort of clogs; or went barefoot. But in travelling they uſed ſhoes, which were indeed a ſort of ſhort boots, reaching a little way up the legs *. Hence, when our Saviour ſent his twelve diſciples to preach in the neighbouring towns, deſigning to convince them by their own experience of the extraordinary care of divine providence over them, that they might not be diſcouraged by the length and danger of the journies they would be called to undertake; I ſay, on this account he ordered them to make no proviſion for their preſent journey, particularly,

O 2 not

(a) 2 Kings iv 29.   (b) John xiii. 4.
* See Wagenſeil. Sotah, p. 664. edit. Altdorf. 1674. or in Miſhn. Surenhuſii, tom. 3. p. 261. Lightfoot's Horæ hebr. Matt. x. 10. Sagittarius de Nudipedalibus veterum, cap. i. §. xix. et ſeq. apud Syntagma Diſſertationum. tom. i. p. 272. et ſeq. Rotterod 1699. But Bynæus is of opinion, that ſhoes and ſandals are the ſame, de Calceis Hebræorum, lib. i. cap. vi. §. ix. x. p. 90,—98. Dordrac. 1715.

not to take fhoes on their feet, but to be fhod
with fandals (a).

The ethiopian chriftians have indeed found
out another reafon for the Ifraelites being commanded to eat the firft paffover with fhoes on
their feet ; namely, becaufe the land of Egypt
was polluted ; whereas at mount Sinai God
commanded Mofes to put off his fhoes from his
feet, becaufe the place was holy ; and for this
reafon the Ethiopians fay, it is a cuftom with
them to be barefoot in their churches *.

Again, they were to eat the paffover with
ftaves in their hands, fuch as were always ufed
by travellers in thofe rocky countries, both to
fupport them in flippery places, and defend
them againft affaults (b).   Of this fort was
probably Mofes's rod which he had in his
hand, when God fent him with a meffage to
Pharaoh (c), and which was afterwards ufed as
an inftrument in working fo many miracles.
So neceffary in thefe countries was a ftaff, or
walking ftick on a journey, that it was a ufual
thing for perfons when they undertook long
journeys, to take a fpare ftaff with them, for
fear one fhould fail.   When Chrift, therefore,
fent his apoftles on that embaffy, which we
mentioned before, he ordered them not to take
ftaves, μητε ραϐδας (d), that is, only one ftaff or
walking ftick, without making provifion of a
fpare one, as was common in long journeys ;
or as it is in St. Mark (e), " fave a ftaff only."
If therefore we adhere to the common reading
in

(a) Matt. x. 10. compared with Mark vi. 9.
* Damianus Goenfis de moribus Æthiopum, cited by
Sagittarius de Nudipedalibus veterum, cap. ii. §. xv. ubi
fupra, p. 305, 306. Rotterod. 1699.   (b) See Gen.
xxxii. 10.   (c) Exod. iv. 2.   (d) Luke ix. 3.
(e) Mark vi. 8.

in the parallel paffage in St. Matthew, where
Chrift bad them take μητε ραϐδον, not a ftaff (a),
it muft be underftood of a fpare ftaff. Neverthelefs many copies have ραϐδυς in this place,
which is followed in our tranflation.

Now thefe circumftances were plainly peculiar to the firft paffover ; for when the children
of Ifrael were fettled in the land of Canaan,
they no longer eat the pafchal lamb in the pofture of travellers, but like men at reft and
eafe, fitting or rather lying on couches; the
pofture in which our Saviour and his difciples
eat the paffover (b).

The pafchal lamb was to be eaten with unleavened bread ; in the Hebrew מצות matfoth,
which fome derive from מצץ matfets, or מצה
matfah, compreffit, becaufe bread made without yeaft or leaven is heavy and clofe, as if
preffed together. Bochart rejects this derivation,
and derives it from an arabic word, with the
fame radicals, which fignifies pure and fincere*,
and fo מצות matfoth, fignifies bread made of
pure flour and water, without any mixture. This
fuits beft with the apoftle's allufion : " Therefore let us keep the feaft, not with old leaven,
neither with the leaven of malice and wicked-
nefs ; but with the unleavened bread of finceri-
ty and truth (c)."

The reafon of the injunction to eat the pafchal lamb with unleavened bread was, partly,
to remind them of the hardfhips they had fuf-
tained in Egypt, unleavened being more heavy
and lefs palatable, than leavened bread ; and it
is, therefore, called the bread of affliction (d) ;

O 3　　　　　　　and

(a) Matt. x. 10.　　(b) John xiii. 23.
* Bochart. Hieroz. lib. ii. cap. L. p. 601.
(c) 1 Cor. v. 8.　　(d) Deut. xvi. 3.

and partly to commemorate the fpeed of their deliverance or departure from thence, which was fuch, that they had not fufficient time to leaven their bread; it is exprefsly faid, that their "dough was not leavened, becaufe they were thruft out of Egypt and could not tarry (*a*);" and on this account, it was enacted into a ftanding law, "Thou fhalt eat unleavened bread, even the bread of affliction; for thou cameft forth out of Egypt in hafte (*b*)." This rite, therefore, was not only obferved at the firft paffover, but in all fucceeding ages.

The fallad, or fauce, of bitter herbs was doubtlefs prefcribed for the fame reafon, namely to be a memorial of that fevere bondage in Egypt, which "made their lives bitter to them (*c*);" and poffibly alfo, to denote the hafte they were in, which laid them under a neceffity of taking up with fuch wild herbs as were readieft at hand. We have not any account, what herbs in particular thefe were, except from the conjectures of the rabbies, which are not worth our attention *.

To this fallad, or fauce, the latter Jews, as Godwin obferves, add another, of fweet and bitter things, as dates, figs, raifons, vinegar, and other ingredients, pounded and mixed up together to the confiftence of muftard, which they call חרוסת charofeth, and make to be a memorial of the clay in which their fathers laboured

(*a*) Exod. xii. 39.
(*b*) Deut. xvi. 3.
(*c*) Exod. i. 14.

* Mifhn. tit. Pefachim, cap. 2. §. 6. tom. 2. p. 141. edit. Surenhus. Their opinion is difcuffed at large, by Bochart, Hierozoic. lib. ii. cap. L. oper. tom 2. p. 603, —609.

boured in the land of Egypt *. Some imagine, this was the ſauce in which our Saviour dipt the ſop that he gave to Judas (a).

It was further preſcribed, that they ſhould eat the fleſh of the lamb, without breaking any of his bones (b). This the later Jews un-derſtand, not of the leſſer bones, but only of the greater, which had marrow in them †. Thus was this rite alſo intended to denote their being in haſte, not having time to break the bones and ſuck out the marrow ‡. But it had likewiſe a typical meaning, of which we ſhall have occaſion to take notice hereafter.

7thly, It was ordered, that nothing of the paſchal lamb ſhould remain till the morning; but, if it was not all eaten, it ſhould be con-ſumed by fire (c). The ſame law was extended to all euchariſtical ſacrifices (d); no part of which was to be left or ſet by, leſt it ſhould be corrupted, or converted to any profane or com-mon uſe. An injunction, which was deſigned, no doubt, to maintain the honour of ſacrifices, and teach the Jews to treat with reverence what-ever was conſecrated, more eſpecially, to the ſervice of God.

As to the firſt paſchal ſacrifice, it was the more neceſſary that it ſhould all be eaten or conſumed that night, as the Iſraelites were to march out of Egypt early the next morning. Otherwiſe they would have been obliged either

O 4   to

---

* Maimon. de Solemnitate Paſchatis, cap. vii. §. xi. p. 889. Crenii Faſciculi ſeptimi.

(a) John xiii. 26.   (b) Exod. xii. 46.

† Vid. Bochart. Hierozoic. lib. ii. cap. L. oper. tom. 2. p. 609.

‡ Maimon. Moreh Nebhoch. part iii. cap. xlvi. p. 483. Baſil. 1629.

(c) Exod. xii. 10.   (d) Levit. xxii. 30.

to ſubmit to the inconvenience of carrying the
remainder of it along with them, or to the diſ-
agreeable circumſtance of leaving it behind,
them, to the contempt of the Egyptians. Moreover, this law with reſpect to ſacrifices might
be made ſo comprehenſive and general, on the
ſame account that induced Hezekiah to break
in pieces the brazen ſerpent (a); that is, to prevent the abuſe of ſuch relicks to ſuperſtitious
uſes, and to diſcountenance the cuſtom of the
heathen idolaters, who reſerved ſome part of
their ſacrifices for any purpoſes they thought
proper; as Herodotus * informs us concerning
the antient Perſians, and as ſeems to be intimated in the ſixth chapter of the apochryphal
book of Baruch, where the prieſts are ſaid " to
ſell and abuſe the things that were ſacrificed to
idols; and in like manner their wives laid up
part thereof in ſalt (b)." From whence we may
naturally derive the like ſuperſtitious cuſtom of
ſome women among Chriſtians, who procure
and lay up ſome part of the bread, which has
been uſed in the Lord's ſupper, to cure their
children of the whooping cough.

8thly, It was enjoined the Iſraelites at the
firſt paſſover, that they ſhould keep in their
own houſes all that night, " and none of them
ſhould go out of the door of his houſe till the
morning," leſt they ſhould be expoſed to the
deſtroying angel (c). We are not to ſuppoſe,
the angel could not have diſtinguiſhed an
Iſraelite from an Egyptian, if he had met him
in the ſtreet; but, they were hereby intended
to

(a) 2 Kings xviii. 4.
* Herodot. Clio, cap. 132. p. 55. edit. Gronov.
(b) Baruch vi. 28.   (c) Exod. xii. 22, 23.

to be inſtructed, that their ſafety lay in being
under the protection of the blood of the lamb,
which was ſprinkled upon the door-poſts of
their houſes, as an emblem and type of ſpiritual ſalvation by the blood of Chriſt. This
rite, however, was peculiar to the firſt paſſover,
and not obſerved in ſucceeding ages ; otherwiſe, Chriſt and his apoſtles would not have
gone to the mount of Olives the ſame evening on which they had been eating the paſs-
over (a).

Having thus conſidered the rites of the paſs-
over, we are

3dly, to enquire into the ſignification of them.

That the paſſover had a typical reference to
Chriſt, we learn from the apoſtle's calling him
" our paſſover (b) :" Godwin has drawn out a
catalogue of thirteen articles in which this type
reſembles its antitype, and a larger and more
particular one may be found in the chapter, de
Paſchate, of Witſius's Œconomia Fœderis, under four general heads : The firſt reſpecting the
perſon of Chriſt :—the ſecond, his ſufferings :
the third, the fruits and effects of them :—
and the way in which we are to obtain an intereſt in theſe fruits and effects. We ſhall
briefly ſelect a few of the particulars under each
of theſe heads.

1ſt, The perſon of Chriſt was typified by
the paſchal lamb. On which account, as well
as in reſpect to the lamb of the daily ſacrifice,
he is often repreſented under the emblem of a
lamb. " Behold the lamb of God," ſaith John
the baptiſt (c). The fitneſs and propriety of
this

(a) Matt. xxvi. 30.   (b) 1 Cor. v. 7.
(c) John i. 29, 36.

this type or emblem conſiſts, partly, in ſome natural properties belonging to a lamb; and, partly, in ſome circumſtances peculiar to the paſchal lamb. A lamb being, perhaps, the leaſt ſubject to choler of any animal in the brute creation, was a very proper emblem of our Saviour's humility and meekneſs; and of his inoffenſive behaviour (a); for he, by whoſe precious blood we were redeemed, was "a lamb without blemiſh and without ſpot (b):" and likewiſe of his exemplary patience and ſubmiſſion to his father's will under all his ſufferings and in the agony of death; for though he was "oppreſſed, and afflicted, yet he opened not his mouth (c)." By his almighty power he could have delivered himſelf, out of the hands of his enemies, as he had done on former occaſions (d); but behold, the lion of the tribe of Judah now transformed into a lamb, by his obedience to his father's will, and compaſſion to the ſouls of men.

There were, alſo, ſome circumſtances peculiar to the paſchal lamb, which contributed to its fitneſs and propriety as a type and emblem of Chriſt. Such as its being ordered to be free from all blemiſh and natural defect, that it might the better repreſent the immaculate ſon of God, who was made without ſin, and never did any iniquity (e); that it was to be taken out of the flock, therein repreſenting that divine perſon, who, in order to his being made a ſacrifice for our ſins, did firſt become

---

(a) Matt. xi. 29.
(b) 1 Pet. i. 19.
(c) Iſaiah liii. 7.
(d) Luke iv. 29, 30. John viii. 59.
(e) Heb. vii. 26.

come one of us by taking our fleſh and blood, and "was made in all things like to his bre-thren (a.'

The paſchal lamb was to be a male of the firſt year, when the fleſh was in the higheſt ſtate of perfection for food; more fitly to repreſent the "child that was to be born," "the ſon that was to be given (b)," to us, and the excellency of the ſacrifice he was to offer for us, after he had lived a ſhort life among men. Once more,

The paſchal lamb was to be taken out of the flock four days before it was ſacrificed. This circumſtance, if we underſtand it of ſuch pro-phetic days as are mentioned in the fourth chap-ter of Ezekiel, is perfectly applicable to Chriſt, who left his mother's houſe and family, and en-gaged publickly in his office as a Saviour, four years before his death.

2dly, The ſufferings and death of Chriſt were alſo typified by the paſchal lamb in vari-ous particulars. For inſtance, that lamb was to be killed "by the whole aſſembly of the congregation of Iſrael (c);" and ſo the whole eſtate of the Jews, the prieſts, ſcribes, elders, rulers, and the populace in general (d), con-ſpired in the death of Chriſt. The paſchal lamb was to be killed by the effuſion of its blood, as pointing out the manner of Chriſt's death; in which there was an effuſion of blood on the croſs. It was to be roaſted with fire, as repreſenting its antitype enduring on our ac-count the fierceneſs of God's anger, which is ſaid to "burn like fire (e)." Hence that com-plaint of our ſuffering Saviour in the prophecy concern-

(a) Heb. ii. 14, 17.   (b) Iſai. ix. 6.
(c) Exod. xii. 6.   (d) Compare Mark xiv. 43. with
Luke xxiii. 13.   (e) Pſal. lxxxix. 46. Jerem. iv. 4.

concerning him in the twenty-ſecond Pſalm, " My heart is like wax, it is melted in the midſt of my bowels; my ſtrength is dried up like a potſherd, and my tongue cleaveth to my jaws (*a*)."

There was, further, a remarkable correſpondence betwixt the type and the antitype, with reſpect to the place and time in which each was killed as a ſacrifice. The place was the ſame as to both; namely, " the place which the Lord ſhould chuſe to put his name there," which from the reign of David was at Jeruſalem: and the time was alſo the ſame; for Chriſt ſuffered his agonies on the ſame evening on which the paſſover was celebrated; and his death the next day, betwixt the two evenings, according to the moſt probable interpretation of that phraſe, namely, betwixt noon and ſun ſet.

3dly, Several of the happy fruits and conſequences of the death of Chriſt were remarkably typified by the ſacrifice of the paſchal lamb; ſuch as protection and ſalvation by his blood, of which the ſprinkling of the door poſts with the blood of the lamb, and the ſafety which the Iſraelites by that means enjoyed, from the plague that ſpread through all the families of the Egyptians, was a deſigned and illuſtrous emblem. It is in alluſion to this type, that the blood of Chriſt is called " the blood of ſprinkling (*b*)."

Immediately upon the Iſraelites eating the firſt paſſover, they were delivered from their egyptian ſlavery, and reſtored to full liberty, of which they had been deprived for many years;

_____

(*a*) Pſal. xxii. 14, 15.　(*b*) 1 Pet. i. 2. Heb. xii. 24.

years; and ſuch is the fruit of the death of Chriſt, in a ſpiritual and much nobler ſenſe, to all that believe in him; for he hath thereby " obtained eternal redemption for us," and " brought us into the glorious liberty of the children of God (a)."

4thly, The ways and means, by which we are to obtain an intereſt in the bleſſed fruits of the ſacrifice of Chriſt, were alſo repreſented by lively emblems in the paſſover, namely, by the ſprinkling of the blood of the lamb on the door poſts, and by eating the fleſh of it. The door poſt may be underſtood to ſignify the heart of man, which is the gate, or door, by which the king of glory is to enter (b); and which is as manifeſt in the ſight of God, as the very doors of our houſes are to any one that paſſes by them (c). The ſprinkling of the blood on the door poſts may therefore ſignify the purify-ing of the heart by the grace of Chriſt, which he purchaſed for us by his blood. This ſeems to be the apoſtle's alluſion in the following ex-preſſion, " Having your hearts ſprinkled from an evil conſcience (d)."

By eating the fleſh of the lamb we have no difficulty to underſtand faith in Jeſus Chriſt, ſince Chriſt himſelf has expreſſed ſaving faith in him by the metaphor of eating his fleſh, pro-bably in reference to the paſſover (e).

It is worthy of our notice, that the lamb was to be roaſted whole, and was to be all eaten, and none of it left: which may fitly ſignify, that, in order to our obtaining the be-nefits of Chriſt's ſacrifice, we muſt receive him,

---

(a) Heb ix. 12.   Rom. viii. 21.   (b) Pſal. xxiv. 7.
(c) 1 Sam. xvi. 7.   (d) Heb. x. 22.   (e) John vi. 53.

him, submit to him, and trust upon him in all
his characters and offices, as our prophet, our
priest and our king; nor are we to expect, that
he will redeem and save us from the wrath to
come, if we will not at present have him to
reign over us.

The passover was to be eaten with bitter
herbs; which, besides its being an intended
memorial of the afflictions of the Israelites in
Egypt, may fitly signify, that repentance for
sin must accompany faith in Christ; and also,
that, if we are partakers of the benefits of
Christ's sufferings, we must expect, and be
content, to be in some measure partakers likewise of his sufferings. To this purpose the
apostle speaks of " the fellowship of his sufferings (a);" and elsewhere saith, " that if we suffer with him, we shall also reign with him (b)."

The passover was also to be eaten with unleavened bread; which St. Paul interprets to
signify sincerity and purity of heart, in opposition to malice, wickedness and falshood; and
which must necessarily accompany faith in Christ
in order to his being our passover, that is, our
protector from the wrath of God, and our redeemer from spiritual bondage and misery (c).

It was further ordered, that in eating the
paschal lamb they should " not break a bone
of it;" a circumstance in which there was a
remarkable correspondence betwixt the type and
the antitype (d).

Perhaps there is more fancy, than judgment,
in that mystical interpretation, which some have
put on this circumstance; who by the bones
understand

(a) Phil. iii. 10.   (b) 2 Tim. ii. 12.   (c). 1 Cor.
v. 7, 8.   (d) John xix. 33, 36.

underſtand thoſe ſecrets of God, or thoſe hard and difficult things in the divine counſels, which we are not able to comprehend, and which we ſhould, therefore, be humbly content to be ignorant of without too curiouſly and anxiouſly ſearching into them; according to the advice of Moſes, " Secret things belong to the Lord our God, but thoſe which are revealed, to us and to our children for ever, that we may do all the words of this law (a)."

None, who were legally unclean and polluted, might eat the paſſover; which may further hint to us that purity and holineſs are neceſſary and incumbent on all that would partake of the benefit of Chriſt's ſacrifice; for " what fellowſhip hath righteouſneſs with unrighteouſneſs? what communion hath light with darkneſs? what concord hath Chriſt with belial (b)."

The Iſraelites were to eat their firſt paſſover in the habit and poſture of travellers; which, in the myſtical ſenſe, may ſignify, that ſuch as enter into covenant with God through Chriſt, muſt be reſolved. upon, and ready to go forth to, every duty to which he calls them. They are not to look on this world as their home; but, remembering that they are travelling towards heaven, they are to bear that bleſſed world much upon their thoughts, and to be diligent in preparing for their entrance into it. To this purpoſe are we exhorted " to gird up the loins of our minds and to be ſober;" to " ſtand, having our loins girded about with truth;" and, " as pilgrims and ſtrangers, to abſtain from fleſhly luſts, which war againſt the ſoul (c)."

In

(a) Deut. xxix. 29.   (b) 2 Cor. vi. 14, 15.
(c) 1 Pet. i. 13.   Epheſ. vi. 14.   1 Pet. ii. 11.

In all theſe expreſſions there ſeems to be ſome reference to the habit and poſture of the Iſraelites at the firſt paſſover.

They were to eat the paſſover in haſte; and thus we muſt " flee for refuge to lay hold on the hope ſet before us (*a*);" muſt not delay and trifle, but " give diligence to make our calling and election ſure (*b*);" for the kingdom of heaven is ſaid to " ſuffer violence, and the violent take it by force (*c*).".

In the laſt place, the Iſraelites were to eat the paſſover, each family in their own houſe; and none might go out of the houſe any more that night, leſt the deſtroying angel ſhould meet and kill him. By the houſes may be underſtood the church of Chriſt, in which only we are to expect communion with him and ſalvation by him; and having entered into it, we muſt not go out again, leſt we meet with the doom of apoſtates (*d*), which is dreadful beyond deſcription *.

Of the feaſt of unleavened bread.

Having treated pretty largely of the paſſover, we proceed to the feaſt of unleavened bread, which

---

(*a*) Heb. vi. 18.   (*b*) 2 Pet. i. 10.
(*c*) Matt. xi. 12.   (*d*) See Heb. vi. 4,—6. x. 39.
2 Pet. ii. 20, 21.

* Beſides Witſius, ſee Mather on the types, p. 521,—520. Dublin. 1685

On the ſubject of the paſſover in general, with the reſt of the authors already quoted, ſee Lightfoot, in his temple ſervice, chap. 12, 13, 14. and Spencer de legibus Hebræor. lib. ii. cap. iv. tom. i. p. 293,—310. In Witſii Œconom. fœderis is a good abridgement of what Bochart hath ſaid on the ſubject.

which immediately followed it, and was kept
ſeven days, from the fifteenth of the month
Niſan, to the twenty-firſt, incluſive ; as appears from the two following paſſages : the firſt
from the book of Exodus, "In the firſt month,
on the fourteenth day of the month at even ye
ſhall eat unleavened bread, until the one and
twentieth day of the month at even (*a*):" Again,
from the book of Numbers, "In the fourteenth
day of the firſt month is the paſſover of the
Lord; and in the fifteenth day of this month
is the feaſt ; ſeven days ſhall unleavened bread
be eaten ;: in the firſt day ſhall be an holy convocation (*b*)." When therefore it is ſaid in the
ſixteenth chapter of Deuteronomy, "Six days
ſhalt thou eat unleavened bread, and on the
ſeventh ſhall be a ſolemn aſſembly(*c*)," it cannot
be meant that they were to uſe unleavened
bread ſix days only ; but that having eaten it
ſix days, they ſhould conclude the feſtival on
the ſeventh with a ſolemn aſſembly, continuing
to eat unleavened bread on this day, as they
had done on the ſix preceding. The ſamaritan
text and the ſeptuagint, read likewiſe in the
thirteenth chapter of Exodus, "ſix days ſhalt
thou eat unleavened bread (*d*)," and not ſeven,
as it is in the hebrew copy and the targum.

The very day of the paſſover, viz. the fourteenth of Niſan, is called the firſt day of unleavened bread, both by St. Matthew and St.
Mark (*e*) ; whereas, according to the paſſage
before cited, from the book of Numbers, the
fifteenth day of the month being ſaid to be the
firſt day of the feaſt, that is, of unleavened

(*a*) Exod. xii. 18.   (*b*) Numb. xxviii. 16, 17.
(*c*) Deut. xvi. 8.   (*d*) Exod. xiii. 6.   (*e*) Matt. xxvi.
17.   Mark xiv. 12.

bread, the day of the paſſover was the day before the firſt day of unleavened bread.   Some
therefore ſuppoſe, that πρωτη is put by the evan-
geliſts for προτερα; as it is in the firſt chapter of St. John, where John the baptiſt ſays,
" He that comes after me," πρωτος μϵ ην, that is,
προτερος, " was before me (a)."   Thus πρωτη
ημϵρα των αζυμων, ſhould be rendered not " the
firſt day of the feaſt," but " the day before the
feaſt of unleavened bread*."   I apprehend,
however, there is no need, in order to ſolve the
difficulty, to have recourſe to this more un-
uſual meaning of the word πρωτος : for theſe
two feaſts, the paſſover and that of unleavened
bread, though diſtinct in themſelves, yet followed cloſe upon one another, and being unit-
ed into one continued feſtival for eight days together, hence the name of either of them came
to be uſed for both.   The feaſt of unleavened
bread is called the paſſover by St. Luke (b) ;
and why then may not the feaſt of the paſſover
be called the feaſt of unleavened bread by
St. Matthew and St. Mark, eſpecially ſince
the paſſover alſo was eat with unleavened
bread? and this, notwithſtanding the feaſt of
unleavened bread, properly ſo called, did not
begin till the next day ; at leaſt, not till the
evening of the paſchal day ; for it muſt be remembered, the Jews celebrated their ſabbath,
and all ſacred feſtivals, from evening to evening.   This, indeed, gives us the hint of another ſolution, which is eſpouſed by ſome ;
namely, that the paſchal day is called the firſt
day of unleavened bread, becauſe the feaſt of
unleavened bread began on the evening of that
day

(a) John i. 30.
* Reland. Antiq. part. iv. §. iii. p. 456. edit. 3. 1717.
(b) Luke xxii. 1.

day *. But the former folution is, I think, the more fatisfactory.

During the whole continuance of this fefti-val they might not eat any leavened bread, nor fo much as have it in their houfes (a). Care, therefore, muft be taken, before the feaft be-gan, to "purge out the old leaven;" as the apoftle, in allufion to this rite, expreffes it (b). Concerning this matter the modern Jews are fuperftitioufly exact and fcrupulous. The maf-ter of the family makes a diligent fearch into every hole and crevice throughout the houfe, left any crumb of leavened bread fhould re-main in it; and that not by the light of the fun or moon, but of a candle. And in order that this exactnefs may not appear altogether fuperfluous and ridiculons, care is taken to con-ceal fome fcraps of leavened bread in fome cor-ner or other, the difcovery of which occafions mighty joy. This fearch, neverthelefs, ftrict as it is, does not give him entire fatisfaction. After all he befeeches God, that all the leaven-ed bread which is in the houfe, as well what he has found, as what he has not, may become like the duft of the earth, and be reduced to nothing. And as they are thus fuperftitioufly careful in purging out the old leaven, fo they are no lefs exact and fcrupulous about making their bread for the feaft, left there fhould be any fermentation in it, or any thing like leaven mixed with it. For inftance, the corn of which it is made, muft not be carried to the mill on the horfe's bare back, left the heat of the horfe fhould make it ferment; the fack, in which it is put, muft be carefully examined, left there

P 2 fhould

* Reland. ubi fupra, p. 455, 456.
(a) Exod. xii. 15, 18, 19. (b) 1 Cor. v. 7.

ſhould be any remainder of old meal in it, which might prove like leaven to the new meal; the dough muſt be made in a place not expoſed to the ſun, leſt the heat of the ſun ſhould make it ferment; and it muſt be put into the oven immediately after it is made, leſt it ſhould ferment itſelf *.

From the Jews, probably, the roman catholicks have borrowed many ſuperſtitious niceties about the corn and dough, of which they make their hoſts.

The puniſhment to be inflicted on any, who neglected to cleanſe their houſes from leaven againſt the feaſt, is, in the judgment of the rabbies, ſcourging †. But the penalty for eating leavened bread during this feſtival, is, according to the law of God, to be " cut off from the congregation of Iſrael (a) :" the ſame puniſhment, which is threatned to the neglect of circumciſion (b), and to ſeveral other treſpaſſes, both againſt the moral and ceremonial laws; as to wilful ſinning in contempt of the divine authority (c), to profaning the ſabbath (d), to the eating of fat and blood (e), and to ſeveral other violations of the law. But what this כרת chereth, as the rabbies call it from כרת charath, ſecuit, or cutting off, ſignified is rather differently conjectured by various writers, than certainly determined by any. Some make it to ſignify excommunication; others

thers

---

* See Buxtorf. Synag. judaic. cap. xvii. p. 394,—398. edit. 3. Baſil. 1661. and Maimon. de ſolennitate Paſchatis, cap. ii,—v. p. 843,—877. Crenii Faſcicul. ſeptimi.

† Maimon. de ſolennitate Paſchatis, cap. i. p. 838,— 843. Crenii Faſcicul. ſeptimi.

(a) Exod. xii. 19.   (b) Gen. xvii. 14.
(c) Numb. xv. 30, 31.   (d) Exod. xxxi. 14.
(e) Levit. vii. 25, 27.

thers death, to be inflicted by the magiſtrate; others death by the immediate hand of God. Others ſay it was making a man childleſs, ſo that his family and his name periſhed in Iſrael. Maimonides would have it be the extinction both of the ſoul and body, or periſhing like the brutes; and Abarbanel, the loſs of future happineſs *. But hardly any one of theſe ſenſes will ſuit all the caſes, in which this puniſhment is threatned. It could not mean excommunication from the church of Iſrael, when it is threatned to the neglect of circumciſion, becauſe no perſon was a member of that church till he was circumciſed. Nor could it mean death to be immediately inflicted by the hand of God, ſince the Iſraelites neglected circumciſion with impunity, during their journey in the wilderneſs, for forty years together (a). Nor could it ſignify the ſame puniſhment, when threatned to the neglect of the paſſover; ſince that ordinance was ſhamefully neglected during ſeveral wicked reigns of the jewiſh kings, till Hezekiah, and after him Joſiah, revived it (b). It is moſt probable, that כרת chereth, is a general name for ſeveral ſorts of puniſhment, which were to be determined by the nature of the offence. Sometimes it ſeems to import puniſhment by the judge, and ſometimes, by the more immediate hand of God †.

The firſt and laſt days of the feaſt of unleavened bread, were to be kept as ſabbaths,

P 3

holy,

---

* Abarbanel. Diſſert. de pœnâ Excidii, ad calcem Buxtorf. Diſſert. de Sponſalibus et Divortiis.   Where theſe ſeveral opinions are examined.

(a) Joſh. v. 5.   (b) 2. Chron. xxx. xxxv.

† Mr. Selden hath treated largely on the chereth, de Jure Nat. et Gent. lib. vii. cap. ix. and de Syned. lib. i. cap. vi.

holy, and free from all servile work, except dreffing of victuals, which was unlawful on the weekly fabbath (a); and they were likewife to be folemnized by a holy convocation. But we find no precept concerning the keeping the five intermediate days, befides their abftaining from leavened bread, and offering certain facrifices on each of them (b). However, the rabbies have abundantly fupplied thefe defects by their comments; they allow the time to be fpent in mirth, and all lawful recreation; and fome of them allow works of neceffity to be performed, while others think it unlawful even to take up a ftraw, or to pick their teeth *.

One remarkable offering, that was to be made at this feaft, was the fheaf of the firft fruits of the harveft (c). For though this feaft was kept foon after the vernal equinox, yet in that warm climate the barley, which was ufually fown in November, became ripe at this feafon. But if it happened, that the harveft was not forward enough to be fit to cut at the middle of Nifan, they intercalated a month, which they called Veadar, and the next Nifan, and fo put off the feftival a month longer †.

The day, on which this offering was made, is faid to be " the morrow after the fabbath (d)." By which though fome have underftood the weekly fabbath that fell in the time of this feftival, yet the Jews more generally underftand by
it

(a) Compare Exod. xii. 16. with chap. xxxv. 3.
(b) Numb. xxviii. 17.—25.
* See thefe and various other particulars in Buxtorf's Synag. judaic. cap. xix. p. 430,—433. edit. 3.
(c) Levit. xxiii. 10, 11.
† See Lightfoot, Horæ hebr. Matt. xii. 1.
(d) Levit. xxiii. 11.

it the firſt day of the feaſt ; according to which ſenſe, the ſeptuagint renders it τη επαυριον της πρωτης, "the morrow after the firſt." The targum of Onkelos renders it, "after the feaſt day ; and Joſephus ſays expreſsly, τη δευτερα των αζυμων ημερα, &c. on the ſecond day of unleavened bread, which is the ſixteenth of Niſan, they take of the fruits of the harveſt, which they have not touched before ; and eſteeming it their duty firſt to pay due honour to God, from whom they have received their liberal ſupply, they offer him the firſt fruits of the barley *.

The rabbies inform us, that this ſheaf was gathered and prepared for the offering, with a great deal of ceremony ; which, as we have no account of it in ſcripture, we paſs over in ſilence †.

The moral ſignification of this rite, the offering of the firſt fruits, was undoubtedly, to be an acknowledgment of his goodneſs, "who gives rain, both the former and the latter rain, in its ſeaſon, and reſerves to men the appointed weeks of harveſt (a) ;" and alſo of his right to, and propriety, in thoſe bounties of his providence, in conſequence of which he may beſtow, or take them away, as he pleaſes (b) ; and likewiſe, to teach them to look up to God

P 4   for

---

* Joſeph. Antiq. lib. iii. cap. x. §. 5. p. 177, 178. edit. Haverc. ſee alſo Lightfoot. Horæ hebraic. Act. vii. 1.

† See Ainſworth on Levit. xxiii. 10. Lightfoot's templeſervice, chap. xiv. §. 2. Outram de Sacrificiis, lib. 1. cap. viii. §. 6. p. 87. London 1677. Miſhn. tit. Sotah, cap. vii. §. 3. not. Wagenſeil. tom. 3. p. 259, 260. edit. Surenhus. et tit. Menachoth, cap. 10. cum not. Bartenor. et Maimon. tom. 5.

(a) Jerem. v. 24.   (b) Hoſ. ii. 8, 9.

for his bleſſing to render their earthly enjoy-
ments and poſſeſſions profitable and delight-
ful (*a*).

There might alſo be a typical ſignification of
this rite, as referring to the reſurrection of
Chriſt, whoſe ſacrifice and death had been juſt
before repreſented by that of the paſchal lamb,
and which is compared by our Lord himſelf
to corn falling into the ground and dying, after
which it ſprings up and brings forth fruit (*b*).
Accordingly the apoſtle ſaith, as it (*c*) ſhould
ſeem in reference to this type, " Now is Chriſt
riſen from the dead, and is become the firſt
fruits of them that ſlept *."

(*a*) 1 Tim. iv. 4, 5.   (*b*) John xii. 24.
(*c*) 1 Cor. xv. 20.
    * On the ſheaf of the firſt fruits, ſee alſo Reland. Antiq.
part. iv. cap. iii. §. viii. p. 464,—466. Hottingeri Annot.
in Godwin. lib. iii. cap. v. §. 3. not. 3. Francof. 1716.

On the feaſt of unleavened bread, ſee the authors before referred to, on the paſſover.

CHAP. V.

Of the feaſt of Pentecoſt.

THE Pentecoſt was the ſecond of the three grand feſtivals in the eccleſiaſtical year, at which all the males were to appear before the Lord at the national altar.

It is called by ſeveral names in the old teſtament; as, the feaſt of weeks, the feaſt of harveſt, and the day of the firſt fruits. In the new teſtament it is ſtiled pentecoſt; and the rabbies have other names for it, calling it " the day of giving the law," and עֲצֶרֶת gnatſereth, the word which we render " a ſolemn aſſembly."

ıſt. It is called " the feaſt of weeks (*a*)," becauſe it was celebrated ſeven weeks, or a week of weeks, after the paſſover; or rather, after the firſt day of the feaſt of unleavened bread; for the computation of the ſeven weeks began with the ſecond day of that feaſt, and the next day after the ſeven weeks were compleated, was the feaſt of pentecoſt. Thus it is ſaid in Leviticus, " Ye ſhall account unto you from the mor-

(*a*) Exod. xxxiv. 22.

morrow after the ſabbath, from the day that
ye brought the ſheaf of the wave offering;
ſeven ſabbaths ſhall be compleat; even to the
morrow after the ſeventh ſabbath ſhail ye
number fifty days (*a*)." By the ſeven ſabbaths
here mentioned, we are to underſtand ſeven
weeks; and ſo it is rendered in the targum and
in the ſeptuagint; in which ſenſe we find the
word σαββατον uſed in the new teſtament: the
Phariſee in the parable ſaith, νηςευω δις τε σαβ-
βατε, " I faſt twice a week;" that is, on the
ſecond and fifth days, on which faſting was recommended by the tradition of the elders; and
which were accordingly kept every week, as
faſts, by the devout Jews. And in the firſt
verſe of the twenty eighth chapter of Matthew,
μιαν σαββατων evidently ſignifies the " firſt day
of the week."

The rabbies lay great ſtreſs upon the precept
to count the ſeven ſabbaths, or weeks. And
Maimonides remarks, that it was to the honour
of this feſtival, that they were obliged to count
the days of its approach from the preceding
paſſover, as a man, expecting his beſt and moſt
faithful friend at an appointed time, is accuſtomed to number the days and hours till his arrival *. Accordingly the modern Jews make
an act of devotion of counting the days from
the paſſover to the pentecoſt; beginning the
computation with a ſolemn prayer, or benediction, in this form: " Bleſſed art thou, O Lord
our God, the Lord of the world, who haſt
ſanctified us with thy precepts, and commanded
us to number the days of the harveſt; and this

is

(*a*) Levit. xxiii. 15, 16.
* Maimon. Moreh. Nebhoch, part. iii. cap. xliii. p.
471.

is the firſt day." Thus they go on with their
prayer, or benediction, till the ſeventh day;
then they add, "Now there is one week;" and
ſo they proceed with the ſame act of devotion
every day to the evening of the pentecoſt *.

This counting is, in ſome places, performed
publickly in the ſynagogue. But whether it be
thus performed or not, every maſter of a family is obliged to do it every evening at home †.

Now ſince there were ſeven weeks compleat
betwixt the firſt day of the feaſt of unleavened
bread and the day of pentecoſt, it is made matter of enquiry, on what day of the week that
remarkable pentecoſt fell, when the Holy Ghoſt
was ſhed forth on the apoſtles? which is ſaid to
have been εν τω συμπληρωσαι την ημεραν της Πεντη-
κοσης: the meaning of which is ambiguous, as it
may either ſignify, when the day of pentecoſt
was fulfill'd and over; or, as it is rendered in our
engliſh verſion, " when it was fully come (a)."
The former ſenſe is moſt agreeable to the common meaning of the word πληροω, and the text
is accordingly rendered in the italian verſion,
" when the day of pentecoſt was fully gone."
This ſenſe Dr. Lightfoot prefers, and not without reaſon ‡: for ſince Chriſt eat his laſt paſſover on the ſame day with the reſt of the Jews,
as we have already proved, namely, on the fourteenth of Niſan, which was thurſday; the next
day, on which he was crucified, muſt be the
firſt day of the feaſt of unleavened bread;
therefore the ſixteenth day, the ſaturday, was
the

---

* Hottinger. in Godwin. lib. iii. cap. v. §. v. p. 575,
576.

† See Buxtorf. Synag. judaic. cap. xx. p. 441. edit. 3.

(a) Acts ii. 1.

‡ Horæ hebr. in loc.

the firſt day of the ſeven weeks betwixt that
and the pentecoſt; conſequently the fiftieth
day, or the morrow after the ſeventh ſabbath
or week, which was the day of pentecoſt, muſt
fall on the ſaturday, or the jewiſh ſabbath.

The doctor apprehends, no reaſon can be aſſigned for " the diſciples being all with one
accord in one place," on the day when the
Holy Ghoſt deſcended upon them, more reaſonable and probable, than that they were aſ-
ſembled for the celebration of the Lord's day;
which muſt be, therefore, the next day after the
pentecoſt.　Upon which he further obſerves,
that our Lord, in fulfilling ſeveral types by
which he was repreſented, did not confine himſelf to the day of the type, but deferred the ac-
compliſhment to the day following. It was not
upon the very day of the paſſover, but on the
enſuing day, that " Chriſt our paſſover was ſacrificed for us (a)." It was not on the day,
that the ſheaf of the firſt fruits was offered;
but the next day, that Chriſt became the " firſt
fruits of them that ſlept (b)." In like manner,
he ſuppoſes, the deſcent of the Holy Ghoſt
was not on the day of pentecoſt, but when it
was gone, or the next day after. Neverthelefs
our engliſh verſion, " when the day of pentecoſt was fully come," is ſupported by the uſe
of the word πληροω in ſeveral places of the ſeptuagint, as Dr. Hammond hath fully ſhewn *.
Thus in the evangeliſt Luke, οτε επλησθησαν ημεραι οκτω, which we render, " when eight days
were accompliſhed for circumciſing the child(c),"
muſt ſignify, not when the eighth day was over,
but

(a) 1 Cor. v. 7.　　　(b) 1 Cor. xv. 20.
* See Hammond in loc.
(c) Luke ii. 21.

but when it was come, for on that day, according to the law, circumciſion was to be perform-
ed(a). Suppoſing, then, it was the very day
of pentecoſt when the diſciples were thus aſſem-
bled, and the Holy Ghoſt came upon them, it
might neverthelefs be the firſt day of the week,
or the Lord's day; for as the Jews reckoned
all their ſacred and feſtival days from the evening, ſo we have the teſtimony both of Rabbi
Solomon and Maimonides *, that they began
the computation of the ſeven weeks from the
evening of the ſixteenth of Niſan †. Inſomuch
that the ſaturday, on which our Saviour lay in
the ſepulchre, was not one of the forty-nine
days which made ſeven weeks compleat; but
that evening and the firſt day of the week on
which Chriſt roſe from the dead, made the firſt
day of the firſt week; and conſequently friday
evening and ſaturday were the forty ninth, and
the Lord's day was the fiftieth, or the day of
pentecoſt. Thus it appears, that according to
the manner in which the ſcribes computed the
ſeven weeks, the day of pentecoſt that year,
when the Holy Ghoſt deſcended upon the apoſtles, was the firſt day of the week.

According to the computation of the Baithu-
ſians, and Karraites, the day of pentecoſt always fell on the firſt day of the week; for by
" the ſabbath on the morrow after which the
ſheaf was offered," and the computation of the
ſeven weeks began, they underſtand the weekly
ſabbath,

(a) Levit. xii. 2, 3.
* R. Solom. cited by Meyer in not. ad Megillath Taa-
nith, cap. 1. p. 7. ad calcem Tractat. de tempor. et feſtis
Hebræorum. Maimon. de Sacrificiis jugibus, cap. vii. §.
xxii. p. 477. Crenii Faſcic. Sexti.
† See alſo Megillath Taanith, ubi ſupra, p. 4,—6.

ſabbath, (or the ſabbath of the creation, as the
ſcribes call it,) which fell in the paſchal week.
So that, according to them, the firſt day of the
week was always the firſt day of the forty nine
days or ſeven weeks ; and conſequently the fiftieth day, or pentecoſt, was always the firſt day
of the week *.

2dly, It was called " the feaſt of harveſt(a):"
on the following account, according to the learned Mr. Joſeph Mede, becauſe, as the harveſt
began at the paſſover, ſo it ended at pentecoſt†.
Bochart is of the ſame opinion, who ſaith, that
as about the time of the paſſover the ſickle was
brought out for cutting the corn, ſo about pentecoſt it was laid up again, the harveſt being
entirely finiſhed ‡.   And it is likewiſe the ſentiment of Godwin.   But it doth not ſeem to be
juſtly founded ; for at this feaſt the firſt fruits
of their wheat harveſt were brought and offered
to God ; on which account it was called " the
feaſt of harveſt," as that name is explained :
" the feaſt of harveſt, the firſt fruits of thy
labour, which thou haſt ſown in the field."
Now as the firſt fruits of the barley harveſt were
offered

* R. Obad. de Bartenora in Miſhn. tit. Chagigah, cap.
ii. §. 4. p. 419. Megillath Taanith, ubi ſupra. See the
diſpute concerning this computation in Meyer. de tempor.
et feſtis Hebræor. part. 2. cap. xiii. §. xxi,—xxiv. p. 295,
—297. Reland. Antiq. part. iv. cap. iv. §. iii, iv. p. 474,
—476. edit. 3. Liber Cozri, part. iii. §. xli. p. 217. cum
not. Buxtorf. in loc. p. 218, 219. Lightfoot, Horæ hebr.
Act. ii. 1. Selden. de Anno civili Judæorum, cap. vii.

(a) Exod. xxiii. 16.

† Mede's Diatrib. diſc. xlviii. p. 269. of his works.

‡ Bochart. Hieroz. part. 1. lib. iii. cap. xiii. oper.
tom. 2. p. 857. edit. 1712. See alſo Fuller. Miſcell. lib.
iii. cap. xi. apud Criticos ſacros, tom. 9. p. 2362. edit.
Londin.

offered at the very beginning of it, as we have
ſhown in the laſt chapter, ſo it is reaſonable to
ſuppoſe, the firſt fruits of the wheat harveſt were
likewiſe offered at the beginning of it, and not
delayed till it was over, and all brought into
the barns.   Hence

· 3dly, Another name of this feaſt is, "the
day of the firſt fruits (a)," as it is called in the
twenty eighth chapter of the book of Numbers,
becauſe on that day they were to "offer a new
wheat offering unto the Lord of two loaves of
fine flour baked with leaven (b)," as we are informed in Leviticus; and theſe were to be ac-
companied with animal ſacrifices, namely, ſeven
lambs, without blemiſh, of the firſt year, and
a bullock and two rams, for a burnt-offering,
a kid of the goats for a ſin-offering, and two
lambs of the firſt year for a ſacrifice of peace-
offerings (c)."

It may to us ſeem very ſtrange, that the
wheat harveſt ſhould not begin in Judea till
ſeven weeks after the barley harveſt; whereas
we are accuſtomed to ſee them both together.
It was otherwiſe in the eaſtern countries *; in
Egypt particularly, "the barley, it is ſaid,
was ſmitten with the hail, for it was in the ear,
whereas the wheat and the rye were not ſmitten,
for they were not grown up (d)."

It is enquired, why leaven was uſed in the
bread offered at pentecoſt; whereas it was expreſsly forbidden at the paſſover?

The

(a) Numb. xxviii. 26.   (b) Levit. xxiii. 16, 17.
(c) ver. 18, 19.
   * Vid. Bochart. ubi ſupra, p. 857, 858.
(d) Exod. ix. 31, 32.

The rabbies ſay, becauſe their bread at the paſſover was in commemoration of their ſudden departure out of Egypt, when they could not ſtay to have it leavened; but the loaves offered at pentecoſt, were in behalf of the bread which they were ordinarily to eat *.

4thly, This feaſt is ſtiled in the new teſtament Πεντηκοϛη, that is, the fiftieth; becauſe it was kept fifty days after the paſſover. Paſor in his lexicon ſuppoſes the word ημερα to be underſtood, with which the feminine adjective Πεντηκοϛη agrees. This, however, would make a ſad tautology of the expreſſion in the Acts, την ημεραν της Πεντηκοϛης (a).

5thly, The rabbies call this feaſt " the day of the giving of the law ;" for it is the conſtant opinion of the Jews, that on this day the law was given on mount Sinai, namely, on the fiftieth day from their departure out of Egypt†. This is collected from the nineteenth chapter of Exodus, in the firſt verſe of which it is ſaid, that " in the third month, or in the third new moon, (as the hebrew word קדש chodheſh ſignifies,) when the children of Iſrael were gone forth out of Egypt, the ſame day, (that is, the day of the new moon,) they came to Sinai." Adding, therefore, to this day twenty nine for the laſt month, and fifteen

days

---

* Abarbanel in Lev. iii. cited by Lightfoot in his Temple Service, chap. xiv. §. iv.

(a) Acts ii. 1.

† Maimon. Moreh Nebhoch. part. iii. cap. xliii. p. 471. who makes the deſign of pentecoſt to be a memorial of the giving of the law. Abarbanel, who differs with him as to the deſign of the inſtitution, admits nevertheleſs, that it was celebrated on the ſame day on which the law was given. See Meyer. de tempor. et feſtis Hebræor. part. ii. cap. xiii. §. xvi, xvii. p. 293, 294.

days of the firſt month, it makes forty-five from the time of their departure from Egypt to their arrival at Sinai. To which if we add the day when Moſes went up to God in the mount (a), and the next day when he reported his meſſage from God to the people, and returned their anſwer (b); and the three days more which God gave them to prepare themſelves for his coming down among them (c); there were juſt fifty days from the firſt paſſover to the giving the law at mount Sinai; to which, therefore, according to Maimonides, the inſtitution of this feaſt had a ſpecial regard.

6thly, The rabbies again call this feaſt עצרת gnatſereth *; the word which we render, " ſolemn aſſembly (d);" which, though it is never applied to the pentecoſt in ſcripture, yet they in a manner appropriate it to this feaſt, calling it עצרת gnatſereth, κατ᾽ εξοχην. The reaſon of which might be, as Dr. Lightfoot conjectures, becauſe this feaſt conſiſted of one ſolemn day only, whereas the feaſt of the paſſover and of tabernacles had more †.

The more immediate deſign of this inſtitution ſeems to have been, that they might thankfully acknowledge the goodneſs of God in giving them the fruits of the earth, and beg his bleſſing on the bounties of his providence, by their offering the firſt fruits of their harveſt to

(a) Exod. xix. 3. (b) ver. 7, 8.
(c) ver. 11.
* See the Chaldee Paraphraſe on Numb. xxviii. 26. Miſhn. tit. Gnerachin, cap. 2. §. 3. tom. 5. p. 196. See alſo Reland. Antiq. part. iv. cap. iv. §. iii. p. 472, —474. and Lightfoot's temple ſervice, chap. xiv. §. iv.
(d) Levit xxiii. 36. Deut. xvi. 8.
† Horæ hebr. Act. ii. 1.

him; and it doubtleſs had a typical reference to the firſt fruits of the Holy Spirit, and of converts to Chriſt, after the erection of the goſpel kingdom, by means of Peter's preaching on the day of pentecoſt *.

* See on the pentecoſt, Meyer. de Temporibus et Feſtis Hebræorum, part. 2. cap. xiii. Reland. Antiq. part. iv. cap. iv. Lightfoot, Horæ hebr. Act. ii. 1. and Temple-ſervice, chap. xiv. Leydekker de Republ. Hebræor. lib. ix. cap. v.

CHAP.

CHAP. VI.

Of the feaſt of Tabernacles.

THE feaſt of tabernacles was the third grand feſtival, at which all the male Iſraelites were to attend at the national altar (*a*). It derived its name from their dwelling in tabernacles*, or booths, during its celebration (*b*). It is likewiſe called the " feaſt of ingathering in the end of the year (*c*)," becauſe at this ſeaſon the whole harveſt, not only of the corn, but alſo of the vintage and other fruits, for which they were to expreſs their thankfulneſs to God at this feaſt, was compleated (*d*).

It began on the fifteenth day of the month Tiſri, the firſt of the civil and the ſeventh of the eccleſiaſtical year, and was to be celebrated ſeven days : " The fifteenth day of the ſeventh month ſhall be the feaſt of tabernacles for ſeven days (*e*)." To which there was alſo added an eighth day, which was to be obſerved with peculiar ſolemnity : " Seven days ſhall ye offer an offering made by fire unto the Lord; on the eighth day ſhall be an holy convocation unto

Q 2 you,

you, and ye ſhall offer an offering made by fire unto the Lord; it is a ſolemn aſſembly, and ye ſhall do no ſervile work therein (a)." But as the feaſt of tabernacles is expreſſly limited to ſeven days: " The fifteenth day of this ſeventh month ſhall be the feaſt of tabernacles for ſeven days unto the Lord (b); " during which only they are commanded to dwell in tabernacles or booths (c), this eighth day was not ſo properly a part of the feaſt of tabernacles, as another diſtinct feaſt which followed immediately upon it; agreeably to the account which is given in the book of Nehemiah, " They kept the feaſt ſeven days, and on the eighth day was a ſolemn aſſembly according unto the manner (d)." The ſeven days are expreſſly ſaid in Leviticus to have been kept in commemoration of their dwelling in tents in the wilderneſs for forty years (e); the eighth day, therefore, was properly the feaſt of ingathering, on which they were to give thanks for their whole harveſt, " after, as it is expreſſed in the book of Deuteronomy, they had gathered in their corn, and their wine (f)." Indeed there is no mention in this laſt paſſage, of this eighth day, but only of the feſtival of ſeven days. Nevertheleſs theſe being obſerved on a ſeparate account, namely, to commemorate their dwelling in tents in the wilderneſs, we may conclude, that the rejoicing and thankſgiving, enjoined at this feſtival on account of the harveſt, were chiefly if not wholly appropriated to the eighth day. And it is obſervable, that they were commanded to dwell in booths no longer than the ſeven days;

(a) Levit. xxiii. 36.   (b) ver. 34.   (c) ver. 42.
(d) Nehem viii. 18.   (e) Levit. xxiii. 42, 43.
(f) Deut. xvi. 13,—16.

days; a circumſtance, which ſhows, that the eighth day was not obſerved on the ſame account as the ſeven preceding. Nevertheleſs, as the names of the feaſt of the paſſover, and the feaſt of unleavened bread which immediately followed it, are frequently confounded *, ſo the feaſt of tabernacles and of ingathering, though properly diſtinct, yet following cloſe upon one another, are ſometimes ſpoke of as one feaſt, and the name of either indifferently applied to both. It was probably the eighth day, which is ordered to be kept with the ſolemnity of a ſabbath, and not the ſeventh, concerning which there is no ſuch appointment in the law, that is ſtiled by the evangeliſt John, "the laſt and great day of the feaſt (a)," that is, of the feaſt of tabernacles (b).

The firſt day of this feaſt was to be kept as a ſabbath (c), and during that and the ſix following days they were to dwell in tents or booths, made of branches of ſeveral ſorts of trees, which are particularly mentioned (d). The name of the firſt ſort is עץ הדר gnets hadhar, which we render, "goodly trees." The Jews will have it to mean the citron †. The next is called תמר thamar, or the palm. The third is עץ עבת gnets gnabhoth, which ſignifies any thick or buſhy wood; by which the Jews underſtand the myrtle. The laſt is the willow. But when Nehemiah, upon the revival of this feaſt, directed the people what branches to gather, he called ſome of them by different names, which we render olive branches, and pine branches, and myrtle branches (e). Pro-

Q 3 bably,

* See before, chap. 4. p. 209, 210.

(a) John vii. 37. (b) See ver. 2, (c) Levit. xxiii. 39. (d) ver. 40. † Reland. Antiq. part. iv. cap. v. §. ix. Hottinger in Godwin. lib. iii. cap. vi. §. iii. not. 4 p. 581,—584. (e) Nehem. viii. 15.

bably, therefore, the Karraites were right in
their opinion, that it was not the intention of
the law to oblige them to uſe certain trees and
no other, but only ſuch as were fit for the purpoſe, and could be moſt readily procured, in
the places where they dwelt.   Accordingly Moſes named ſuch trees as were moſt common in
his time, and Nehemiah others that were grown
more common in his.   It appears from the paſſage in Nehemiah, that the booths were to be
made of theſe branches; but this is not expreſsly declared of the boughs mentioned in Levitic-
cus.   It is only ſaid, " You ſhall take on the
firſt day the boughs of goodly trees, branches
of palm trees, and the boughs of thick trees,
and willows of the brook ; and ye ſhall rejoice
before the Lord your God ſeven days."   Theſe
boughs and branches the Sadducees underſtand
to be for making their booths ; but the Phari-
ſees, that they were to be carried in their hands *;
which is the practice of the modern Jews to this
day.   They tye together one branch of palm,
three branches of myrtle, and one of willow.
This they carry in their right hands, and in
their left they have a branch of citron, with its
fruit, or at leaſt of pomecitron, when they cannot procure ſuch a branch.   With theſe, every
day of the feaſt, that is, for ſeven days, they
make a proceſſion in their ſynagogues round
their reading deſks, as their anceſtors did round
the walls of Jericho, in token of the expected
downfal of their enemies †.   Under each of
theſe branches a myſtery is comprehended.
The palm, inaſmuch as it bears an inſipid
fruit,

---

* Reland. Antiq. ubi ſupra. See Joſeph. Antiq. lib. iii.
cap. x. §. 4. p. 175. edit. Haverc.

† Buxtorf. Synag. Judaic. cap. xxi. p. 460, 461.

fruit, is an emblem of the hypocrite.   The
myrtle, as it has a fragrant fmell, although it
be barren, refembles thofe who perform good
works without the law.   The willow is an
emblem of the wicked, and the citron of the
righteous *.   They alfo turn about with thefe
branches to the four cardinal points, and fhake
or pufh with them each way, and upwards and
downwards, to drive the devil from them †.
While they are making this proceffion, they
fing Hofannah; whence this feaft is called by
the rabbies, the Hofannah; and fometimes the
branches are called by the fame name.   On the
laft day, which they call Hofanna rabbah, or
the great Hofannah, they make the proceffion
feven times together, in memory of the fiege
of Jericho.   The form of the Hofannah in
their ritual, which they fing on this occafion
is remarkable, " For thy fake, O our creator,
Hofannah; for thy fake, O our redeemer, Hofannah; for thy fake, O our feeker, Hofannah:" as if they befeeched the bleffed trinity,
faith Dr. Patrick ‡, to fave them, and fend
them help.   This feaft is kept with the greateft jollity of any of their feftivals, efpecially
on the eighth day; when, according to the law,
they were to feaft and rejoice upon their having
gathered in their corn and their wine.   Hence,
in the talmud, it is often called חג chag, the
feaft, κατ᾽ εξοχην: and Philo calls it εορτων μεγιϛην,
the greateft of the feafts §; and hence likewife
this jewifh feftival came to be more taken no-

tice

* Buxtorf. Synag. Judaic. cap. xxi. p. 457. edit. 3.
† Buxtorf. cap. xx. p 459.
‡ Patrick on Levit. xxiii. 40.
§ See Wolfii Curæ Philolog. in Joh. vii. 37.

tice of by the heathens than any other. It is
probable King Cecrops took from it the hint of
the law which he ordained at Athens, " that
the mafter of every family fhould after harveft
make a feaft for his fervants, and eat together
with them, who had taken pains with him in
tilling his ground *." And as this jewifh feftival was kept at the time of the vintage, or,
prefently after it, when " they had gathered in
their corn and their wine," it is not unlikely,
that the heathens borrowed their bacchanalia
from it; and this might lead Plutarch into
that egregious miftake, that the Jews celebrated this feftival to the honour of Bacchus; for
he faith in his fympofia †, " that in the time of
the vintage the Jews fpread tables, furnifhed
with all manner of fruits, and lived in tabernacles efpecially of palm and ivy wreathed together, and they call it the feaft of tabernacles;"
" and then a few days after," faith he, (referring I fuppofe to the laft day of the feaft) " they
kept another feftivity, which openly fhows it
was dedicated to Bacchus; for they carried
boughs of palms, &c. in their hands, with
which they went into the temple, the levites,
(who, he fancies, were fo called from Ευιος, one
of the names of Bacchus) going before with
inftruments of mufick, &c."

Although only the firft and laft days of this
feaft were to be kept as fabbaths, there were,
neverthelefs, peculiar and extraordinary facrifices appointed for every day of it (a). On the
firft day, " thirteen young bullocks, two rams
and fourteen lambs of the firft year" were facrificed;

* Macrob. Saturnal. lib. 1. cap. x. p. 231. edit. Gronov.
Lugd. Bat. 1670.
† Plutarch. Sympos. lib. iv. prob. 5. oper. tom. 2. p.
671. edit. Francof. 1620.
(a) Numb. xxix. 12, et feq.

crificed; whereas on the other feſtivals two bullocks ſufficed (a). The next day twelve bullocks were ſacrificed, and ſo on, with the de-
creaſe of one bullock a day, till on the ſeventh
day only ſeven bullocks were offered; which in
all made ſeventy bullocks. The lambs and the
rams alſo were in a double proportion to the
number ſacrificed at any other feſtival. The
doctors give this reaſon for the daily diminution of the number of the bullocks ; the whole
number, ſay they, being ſeventy, was according to the languages of the ſeventy nations of
the world ; and the diminution of one every
day ſignified that there ſhould be a gradual diminution of thoſe nations, till all things were
brought under the government of the Meſſiah*.
Others ſuppoſe this diminution had a reſpect to
the ſeventy years of man's age, which is daily
decaying †.

For the eighth day, though it was properly
a diſtinct feſtival, and was to be kept with extraordinary ſolemnity, fewer ſacrifices were appointed than for any of the foregoing ſeven.
On every one of them two rams were offered
and fourteen lambs ; on this day there were but
half as many ; and whereas ſeven bullocks were
the feweſt that were offered on any of theſe days,
on this there was only one (b). By which, Dr.
Patrick ſaith, God conſulted perhaps the weak-
neſs of mankind, who naturally grow weary
both of the charge and labour of ſuch ſervices,
when

(a) See Numb. xxviii. 11, 19, 27.

* R. Solomon in Numb. xxix. cited by Lightfoot in his
Temple-ſervice, chap. xvi. §. 1.

† Abarbanel in Numb. xxix. cited by Lightfoot, ubi
ſupra.

(b) Numb. xxix. 36.

when they are long continued; and therefore
he made them every day leſs toilſome and expenſive; and put them in mind likewiſe that
the multitude of ſacrifices did not procure their
acceptance with God, and that in length of
time they would come to nothing, and be utterly aboliſhed, to eſtabliſh ſomething better in
their room *.

Before we diſmiſs the ceremonies of this feaſt,
we muſt not forget to mention a very extraordinary one, of which the rabbies inform us,
though there is not the leaſt hint of it in the
law of Moſes, notwithſtanding he gives a more
particular deſcription of this feaſt than of any
other; namely, the drawing water out of the
pool of Siloam, and pouring of it, mixed with
wine, on the ſacrifice as it lay on the altar †.
This they are ſaid to have done with ſuch expreſſions of joy, that it became a common proverb, "He that never ſaw the rejoicing of
drawing water, never ſaw rejoicing in all his
life ‡." To this ceremony our Saviour is ſuppoſed to refer, when " in the laſt day, the
great day of the feaſt, he ſtood and cried, ſaying, If any man thirſt, let him come unto me,
and drink; he that believeth on me, as the
ſcripture hath ſaid, out of his belly ſhall flow
rivers of living water (a):" thereby calling off
the people from their carnal mirth, and feſtive
and

---

* See Patrick in loc.

† See this ceremony deſcribed in Maimon. de Sacrificiis jugibus, cap. x. ſ. vii. p. 494, 495. Crenii Faſcic.
Sexti. in Annot. Conſtant. L'Empereur, ad cod. Middoth,
cap. 2. ſ. 5. p. 67,—69. edit. Lugd. Bat. 1730. or in
Miſhn. Surenhus. tom. 5. p. 343, 344.

‡ Miſhn. tit. Succah, cap. 5. ſ. 1. tom. 2. p. 277. edit.
Surenhus.

(a) John vii. 37, 38.

and pompous ceremonies, to ſeek ſpiritual re-
freſhment for their ſouls. The Jews pretend to
ground this cuſtom on the following paſſage of
Iſaiah, " With joy ſhall ye draw water out
of the wells of ſalvation (a)." This libation
was performed every day of the feaſt, at the
time of the morning ſacrifice * ; but the greater
part of their rejoicing on that occaſion was ad-
journed till evening ; when a wild and ridiculous ſcene of mirth was acted in the court of
the temple, by thoſe who were eſteemed the
wiſe men of Iſrael †, namely, by the elders and
members of the ſanhedrim, the rulers of the
ſynagogues, and doctors of the ſchools, and
ſuch others as were moſt honoured for their age
and piety. All the temple-muſick played, and
theſe old men danced, while the women in the
balconies round the court, and the men on the
ground, were ſpectators. All the ſport was to
ſee theſe venerable fathers of the nation ſkip and
dance, clap their hands and ſing ; and they,
who played the fool moſt egregiouſly, acquitted
themſelves with moſt honour ; for in this they
pretend to imitate the example of David, " who
danced before the Lord with all his might, and
ſaid, I will be yet more vile than this, and be
baſe in my own ſight (b)." In this manner they
ſpent the greater part of the night, till at length
two prieſts ſounded a retreat with trumpets.
This mad feſtivity was repeated every evening,
except

(a) Iſai. xii. 3.
* Maimon. ubi ſupra, §. vi.
† Maimon. in Lulahb, cap. viii. §. 12, et ſeq. See the
quotations in Talmudis Babylonici codex Succah, by Dachs,
not. 1, 2, ad cap. v. §. iv. p. 451, 452. Trajcct ad Rhen.
1726.
(b) 2 Sam. vi. 14, 22.

except on the evening before the ſabbath which
fell in this feſtival, and on the evening before
the laſt and great day of the feaſt. It ſeems,
theſe two evenings were accounted too holy for
ſuch ridiculous gambols *.

We can be at no loſs for a reaſon, why the
feaſt of ingathering, which was annexed to the
feaſt of tabernacles, was celebrated at this ſeaſon of the year, when the vintage, as well as
the corn harveſt, was newly finiſhed; in reſpect
to which the feaſt is ſaid, in the book of Exodus, to be " in the end of the year (a),"
though it was not celebrated till three weeks
after the new civil year began; and ſo the next
words ſeem to explain it, " in the end of the
year, when thou haſt gathered thy labours out
of the field :" In which ſenſe it comes nigh our
autumn, the latter end of the year. Or, perhaps, the phraſe השנה בצאת betſeeth haſhanah,
may admit of a different verſion, for the verb
יצא jatſa, ſignifies not only exiit, but, ortus
eſt, in which ſenſe it is applied to the riſing of
the ſun (b), and to the birth of man (c). Accordingly betſeeth haſhanah may be as juſtly
rendered, in ortu anni, as in exitu anni; in the
beginning as in the end of the year, and may
as properly be applied to the firſt month as the
laſt. But it is not ſo obvious, for what reaſon
the feaſt of tabernacles was fixed to this ſeaſon.
One might naturally expect, that the annual
commemoration of their dwelling in tents in the
wilderneſs, ſhould be celebrated at the ſame
time

* See a larger account of this ceremony in Lightfoot's
Temple-ſervice, chap. xvi. §. iv.
(a) Exod. xxiii. 16.   (b) Gen. xix. 23. Pſal.
xix. 6.   (c) Job i. 21.   1 Kings viii. 19. Iſai.
xi. 1.

time of the year, when either they firft betook
themfelves to tents on their leaving Egypt prefently after the paffover, or when they quitted
their tents upon their entrance into Canaan, a
little before the paffover, which was kept in the
plains of Jericho (*a*).   Whereas this feaft was
appointed to be celebrated at near fix months
diftance from either.

Rabbi Jacob Levita conceives, that as it was
ufual with people in warm climates to live much
in tents or booths in fummer for coolnefs, God
purpofely directed the celebration of this feaft
to be delayed to that feafon of the year when
the cold mornings, winds and rains, ordinarily
obliged them to quit their booths and betake
themfelves to their houfes ; that it might appear, their dwelling in booths at this time was
not for convenience or pleafure, but in obedience to the divine command *. Maimonides, on
the contrary, obferves, that this feaft was wife-
ly fixed to that feafon, when the people might
dwell in booths with the leaft inconvenience,
becaufe the weather was then moderate, and
they were not wont to be troubled either with
heat or with rain †.

Others have, therefore, endeavoured to prove,
that this was the time of the year, when Mofes
came down the fecond time from the mount,
and brought them the joyful news, that God
was appeafed for the fin of the golden calf ;
and that he had accordingly ordered the tabernacle to be reared in token that now he no longer difdained to dwell among them, in memory

---

(*a*) Jofh. v. 10.
* Meyer. de Temporibus et Feftis Hebræor. part. ii. cap.
xvi. §. iv. p. 318, 319.
† Maimon. Moreh Nebhoch. lib. iii. cap. xliii:

ry of which this feaſt is ſuppoſed to be appointed. However, this is aſſigning a quite different reaſon for their dwelling in booths or tabernacles from that which the ſcripture aſſigns; for according to the ſcripture this appointment was deſigned, not in commemoration of God's dwelling in the tabernacle among them, but of their " dwelling in tents forty years in the wilderneſs."

The learned Joſeph Mede's opinion ſeems to be the moſt probable, as well as the moſt ingenious*, namely, that this feaſt was affixed to the time of the year when Chriſt was to be born, and the dwelling in tabernacles was intended as a type of his incarnation ; as St. John ſeems to intimate, when he ſaith, " the word was made fleſh, και εσκηνωσεν εν ημιν, and tabernacled in or with us (a).

We are aſſured by the Apoſtle, that the law in the general had " a ſhadow of good things to come (b)," or a typical reference to Chriſt and the goſpel diſpenſation. It is, therefore, incredible, that any of the three grand feſtivals ſhould be without ſome illuſtrious type of him, or ſhould not point to ſome principal circumſtance concerning him ; as we know the paſſover and the pentecoſt did, the former being a type of his paſſion, the latter of his ſending the firſt fruits of his ſpirit, on his ſetting up the goſpel kingdom. And can it be imagined, that the third principal feaſt, which was more ſolemn than either of the others, having a more extraordinary courſe of ſacrifices annexed to it, ſhould not typically point to ſome grand event concerning him and his kingdom? And to
what

* Mede's Diatrib. Diſc. xlviii. p. 268. of his works, edit. 167.
(a) John i. 14.   (b) Heb. x. 1.

what can we fo naturally apply it, efpecially after the hints St. John has given us in the paffage before quoted, as to the incarnation and birth of our Saviour? The events, then, that were typified by the two former feafts, falling out at the very time of thofe feftivals, it is probable the cafe was the fame as to the feaft of tabernacles, and that Chrift was born at this feftival *.

Of the time of Chrift's nativity.

As to the vulgar opinion, that the birth of Chrift was on the twenty-fifth of December, there is not only no good reafon for it, but the contrary.

It is certain, this day was not fixed upon in the chriftian church, as the day of our Saviour's nativity till after the time of Conftantine, in the fourth century; and then it was upon a miftaken fuppofition, that Zacharias, the father of John the baptift, was the high prieft, and that the day when he burnt incenfe upon the altar in the temple, while the people were waiting without, was the day of expiation, or the tenth of the month Tifri, which fell out that year about the middle of September. As foon as Zacharias had fulfilled the days of his miniftration, John the baptift was conceived, that is, towards the end of September. Our Saviour was conceived fix months after, that is, towards the end of March, and confequently his birth must

---

* On the feaft of tabernacles, befides the Mifhna, tit. Succah, and Dachs. Talmudis babylon. codex Succah, five de Tabernaculorum Fefto, paffim, fee Meyer. de Temporibus et Feftis diebus Hebræor. part. 2. cap. xvi. Reland. Antiq. part. iv. cap. v. Ainfworth on Levit. xxiii. 34,—43. Lightfoot Temple-fervice, chap. xvi. Leidekker. de Republ. Hebr. lib. ix. cap. vii.

muft fall out towards the end of December. This is the ground upon which the feaft of our Saviour's nativity was fixed to the twenty-fifth of December*. However, that it is erroneous, is very evident; for Zacharias was not in the holy of holies, into which the high prieft only entered, when the angel appeared to him; but by the altar of incenfe, which ftood in the fanctuary without the veil (a); at which altar the common priefts performed their daily miniftry. Neither was Zacharias the high prieft; for we are told, that " he was of the courfe of Abia," and that his lot " was to burn incenfe (b);" whereas the high prieft was of no courfe at all, neither did burning incenfe in the moft holy place fall to him by lot, but was part of his proper and peculiar office. Accordingly there is no reafon to conclude, that the day when the angel appeared to Zacharias was the day of expiation, which is the foundation of the common opinion concerning the time of the birth of Chrift.

I add further, that not only is the vulgar opinion of the feafon of his nativity deftitute of any juft ground; but there are good and valid arguments againft it. For inftance,

There was a decree from Cefar Auguftus iffued and executed at this feafon, that all perfons, women as well as men, fhould repair to their refpective cities, to be taxed, or enrolled. This occafioned the Virgin Mary to come to Bethlehem at that time; where fhe was delivered. But furely this decree was not executed in the middle of winter, which was a very fevere feafon in that country, and highly inconvenient for

* Spanhem. Hiftor. Ecclef. Secul. i. Sect. ii. de Nativitate, §. iii. p. 523, 524. et Secul. iv. Sect. vi. de Ritibus, p. 855. edit. Lugd. Bat. 1701.

(a) Luke i. 11.   (b) Luke i. 5, 9.

for travelling, efpecially for fuch multitudes, and in particular for women in Mary's condition ; as may be inferred from what our Saviour faith in the twenty fourth chapter of St. Matthew, concerning the difficulties to which his difciples would be expofed, if their flight, previous to the fiege and deftruction of Jerufalem, fhould happen in the winter (a).

Again, at the time when Chrift was born, there were fhepherds abroad in the fields by night watching their flocks ; certainly a very unfeafonable fervice for the winter in Judea, if we may judge of the weather in that country, and at that feafon, by the Pfalmift's defcription : " He giveth fnow like wool, he fcattereth the hoar froft like afhes ; he cafteth forth his ice like morfels; who can ftand before his cold (b)?"

Upon the whole, there is great probability, that Chrift was not born in December. But, though we do not pretend to be certain of the real time when he was born, there are, however, feveral reafons to incline us to believe, it was at the feaft of tabernacles ; particularly, as was hinted before, the fynchronifm of the type and the antitype in the two other principal feafts ; and the fame, therefore, was probably the cafe as to this feaft.

Again, Dr. Lightfoot has offered feveral arguments, to prove that Chrift was baptized at the time of the feaft of tabernacles *. But when he was baptized, he was ωσει ετων τριακοντα αρχομενος, that is, entering on his thirtieth year (c) ; confequently this was the fame time of the year in which he was born.

_____

(a) Matt. xxiv. 20.   (b) Pfal. cxlvii. 16, 17.
* See his Harmony on Luke iii. 21.
(c) Luke iii. 23.

Further, Jofeph Scaliger obferves, that the twenty four courfes of the priefts, which went through the year, began with the month Nifan about the vernal equinox ; and that confequently the eighth courfe, to which Zacharias belonged, miniftred in the latter part of July. If from thence you reckon the five months to the virgin's conception, and nine more for her geftation, the birth of Chrift will fall in the latter end of September, that is, at the feafon of the feaft of tabernacles *.

* See Scalig. Fragment. p. 58, 59. ad calcem emend. Temp. Mede's Diatrib. difc. xlviii. on Deut. xvi. 16. Chrift's birth miftimed, a Tract. No. iv. in the Phenix, 1707. and in defence of the common opinion, Selden on the Birth-day of our Saviour, apud Opera, vol. 3. tom. 6. p. 1405. et feq.

CHAP.

CHAP. VII.

Of the feaſt of Trumpets and New Moons.

HAVING conſidered the three grand feſtivals, at which all the male Iſraelites, who were able, were obliged to aſſemble at the national altar, we proceed to conſider the leſſer feaſts, of which ſome were menſtrual, others annual. The menſtrual were the new moons, which were kept on the firſt day of every month ; and of theſe one was more remarkable and to be obſerved with greater ſolemnity than the reſt ; namely, on the firſt day of the month Tiſri. This is ſtiled the " feaſt of trumpets."

It is proper firſt to conſider the common new moon feaſt, of which we find no other inſtitution in the law of Moſes, than meerly a preſcription of certain ſacrifices to be offered on the day of the new moon, or which is the ſame, on the firſt day of the month, over and above the ſacrifices that were daily offered (a).

The ſacrifices, preſcribed on this occaſion, are two young bullocks, one ram and ſeven

R 2   lambs

(a) See Numb. xxviii. 11,—15.

lambs for a burnt-offering, and a kid of the goats for a ſin-offering, to be attended with meat-offerings and drink-offerings, as uſual in other ſacrifices.

The number of the animal ſacrifices are eleven, for which the hebrew doctors have deviſed the following reaſon, becauſe the lunar year falls ſhort of the ſolar by eleven days *. We find only one precept more in the law of Moſes concerning theſe new moons; namely, that " in their ſolemn days, and in the beginning of their months, they ſhall blow with the trumpets over their burnt-offerings, and over the ſacrifices of their peace-offerings (a)." But this is rather to be conſidered as a ceremony attending the ſacrifices, than as peculiar to the new moon days; for the ſame thing is enjoined at their other ſolemn ſacrifices, or on their other ſolemn days, at the ſeveral feaſts which are inſtituted in the twenty-third chapter of Leviticus, which were to be proclaimed as holy convocations (b), and this was always done by ſound of trumpets (c).

Indeed in the eighty-firſt Pſalm this ſeems to be mentioned as a rite peculiar to the new moon : " Blow up the trumpet in the new moon, at the time appointed, on the ſolemn feaſt day (d)." But it is probable the new moon, here mentioned, was the feaſt of trumpets, or the new moon at the beginning of the month Tiſri ; for the uſe of which feſtival Dr. Patrick ſuppoſes this Pſalm was compoſed. This was the chief new moon of the year, and was diſtinguiſhed from the reſt by peculiar rites, particu-

---

* Reland. Antiq. part. iv. cap. vii. §. iv. p. 510. edit. 3. (a) Numb. x 10.　(b) Levit. xxiii. 2.　(c) Numb. x. 7, 8.　(d) Pſal. lxxxi. 3.

particularly by the blowing of trumpets, as we
ſhall ſee hereafter.

The trumpet, or muſical inſtrument, of
which Aſaph here ſpeaks as to be ſounded on
the new moon to which he refers, was the
שופר ſhophar, made of horn, and therefore
ſometimes rendered the cornet; whereas the
inſtrument uſed on the ordinary new moons,
or at the beginning of their months, was the
חצצרה chatſotſerah (a), which was made of ſilver (b).   Of both theſe inſtruments we have
formerly given an account *.

The new moon to which Aſaph refers,
was to be kept as a ſabbath, for it is called a
ſolemn feaſt-day.   But I do not find the ordinary new moons ever ſo ſtiled; nor does it appear by the law of Moſes, that they were to be
obſerved as ſacred feſtivals, or ſabbath-days,
in which no ſervile work was to be done.   They
are not mentioned among the ſacred feaſts in
the twenty-third chapter of Leviticus.   Nor
is any thing preſcribed on thoſe days more
than the offering of the ſacrifices already
mentioned.   Nevertheleſs ſacrifices relating to
and implying devotion in the offerers, thoſe
days were accounted more ſacred than common
ones, and were accordingly obſerved by pious
Iſraelites for the exerciſes of devotion; they
uſed at theſe ſeaſons to repair to the prophets,
or other miniſters of God, to hear his word.
This occaſioned the Shunamite's huſband enquiring, for what end ſhe deſired to go to the
prophet that day, "when it was neither new
moon, nor ſabbath;" a plain intimation, that

it

(a) Numb. x. 10.   (b) ver. 2.
* See vol. 1. p. 276, 277.

it had been her cuſtom to do it on thoſe days..
The new moons and ſabbaths are ment.oned
together, as days of publick worſhip, by ſeveral of the prophets. "It ſhall come to paſs,
ſaith the prophet Iſaiah, that from one new
moon to another, and from one ſabbath to another, ſhall all fleſh come to worſhip before me,
ſaith the Lord (a)." Again, "thus ſaith the
Lord God, (by the prophet Ezekiel,) the gate
of the inner court, that looketh towards the
eaſt, ſhall be ſhut the ſix working-days; but
on the ſabbath it ſhall be opened, and on the
day of the new moon it ſhall be opened (b)."
And in the following remarkable paſſage of the
prophet Amos, "Hear this, O ye that ſwallow
up the needy, even to make the poor of the
land to fail, ſaying, when will the new moon
be gone, that we may ſell corn? and the ſabbath, that we may ſet forth wheat, &c (c)." It
appears from this paſſage, that though the law
did not expreſsly require, that they ſhould abſtain from ſervile work on the new moon, as it
did on the ſabbath; worldly buſineſs, notwithſtanding, was in a good meaſure, laid aſide on
thoſe days.

Beſides the publick, national ſacrifices that
were to be offered on the new moons, it was
cuſtomary to make feaſts, probably on the
more private ſacrifices offered by particular perſons and families (d).

In the opinion of the rabbies, whilſt men are
allowed to follow their vocations on the new
moons, as on other days; the women were exempted from all labour. For they pretend,
the

(a) Iſai. lxvi. 23.   (b) Ezek. xlvi. 1.   (c) Amos
viii. 5.   (d) See 1 Sam. xx. 5, 6.

the new moon is in a peculiar manner the feſtival of the women, in commemoration of their
liberality at the time of erecting the tabernacle,
in contributing their moſt valuable jewels to
promote the magnificence of the divine ſervice,
which memorable action was performed, they
ſay, on the new moon of the month Niſan *.

It does not appear in ſcripture by what method the ancient Jews fixed the time of the
new moon, and whether they kept this feaſt on
the day of the conjunction, or on the firſt day
of the moon's appearing. The rabbies are of
the latter opinion. They tell us, that for want
of aſtronomical tables, the Sanhedrim, about
the time of the new moon, ſent out men to
watch upon the tops of mountains, and give
immediate notice to them of its firſt appearance; upon which a fire was made on the top
of mount Olivet, which, being ſeen at a diſtance, was anſwered by fires on the tops of o-
ther mountains, and they in like manner by
others ſtill more remote; by which means the
notice was quickly ſpread through the whole
land. But experience at length taught them
that this kind of intelligence was not to be depended on, the Samaritans, and other prophane
perſons, ſometimes kindling ſuch fires on the
tops of mountains at a wrong ſeaſon on purpoſe to deceive the people, and diſturb the order of the ſacred feſtivals. In later time, therefore, the Sanhedrim was forced to ſend expreſſes on this occaſion to all parts of the country.

It is further added, that becauſe of the uncertainty that would attend this way of fixing

R 4   the

---

* See Buxtorf's Synag. judaic. cap. xxii. p. 473, 474.
edit. 3. et Le dekker. de Republ. Hebræor. lib. ix. cap. ii.
p. 538, 539. Amſtel 1704.

the time of the new moon, eſpecially in cloudy weather, they obſerved two days, that they might be ſecure of being in the right *. Hence they account for Saul's expecting David at his table two days ſucceſſively, on the feaſt of the new moon (a).

The modern Jews keep this feſtival, by repeating certain prayers in their ſynagogues, and afterwards by feaſting in their own houſes †; and ſome devotees faſt on the vigil of it ‡.

Many of them add another ceremony about three days after. They meet in companies in the night in ſome open place, when they bleſs God in a prayer of conſiderable length, for having created the moon, and for having renewed her, to teach the Iſraelites that they ought to become new creatures. Then they leap up thrice in the air as high as they are able, and ſay to the moon, " As we leap up towards thee without being able to touch thee, ſo may it be impoſſible for our enemies to riſe up againſt us to hurt us ‖."

The reaſon of God's appointing peculiar ſacrifices to be offered at the new moon, might be in part, to make the time of it more carefully obſerved; which was a matter of conſiderable importance, not only to prevent confuſion in their chronology, ſince they reckoned by lunar months; but likewiſe, becauſe the true time of obſerving all their great feſtivals depended upon it. Nevertheleſs I conceive the chief reaſon of this inſtitution was to preſerve the Iſraelites from the idolatry of the heathens, who uſed to offer ſacrifices to the new moon.

Thus

---

* See above, chap. 1. p. 120, 121. (a) 1 Sam. xx. 24.
† Buxtorf. Synag. cap. xxiv. p. 500, 504. ‡ Buxtorf. cap. xxiii. p. 489. ‖ See baſnage's Hiſtory of the Jews, book v. chap. xiv. §. ix. p. 451, 452.

Thus among the Athenians, the firſt day of the month was τη ιερωτατη ημερων, a moſt holy day, as Plutarch ſtiles it*. And there was a law, ταις νεμηνιαις θυειν, to offer ſacrifices on the new moons†. Some indeed have obſerved ſo great a reſemblance in ſeveral articles of the athenian law, to that of Moſes, as to ſuſpect that the athenian lawgiver took the hint of many of them from the jewiſh inſtitutions. Be that as it will, nothing is more likely than that as the ſun and the moon were the principal idols the heathens worſhiped, it was uſual for them to pay their devotions to the moon, pro-bably by ſacrifices, chiefly at the time of her firſt appearing after the change. In order, therefore, to check this ſpecies of idolatry, God commanded the Iſraelites to offer ſolemn ſacrifices to him at the ſame time, that the hea-thens were ſacrificing to the moon. Accord-ingly it is very obſervable, that the ſin-offering on this occaſion, which was to be a kid of the goats, is particularly and expreſsly directed to be offered to Jehovah (a). The deſign of this, Grotius obſerves, was to put them in mind of the right object of worſhip, at a time when they were in peculiar danger of being ſeduced to offer ſacrifices to the moon after the manner of the heathens. Which remark is the more worthy of notice, in that, though in the ſame chapter a goat is ordered to be ſacrificed for a ſin-offering, both at the feaſt of the paſſover and at pentecoſt (b); yet it is not ſaid in either inſtance,

---

* Plutarch. de vitando ære alieno, oper. tom. 2. p. 828. A. edit. Francof. 1620.

† Vid. Petiti Comment. in Leges Atticas, lib. i. tit. 1. p. 85.

(a) Numb. xxviii. 15.   (b) ver. 22,—30.

ſtance, that it muſt be offered to Jehovah, though it was, no doubt, ſo intended ; in all probability becauſe there was no ſuch danger of this kind of idolatry at thoſe ſeaſons, as there was at the new moon. Maimonides likewiſe hath obſerved that " this ſin-offering is ſo pe-culiarly ſaid to be unto the Lord, leaſt any ſhould think this goat to be a ſacrifice to the moon after the manner of the Egyptians, who uſed to ſacrifice one to the moon at this time, as they did to the ſun at his riſing *." And it ſeems, among the heathens, the goat was a favourite ſacrifice to the moon, becauſe the horns of that animal ſomewhat reſemble the new moon †. Thus much for the common new moon.

The new moon which began the month Tiſri, the ſeventh of the eccleſiaſtical, but the firſt of the civil year, was to be obſerved with more than ordinary ſolemnity, not only with ſeveral ſacrifices additional to thoſe that were offered on other new moons ; but it was to be kept as a ſabbath, in which they were to have a holy convocation, and to do no ſervile work. And beſides the ſounding the trumpets over the ſacrifices, as on the other new moons and ſolemn feſtivals ; this was to be " a day of blowing the trumpets(a)," that is, as the an-cient Jews underſtand it, they were to be blown from morning to evening ‡ ; at leaſt it imports they were to be blown more on this day than on any other.

This

---

* Moreh Nebhoch. part. iii. cap. xlvi. præſertim p. 488.
† Spencer de Legibus Hebræor. lib. iii. differt. iv. cap. 1. ſect. v. p. 814. tom. 2. edit. Cantab. 1727.
(a) Numb. xxix. 1.
‡ Munſter. in loc. et Buxtorf, Synag. cap. xxiv. p. 504.

This day is alfo called " a memorial of blow-ing of trumpets (*a*)."

The fcripture no where exprefsly affigning the reafon of this feftival, and particularly of the blowing of trumpets, from whence it is called the feaft of trumpets, the learned are very much divided about it.   Maimonides thinks it was in-ftituted to awaken the people to repentance a-gainft the annual faft or great day of expiation, which followed nine days after.   He makes the found of the trumpet on this day to be in effect faying, " Shake off your drowfinefs ye that fleep, fearch and try your ways, remember your creator and repent, bethink yourfelves and take care of your fouls, &c*.

Some have fuppofed, that the apoftle refers to this ufe and meaning of blowing the trum-pets, in the following paffage of the epiftle to the Ephefians, " Wherefore he faith, Awake, thou that fleepeft, and arife from the dead, and Chrift fhall give thee light (*b*)."   Accordingly they make the nominative cafe to λεγει, he faith, to be Θεος, God, as fpeaking by the voice or found of the trumpet.   To this it may be ob-jected, not only that there is no intimation in fcripture, that the trumpets were blown for the purpofes Maimonides imagines ; but likewife that the apoftle would hardly have referred to a jewifh ceremony, as if the meaning of it were well known, when he was writing to the Gentiles,

who

(*a*) Levit. xxiii. 24.   See the inftitution of this feftival, Numb. xxix. 1,—6.   Levit. xxiii. 24, 25.

* Maimon. de poenitentiâ cap. iii. §. vi. p. 56. edit. et verf. Clavering. Oxon. 1705.   See alfo Moreh Nebhoch. part. iii. cap. xliii. p. 471, 472. edit. Buxtorf. 1629. and Shom Tobh on Maimonides, quoted by Hottinger on God-win. lib. iii. cap. vii. §. vi. not. 4. p. 601.

(*b*) Ephef. v. 14.

who probably were unacquainted with the ceremony itſelf, and much more with its deſign and
intention. Others therefore ſuppoſe the nominative caſe to λεγει is γραφη, the ſcripture, or
God ſpeaking in the ſcripture, and that there is
a reference to the following paſſage of Iſaiah,
" Ariſe, ſhine, for thy light is come, and the
glory of the Lord is riſen upon thee (a) : "
quoted by the apoſtle, though not verbatim, yet
according to the ſenſe ; while others apprehend
the alluſion is not ſo much to any particular
paſſage, as to the general and principal deſign
of the ſacred oracles, which evidently is, to a-
waken, convert and ſave ſinners.

It is an ingenious conjecture of Heuman-
nus *, that this paſſage is taken out of one of
thoſe hymns, or ſpiritual ſongs, which were
in common uſe in the chriſtian church in thoſe
times, and which are mentioned by the apoſtle
in a ſubſequent paſſage, ' " Speaking to yourſelves in pſalms and hymns and ſpiritual
ſongs (b)." This author obſerves, that it conſiſts of three metrical lines,

$$\text{Εγειραι ο καθευδων,}$$
$$\text{Και αναϛα εκ των νεκρων,}$$
$$\text{Και επιφαυϲει ϲοι ο Χριϲος.}$$

As for διο λεγει, he makes it to be the ſame
with διο λεγεται, " wherefore it is ſaid (c)." But,
on ſuppoſition that theſe lines were taken out
of ſome hymns or ſpiritual ſongs, known to
have been compoſed by inſpiration, I ſhould
rather

(a) Iſa. lx. 1.
* Poeciles tom. 2. lib. ii. p. 390. as cited by Wolfius,
Curæ philologicæ in loc.
(b) Epheſ. v. 19.   (c) As in Rom. xv. 10.

rather think the nominative caſe to λεγει may be Θεος, or πνευμα αγιον.   To return to the ſubject we are upon.

It may be further objected to Maimonides and ſome other Jews, who conceive the deſign of blowing the trumpets was to awaken men to repentance, that זכרון תרועה zickron terungnah, which we render " a memorial of blowing the trumpets (a)," properly ſignifies a memorial of triumph, or ſhouting for joy; for, as Dr. Patrick obſerves *, the word תרועה terungnah, is never uſed in ſcripture but for a ſound or ſhout of rejoicing, as the chaldee יבבא jabbaba, by which Onkelos renders it, always ſignifies†.

Other Jews, therefore, make the blowing of the trumpet to be a memorial of Iſaac's deliverance by means of the ram, which was ſubſtituted to be ſacrificed in his ſtead.   Accordingly they ſay, the trumpets blown on this day muſt be made of rams horns; and ſuch are thoſe which the modern Jews blow in their ſynagogues ‡.

They ſound the horn thirty times, ſometimes ſlow; and ſometimes quick.   If the trumpeter ſounds it clear and well, they reckon it a preſage of a happy year; if otherwiſe, they expreſs their concern by the ſadneſs of their countenances, eſteeming it an unfavourable omen. When he hath done, the people repeat theſe words loudly and diſtinctly §, " Bleſſed is the people that know the joyful ſound; they ſhall walk, O Lord, in the light of thy countenance (b). And when they return from the ſynagogue,
their

(a) Levit. xxiii. 24.   * Patrick on Numb. xxix. 1.
† See Chaldee Paraphraſe on Numb. xxix. 1.
‡ Abarbanel in Levit. xxiii. 24.   § Buxtorf. Synag.
Judaic. cap. xxiv. p. 502.   (b) Pſal. lxxxix. 15.

their ſalutation to one another is, " Mayeſt thou be written in a good year ;" the reply, " And thou alſo *."

Some of the chriſtian fathers, particularly Baſil † and Theodoret ‡, make the ſounding of the trumpets on this day, to be a memorial of the giving of the law at mount Sinai, which was attended with the ſound of a trumpet (a). But the opinion, more generally embraced both by Jews and Chriſtians, is, that it was a memorial of the creation of the world, at which the " ſons of God ſhouted for joy (b) ;" and which is ſuppoſed, not altogether without reaſon, to have been at this ſeaſon of the year. The month Tiſri, therefore, was not only anciently, but is ſtill, reckoned by the Jews the firſt month of the year ; and the feaſt of tabernacles, which was kept in this month, was ſaid to be תקופת השנה tekuphath haſhanah (c). which we render, " at the end," but in the margin more truly, " at the revolution of the year ;" importing, that at this ſeaſon the year had revolved, and was beginning anew. So that the feaſt of trumpets was indeed the new years day, on which the people were ſolemnly called to rejoice in a grateful remembrance of all God's benefits to them through the laſt year, which might be intended by blowing the trumpets ; as well as to implore his bleſſing upon them for the enſuing year, which was partly the intention of the ſacrifices on this day offered.

The modern Jews have a notion, which they derive from the miſhna §, that on this day God

judges

---

* Buxtorf. p. 497, 498.   † Baſil. in Pſal. lxxxi.

‡ Theodoret. Quæſtiones in Levit. Quæſt. 32.

(a) Exod. xix. 16.   (b) Job xxxviii. 7.   (c) Exod. xxxiv. 22.

§ Miſhn. tit. Roſh haſhanah. cap. 1. §. 2. tom. 1. p. 311.

judges all men, who pafs before him as a flock before the shepherd. Therefore, as Basnage faith, their zealots spend, some a whole month before hand, others four days, and especially the eve of this feast, in confessing their sins, beating their breasts, and some in lashing their bare backs by way of pennance, in order to procure a favourable judgment on this decisive day. He adds, if Christians should be told that they have derived their vigils, their whip-cord discipline, and the merit annexed to them from the Jews, though they would not be pleas-ed, it is neverthelefs probable*.

As for the long account, which Godwin gives us of the tranflation of feasts, it is mere rabbi-nical trifling, without the leaft foundation in the facred oracles, and of confequence, utterly un-worthy our attention†.

---

* See Bafnage's Hiftory of the Jews, book v. chap. xiii. On the Feaft of Trumpets, fee Meyer. de Tempor. et Feftis Diebus Hebræor.

† Vid. Bochart. Hieroz. part. 1. lib. ii. cap. 1. oper. tom. 2. p. 561, 562. Lugd. Bat. 1712.

CHAP. VIII.

Of the day of Expiation.

GODWIN ftiles this day the feaft of expiation, whereas it was altogether a faft, a
day of deep humiliation, and of " afflicting their
fouls (*a*)." Neverthelefs he is fo inconfiftent with
himfelf, that he underftands the faft mentioned
in the account of St. Paul's voyage to Rome (*b*),
to be meant of the day of expiation. It is true
there is no exprefs injunction in the law of Mofes nor any where in the Old Teftament to faft
on this folemnity. But that it was underftood
to be a faft by the Jews, appears from Jofephus * and Philo †, who both ftile this day
νησεια, " the faft." The rabbies commonly
diftinguifh it by the name of צומא רבה tfoma
rabba, the great faft ‡. Tertullian likewife,
                                        fpeak-

(*a*) See an account of the inftitution of this annual folemnity, Levit. xvi. and chap. xxiii. 27,—32.

(*b*) Acts xxvii. 9.

* Jofeph. Antiq. lib. iii. cap. x. §. 3. p. 172.

† Philo de Vitâ Mofis, lib. ii. oper. p. 508. F. edit.
Colon. Allobr. 1613.

‡ Midrafch Ruth. 46. 4. et Echa Rabbati. 80. 1. quoted
by Reland, Antiq. part. iv. cap. vi. §. 1. p. 492.

speaking of the two goats that were offered on this day, faith, jejunio offerebantur, they were offered on the faft *.

As for the faft mentioned in the account of St. Paul's voyage, and concerning which it is faid, that " failing was now dangerous, becaufe the faft was now paft (a)," Caftalio, not being able to conceive what a jewifh faft could have to do with failing, fuppofes there is an error in the greek copy, and that inftead of νηϛειαν, it fhould be νηνεμιαν, which fignifies calm weather; and according to him the meaning is, that failing was now dangerous, becaufe the fine weather, or calm feafon, was now over. However, all the manufcripts and ancient verfions remonftrate againft this emendation; and indeed there is no need of it, to fupport even Caftalio's own fenfe of the paffage; for this jewifh faft being kept on the tenth day of the month Tifri, a little after the autumnal equinox, it is in fact the fame thing to fay, the faft was already paft, or the calm feafon of the year was over.

Before the invention and ufe of the compafs, failing was rarely practifed in the winter months; and it was reckoned very dangerous to put to fea after the autumnal equinox. Hefiod obferves, that at the going down of the pleiades navigation is dangerous†; and the going down of the pleiades, he faith, was in autumn, when after harveft they began to plow‡. Again, speaking of fafe and profperous failing, for which he allots fifty days after the fummer fol-

---

* Tertullian adverfus Judæos, cap. xiv. oper. p. 201. C. edit. Rigalt.

(a) Acts xxvii. 9.

† Hefiod. Opera et Dies, lib. ii. l. 236,—240.

‡ Hefiod. lib. ii. l. 2.

ftice, he admonifhes to make hafte, and get
home before the time of new wine, and the autumnal ftorms, which made the fea difficult and
dangerous *. Philoftratus, in his life of Apollo-
nius Tyaneus †, faith, that at the latter end of
autumn the fea was more unfettled. And Philo
fpeaks of the beginning of autumn as the laft
feafon that was fit for navigation ‡. Thefe tef-
timonies fufficiently demonftrate, that when the
facred hiftorian declares, that " failing was now
dangerous, becaufe the faft was already paft,"
he fpeaks according to the common fenfe and
apprehenfion of thofe times ; and he likewife
afcertains the feafon of the year, when this faft
was kept, to be about, or foon after the autumnal equinox ; which anfwering to the time
of the day of expiation among the Jews, renders it highly probable, that this was the particular faft to which the writer of the Acts refers. As to the objection of Erafmus Schmidius §, that it is improbable thefe alexandrian
mariners fhould denominate the feafons of the
year from jewifh fafts or feftivals, he fhould
have obferved, that the paffage under confideration is not the words of the alexandrian mariners, but of Luke the hiftorian, who was a
Jew by nation, and no doubt therefore, denominated the feafons from fome jewifh faft, according to the cuftom of his country.

Scaliger ‖ conceives the faft here referred to,
was that in the month Tebeth, or the tenth
month,

* Hefiod. lib. ii. l. 281,—295.
† Philoftrat. in vitâ Apollonii. lib. iv. cap. iv. p. 168.
A. edit. Paris. 1608.
‡ Philo. Legat. ad Caium, oper. p. 770. B. edit. Colon.
Allobr. 1613.   § Erafmus Schmidius in loc.
‖ De Emendat. Tempor. cited by Wolfius, Curæ Philo-
log. in Act. xxvii. 9.

month, anfwering to our December or Janua-
ry; which faft is mentioned by the prophet
Zechariah (a), and was kept in memory of Nebuchadnezzar's fitting down before Jerufalem,
to befiege it, on the tenth day of the month (b).
Scaliger has been followed in this opinion, by
feveral others; but is confuted by Hafæus *,
who fhows, that failing was abfolutely difufed,
both by the Romans and Greeks, in the depth
of winter. The Romans fhut up the fea, or
forbad failing from the third of the ides of
November to the fixth of the ides of March,
that is, from November the twenty-fecond to
March the twenty-firft; and it appears by
Theophraftus †, that the Greeks opened the
fea at their Dionyfia, or feaft of Bacchus,
which was kept in March. It is therefore,
altogether improbable, or rather incredible, that
the fhip in which Paul failed, fhould put to fea
foon after the faft of the tenth month. It remains then, that the faft here intended, muft
be the day of expiation, which fell out in our
September or October.

This account from Hafæus will likewife explain the reafon of Paul's and his companions
ftopping three months at Melita, before they
could get a paffage to Italy. " After three
months we departed in a fhip of Alexandria,
which had wintered in the ifle (c)." Now,
fuppofing they firft put to fea at the beginning or middle of October, yet failing flowly,
and much time being fpent before their fhip-

(a) Zech. viii. 19.   (b) 2 Kings xxv. 1.
* See his Difcourfe de Computatione Menfium Paulini
Itineris, in the Bibliotheca Bremenfis, Clafs. 1. p. 17. &
feq.   † Theophraft. Charact. Ethic. cap. iv. alias 3.
(c) Acts xxviii. 11.

wreck (a), probably they did not arrive at Melita till the middle of December; and there they were forced to stay till the sea was opened in the spring, or till the law allowed them to put to sea again, in March.

Upon the whole, as there is great reason to conclude, that the fast which was lately past at the beginning of Paul's voyage, was the day of expiation; we may from hence infer, that this day was kept as a fast by the Jews; though as we before observed, fasting is not expressly enjoined in the mosaick institution; unless it was included, or, as some have thought, directly intended in the words, " Ye shall afflict your souls (b)." This seems to be the meaning of the same expression in the following passage of Isaiah, " Is it such a fast that I have chosen? a day for a man to afflict his soul? is it to bow down his head as a bulrush, and to spread sackcloth and ashes under him? wilt thou call this a fast, and an acceptable day to the Lord (c)?" Among the several external rites here particularly specified, as belonging to a fast, and as carefully observed by the hypocritical Jews, there is nothing said of their abstinence from food, which undoubtedly belonged to a fast, and might naturally have been expected to have been mentioned on this occasion, unless it be intended by the phrase, " afflicting their souls." By the soul we may understand the sensitive part of man, which is afflicted by fasting. Accordingly David saith, that he had " humbled his soul with fasting (d)." The word here translated humbled, is the same which in Leviticus

is

(a) Acts xxvii. 7, 9. (b) Levit. xvi. 29.
(c) Isai. lviii. 5. (d) Psal. xxxv. 13.

is rendered, afflicted. And if by the foul we underftand the rational foul or mind, fome have obferved a natural connection betwixt afflicting the foul with a deep penitential fenfe of fin, and bodily fafting ; inafmuch as great grief never fails to pall the appetite, and incline men to faft ; and therefore " afflicting their fouls" very naturally implies abftinence from food.   Hence, perhaps, the light of nature hath led men to practice fafting, as a proper token and evidence of inward contrition.   Thus the Ninevites, though heathens, proclaimed a faft of ftrict abftinence from food, when they were threatened with fpeedy deftruction (a). We find, indeed, no fcripture example of re-ligious fafting before the inftitution of this an-nual-faft by Mofes ; yet this filence concerning it will by no means prove it was never prac-tifed. But from the time of Mofes the jewifh hiftory abounds with inftances and examples of this fort. After the unexpected defeat before Ai, Jofhua and all the elders of Ifrael conti-nued proftrate before the ark from morning to night (b) ; which muft therefore be without eat-ing.   The fame was practifed by the eleven tribes, upon the defolation which had befallen the tribe of Benjamin : they " wept, and fat there before the Lord, and fafted that day un-till evening (c)."   And again by all the peo-ple at Mizpeh, in token of their repentance for having ferved Baalim and other ftrange gods (d) ; and particularly by David, in hopes of faving the life of the child which he had by Bathfheba (e), and on other occafions, when, as

S 3   he

(a) Jon. iii. 5, 7.   (b) Jofh. vii. 6.   (c) Judg. xx. 26.   (d) 1 Sam. vii. 6.   (e) 2 Sam. xii. 16.

he faith in the before-cited paſſage, he " humbled his ſoul with faſting."

Beſides the annual faſt in the ſeventh month, we read of three others kept by the Jews after their return from the captivity; one in the fourth month, another in the fifth, another in the tenth (a). The later Jews had ſo multiplied them, that they filled almoſt half their kalendar.

According to the rabbies, the faſt we are now ſpeaking of was to be obſerved with extraordinary ſtrictneſs; they mention ſix things in particular, which they were that day to abſtain from, namely, eating, drinking, waſhing, anointing themſelves, wearing ſhoes, at leaſt thoſe made of leather, and the uſe of the marriage bed *.

This faſt being called a ſabbath, and being kept like a ſabbath, by their abſtaining from all ſervile work (b), as probably their other faſts were, might occaſion the error of thoſe heathen writers, who repreſent the Jews as faſting on their weekly ſabbaths. Suetonius cites Octavius ſaying, in an epiſtle to Tiberius, " Ne Judæus quidem, mi Tiberi, tam diligenter ſabbatis jejunium ſervat quam ego hodie ſervavi : a Jew does not obſerve the faſt of his ſabbath ſo carefully, as I have done to day †." And Juſtin ſaith of Moſes, Quo (ſc. ad montem Synæ) ſeptem dierum jejunio per deſerta Arabiæ cum populo ſuo fatigatus, cum tandem
veniſſet

(a) Zech. viii. 19.

* Miſhn. tit. Joma, cap. 8. §. 1. tom. 2. p. 252. Surenhus.

(b) Lev. xvi. 31.

† Sueton. in vit. Octav. cap. lxxvi. p. 473, 474. tom. 1. edit. Pitiſci, Traject. ad Rhen. 1690.

veniſſet, ſeptimum diem, more gentis ſabbatum appellatum, in omne ævum jejunium ſacravit, quoniam illa dies famem illis erroremque finierat: that arriving at mount Sinai, after wandering and faſting in the deſerts of Arabia ſeven days, he conſecrated every ſeventh day, called the ſabbath, for a perpetual faſt, becauſe that day had put a period to their wandering and hunger *.

This annual faſt is called in the hebrew יום הכפרים jom hacchipurim, the day of atonement κατ' ἐξοχην (a), becauſe of the extraordinary expiatory ſacrifices offered thereon, and becauſe the rites, which the law preſcribed to be then uſed, were more eminently typical of the miniſtry of our great high prieſt Jeſus Chriſt, and of the atonement made by him for the ſins of his people, than thoſe which appertained to any other feſtival. And whereas other expiatory ſacrifices atoned for particular ſins, and the ſins of particular perſons, the Jews ſay, the ſacrifices of this day atoned for all the ſins of the foregoing year, and that of the whole nation †. They add likewiſe, that on this day ſatan had no power to do any harm to their nation, as he had on the other three hundred and ſixty four days of the year. Which opinion is abundantly confirmed by the cabbaliſts; for they find that the letters of the word, השטן haſatan, make, according to their gematria, three hundred ſixty and four ‡.

S 4

Several

---

* Juſtin. lib. xxxvi. cap. ii. §. 14. p. 524. edit. Grævii, Lugd. Bat. 1701.

(a) Lev. xxiii. 27.

† Miſhn. tit. Joma, cap 3. §. 8. with reſpect to offences againſt their neighbours, the expiation was on condition the offended perſons were appeaſed. See §. 9.

‡ Buxtorf. Synag. Judaic. cap. xxvi. p. 535. edit. 3.

Several reasons are assigned by the Jews, for God's fixing this annual fast and expiation to the tenth day of the month Tisri. For instance, their tradition saith, this was the day on which Adam repented of his transgression, and God was reconciled to him; and the day also on which Abraham was circumcised; and therefore they were in so particular a manner to repent of and atone for their transgressions of God's covenant, on this day, when they (as being included in their father Abraham) were first taken into covenant with God[*].

Further, the rabbies tell us, this was the day on which Moses came down the last time from the mount, having received the second table from God, with an assurance of his having pardoned their sin of the golden calf; and therefore it was annually to be kept as a day of expiation and plenary remission[†].

It was probably on this last jewish tradition, that Mohammed founded the institution of his annual fast on the month Ramadan, in which he saith, the Coran, was sent down from heaven[‡].

On these jewish traditions we can have no dependance; nor need we be solicitous to discover the reason of God's appointing the tenth of the month Tisri for the day of expiation in preference to any other, since the absolute silence of scripture concerning it is a sufficient indication,

---

[*] Abarbanel in Levit. xxiii. cited by Meyer. de Temporibus & Festis Hebræor. part. 2. cap. xv. §. iii. p. 309, 310. and more fully by Nicolai, Annot. in Cunæum de Republ. Hebræor. lib. ii. cap. iv. not. 1. p. 223, 224. Lugd. Bat. 1703.

[†] Maimon. Moreh Nebhoch. part. iii. cap. xliii.

[‡] Sale's translation of the Coran, chap. 2. p. 21.

indication, that the knowledge of it is of no
importance.

We have only to obferve further concerning
the time of this faft, that it was to be kept
from evening to evening (a) : which expreffion, as it is peculiar to this day, and is not
ufed concerning the weekly fabbath or any o-
ther feftival, the Jews underftand to import
more than a natural day; or that this faft was
to comprehend the evening, or fome of the
latter part, of the ninth day, as well as the
whole tenth. Although, therefore, the tenth
day of the month is appointed for the day of
atonement (b), yet it is faid (c), " ye fhall afflict your fouls in the ninth day at evening."
Accordingly they are faid to have begun this
half an hour before fun fet on the ninth, and
to have continued it till half an hour after fun
fet on the tenth.   So that this fabbath was an
hour longer than any other *. It is therefore
called in the Talmud יומא Joma, the day by
way of eminence, and by the helleniftic jews,
σαββατον σαββατων.

We now proceed to the confideration of thofe
rites, with which the day of expiation was to
be obferved. And here from the rabbies I
might give you a long detail of thofe which
were preparatory, and were ufed for feveral
days before hand; efpecially relating to the
highprieft, who on this day was to perform the
moft folemn part of all his miniftry. They tell
us, that leaving his own houfe, he conftantly re-
fided in an apartment of the temple for a week
before,

(a) Lev. xxiii. 32.   (b) Lev. xxiii. 27.
(c) ver. 32.
* Maimon. de Solennitate expiationum, cap. i. §. vi.
p. 823, 824. Crenii Fafcicul. feptimi.

before, and during every day practised the sacred rites, such as sprinkling the blood of the daily facrifices, burning incenfe, &c. that he might be expert in performing the peculiar duties of his office on the day of expiation. And left after all he fhould be ignorant or unmindful of them, the Sanhedrim fent elders to read the ceremonial to him, to direct him in the service, requisite on this occafion, and to fwear him not to make any alteration it it *. But as Bafnage very juftly obferves, the Talmudifts make no fcruple to invent ceremonies unknown to their fathers † ; we fhall therefore pafs over the rites mentioned by them without any further notice, and attend only to those that are prefcribed in the divine law.

Befides fafting, fpoken of before, this day was to be kept with all the ftrict and religious regard of a fabbath (a), and with offering facrifices, firft, for the highprieft and his family, and then for the people (b).

The victims, offered on this day, including the daily burnt-offerings, were fifteen. The two firft were a bullock and a ram, and were defigned to make atonement for the " highprieft himfelf, and for his houfe ;" by which is probably meant the other priefts, and perhaps the whole tribe of Levi ; for the priefts are
called

---

* Mifhn. tit. Joma, cap. 1. §. 1,—5. p. 206,—209. tom. 2. edit. Surenhufii. Maimon. de Solenni Die Expiationum, cap. i. §. iii,—v. p. 653,—655. Crenii Fafcic. feptimi. See alfo Buxtorf. de Synag. cap. xxv, xxvi.

† Bafnage's hiftory of the Jews, book v. chap. xiii. §. vi. p. 448.

(a) Lev. xxiii. 32. xvi. 29. 　　　　(b) Heb. vii. 27. See an account of thefe facrifices in Lev. xvi. 3, 5, 8. and Numb. xxix. 7,—11.

called "the houſe of Aaron (a)." However, rabbi Jehuda, underſtanding by the highprieſt's houſe chiefly his wife, makes it ſo neceſſary for him to have a wife on this day, that if ſhe died, he muſt marry another; that he might ſatisfy the law, by making expiation for himſelf and his wife. But this opinion is rejected by the other rabbies *.

Of the victims, none are more remarkable than the two goats, which the high-prieſt was to receive from the congregation, and to ſet them before the tabernacle; caſting lots, which of the two ſhould be immediately ſacrificed, and which ſhould be ſent alive into the wilderneſs, after the ſins of the people had been confeſſed over him, and laid as it were upon him. The manner in which theſe lots were caſt, does not appear in ſcripture. But if we may credit the rabbies, there was an urn brought to the high-prieſt, into which he threw two wooden lots, on one of which was written, "For the Lord;" on the other, "For עזאזל gnazazel; the word which we render, the ſcape goat. After he had ſhaken them, he put both his hands into the urn, and brought up the lots, one in each hand; and as the goats ſtood one on each ſide of him, their fate was determined by the lot that came up in the hand next to them. If the right hand brought up the lot for the Lord, they regarded it as a good omen. This, they ſay, fell out through the whole prieſthood of Simeon the Juſt. If the left hand brought up that lot, they accounted it as a bad

---

(a) Pſal. cxv. 10, 12. and cxxxv, 19.

* Miſhn. tit. Joma, cap. 1. §. 1. cum notis Maimon. & Bartenor. in loc. p. 206. tom. 2. edit. Surenhus.

a bad omen, and an indication that God was not pacified *.

The goat, on which the lot fell for life, is called in the Hebrew עזאזל gnazazel (a) : concerning the meaning of which word there are divers opinions. The chief are the three following :

1ft, The moſt common opinion is, · that עזאזל gnazazel is a name given to the goat itſelf, on account of his being let go ; as being derived from עז gnez a goat and אזל azel, abiit, to go away. Thus it is explained by Buxtorf †, and by Paulus Fagius ‡ and many others § ; and ſo it was underſtood by our tranſlators ; who therefore render it a ſcape goat ; the ſeptuagint likewiſe renders it αποπομπαιος, and the vulgate emiſſarius. To this interpretation it is, however, objected, that עז gnaz, ſignifying a ſhe goat, אזל azel, which is the third perſons maſculine, cannot agree with it. Bochart, therefore, derives gnazazel from the Arabick word gnazala, ſignifying to remove or ſeparate ; and underſtands by it a ſeparate place or wilderneſs ‖. But others perceive no occaſion to have recourſe to the Arabick, as with reſpect to compound words ſuch an enallage generis is not uncommon in the Hebrew **.

adly,

* Miſhn. tit. Joma, cap. 3. §. 9. p. 223. tom. 2. & Maimon. de Solenni Die Expiationum, cap. iii. §. i,—iii. p. 665,—668. Crenii Faſcic. Septimi.

(a) Lev. xvi. 8.

† Buxtorf. Lexic. Hebraic. & Chaldaic. in verb.

‡ Fagius in loc. apud Criticos Sacros.

§ Franciſc. Turretine de Veritate Satisfact. Chriſti, part. iii. §. xxiv. p. 141. Genevæ, 1666.

‖ Bochart. Hierozoic. part. 1. lib. ii. cap. liv. p. 653 & ſeq.

** Vid. Witſii Œconom. Fœder. lib. iv. cap. vi. §. liii. p. 506. edit. Leovard. 1677. Mr. Jones, in his M. S. lectures

2dly, The second opinion, espoused by Le Clerc *, is, that gnazazel was the name of a place, either a mountain or cliff, to which the goat was led, and from thence, as the rabbies say, he was cast down and killed †. In favour of this it is alledged, that the words in the sixteenth chapter of Leviticus, "He that let go the goat לעזאזל. langnazazel," cannot be properly rendered any other way than, to gnazazel ; which intimates, that gnazazel must be a place.

To this it is objected, that those who have examined the geography of the holy land, have never been able to point out any place of that name, except in an anonymous writer of very little credit, mentioned by Aben Ezra, who speaks of such a mountain near Mount Sinai, which must have been too far distant, for the
scape

---

lectures on Godwin, observes, that the word עז gnez, seems to be of the epicene gender. Non diffitendum est quidem, inquit ille, quin עז gnez, quam plurimum in scripturis usurpatur in genere fæmineo; sed non inde sequitur quod ea vox nunquam in masculino fuit usurpata ; revera vero potius vox epicena videtur, quæ utrique generi tribui possit, quum pluralem format more masculinorum ; & quod revera ita est ex Gen. xxx. 32, 33. constare videtur; procul dubio enim hircos æque ac capras habuit Labanus, & quamvis ibi Com. 35. usurpantur adjectiva fæminei generis, tamen cap. xxxi. 8. eadem adjectiva de iisdem rebus in masculino usurpantur.

* This is the opinion of R. Bechai, R. Solomon, R. Levi Ben Gerson, Aben Ezra, and other jewish writers, and of Cunæus, Vatablus, Schindler, and other Christians. See Nicolai, Annot. in Cunæum, lib. ii. cap. vi. It is likewise the opinion of Hottinger. See his notes on Godwin.

† Mishn. tit. Joma, cap. 6. §. 6. cum not. Sheringham. tom. 2. p. 243, 244. edit. Surenhus. Targum Jonathan Ben Uziel in Lev. xvi. 10. apud Walton Polyglot. tom. 4. Maimon. de Solenni Die Expiationum, cap. iii. § vii. p. 674. Crenii Fascicul. septimi.

scape-goat to have been conducted thither from Jerusalem. Besides, Moses usually prefixes the word mount to the proper name of any mountain; as Mount Hebor, Mount Geri-zim, &c*.

3dly, The third opinion is that of Spencer †, who is followed by Witsius ‡, Coccejus §, Altingius ‖, Meyer **, and others; that gnazazel was the name of the devil, who was worshipped by the Heathens, and particularly by the Egyptians, in the form of a goat ††. Hence Juvenal saith, of Egypt,

——Nefas illic fœtum jugulare capellæ,

Sat. xv. l. 11.

because there the goat was honoured as a God.

According to this interpretation of gnazazel, it is supposed by some, that both the goats were typical of Christ, that which was sacrificed signifying his death, and the other which was sent to gnazazel, his being exposed to and overcom-

ing

* See Bochart. Hierozoic. part. i. lib. ii. cap. liv. p. 653. Spencer de Legibus, lib. iii. Dissert. viii. cap. i. sect. i. p. 1040.

† Spencer, ubi supra, sect. ii. p. 1041.

‡ Le Œconom. Fœder. lib. iv. cap. vi. §. lxv, lxvi. p. 513. edit. Leovard. 1677. & Ægyptiaca, lib. ii. cap. ix. §. iii. p. 120. Amstel. 1696.

§ Comment. in Heb. ix. 25.

‖ Alting. ad Lev. xvi. oper. tom. 1. p. 82, 83.

** Meyer. de Festis Hebræor. part. ii. cap. xv. §. xvi. p. 315, 316.

†† Herodot. Euterp. cap. 46. p. 106, 107. édit. Gronov. Maimon. Moreh Nebhoch. part. iii cap. xlvi. p. 480. See various testimonies to the same purpose in Bochart. Hieroz. part. i. lib. ii. cap. liii. p. 641. & part. ii. lib. vi. cap. vii. p. 828, 820. compare Lev. xvii. 7. and 2 Chron. xi. 15. in the Hebrew שעירים sengnirim, hirci.

ing the power of the devil.   Dr. Patrick objects
to this opinion, that though it hath been efpoufed
by very great men, it is difficult to conceive,
that, when the other goat was offered to God
on his altar, this fhould be fent among the demons who delighted in defart places.   Nor will
it accord with the hebrew text, which faith,
this goat was for gnazazel, as the other was
for the Lord.   Now furely none will imagine,
that both thefe goats being "fet before," and
prefented to "the Lord," as equally confecrated to him (*a*), he would order one of them
for himfelf, and the other for the devil; efpecially as he foon after exprefsly commanded the
Ifraelites "no more to offer their facrifices unto devils," שעירים fengnirim, Hircis, five Dæ-
monibus hirci-formibus (*b*).   And though Spencer will not allow, that the goat, which, he
faith, was fent to gnazazel, or to the devil,
was to be confidered as a proper facrifice to
him, but only as being delivered into his power, and given up to his difpofal; neverthelefs
as the former goat, upon whom the lot to the
Lord fell, was a facrifice to the Lord, fo the
fame expreffion being ufed concerning the goat
on whom fell the lot to gnazazel, if the word
gnazazel means a demon, it would feem to
imply a facrifice to that demon; but granting
the fending the goat to that demon was not
properly a facrifice, or an act of religious worfhip, it feems however to have been a rite,
which might fo eafily have been interpreted
into an encouragement of demon-worfhip, that
it is very difficult to conceive of it as a divine
inftitution.

Upon

(*a*) Lev. xvi. 10.   (*b*) Lev. xvii. 7.

Upon the whole, though we cannot arrive at abſolute certainty in this matter, the firſt opinion appears moſt probable; and that, as the ſacrifice-goat was typical of the expiation of ſin by the ſacrifice of Chriſt, the ſcape-goat, which was to have the ſins of the people confeſſed over him, and as it were put upon him, and then to be ſent away alive into ſome deſart place, where they would ſee him no more, was intended to ſignify the effect of the expiation, namely, the removing of guilt, inſomuch that it ſhould never more be charged on the once pardoned ſinner *.

The rites attending the publick ſervice of this day were chiefly performed by the high-prieſt, who had more to do on this than any other day of the year, or perhaps all the reſt together. He was to kill and offer the ſacrifices, and ſprinkle their blood with his own hands (a). He was dreſſed, therefore, in a manner ſuitable to this ſervice, with only a ſingle linen veſt and breeches, and with a linen girdle and mitre (b). Theſe the Jews called the white garments, as diſtinguiſhed from the other four, which compleated the pontifical habit, wherein the high-prieſt miniſtred on other occaſions, and which were ſtiled the golden garments, becauſe they had a mixture of gold in them; namely, the blue robe, adorned at the bottom with golden bells and pomegranates;

the

---

* On this ſubject, ſee Friſchmuthi Differt. duæ de Hirco Emiſſario, apud Theſaur. theolog. philolog. tom. 2. p. 914. & ſeq. Deylingii Obſervat. Sacræ, part. i. Obſerv. xviii, de Hirco Emiſſario Chriſti Figurâ, Spencer. de Hirco Emiſſario, apud Leg. Hebræor. lib. iii. Differt. viii. and Bochart. Hieroz. part. i. lib. ii. cap. liv.

(a) Lev. xvi. 11,—15.   (b) ver. 4.

the embroidered ephod with its curious girdle;
the breaſt plate, enriched with jewels ſet in
gold; and the golden fillet or crown upon the
mitre.   Whenever the high-prieſt miniſtred on
other occaſions, he was dreſſed in theſe eight
garments *.   On the day of expiation he wore
only the four which were common to him and
the other prieſts.   Some conceive, this was deſigned as a token of humility, this day being
appointed for the confeſſion of ſins and for repentance.   There was alſo another good reaſon,
why he ſhould on this occaſion be dreſſed like an
ordinary prieſt, becauſe he was to do the work of
one; in killing and offering the ſacrifices, which
being a laborious employment required him to
be thinly clad; and his upper garments to be
laid aſide.   Beſides, as ſome of it was but dirty
work, performing it in theſe veſtments, which
were rich and finely embroidered; would have
been altogether improper.

· The grand peculiarity in the ſervice of this
day, was the high-prieſt's entering into the holy of holies, which was not permitted at any
other time (a).   And as it was his peculiar priviledge thus to draw nearer to God, or to the
tokens of his ſpecial preſence, to the ark; to
the mercy-ſeat and to the ſheckinah, than was
allowed any other mortal, Philo makes him on
this occaſion, to be transformed into ſomewhat
more than man.   To which purpoſe he cites a
paſſage of Leviticus in the following manner,
Οταν---εισιη εις τα αγια των αγιων, ſcilicet ο μεγας
ιερευς, ανθρωπος εκ εσαι εως αν εξελθη.   Quum in-
greſſus fuerit, nempe magnus ſacerdos, in ſanc-

* See theſe garments deſcribed in Exod. xxviii. and a-
bove, vol. 1. book 1. chap. 5. p. 212.—246.
(a) Lev. xvi. 2, &c. compared with Heb. ix. 7.

ta fanctorum, non erit homo, donec egreffus
fuerit *. But this conceit is built on a fad mif-
reprefentation of the paffage, for the words are
thefe, Πας ανθρωπος εκ εςαι εν τη σκηνη, "there
fhall be no man in the tabernacle, when he,"
the high-prieft, "goes in to make an atonement in the holy place (a)."

It is queried, whether on this day the high-
prieft entered more than once into the moft holy place. It fhould feem by the ritual in the
fixteenth chapter of Leviticus, that he muft
do it three or four feveral times; in order to
carry in, firft, the cenfer full of burning coals
in one hand, and the incenfe in the other (b):
Secondly, the blood of the bullock, which was
facrificed for himfelf and his houfe (c): Thirdly, the blood of the goat of the fin-offering
for the people (d): And it may be, fourthly,
as the rabbies fay, to bring out the cenfer and
the pot which contained the incenfe. Thus,
according to them, he entered into the holy of
holies on this one day four feveral times †;
whereas fome chriftian writers, on the contrary,
have afferted, that he entered only once; fuppofing it to be fo declared by the apoftle, when
he faith, "Into the fecond [tabernacle] went
the high-prieft alone once every year (e)." Befides,

---

* Philonis lib. fecund. de Somniis, oper. p. 880. F.
edit. Colon. Allobr. 1613.
  (a) Lev. xvi. 17.   (b) ver. 12.   (c) ver. 14.
(d) ver. 15.
  † Maimonides & Bartenora in Mifhn. tit. Chelim. cap. i.
§. 9. tom. 6. p. 23. & Mifhn. tit. Joma, cap. 5. §. 1. p.
231. §. 3. p. 234. §. 4. p. 235. cap. 8. §. 4. p. 248.
edit. Surenhus. Maimon. de Solenni Die Expiationum,
cap. iv. §. i. p 681. §. ii. p. 682, 683, 686. Crenii Fafcicul. feptimi.
  (e) Heb. ix. 7.

fides, they alledge that if he had entered oftener he would have failed in that particular,
of being what the apoftle reprefents him to be,
a type of Chrift *, " who entered once into
the holy place (a)."

To this it is replied, that the high-prieft
might properly enough be faid to enter in only
once, that is, one day in the year, though he
entered in ever fo many times on that day.   In
like manner all the male Ifraelites are faid to
appear before the Lord, or at the national altar, three times in the year, that is, at three
different feafons, or on the three grand feftivals: But no one would fuppofe, they were
permitted to vifit the temple no more than once
at each of thofe feftivals, efpecially confidering
that two of them lafted each for the fpace of a
week †.

The fervice, performed by the high-prieft in
the inmoft fanctuary, was burning incenfe, and
fprinkling the blood of the facrifices before the
mercy-feat ; which he was to do with his finger
feven times (b).   The fame number of fprink-
lings of the blood of the fin offerings of the
congregation, is required on another occafion (c) ; and likewife of the blood of the red
heifer, which was burnt, in order to make the
water of feparation with its afhes (d).   The
fame rite is prefcribed for the cleanfing of a
leper (e), in dedicating the altar (f), and at the

T 2 confe-

---

* See Wilkens de Functione Pontificis maxim. ad Hebr.
ix. 7. Differt. ii. cap. iii. præfertim à §. x. ad fin. capitis,
p. 763,—765. tom. 2. Thefauri theologico-philolog.
   (a) Heb. ix. 12.
   † Vid. Deylingii Obfervat. Sacræ, part. 2. obferv. xiii.
§. xvi,—xxx. p. 184,—198.
   (b) Lev. xvi. 14.   (c) Lev. iv. 6.   (d) Numb.
xix. 4.   (e) Lev. xiv. 7.   (f) Lev. viii. 11.

confecration of the priefts (a). Some perfons
difcover a great deal of myftery in this number feven, obferving that it is much ufed on
other occafions. Jericho was befieged feven
days, on each of which feven priefts were to
blow with feven trumpets (b). Seven priefts
alfo blew with feven trumpets before the ark,
when David brought it home (c). Naaman is
ordered by the prophet Elifha to wafh himfelf
in Jordan feven times (d). In the book of the
Revelation we read of the feven fpirits of
God (e), of the book with feven feals (f), of
feven angels with trumpets (g), and of feven
phials full of the wrath of God (h). Every
feventh day was the fabbath, every feventh
year was a year of reft unto the land, in which
there was no plowing, or fowing; and feven
times feven years brought the jubilee. Seven
was alfo much regarded in the number of victims offered on extraordinary occafions. Job
offered feven bullocks, and feven rams for his
friends (i). David facrificed the fame number
of victims on occafion of his bringing the ark to
the place he had prepared for it (k). Hezekiah
offered victims by fevens, when he abolifhed
idolatry, and reftored the true religion (l).
Nay, it appears, that the number feven was
highly regarded and thought of great efficacy
in religious actions, not only by the Jews, but
by the Heathens. Balak king of Moab offered, by the direction of Balaam, feven oxen and
feven rams upon feven altars (m). Apuleius
faith,

(a) Exod. xxix. 21. compared with ver. 35.
(b) Jofh. vi.   (c) 1 Chron. xv. 24.   (d) 2 Kings v.
10.   (e) Rev. v. 6.   (f) ver. 1.   (g) Rev viii. 2.
(h) Rev. xv. 7.   (i) Job xlii. 8.   (k) 1 Chron. xv.
26.   (l) 2 Chron. xxix. 21.   (m) Numb. xxiii. 1, 2.

faith, Defirous of purifying myfelf, I wafh in the fea, and dip my head feven times in the waves; the divine Pythagoras having taught, that this number is above all others moft proper in the concerns of religion *.

The high-prieft is ordered to fprinkle the blood eaftward (a); in the appointment of which circumftance likewife fome have difcovered a profound myftery; that whereas the priefts in all the other parts of their fervice turned their faces to the Weft, the high-prieft in performing this chief part of his miniftry difpofed his face towards the Eaft, "as turning his back upon the beggarly elements of this world," and as reprefenting him whofe name is the Eaft; for fo the feptuagint and the vulgate render the hebrew word נמצ Tfemach, in the fixth chapter of Zachariah, "Behold the man whofe name is, as we render it, the branch (b);" but according to the verfions juft mentioned, ανατολη, or Oriens. However, the true reafon of his fprinkling the blood eaftward is evidently, becaufe the mercy-feat before which he was to fprinkle it ftood on the Eaft fide of the holy of holies, the fide by the veil, which parted it from the fanctuary. It is faid, "he fhall fprinkle it upon the mercy-feat, and before the mercy-feat;" by which one would think he fprinkled the mercy-feat itfelf with fome of the blood. But the Jews unanimoufly underftand

T 3   it

---

* Apuleius de Afino aureo, lib. xi. ab init. Thofe who would fee more concerning the number, feven, and its fuppofed myfteries, may read St. Jerom on Amos v. 3. and Philo de Opificio Mundi, oper. p. 15,—21. de Legis Allegor. lib. 1. p. 31,—33. de Decalago, oper. p. 585, 586. edit. Colon. Allobr. p. 1613.

(a) Lev. xvi. 14.   (b) Zech. vi. 12.

it otherwife; and indeed עַל־פְּנֵי gnal-penè, which we render, " upon," may as well be tranſlated, "' towards ;" or, as we expreſs it, " over againſt the face of the mercy-ſeat." The difference betwixt עַל־פְּנֵי gnal-penè and לִפְנֵי lippenè, which we render, " upon," and " before," is only this, that the former ſignifies towards the top, and the latter towards the lower part of the mercy-ſeat *.

The rabbies repreſent the high-prieſt as waſhing himſelf all over, and changing his dreſs ſeveral times, during the ſervice of this day, ſometimes wearing the white and ſometimes the golden veſtments †.

As to the ſpiritual or evangelical meaning of theſe rites, the apoſtle hath very particularly explained them in the ninth chapter of the epiſtle to the Hebrews. As the high-prieſt was a type of Chriſt, his laying aſide thoſe veſtments which were " made for glory and for beauty (a)", and appearing only in his white garments, might ſignify our Lord's ſtate of humiliation, when he " laid aſide the glory which he had with the father before the world was," and " was made in faſhion as a man."

The expiatory ſacrifices, offered by the high-prieſt, were typical of the true expiation which Chriſt made for the ſins of his people by the ſacrifice of himſelf; and the prieſt's confeſſing the

* Deylingii obfervat. facræ, part. 2. obferv. xiii. §. xxvi, xxvii. p. 194, 195.
† Vid. Reland. Antiq. part. iv. cap. vi. Miſhn. tit. Joma, cap. 3. §. 3,—7. p. 218,—221. cap. 4. §. 5. p. 230. cap. 8. §. 3, 4. p. 247, 248. tom. 2. Surenhus. Maimon. de Solenni Die Expiationum, cap. ii. §. 1,—vi. p. 658,—662. cap. iv. §. i. p. 678. §. ii. p. 685, 686. Crenii Faſcic. feptimi.
(a) Exod. xxviii. 2.

the fins of the people over, and putting them
upon the head of the fcape-goat (*a*), was a
lively emblem, of the imputation of fin to
Chrift, " who was made fin for us (*b*) ;" for
" the Lord hath laid on him the iniquity of us
all (*c*)."   And the goat's " bearing upon him
all the iniquities of the Jews into a land not
inhabited (*d*)," fignifies the effect of Chrift's facrifice in delivering his people from guilt and
punifhment.   The prieft's entering into the holy of holies with the blood of the facrifice, is
interpreted by the apoftle to be typical of Chrift's
afcenfion, and heavenly interceffion for his people in virtue of the facrifice of his death *.

(*a*) Lev. xvi. 21.   (*b*) 2 Cor. v. 21.   (*c*) Ifa. liii. 6.
(*d*) Lev. xvi. 22.
   * For a more particular account of the fpiritual defign
of the rites attending the fervice of the day of expiation,
fee Witfius de Œconom. Fœderum, lib. iv. cap. vi. §. lviii.
   Concerning the day of expiation, fee the commentators
on the fixteenth chapter of Leviticus, particularly Ainfworth ; Lightfoot's temple fervice, and the mifhnical tract,
Joma, with Sheringham's notes.

C H A P. IX.

Of the fabbatical Year or feventh Year's Reſt.

AMONG the πτωχα ϛοιχεια or beggarly elements, of the jewiſh difpenfation, the apoſtle mentions days, and months, and times, and years (a). For befides the weekly fab-baths, or days of reſt, the law prefcribed the obfervance of the monthly new-moons, and annual feſtival feafons, fuch as the paſſover, pentecoſt, feaſt of tabernacles, &c. which are the καιροι or times, to which the apoſtle refers ; and likewife whole years, to be obſerved with pe-culiar regard after certain returning periods, fuch as every feventh year, called the fabbati-cal year ; and every feven times feventh, ſtiled the jubilee.

It is the former which falls under our pre-fent confideration * ; and in the law of Mofes it is diſtinguiſhed from all others by feveral names. It is fometimes called שנה השבעית
ſhanah

(a) Gal. iv. 9, 10.
* The inſtitution of the fabbatical year is in Exod. xxiii. 10, 11. Lev. xxv. 2,—7. Deut. xv. 1,—18. and xxxi. 10,—13.

fhanah hafhebingnith, the feventh year κατ'
ἐξοχην: fometimes, שבת הארץ fabbath haarets,
the fabbath or reft of the land ; and fometimes
שמטה ליהוה fhemittah Laihovah, the releafe
of the Lord.

The peculiar obferyances of this year were
the four following.

1ft, A total ceffation from all manner of a-
griculture.

2dly, Leaving all the fpontaneous product
of the ground to be ufed and enjoyed in common ; fo that no perfon was to claim any peculiar property.

3dly, The remiffion of all debts from one
Ifraelite to another.

4thly, The publick reading of the law at the
feaft of tabernacles.

Before we confider thefe feveral particulars,
there are two chronological queftions to be
briefly difcuffed.

1ft, From whence the computation of the
fabbatical year commenced ; and

2dly, At what feafon of the year it began.

1ft, It is made a queftion, from whence the
computation of the fabbatical year commenced,
or how foon it began to be obferved by the
Jews.   In the general it was, when they came
into the land of Canaan.   For they received
this command, while they were yet in the wildernefs, " When ye come into the Land, which
I give you, then fhall the land keep a fabbath
to the Lord (a)."   Neverthelefs, it is far from
being fettled, what year after their entrance
into Canaan was obferved, as their firft fabbatical year.   Archbifhop Ufher * determines it

tq

to be the seventh year after the manna ceased,
from which time the Israelites lived upon the
fruits of the land of Canaan (a); and six years
being taken up in the conquest and division of
the land, the seventh proved in all respects a
year of rest, when they peaceably enjoyed the
fruits of their victories, and of the country
they had subdued.

Nevertheless, others observing, that the sabbatical year is enjoined to be observed after six
years of agriculture, " Six years thou shalt
sow thy field, and six years thou shalt prune
thy vineyard, and gather in the fruit thereof,
but in the seventh year shall be a sabbath of rest
unto the land (b):" I say, others for this reason conceive it more probable, that the six
years preceding the sabbatical year, did not
commence till after the conquest and division of
the land. For it is not to be supposed, that
they could apply themselves to agriculture, till
they had actually conquered it, or that they
would do it, till each man's property was af-
signed him. Now the year, in which Joshua
divided the land, may be thus computed: Caleb was forty years old, when Moses sent him
from Kadesh-barnea to spy out the land (c);
and this was in the autumn of the second year
from their exodos, or at the season, when the
grapes, pomegranates and figs were ripe, of
which the spies brought a sample with them (d).
But Caleb was eighty-five years old at the time
of the division of the land (e); it was, therefore, forty-five years since he went as a spy;
to which adding one year and a half before
elapsed

(a) Josh. v. 12.   (b) Lev. xxv. 3, 4.   (c) Josh.
xiv. 7.   (d) Numb. xiii. 23.   (e) Josh. xiv. 10.

elapfed betwixt that time and the exodos, and the divifion of the land will appear to have been made in the forty-feventh year of their departure from Egypt ; from which fubtracting forty years, the time of their wandering in the wildernefs (a), and there remain fix years and an half from their entrance into Canaan to the divifion of the land, which was compleated the latter end of the fummer. Infomuch that every man's property was affigned him againft the enfuing feed time, with which began the fix years that preceded the firft fabbatical year. Probably, therefore, the firft fabbatical year was not kept till the fourteenth year from their entrance into Canaan *.

2dly, The other chronological queftion is, at what feafon the fabbatical year began, whether with the month Nifan in the fpring, or Tifri in autumn; or in other words, whether the fabbatical year was reckoned by the ecclefiaftic, or civil computation.

This queftion, though not exprefsly determined by the mofaick law, is, I apprehend, not very difficult to be decided. That the fabbatical year followed the civil computation, beginning with the month Tifri, may be ftrongly inferred from a paffage in the twenty-fifth chapter of Leviticus (b), where they are commanded to " fow their fields and prune their vineyards, and gather the fruit thereof, for fix years fucceffively, and to let the land reft," or lie fallow, " on the feventh." Doubtlefs therefore the feventh, or fabbatical year began after the harveft and fruits were gathered in,

and

(a) Numb. xiv. 33, 34.
* Maimon. de Anno Sabbatico & Jubilæo, cap. x. §. ii.
(b) Lev. xxv. 3, 4.

and againſt the uſual ſeaſon of ploughing and
ſowing. It muſt then have begun in autumn * ;
for had it begun with the month Niſan, they
muſt have loſt a crop of the laſt year's ſowing, as well as have neglected the ſeed time
for the next year; which is inconſiſtent with
the law in the twenty-third of Exodus (a),
" Six years ſhalt thou ſow thy land, and gather
in the fruits thereof."

We proceed to conſider the particular obſer-
vances of the ſabbatical year. The,

1ſt, is the total ceſſation from all manner of
agriculture. " Thou ſhalt neither ſow thy
field, nor prune thy vineyard (b)." If it be
aſked, what they were to live upon during this
year, the anſwer is,

1ſt, They were allowed to eat whatever the
land and fruit-trees produced ſpontaneouſly,
without ploughing and pruning; only the proprietors of the ground and trees were not to
look upon the product of that year as peculiarly their own, but all was to be in common;
as will be ſhowed under another head. Now
ſome crop would riſe this year from the corn
ſhed in the laſt harveſt, and from what was
ſcattered in winnowing, which they performed
abroad in the fields. But

2dly, The queſtion is beſt anſwered by God
himſelf, " I will command my bleſſing upon
you in the ſixth year, and it ſhall bring forth
fruit for three years (c):" that is, for part of
the ſixth, the whole ſeventh, and part of the
eighth, till harveſt come, reckoning the years
to begin with Niſan. Thus one whole year
and

* Miſhn. Roſh haſhanah, cap. 1. §. 1. p. 300. tom. 2.
(a) Exod. xxiii. 10. (b) Lev. xxv. 4.
(c) Lev. xxv. 21.

and part of two others were called three years ;
as one whole day and part of two others, during which our Saviour laid in the Sepulchre,
are termed three days, and three nights (a),
τρεις ημερας και τρεις νυκτας, which is a hebraifm
of the fame import with the greek word νυχθη-
μερα, or three natural days *.

This divine promife of an extraordinary
blefling on the fixth year is doubtlefs to be
underftood conditionally, on fuppofition of their
obedience to the law of God. When therefore they became negledtful on this head, and
frequently revolted to idolatry, it is reafonable
to fuppofe God, in a great meafure at leaft,
witheld that extraordinary blefling. Whereupon, as one fin frequently leads to another,
they alfo frequently negledted the obfervance
of the fabbatical year. And on that account,
as Mr. Mede obferves, the Lord, agreeably to
what he had foretold and threatned (b), caufed
them to be carried captive, and the land to be
wafte for feventy years, without inhabitant,
till it had fulfilled the years of fabbath which
they obferved not. For their idolatry he gave
them into the hand of their enemies, the Gentiles ; and moreover, for their fabbatical facri-
ledge, he caufed them, not only to be made
captives, but carried away into a ftrange country, and their land lay defolate for feventy
years †. This making profit of their land on
the

(a) Matt. xii. 40.
  * See Reland. Antiq. part. iv. cap. 1. §. xx, xxi. p.
442,—444. edit. 3. Kidder's Demonftration of the Meffias, part. i. chap. viii. p. 104. part. ii. chap. iii. p. 61,
—64. edit. 2. fol. London, 1726.
  (b) Lev. xxvi. 34. compared with 2 Chron. xxxvi. 21.
  † Mede's Diatrib. Difcourfe xxvii. p. 123. of his
works.

the fabbatical year, as well as not remitting
debts upon that year, as the law enjoined them,
was " the iniquity of their covetoufnefs for which
the Lord was wroth with them, and fmote
them (a)." Indeed, after they had been thus
chaftifed for their difobedience, they grew fuperftitioufly fcrupulous, rather than religioufly
obedient, in obferving the fabbatical year.
Neverthelefs it does not appear, God ever renewed the extraordinary bleffing on the fixth
year, which he firft promifed them, and they
had fhamefully forfeited. So that in after-
ages the fabbatical year was always a year of
fcarcity. Hence, when Alexander the great,
by a wonderful providence, was diverted from
his purpofe of deftroying Jerufalem, and on the
contrary, became moft kindly difpofed towards
the Jews, bidding them afk what they had to
defire of him ; they petitioned for an exemption every feventh year from paying tribute,
becaufe, according to their law, they then
neither fowed nor reaped *. Hence alfo our
Saviour, forewarning his difciples of the ap-
proaching calamities of Jerufalem and Judea,
whereby they would be obliged to quit their
habitations and their country, advifes them to
pray that their flight might not be in the winter, nor εν σαββατω (b), which is moft naturally to be underftood of the fabbatical year ;
when provifions being fcarce would make it
doubly inconvenient to be forced to travel and
fojourn among ftrangers.

2dly,

(a) Ifai. lvii. 17.
* Jofeph. Antiq. lib. xi. cap. viii. or Prideaux's Connect. part. i. book vii. fub A. ante Chrift. 332.
(b) Matt. xxiv. 20.

2dly, Another obſervance, belonging to the ſabbatical year, was leaving the ſpontaneous product of the fields and fruits-trees to be uſed and enjoyed in common ; ſo that no perſons were to claim any peculiar property in them. For, although the product of this year was to be for the poor and the beaſts of the field (*a*), yet the proprietors of the fields and vineyards were not excluded from ſharing it in common with others ; as appears from the following paſſage, " The ſabbath of the land ſhall be meat for you, for thee and for thy ſervant (*b*) :" where the word ſabbath means the fruit that grew on the ſabbatical year; as elſewhere (*c*), the ſabbaths of the Lord ſignify the ſacrifices offered on the ſabbath days.

On this year, therefore, the whole land was one common field, in which none were conſidered as having any diſtinct property, but every rich and poor Iſraelite, and foreigner who happened to be in the country, nay, men and beaſts were fellow commoners. So that, as Maimonides ſaith, whoever lock'd up his vineyard, or hedged in his field on the ſeventh year, broke a commandment; and ſo likewiſe, if he gathered in all his fruits into his houſe. On the contrary, all was to be free, and every man's hand alike in all places *.

Since beaſts are mentioned in the law as fellow commoners with men, the Jews, according to Maimonides, were over careful, that they ſhould have an equal ſhare with themſelves. So that when there was no longer any fruit for the beaſts of the field, they would not eat of what they

(*a*) Exod. xxiii. 11.   (*b*) Lev. xxv. 6, 7.   (*c*) Lev. xxiii. 38.
* Maimon. de Anno Sabbatic, & Jubilæo, cap. iv. §. 24.

they had gathered for themſelves, but threw it
out of their houſes *.

3dly, The next obſervance, attending the
ſabbatical year, was the remiſſion of all debts
from one Iſraelite to another (*a*). The rabbies
have deviſed ſuch a number of exceptions to
this law, as in a manner wholly to defeat it.
They ſay, for inſtance, he that lends upon a
pawn, is not bound to releaſe ; that mulcts, or
fines for defaming a man, &c. are not to be releaſed ; that if a man was caſt at law in a certain ſum to be paid to another, it was not to
be releaſed ; and that if a man lent money on
the expreſs condition that the debt ſhould not
be releaſed on the ſabbatical year, he was not
bound to releaſe it †.

Some of them will have the releaſe to ſignify no more, than that the debt ſhould not be
claimed in that year ; but that after the expira-
tion of it, it might be demanded ‡. Thus
they make void the commandment of God by
their traditions ; for the law ſeems plainly to
require an abſolute diſcharge of all debts from
one Iſraelite to another, though it did not extend to debts owing them by foreigners or
heathens. The only point in this law, which
can well bear diſpute, is, at what time the
diſcharge was to be given to the debtor, whether at the beginning or at the end of the year.
Maimonides § underſtands, that it was not to
be given till the end ; becauſe it is ſaid, " At
                                                 the

---

* Maimon. ubi ſupra, cap. vii.
(*a*) Deut. xv. 1,—3.
† Miſhn. tit. Shebingnith, cap. 10. præſertim, § 2,—4.
p. 195, 196. tom. 1.
‡ Maimon. de Anno ſabbat. cap. 9.
§. Maimon. de Anno ſabbatic. & Jubilæo, cap. 9. §. 4.

the end of every feventh year ye fhall make a releafe (*a*)." Others conceive, I apprehend on jufter grounds, that the releafe took place at the beginning, or that the debtor was freed from his obligation as foon as the fabbatical year commenced. For in a parallel cafe, the releafe of a hebrew fervant, we find this phrafe, " at the end of feven years," means in the feventh year, as foon as the fix years fervice was compleated (*b*). " At the end of feven years let ye go, every man, his brother, an Hebrew, which hath been fold unto thee; and when, he hath ferved thee fix years, thou fhalt let him go free from thee."

The whole feventh year, then, is called the end of the feven years, as being the laft of the week of years; in like manner, as we call the whole Saturday the end of the week.

Some alfo refer to the fabbatical year the releafe of the hebrew fervants, or flaves; who had liberty to go out free on the feventh year. But in that cafe, the feventh year feems rather to mean the feventh from the beginning of their fervitude *; becaufe it is faid, " If thou buy an hebrew fervant, fix years he fhall ferve you, and in the feventh year he fhall go free (*c*)." Again, " When he has ferved thee fix years, then fhalt thou let him go free from thee (*d*)."

The year of manumiffion could not therefore be the fabbatical year, unlefs the fervitude commenced immediately after the laft fabbatical year. Although, therefore, the mention of

---

(*a*) Deut. xv. 1.

(*b*) See Deut. xv. 12, 18. compared with Jer. xxxiv. 14.

* Maimon. de Servis, cap. ii. §. 2, 3.

(*c*) Exod. xxi. 2.   (*d*) Jer. xxxiv. 14.

the releaſe of hebrew ſervants may ſeem to be introduced in this place a little out of its proper courſe, we ſhall notwithſtanding take this opportunity briefly to comment upon the law concerning them in the twenty firſt chapter of Exodus (a). I would eſpecially remark, that in caſe ſuch a ſervant, or ſlave, ſhould voluntarily renounce his proffered liberty, and chuſe to abide with his old maſter, he was to be brought before the judges, that it might appear he was not forcibly or fraudulently detained againſt the law, but ſtaid with his own conſent (b). Upon which his ear was to be bored with an awl to the door poſt of his maſter's houſe, in token that he was now affixed to his houſe and ſervice for life, or at leaſt till the year of the jubilee. This jewiſh cuſtom was borrowed by other nations; particularly, by the Arabians; as appears from a paſſage of Petronius Arbiter*, where he introduces one Giton expreſſing himſelf in theſe terms, Circumcide nos, ut Judæi videamur; & pertunde aures, ut imitemur Arabes. Juvenal puts the following expreſſions in the mouth of a Libertinus,

——————————————— Quamvis
Natus ad Euphratem, molles quod in aure feа
    neſtræ
Arguerint, licet ipſe negem.
Satyr. 1. l. 104.

It is generally ſuppoſed by the commentators, that the pſalmiſt refers to this rite in the
fourth

(a) Exod. xxi. 1,—6.   (b) ver. 5, 6.
* Petron. Arbitri Satyricon, p. 364. edit. Michael. Hadrian. Amſtel. 1669.

fourth Pfalm, " Sacrifice and offering thou
didſt not deſire; mine ears haſt thou opened (a): Or," as the margin tranſlates the verb
כרית caritha, " My ears haſt thou digged."
But the apoſtle, quoting this paſſage, which
he applies to Chriſt, renders it, σωμα δε κατηρ-
τισω μοι, " a body haſt thou prepared me (b):"
which is a quotation of the apoſtle's from the
Septuagint, though it manifeſtly differs from
the hebrew text; and great uſe hath accordingly been made of it, to prove the authority of
that verſion. It cannot, however, be eaſily
imagined, he would follow the feptuagint in
preference to the hebrew original, when he
was writing to thoſe who were Hebrews, and
would probably object againſt ſuch a citation.
The commentators have endeavoured to ſhow
that the quotation is made κατα διανοιαν though
not κατα λεξιν, according to the ſenſe, though
not according to the letter*.

The learned Mr. Peirce obſerves, that the
authority of the feptuagint, and of an inſpired
apoſtle, ſhould weigh more with us than that
of our preſent hebrew copies, which may have
been corrupted through the miſtake of tran-
ſcribers; and that in this caſe the Hebrew
ſhould be corrected by the Greek. He conjectures, therefore, that the word אזנים ofnaim,
aures, was in the true copy אז־גוף as-guph,
tunc corpus. We have other inſtances of the
like miſtakes of joining two words in one. In
the fifteenth verſe of the third chapter of Iſaiah,
מה לכם mah lachem, quid vobis, as it is in the
Keri, is made one word in the Chetibh, מלכם
mallachem, which fignifies their king; but in
that

(a) Pfal. xl. 6.   (b) Heb. x. 5.
See Whitby, Pool, &c. in loc.

that place it carries no fenfe at all. As for the change of גוף guph, into נים naim, it is not very improbable, confidering the fimilitude of the ג gimel and נ nun, the ' jod and ו vau, and the ף phe, final, and ם mem, final; for if the long ftroke of the ף phe, below the line was obfcure, it might eafily be miftaken for mem claufum.

Indeed the word גוף guph, is not found in the hebrew bible; but we have גופה guphah, the feminine; and גוף guph, is frequently ufed by the rabbies. Perhaps, therefore, it might be an απαξ λεγομενον in the claufe under confideration. However, if that be difliked, we need only read גוה gevah, which the feventy elfewhere render σωμα (a). As for the verb ברה charah, Stockius fhows, its proper meaning is paravit *. So that according to this conjectural criticifm, the claufe is literally rendered, by the feptuagint and by the apoftle, σωμα κατηςτισω μοι, "a body haft thou prepared me."

Dr. Doddridge † brings another folution of the words from monfieur Saurin, who fuppofes, that the feptuagint chofe to explain the phrafe of boring the ear, by that of preparing the body for fervice; as better known to thofe for whom the verfion was intended; and therefore to be preferred alfo by the apoftle, who though he directs this epiftle to the Hebrews, to whom the other cuftom might be well known, yet intended it for general ufe ‡.

We return to the fabbatical year. The

4th,

(a) See Job xx. 25.
* See Stockii Clavis Vet. Teft. in verb.
† Doddridge in loc.
‡ Saurin's Serm. vol. xi. p. 17,—23.

4th, Obfervance, which we mentioned, was the publick reading of the law at the clofe of it at the feaft of tabernacles (*a*) As mens minds were now free from cares by the releafe of their debts, it might be fuppofed they would the better attend to God's law. This, there-fore, was a proper opportunity for the publick reading it to the people.

As for the general reafon, on which the law concerning the fabbatical year was grounded, it was no doubt partly political and civil; to prevent the land from being worn out by continual tilling * : partly religious; to afford the poor and labouring people more leifure one year in feven, to attend to devo-tional exercifes : and partly myftical, typifying that fpiritual reft, which Chrift will give to all who come unto him (*b*). Some, both Jews and Chriftians, make the fabbatical year to be typical of the Millennium. For as the law confecrates the feventh day and the feventh year, they conclude the world will laft fix thoufand years in the ftate in which we now fee it; or, as R. Elias in the Talmud expreffes it, two thoufand years without the law, two thoufand under the law, and two thoufand un-der the Mefliah †. After which comes the grand fabbath of one thoufand years. This no-tion, though it be perhaps without any fuffi-

U 3   cient

(*a*) Deut. xxxi. 10, 11.

* Maimon. Moreh Nebhoch. part. iii. cap. xxxix. Philo de Execrationibus, oper. p. 724, B. C. edit. Colon. Allobr. 1613.

(*b*) Matt. xi. 28.

† Vid. Cocceii Sanhedrim & Maccoth, apud Excerpt. Gemar. Sanhedr. cap. xi. §. xxix. p. 346. edit. Am-ftel 1629.

cient ground, might be improved into an argument ad hominem, to convince the Jews,
that the Meſſiah muſt be already come; ſince
the world is gone far more than half way
through the laſt two thouſand years of the
ſix thouſand, allowed by their tradition for its
continuance; during which period, therefore,
if at all, muſt be the reign of the Meſſiah. *

* See on this ſubject the Commentators on Deut. xv,
particularly Ainſworth. See alſo Reland. Antiq. Hebr.
part. iv. cap. viii. §. xiii,—xvii.

CHAP. X.

The JUBILEE.

THE jubilee was the grand fabbatical year, celebrated after every feven feptenaries of years; namely, every forty-ninth or fifteenth year. This was a year of general releafe, not only of all debts, like the common fabbatical year, but of all flaves; and of all lands and poffeffions which had been fold, or otherwife alienated from the families and tribes to which they originally belonged (a).

The critics are not agreed about the etymology of the word יובל Jobel. Some derive it from Jubal, who was the inventor of mufical inftruments (b); and fuppofe, that this year was named after him, becaufe it is a year of mirth and joy, on which mufick is a common attendant; or, as we fay in Englifh, a jovial time, the word jovial being perhaps a corruption of the hebrew word Jobel; or elfe, becaufe it was ufhered in with the mufical found

U 4 of

of the trumpet through the whole land *. O-
thers, particularly R. David Kimchi, tell us,
that Jobel fignifies a ram in the Arabick;
and that this year was fo called, becaufe it
was proclaimed with trumpets made of rams
horns †. With him the rabbies in general
agree ‡. Bochart, however, is of opinion, there
were never any trumpets made of rams horns,
they being very unfuitable for fuch a purpofe,
and that the phrafe שופרות היבלים fhopheroth
hajjobhelim, which in the fixth chapter of
Jofhua we render trumpets of rams horns (a),
means only fuch trumpets, as were to be ufed
in proclaiming the jubilee; which, it is far
more probable, were made of the horns of
oxen, than of rams §.

Hottinger is of opinion ‖, that Jobel is a
word invented to imitate the found of the inftrument, and that it does not therefore fignify
the trumpet itfelf, but the found it made (b).
Dr. Patrick efpoufes this etymology, and conceives this year was called Jobel from the found
then every where made; as the feaft of the
paffover was ftiled Pefach, from the angel's
paffing over the Ifraelites when he flew the
Egyptians **.

There

---

* See Mafius ad Jofh. vi. 4. apud Criticos Sacros.
† R. D. Kimch. in Lev. xxv.
‡ R. S. Jarchi in Lev. xxv. and the Chaldee Paraphraft
fometimes explains יובל jobel by דיכרא dichra, a ram,
particularly in Jofh. vi. 4.
(a) Jofh. vi. 4.
§ Bochart. Hierozoic. part. i. lib. ii. cap. xliii. oper.
tom. 2. p. 425, 426.
‖ Joh. Hen. Hottinger. Analect. hiftorico-theolog, Differt. iii. & Joh. Hen. Hottinger. jun. Annot. in Godwin.
(b) See Exod. xix. 13. and other places.
** Patrick on Levit. xxv. 10.

There is another opinion, which bids as fair
for probability as any of the former, that Jobel
comes from יבל jabal, in hiphil הביל hobil,
which signifies to recall, restore, bring back,
&c. because this year restored all slaves to their
liberty, and brought back all alienated estates
to the families to which they originally belonged *. Accordingly the septuagint renders
Jobel, αφεσις, a remission (a); and Josephus
saith, it signifies ελευθεριαν, liberty †.

As the learned are not agreed about the etymology of the name, so neither about the year
in which the festival was to be celebrated; whether every forty-ninth, or every fiftieth; and
it is hard to say, which of these opinions hath
the most eminent, or the most numerous advocates. On the former side are Joseph Scali-
ger ‡, Petavius §, Jacobus Capellus ||, Cunæ-
us **, Spanheim ††, Usher ‡‡, Le Clerc §§,
and

---

* Fuller. Miscell. sacr. lib. iv. cap. viii. apud Criticos
Sacros, tom. ix.

(a) Lev. xxv. 10.

† Joseph. Antiq. lib. iii. cap. xii. §. 3. p. 184.

‡ Scaliger de Emendat. Tempor. lib vii. p. 782. D,
Colon. Allobr. 1629. Canon. Isagog. lib. i. p. 55. ad
calcem Thesaur. Tempor. Amstel. 1658. & Animadvers. in
Chronic Eusebii, p. 15.

§. Petav. Rationar. Tempor. part. 2. lib. ii. cap. vii.
p. 87, & seq. edit. Paris 1673. & de Doctrin. Tempor.
lib. ix. cap. xxvii.

|| Jacob: Capell. Histor. Sacr. & exotic. ad A. M. 2549.

** Cunæus de Republ. Hebr. lib. i. cap. vi. p. 54,
& seq.

†† Spanhem. Chronolog. Sacra, part. i. cap. xvi. p. 84,
—86. apud oper. geograph. chronolog. & histor. Lugd.
Bat. 1701.

‡‡ Usser. Annal. A. M. 2609. Jubilæus primus. A. M.
2658. Jubilæus secundus. See p. 24. A. M. 2707. Jubilæus tertius. p. 25. edit. Genev. 1722.

§§ Cleric. in Lev. xxv. 10.

and many others; on the latter, the Jews in
general *, many of the chriftian fathers, and
among the moderns Fagius †, Junius ‡, Hot-
tinger§, Schindler‖, Leidekker **, Leufden ††,
Meyer ‡‡, Calmet §§, &c.

The ground of the former opinion is chiefly
this, that the forty-ninth year being of courfe
a fabbatical year, if the jubilee had been kept
on the fiftieth, the land muft have had two
fabbaths, or muft have lain fallow two years
together, fince all agriculture was forbid on the
jubilee, as well as on the fabbatical year.

Now this is thought an unreafonable fuppofition, fince in all likelihood, without a miracle,
it muft have produced a dearth. If the law,
therefore, had carried any fuch intention,
one might have expected a fpecial promife,
that the forty-eighth year fhould bring forth
fruit for four years, as there was, that the fixth
year fhould bring forth fruit for three.

On the other hand it is alledged, that the
fcripture declares for the fiftieth year (a): "And
ye

---

* See Chaldee Paraphraft on Lev. xxv. Maimon. de
Anno Sabbatico & Jubileo. cap. x. §. vii. R. Menachem,
in Lev. xxv.

† Fagius in Lev. xxv. 10.

‡ Junius & Tremellius in loc.

§ Hottinger Annot. in Godwin. lib. iii. cap. x. §. 1;
Annot. 1. p. 635, 636.

‖ Schindler. Lexic. Pentaglot. in verb. יובל.

** Leidekker. de Republ. Hebræor. lib. v. cap. xiv.
§. iv. p. 323. Amftel. 1704.

†† Leufden. Philolog. hebræo-mixt. Differt. xli. p. 290.
edit. Ultrajecti, 1682.

‡‡ Meyer. de Tempor. & Feft. Hebræor. part. 2. cap.
xviii. §. vii,—xlix. p. 343,—358. edit. 2. Amftel. 1724.
where he confiders the argument at large.

§§ Calmet on the word jubilee.

(a) Lev. xxv. 10, 11.

ye fhall hallow the fiftieth year, and proclaim liberty throught all the land unto all the inhabitants thereof; it fhall be a jubilee unto you, and ye fhall return every man unto his poffeffion, and ye fhall return every man unto his family; a jubilee fhall that fiftieth year be unto you." Befides, if the law had meant, that the forty-ninth fhould be the jubilee, there would have been no need of forbidding fowing, reaping, &c. on the jubilee, becaufe that being the fabbatical year it was forbidden in the preceding law relating to that year (a).

As to the fuppofed dearth, the gentlemen on this fide of the queftion conceive, there could be no danger of that while God protected the nation by a fpecial providence; and efpecially, fince we have an inftance of their living without any harveft for two years together, when the Affyrians had trodden down or fpoiled the crop of one year, and the next was probably a fabbatical year; and yet there was no famine, but they had fufficient to eat of that which grew of itfelf (b).

The authors of the univerfal hiftory have endeavoured to reconcile thefe two opinions; obferving, that as the jubilee began in the firft month of the civil year, which was the feventh of the ecclefiaftical, it might be faid to be either the forty-ninth or fiftieth, according as the one or the other of thefe different computations was followed *.

The jubilee began on the tenth day of the month Tifri, at the evening of the day of atone-

(a) Lev. xxv. 4, 5.	(b) 2 Kings xix. 29.
* Univerfal Hiftory, Hift. of the Jews, book i. chap. vii. Laws relating to the jubilee, not, R.

atonement (*a*). A time, faith Dr. Patrick, very
fitly chosen; for they would be better disposed
to forgive their brethren their debts, when they
had been craving pardon of God for their own.
To which we may add, that when their peace
was made with God by the sacrifices of atonement, it was the proper time to proclaim liberty and joy throughout the land.

The peculiar observances of the jubilee beyond those of the common sabbatical year were
the following,

1st, That it was proclaimed by the sound of
the trumpet throughout the whole land. Maimonides faith, every private man was to blow
with a trumpet, and make a sound nine times *.

2dly, The jubilee was a year of general re-
lease of all slaves and prisoners. Even such as
had voluntarily relinquished their freedom, at
the end of their six years service, and had had
their ears bored in token of perpetual servitude,
were yet set free at the jubilee; for " then they
were to proclaim liberty throughout all the land
to all the inhabitants thereof (*b*)."

3dly, In this year all estates, which had been
sold, were returned back to their former proprietors, or to the families to which they originally belonged; by which means it was provided, that no family should be sunk and ruin-
ed and doomed to perpetual poverty; for the
family estate could not be alienated for longer
than fifty years. The nearer, therefore, the
jubilee was, the less was the value of the pur-
chase of an estate (*c*). This law of the Jews
was

(*a*) Lev. xxv. 9.
* Maimon. de Anno Sabbat. & Jubilæo, cap. 10.
(*b*) Lev. xxv. 10.   (*c*) ver. 15, &c.

was famous among the Heathens, fome of whom copied after it. Diodorus Siculus faith, It was not lawful for the Jews, τυς ιδιος κληρυς πωλειν, to fell their own inheritances * ; and Ariftotle, in his politicks †, faith of the Locrians, that they were prohibited by their laws from felling their antient poffeffions.

The reafon and defign of the law of the jubilee was partly political, and partly typical.

1ft, It was political, to prevent the too great oppreffion of the poor, as well as their being liable to perpetual flavery. By this means the rich were prevented from accumulating lands upon lands, and a kind of equality was preferved through all their families. Never was there any people fo effectually fecured of their liberty and property, as the Ifraelites were; God not only engaging fo to protect thofe invaluable bleffings by his providence, that they fhould not be taken away from them by others; but providing, in a particular manner by this law, that they fhould not be thrown away through their own folly; fince the property, which every man or family had in their dividend of the land of Canaan, could not be fold or any way alienated for above half a century. By this means alfo the diftinction of tribes was preferved, in refpect both to their families and poffeffions; for this law rendered it neceffary for them to keep genealogies of their families, that they might be able, when there was occafion, on the jubilee year to prove their right to the inheritance of their anceftors. By this means it was certainly known, of what tribe and family the Meffias fprung. Upon which

Dr.

* Dicd. Sicul. lib. xl.
† Arift. Politic, lib. ii. cap. 7. See alfo lib. vi. cap. 4.

Dr. Allix obferves, that God did not fuffer them to continue in captivity out of their own land for the fpace of two jubilees, left by that means their genealogies fhould be loft or confounded.

A further civil ufe of the jubilee might be for the readier computation of time. For, as the Greeks computed by Olympiads, the Romans by Luftra, and we by centuries, the Jews probably reckoned by jubilees; and it might, I fay, be one defign of this inftitution to mark out thefe large portions of time for the readier computation of fucceffive years of ages.

2dly, There was alfo a typical defign and ufe of the jubilee; which is pointed out by the prophet Ifaiah when he faith in reference to the Meffiah, "The fpirit of the Lord God is upon me, becaufe the Lord hath anointed me to preach good tydings unto the meek, he hath fent me to bind up the broken hearted, to proclaim liberty to the captives, and the opening of the prifon to them that are bound, to proclaim the acceptable year of the Lord (a)." Where " the acceptable year of the Lord," when " liberty was proclaimed to the captives," and " the opening the prifon to them that were bound," evidently refers to the jubilee; but, in the prophetick fenfe, means the gofpel ftate and difpenfation, which proclaims fpiritual liberty from the bondage of fin and fatan, and the liberty of returning to our own poffeffion, even the heavenly inheritance, to which, having incurred a forfeiture by fin, we had loft all right and claim.

I have only further to obferve, that this jubilee of the Jews hath been in fome fort imitated

tated

_____
,a) Ifa. lxi. 1, 2.

rated by the pope; who, after a certain returning period, proclaims a jubilee, in which he
grants a plenary indulgence to all finners, at
leaft to as many as vifit the churches of St.
Peter and St. Paul at Rome.   The jubilee was
firft eftablifhed by pope Boniface VIII. anno.
1300. and was only to return every hundredth
year; but the firft celebration brought fuch
ftores of wealth to Rome, that Clement VI.
reduced the period to fifty years; afterwards
Urban VI. appointed the jubilee to be held
every thirty-five years; and Sextus IV. brought
it down to twenty-five *.

One of our kings, Edward III. caufed his
birth-day, when he was fifty years of age, but
neither before nor after, to be obferved in the
manner of a jubilee; this he did by releafing
prifoners, pardoning all offences, treafon itfelf
not excepted, and granting many priviledges to
the people †.

---

* See on this fubject, Dieteric. Antiq. Biblicæ, ex Lev.
xxv. 4. p. 220, & feq. edit. Giffæ & Francof. 1671.

† Polydor. Virgil. Hiftor. Anglican. lib. xix. p. 494.
Lugdun. Bat. 1651.

C H A P.

C H.A P. XI.

The Feasts of Purim and of Dedication.

BESIDES the sacred festivals, already considered, no other were appointed by the law of Moses. However, the Jews, in process of time, added several others; two of which are to be the subject of this chapter, namely, the feast of purim, of the occasion and institution of which we have an account in the book of Esther (a); and the feast of dedication, mentioned by the evangelist John (b). They were both of them annual festivals, and observed in commemoration of national mercies and deliverances.

The former, the feast of purim, was instituted by Mordecai to commemorate the deliverance of the Jews from Haman's conspiracy, of which we have an account in the book of Esther. Many suppose, that in this he had a special direction from God, delivered by some prophet, perhaps Haggai, or Malachi. But if so, it is strange that the sanction of divine authority

(a) Esth. ix. 20,—ult.   (b) John x. 22.

thority ſhould not be expreſsly ſtamped on the
inſtitution, and that the name of God ſhould
not be mentioned ſo much as once, in the hiſtory of it or of the events relating to it. Thus
much is certain, it hath had the effect, which
meer human inſtitutions in matters of religion
very commonly have, to occaſion corruption
and licentiouſneſs of manners, rather than to
promote piety and virtue. Though ſtill celebrated by the Jews with great ceremony, it is
a time of general riot and debauchery; and
they make it a ſort of rule of their religion to
drink, till they can no longer diſtinguiſh betwixt the bleſſing of Mordecai and the curſing
of Haman *. Inſomuch that archbiſhop Uſher
very juſtly ſtiles the feaſt of purim the bacchanalia of the Jews †.

This feſtival was to be kept two days ſuccef-
ſively, the fourteenth and fifteenth of the month
Adar (a) In the intercalatory year, therefore,
when there are two adars, it is kept twice
over ‡; the firſt time with leſs ceremony, which
they call the little purim; the ſecond, in the
veadar, with more ceremony, which they term
the great purim §. On both days of the feaſt
the modern Jews read over the Megillah, or
book of Eſther, in their ſynagogues. The
copy there read muſt not be printed, but writ-

* Talmud. cod. Megillah, fol. 7, 2. quoted by Buxtorf.
ſynag. Judaic. cap. xxix. p. 559. edit. 3. in Lexic.
Talmud. ſub voc. כםם p. 324. and by Leuſden. Philolog. Hebræo-mixt. Differt. xl. p. 285. edit. 2. Ultraject. 1682.
† Uſſer. Annales, ſub A. M. 3495. p. 88. edit. Genev. 1722.
(a) Eſth. ix. 21.
‡ Miſhn. tit. Megillah, cap. i. §. 4. tom. 2. p. 389.
§ Buxtorf. Synag. lib. xxix. ſub fin.

ten on vellum in the form of a roll; and the
names of the ten ſons of Haman are written in
it in a peculiar manner, being ranged, they
ſay, like ſo many bodies hanging on a gibbet.
The reader muſt pronounce all theſe names in
one breath. Whenever Haman's name is pronounced, they make a terrible noiſe in the ſynagogue; ſome drum with their feet on the floor,
and the boys have mallets, with which to
knock and make a noiſe*. They prepare themſelves for their carnival by a previous faſt,
which ſhould continue three days in imitation
of Eſther's (a); but, for the generality, they
have reduced it to one day †.

We may here take occaſion to conſider three
queſtions, ſtarted upon the ſtory to which this
feſtival relates.

1ſt, When, and in whoſe reign, the affair
happened, which it is intended to commemorate.

2dly, For what reaſon Mordecai refuſed to
pay that reſpect to Haman, the neglect of
which ſo much incenſed him againſt the Jews.

3dly, Why Haman caſt lots, in order to fix
the day for the maſſacre of the Jews.

1ſt, The firſt queſtion is, when, and in what
king's reign, this affair happened. Though it
was doubtleſs after the kingdom of Judah returned from its captivity, yet the ten tribes ſtill
continued in their diſperſion, from which they
have not been recovered to this day. Accordingly the Jews are ſaid, at that time, to have
been diſperſed through all the provinces of
Ahaſuerus's kingdom, " who reigned from In-
dia

(a) Eſth. iv. 16.
* Buxtorf. Synag. Judaic. cap. xxix. p. 555,—558.
† Hottinger in Godwin. lib. iii. cap. xi. annot. 1. p.
643.

dia even to Ethiopia over one hundred twenty
and feven provinces (a):" But who this Ahafuerus was, is a queftion upon which chronologers are much divided. Ufher * takes him
to be Darius the fon of Hyftafpes, who pro-
moted the building the temple at Jerufalem (b).
Scaliger thinks it was Xerxes, who was Darius's fucceffor †.   J. Capellus ‡ is perfwaded,
this Ahafuerus was Ochus, one of the laft
kings of Perfia; for in his reign Alexander the
great was born, who brought the perfian empire
to its period.   Dr. Patrick, in fupport of this
opinion, obferves, that Ochus's perfian name
was Achafh, to which Verofh being added as
his firname, he was called by the perfians Ach-
af-verofh; which the Greeks tranflated Ahafuerus §.   Rollin ‖ fuppofes him to have been
Cambyfes.   I take the opinion of Prideaux **
to be the moft probable of any, that Ahafuerus was Artaxerxes Longimanus; through
whofe favour to the Jews Ezra and Nehemiah
compleated the reftoration of the kingdom of
Judah, and rebuilt Jerufalem.   It is likely,
his extraordinary kindnefs to that people was
owing to the influence of his queen Efther; it
is particularly remarked, that when Nehemiah

X 2   obtained

(a) Efth. i. 1.   iii. 8.
* Uffer. Annal. A. M. 3483. p. 85.
(b) Ezra vi.
† Scalig. de Emendat. Tempor. p. 585. & feq. præ-
fertim, p. 591,—593.
‡ Hiftor. Sacr. & Exotic. A. M. 3640. & 3650.
§ Patrick on Efth. i. i.
‖ Rollin's ancient hiftory, vol. 2. book 4. chap. 2.
** Prideaux's Connect. part. i. book iv. fub anno ante
Chrift. 465. p. 361,—364. vol. 1. edit. 10. See alfo Cle-
rici Annot. in Efth. i. 1.

obtained his commiſſion to rebuild and fortify
Jeruſalem, the queen was ſitting by (*a*).

As for the name אחשורוש Achaſh-veroſh,
it ſeems rather to have been a title common to
the kings of Media and Perſia, than a proper
name of any of them. It is evidently com-
pounded of the perſic word אחש Achaſh, dig-
nitas, which the rabbies commonly uſe for,
magnus, and ראש roſh, caput, ſummitas,
dux, princeps *. So that Achaſh-veroſh ſignifies magnum caput, five magnus princeps ; and
was, as ſome think, nomen gentilitium, the
name of all their kings, as Pharaoh was of all
the kings of Egypt. Accordingly this name or
title is alſo given, as is commonly thought, to
Cambyſes, in the fourth chapter of Ezra (*b*).
Nevertheleſs it might be given to Artaxerxes
κατ' ἐξοχεν. The

2d. Queſtion is, for what reaſon Mordecai
refuſed to pay that reſpect to Haman, the neglect of which ſo much incenſed him againſt the
Jews (*c*).

This queſtion can be only anſwered conjec-
turally. Some think the reaſon was, becauſe
Haman was an Amalekite; and the Iſraelites
had been commiſſioned from God to deſtroy
that whole nation, becauſe of the injuries they
had formerly done them (*d*). But this hardly
ſeems to be a ſufficient account of Mordecai's
refuſing civil reſpect to Haman, who was firſt
miniſter of ſtate ; eſpecially when by ſo doing
he

(*a*) Nehem. ii. 6.
* Vid. Pfeifferi Exercitationes ad calcem Dubior. Vexa-
tor. Exercitat. iii. de Linguâ Protoplaſt. p. 67. edit. 3.
Lipſiæ.
(*b*) Ezra iv. 6.   (*c*) See Eſth. iii, 1,—6.
(*d*) Deut. xxv. 17,—19.

he expoſed his whole nation to imminent danger. Beſides, if nothing but civil reſpect had been intended to Haman, the king need not have injoined it on his ſervants, after he had made him his firſt miniſter and chief favourite (a); they would have been ready enough to ſhow it on all occaſions. Probably, therefore, the reverence ordered to be paid this great man was a kind of divine honour, ſuch as was ſometimes addreſſed to the perſian monarchs themſelves; which being a ſpecies of idolatry, Mordecai refuſed it for the ſake of a good conſcience. And perhaps it was Haman's underſtanding that his refuſal was the reſult of his jewiſh principles, that was the very thing which determined him to attempt the deſtruction of the Jews in general, knowing they were all of the ſame mind. As to the

3d. Queſtion, why Haman caſt lots, in order to fix the day for the maſſacre of the Jews (b); from whence the feaſt of purim, which is a perſic word and ſignifies lots *, took its name (c); it was no doubt owing to the ſuperſtitious conceit, which antiently prevailed, of ſome days being more fortunate than others for any undertaking; in ſhort, he endeavoured to find out, by this way of divining, what month, and what day of the month, was moſt unfortunate to the Jews, and moſt fortunate for the ſucceſs of his bloody deſign againſt them. It is very remarkable, that while Haman ſought for direction in this affair from

X 3   the

(a) Eſth. iii. 1, 2.   (b) Eſth. iii. 7.
* Vid. Pfeifferi Dubia Vexat. centur. iii. lec. xxix. p. 486, 487. edit. 3. Lipſiæ.
(c) Eſth. ix. 26.

the perſian idols, the God of Iſrael ſo overruled the lot, as to fix the intended maſſacre to
almoſt a year's diſtance, from niſan the firſt
month to adar the laſt of the year; in order
to give time and opportunity to Mordecai and
Eſther to defeat the conſpiracy. Thus much
for the feaſt of purim *.

The feaſt of dedication is in Greek termed
εγκαινια (a), from εγκαινιζω renovo, inſtauro; a
word commonly uſed by the antient chriſtian
writers, for an annual feſtival kept in commemoration of the building of cities, or dedication of churches. Thus Codinus, in his Origines Conſtantinopolis, ſaith, τα εγκαινια της πο-
λεως γεγονε και προσηγορευθη Κωνσταντινωπολις: En-
coenia urbis fuerunt celebrata, & Conſtantinopolis fuit appellata †; and Euſebius, in his
eccleſiaſtical hiſtory, ſpeaks of the εγκαινιαν εορ-
ται ‡, meaning the feaſts of the dedication of
Churches. There is no doubt the εγκαινια,
mentioned by St. John, were celebrated in
commemoration of the dedication of the temple. Now the ſeaſon of the year, when this
feſtival was obſerved, will enable us eaſily to
determine, what dedication of the temple it
muſt refer to. The evangeliſt ſaith, " it was
then winter;" it could not therefore be obſerved in commemoration of the dedication of Solomon's temple; for that was in the ſeventh
month, or autumn (b); nor of the ſecond, or
Zerobabel's

---

* See on this ſubject Schickard. Oratiuncula de Feſto
Purim, apud Criticos ſacros, tom. viii.

(a) John x. 22.

† See Suiceri Theſaur. ad voc. Εγκαινια.

‡ Euſeb. Eccleſ. Hiſt. lib. x. cap. iii. p. 463, 464,
edit. Cantab. 1720.

(b) 1 Kings viii. 2.

Zerobabel's temple ; for that was in the month adar in the ſpring (*a*). The feſtival here intended, muſt, therefore, be that inſtituted by Judas Maccabeus, on his having purified the temple and the altar from the pollution of Antiochus Epiphanes ; which was celebrated for eight days ſucceſſively, in the month chiſſau about the winter ſolſtice (*b*). It is mentioned by Joſephus as a feſtival much regarded in his time *.

The circumſtance of Chriſt's walking in the temple at this feaſt (*c*), is alledged by Doctor Nichols †, Prideaux ‡ and others in favour of the obſervance of ſacred feſtivals of mere human inſtitution ; for though this was ſuch an one, neverthelefs Chriſt honoured it with his preſence. But how will this prove, that our Lord had a more ſacred or religious regard to this feſtival, than it may be proved, he had to the winter, from his walking in the temple at that ſeaſon ? Or if he choſe to come to Jeruſalem and to the temple at that time, when more people frequented the temple ſervice, than ordinarily at any other, the only reaſon might be the opportunity of preaching to greater numbers ; on which account we find the apoſtles likewiſe frequented the ſynagogues upon the

X 4   jewiſh

(*a*) Ezra vi. 15, 16.

(*b*) 1 Macc. iv. 52,—59.

* Antiq. lib. xii. cap. vii. §. 7. p. 617. edit. Havercamp.

(*c*) John x. 23.

† Nicholſii Defenſio Ecclef. Anglican. part. ii. cap. xi. p. 298, 299. Londini, 1707.

‡ Connect. part. ii. book iii. vol. 3. p. 278, 279. edit. 10.

jewiſh ſabbath, even after that inſtitution was abrogated *.

Beſides theſe two feſtivals, we read in ſcripture of ſeveral other feaſts, or faſts, obſerved by the Jews in later ages, though not appointed by the law of Moſes ; as the faſt of the fourth month, on account of the taking of Jeruſalem by the Chaldeans (a) ; of the fifth month, on account of their burning the temple and city (b) ; of the ſeventh month, in memory of the murder of Gedaliah (c) ; and of the tenth month, when the babylonian army began the ſiege of Jeruſalem (d). Theſe faſts are all mentioned together in the eighth chapter of Zechariah (e) ; to which we may perhaps add the feaſt, which Joſephus calls, ξυλοφορια, the feaſt of the wood offering, when the people brought great ſtore of wood to the temple for the uſe of the altar †. This is ſaid to be grounded on the following paſſages in Nehemiah, " We caſt the lots among the prieſts, the Levites, and the people for the wood-offering, to bring it into the houſe of our God, after the houſes of our fathers, at times appointed year by year, to burn upon the altar of the Lord our God, as it is written in the law (f)." Again, " I appointed the wards of the prieſts and the Levites, every one in his buſineſs ; and for the wood-offering at times appointed, and for the firſt fruits (g)."

Beſides

* Vid. Peircii Vindic. Fratrum Diſſent. part iii. cap. xi. p. 381. Londini, 1710 or the Engliſh Tranſlat. part. 3. chap. xi. p. 218. London, 1717.

(a) Jer. lii. 6, 7.   (b) 2 Kings xxv. 8.   (c) ver. 25.
(d) Jer. lii. 4.   (e) Zech. viii. 19.

† Joſeph. de Bell. Judaic. lib. ii. cap. xvii. §. 6. p. 194. Havercamp.

(f) Nehem. x. 34.   (g) Nehem. xiii. 30, 31.

Beſides theſe faſts and feſtivals, the modern jewiſh calendar is crowded with a multitude of others * ; of which, there being no mention of them in ſcripture, it is beſide our purpoſe to take any further notice.

* Vid. Selden. de Synedriis Hebræor. lib. iii. cap. xiii. §. xii.

A P-

APPENDIX,

CONCERNING THE

LANGUAGE

OF THE

JEWS.

APPENDIX,

Concering the

Language of the JEWS.

TO the large account given of the Jews and their religion, chiefly from the facred records of the old Teftament, I fhall now fubjoin a differtation on the languages in which thofe records were written, namely, the Hebrew and the Chaldee. However, as only a fmall part of the later writings are in Chaldee, our chief attention will be paid to the Hebrew. And here we fhall confider

ıft, The antiquity of the language ; and
2dly, The language itfelf.

ıft, As to its antiquity : The Jews are very confident it was the firft and original language, which, they fay, was contrived by God himfelf, and which he infpired Adam with a compleat

pleat

pleat knowledge of *. According;y thofe words, which we tranflate, " Man became a living foul (a)," are rendered in the chaldee paraphrafe of Jonathan, " The breath, breathed into him by God, became in man a fpeaking foul." And to the fame purpofe the paraphrafe of Onkelos. But notwithftanding the confident affertions of the Jews, there are other perfons who have taken the liberty to doubt of this opinion, not only as to the high antiquity of the hebrew language, but as to fuch a divine original of any language at all.

1ft, As to the original of language itfelf. Though the Jews affert, their language was taught to Adam by God himfelf, yet they are not all agreed, how far the divine inftitution reached. Abarbanel fuppofes, God inftructed our firft parents only in the roots and fundamental parts of the tongue, and left the further improvement to themfelves † ; but others, that they received the whole extent and propriety of the language by immediate revelation ‡. The fame opinion hath been embraced by feveral Chriftians, particularly by Eunomius, who becaufe God is introduced by Mofes as fpeaking before the creation of man, maintained that there was in words a certain eternal and immutable nature. But it is difficult to conceive, what connection there can be, for the

moft

---

* Vid. Buxtorf. Differtationes Philologico-theolog. Differt. 1. de Ling. Hebr. orig. & antiquit. §. 17. p. 11,—14. §. 30. p. 20,—23. Bafil. 1662.

(a) Gen. ii. 7.

† Abarbanel in Gen. ii. 19. See Buxtorf. ubi fupra. §. 22. p. 15, 16.

‡ R. Jehudah in libro Cozri & ejus Commentator, R Jehudah Mufcatus. See Buxtorf. ubi fupra, §. 21. p. 14, 15.

moſt part, between ſounds and things, except
what is arbitrary, and fixed by conſent or
cuſtom *. And Gregory Nyſſen expoſes it as
ridiculous and blaſphemous to imagine, God
would turn grammarian, and ſet him down ſub-
tilly to invent names for things †. Dr. Shuckford ‡ conceives, that the original of our ſpeaking was indeed from God; not that he put into Adam's mouth the very ſounds which he
deſigned he ſhould uſe as the names of things;
but only as he made him with the powers of
a man, he had the uſe of an underſtanding to
form notions in his mind of things about him,
and he had power to utter ſounds which ſhould
be to himſelf the names of things, according
as he might think fit to call them. Theſe he
might teach Eve, and in time both of them
teach their children; and thus began and ſpread
the firſt language of the world. Perhaps in
this, as in many other diſputes, the truth may
lie betwixt the extremes. If our firſt parents
had no extraordinary divine aſſiſtance in form-
ing a language, it muſt have been a conſiderable time before they would have been able to
converſe freely together; which would have
been a very great abatement of the pleaſure of
their paradiſaical ſtate. Nevertheleſs, as no
doubt

---

* Etſi homines (inquit Heidegger. Hiſt. Patriarch. tom. 1.
Exercit. xvi. §. iii. p. 443. Amſtel. 1667.) potentiam habeant
ſibi mutuò animi ſui notionem per verba ceu αγγιλες quoſ-
dam νοηματων expromendi, tamen ipſa verba non ſignificare
naturalitèr, hoc eſt per connexionem aliquam naturalem ſeu
ſimilitudinem verborum cum rebus; ſed inveniuntur ex
pacto & placito, vel certè per inſtitutionem & conſuetudi-
nem addiſcuntur.

† Contra Eunom. lib. xii. See Heidegger. Hiſtor. Patriarch. Diſſert. xvi. §. v,—vii. tom. 1.

‡ Shuckford's Connect. vol. i. book ii. p. 111.

doubt God formed them with excellent abilities, it may reasonably be supposed, he left them to exercise those abilities in perfecting a language upon the hints which he had given them *.

But in whatever way the original language was formed,

2dly, In the dispute, which was the original language, other nations have put in their claim, with as much assurance as the Jews. The Armenians alledge, that as the ark rested in their country, Noah and his children must have remained there a considerable time, before the lower and marshy country of Chaldea could be fit to receive them ; and it is therefore reason-- able to suppose, they left their language there, which was probably the very same that Adam spoke.

Some have fancied the Greek the most ancient tongue, because of its extent and copiousness †.

The Teutonic, or that dialect of it which is spoken in the lower Germany and Brabant, hath found a strenuous patron in Geropius Becanus ‡, who endeavours to derive even the Hebrew itself from that tongue.

The pretensions of the Chinese to this honour, have been allowed by several Europeans §. The patrons of this opinion endeavour to support it, partly, by the great antiquity of the Chinese, and their having preserved themselves so many ages, from any considerable mixture

or

* See Heidegger. ubi supra. §. viii, ix.
† Eutych. Annales, p. 50.
‡ See his Origines Antwerpiæ, lib. v. p. 539, & seq.
§ See Webb's Essay towards discovering the primitive language.

or intercourse with other nations. It is a notion advanced by Dr. Allix*, and maintained
by Mr. Whitton with his usual tenacity and
fervor †, that the Chinese are the posterity of
Noah, by his children born after the flood,
and that Fohi, the first king of China, was
Noah.

It is further alledged in favour of the Chinese
language, that confisting of few words, and
those chiefly monosyllables, and having no variety of declensions, conjugations or grammatical rules, it carries strong marks of being the
first and original language. Shuckford faith,
it is so like a first uncultivated essay, that it is
hard to conceive any other tongue to have been
prior to it ; and whether it was itself the original language or not ; in respect to its confisting
of monosyllables, the first language was no
doubt similar to it. For it cannot be conceived,
if men had at first known that plenty of expression which arises from polysyllables, any
people or persons would have been so stupid, as
to reduce their language to words of one syl-
lable only ‡.

As for those which are called the oriental
languages, they have each their partizans ; and
of these the Hebrew and Syriac have most
votes. The generality of eastern writers allow
the preference to the Syriac §, except the Jews,

Vol. II.   Y   who

---

* Reflections on the books of the holy scripture, vol. i.
part. i. chap. xx. p. 112.

† Whiston's Theory, book ii. p. 137 & seq. and his
short view of the chronology, &c. p. 61 & seq. See also
Shuckford's Connection, vo.. i. book i. p. 29. book ii.
p. 98,—104

‡ Shuckford's Connect. vol. i. book ii. p. 123, 124.

§ Theodoret. Quæst. 51. in Gen.

who affert the antiquity of the Hebrew with
the greateft warmth; and with them feveral
chriftian writers agree; particularly, Chryfoftom *, Auftin †, Origen ‡ and Jerom § among
the antients, and among the moderns Bochart ‖,
Heidegger **, Selden ††, and Buxtorf ‡‡.
The chief argument, to prove the Hebrew the
original language, is taken from the names
of perfons mentioned before the confufion of
Babel; which, they fay, are plainly of the hebrew derivation. As אדם Adam, from אדמה.
Adamah, the ground, becaufe God formed
him out of the earth: הוה Eve or Havah,
from היה hajah, vixit, becaufe " fhe was the
mother of all living:" קין Cain from קיה ka-
jah, acquifivit: שת Seth from שות futh, po-
fuit: פלג Peleg from פלג palag, divifit; and
feveral others.

It is faid thefe are plainly hebrew names, and
therefore prove the hebrew language to have
been in ufe when they were given. Befides it
is alledged, the names of fome nations are derived from hebrew names. As Ιωνια, Ionia,
from יון Javan, the fon of Japhet. And fo
likewife, of fome heathen gods; as Vulcan,
which feems to be a corruption of Tubal-Cain;
as

---

* Chryfoftom. Homil. xxx. in Gen. xi. tom. 2. p. 239.

† Auguftin. de Civitat. Dei, lib. xvi. cap. xi, xii.

‡ Origen. Homil. xi. in Numb. xviii.

§ Hieron. in Soph. cap. iii. 18.

‖ Bocharti Phaleg, five Geograph. facr. lib. i. cap. xv.
oper. tom. 1. p. 50, 51. edit. 1712.

** Heidegger. Hiftor. Patriarch. tom 1. Exercitat. xvi.
§. xiv. & feq. tom. 1. p. 455 & feq. Amftel 1667.

†† Selden. de Synedr. lib. ii. cap. ix. §. iii. vol. 1.
tom. 2. p. 1420, 1421.

‡‡ Buxtorf. Differtationes Philologico-theolog. Differt. i.
p. 21 & feq. Bafil. 1662.

as Apollo does of Jubal. But Grotius * and others will not allow this argument to be conclusive, and therefore reply,

1st, There are many more patriarchal names, of which we can find no such hebrew derivation, than there are of which we can ; and it might very likely happen, that among such a multitude of names, some few might answer to the word, which expressed the sense of that original word from whence the name was derived, in whatever language Moses had written. Thus, supposing he had written in Latin, and accordingly translated the name Adam into homo, it would have borne as near a relation to humus, the ground, as it does in the Hebrew to אדמה Adamah.

2dly, We have no reason to conclude the names in the mosaick history were the original names, and not translated by Moses into the language in which he wrote ; since we have a plain instance of such a translation, in his own name ; which, as it was given him by Pharaoh's daughter, an Egyptian, cannot be supposed to have been originally Hebrew ; therefore, not משה Mosheh, as he wrote it, but as it is in the Coptic version Moüsi, from Moü, which in that language signifies water, and si, taken. But Moses, finding the hebrew word משה mosheh, to " draw out," bearing some resemblance in found to his name, and in signification to the occasion of it, translated the Egyptian name Moüsi into the hebrew Mosheh.

3dly, It is said, that several of those names are more pertinently derived from some other of the oriental tongues, than from the Hebrew:

---

* Grotius in Gen. xi. 1.

As Abel, or Hebel, which in Hebrew fignifies
vanity or a vapour, feems not a name very ap-
pofite to Adam's fecond fon; and therefore
Mofes hath affigned no reafon for his being
called by that name. But if it be derived from
the Syriac איל יהב jehab eil, which fignifies,
Deus dedit, it is very proper and expreffive.
So the name Babel, which the hebrew text informs us, was fo called, becaufe God did there
בלל balal, that is, confound the language of
all the earth, may be more naturally derived
from the Syriac; in which tongue Babel, or
Bobeel, fignifies confufion. So that the Syriac,
or perhaps any other of the eaftern tongues,
might be proved by this argument from the
etymology of the names, to have been the original language, as well as the Hebrew.

Le Clerc further advances, that feveral of
thefe names were not the proper names, by
which the perfons were called from their birth;
but cognomina, or firnames, which were given
them afterwards on account of fomething remarkable in their lives; and which an hiftorian
would naturally have tranflated into his own
language. Thus the greek writers fpeak of
Pellufia, a city of Egypt, which was fo called
απο τυ πηλυ, from clay, becaufe it ftood in
clayey ground; yet it can hardly be fuppofed
this was its proper Egyptian name.

Upon the whole Le Clerc's opinion feems to
bid faireft for the truth; that neither the Hebrew, nor Syriac, nor Chaldee, nor any other
language now extant, was the true original
tongue; but that this, and the other oriental
tongues have all fprung from, or are fo many
different dialects of that firft language, itfelf
now loft among them. As the Italian, French
and Spanifh are none of them the language of
the

the ancient Romans, but all derived from
it *.

Having failed in the attempt of tracing up
the hebrew language with any certainty to
Adam, we are now to enquire to what people
or nation it properly belonged after the confusion of Babel.

Those, who are zealous for the high antiquity of the hebrew tongue, tell us, it was preserved, in the midst of that confusion, in the
family of Eber, who, they say, was not con-
cerned in the building of Babel, and confequently did not share in the punishment inflicted
on those that were.

Before we examine this opinion, it may be
no improper digression, to consider briefly the
account we have of that confusion, and of the
origin of different languages in the eleventh
chapter of Genesis ; where we read, that "the
whole earth was of one language, and of one
speech (a)." And again (b) "The Lord said,
Behold the people is one, and they have all one
language." But God said, "Let us go down,
and confound their language, that they may
not understand one another's speech." And
again "The Lord did there confound the lan-
Y 3   guage

* See on this subject Clerici Prolegom. 1. in Pentateuch.
Grotius in Gen. xi. 1. Huetii Demonst. evang. Prop. iv.
cap. xiii. sect. iv. Buxtorf. Dissertat. de Antiquitate Ling.
Hebr. sect. xxvii. Heidegger. Histor. Patriarch. tom. 1.
Exercit. vi. §. x,—xviii. p. 451,—465. Walton Prole-
gom. iii. §. 3,—12. Pfeiffer. Dissert. de Ling. Protoplast.
ad calcem Dub. Vexat. and his Critica Sacra, cap. iii.
Bocharti Phaleg. lib. i. cap. xv. Vitring Observationes,
Dissert. i. cap. i,—v. Father Simon's Critical History,
book 1. chap. 14, 15.

(a) Gen. xi. 1.   (b) ver. 6, 7.

guage of all the earth (*a*)." Now as to the degree of this confufion, and the manner in which it was effected, there is a great diverfity of fentiments.

The modern Jews, as Julius Scaliger informs us *, underftand it not of a multiplication of tongues, but of a confufion of thofe ideas, which they affixed to words. Suppofe, for inftance, one man called for a ftone, another underftood him to mean mortar, having that idea now fixed to the word; another underftood water; and another, fand. But though fuch a different connecting of ideas with the fame words muft needs produce a ftrange confufion among the people, enough to make them defift from their undertaking; neverthelefs this by no means accounts for the diverfity of tongues, which confifts not in the fame words being ufed in different fenfes, but in the ufe of words quite remote, and different from one another.

Others are of opinion that all the confufion, which happened at Babel, was in the people's quarrelling among themfelves, and thereupon bandying into parties, and feparating from each other; which, they fay, is afcribed to God in the fame fenfe, in which it is elfewhere faid, there " is no evil in the city, and the Lord hath not done it;" that is, permitted, and overruled it to the accomplifhment of his own wife and gracious defigns.

As for the different languages now in the world, thefe gentlemen fuppofe, that they all
arofe

(*a*) ver. 9.

* Scalig. Exercitat. in Cardan. 259. fect. 1. cited by Stillingfleet, Origin. Sacr. book iii. chap. v. §. iii. p. 362. edit. 8. 1709.

arose at first from one original language, and
that this variety is no more than must naturally
have happened in so long a course of time;
partly through the difference of climates; which,
it is said, will occasion a difference of pronun-
ciation, and thereby gradually a variation in
languages; and from various other causes,
which are sometimes observed to have so altered the language of some nations, that it hath
hardly been intelligible at the distance of two
or three hundred years. Thus the Salian verses,
composed by Numa, were scarcely understood
by the priests in Quinctilian's time *. Salio-
rum Carmina, saith he, vix sacerdotibus suis
satis intellecta. And we find it no less difficult
to understand the language of our forefathers
three or four centuries ago.

To this hypothesis, that what is commonly
called the confusion of tongues was only a difference of opinions, and the contentions conse-
quent thereupon, it may be objected, that this
does by no means come up to the obvious
meaning of the sacred history, which tells us,
" that God did there," even at Babel, " confound the language of all the earth;" which
before was " one" and the same; implying that
in consequence of this extraordinary procedure
of providence, there was now a diversity of
tongues, which occasioned their " not under-
standing one another's speech:" and likewise,
that several of the present languages are so entirely remote from one another, that with no
reasonable probability can they be supposed to
have sprung from the same original. For

Y 4   though

---

* Quinctil. Institut. Orat. lib. i. cap. vi. p. 45. edit.
Gibson, Oxon. 1693.

though length of time may very much alter a language in its words and phrases, according to the observation of Horace *,

Multa renafcentur, quæ jam cecidere; cadent-
    que,
Quæ nunc funt in honore vocabula, fi volet
    ufus :

Yet what inftance can be produced of meer length of time bringing a whole language out of ufe, and introducing another in the room of it. Befides, the greateft alterations of languages, of which any hiftory, fince that of Babel, informs us, have arifen from the intermixture of people of different languages. Thus the roman language was corrupted and altered by the multitude of foreign flaves, which were kept at Rome. But if all languages had originally fprung from one, fuch an intermixture of the people of different nations muft have tended to prevent the diverfity of language, inftead of promoting it.

    Dr. Shuckford has an hypothefis, I fuppofe, peculiar to himfelf; that the builders of Babel were evidently projectors, and their heads being full of innovations, fome of the leading men among them fet themfelves to invent new words, as particularly polyfyllables, and to fpread them among their companions; from whence in time a different fpeech grew up in one party from that in another, till at length it came to fuch a height, as to caufe them to form different companies, and fo to feparate †.

It

---

* De Arte poeticâ, l. 70.
† Shuckford's Connect. vol. i. book ii. p. 133.

It may be objected to this hypothesis, as well as to the former, that it by no means comes up to the obvious meaning of the sacred history. Besides, Theseus Ambrose * hath started another material objection, that the diversity of languages cannot be supposed to have arisen from choice and contrivance, unless it can be imagined that men would do themselves such a prejudice, as that when they had one common language to represent their conceptions, they should themselves introduce so great an alteration, as would break off that mutual society and converse which even nature itself dictated.

As to what Dr. Shuckford saith, that experience shows, the fear of doing mischief, hath not restrained the projects of ambitious men, it may be replied, that though it may not have restrained them from doing it to others, it surely will restain them from doing it to themselves. And as to what he further alledges, that he sees no detriment arising from the confusion of languages, let experience, and the immense pains men are forced to take in learning foreign languages, which they have occasion for, tell us, whether it be an inconvenience and detriment, or not.

Upon the whole, I can see no reason to depart from the obvious meaning of the historical narrative, which represents the confusion of tongues as the immediate act of God; but think it right to conclude with Calvin, Prodigii loco habenda est linguarum diversitas †.

It

---

* Theseus Ambrof. de caufis mutationis linguarum.
† Calvin. Annot. in Gen. xi. 1, 2.

It would be to little purpose to inquire, in what way and manner these new languages were formed ; for though there are various, they are all uncertain, conjectures about it *.

There is one enquiry more on this head, on which we shall briefly touch ; namely, how many languages arose from the confusion of Babel.

The Jews make them seventy, imagining there were seventy different nations then planted in the world † ; a notion, which they ground on the following passage in Deuteronomy, " When the Most High divided to the nations their inheritance, when he separated the sons of Adam, he set the bounds of the people according to the number of the children of Israel (a)." That is, say they, he divided them into seventy nations, seventy being the number of the children of Israel, when they came into Egypt ‡. Bochart, however, hath given a far more probable sense of this passage, that God so distributed the earth among the several people that were therein, as to reserve, or in his sovereign counsel to appoint, such a part for the Israelites, though they were then unborn, as might prove

a com-

* See Buxtorf. Differt. de Ling. Hebr. confusione, & plurium Linguar. Origine. Vitring. Observat. Differt. i. Stillingfleet's Origines Sacræ, book 3. chap. 5. §. 4. Dr. Wotton's Discourse concerning the confusion of languages, and Dr. Brett's Essay on the same Subject.

† Targum Jonathan in Gen. xi. 7, 8.

(a) Deut. xxxii. 8.

‡ Targum Jonathan. in Deut. xxxii. 8. and R. Bechai, quoted by Buxtorf. apud Differtationes Philologico-theolog. Differt. ii. de Ling. Hebr. Confuf. §. 43. p. 79. where, and in the following pages are many other testimonies to the same purpose.

a commodious fettlement and habitation for them *.

We have no way to determine, how many languages fprung out of the firft confufion. No doubt but their number hath been fince multiplied ; for we have inftances in later ages, of feveral languages growing out of one ; the Italian, French and Spanifh, for .inftance, out of the Latin. And thus probably, feveral eaftern tongues, or dialects arofe out of one ; but whether out of the antediluvian language, or fome other, is by no means certain.

We now return to the enquiry, To what people, after the difperfion of the nations, the hebrew language originally belonged. The opinion of the Jews hath been already mentioned, that it was the language of Heber's family, from which Abraham fprung. But this is gratis dictum, or rather highly improbable ; fince we find Heber's family, in the fourth generation after the difperfion, living in Chaldea, where Abraham was born (a) ; and there is no reafon to think they ufed a different language from their neighbours around them. Now that the Chaldee, and not the Hebrew, was the language of Abraham's country, and of his kindred, appears, in that he fent his fervant to his own country, and to his kindred, to take a wife for his fon Ifaac, namely, Rebekah (b) ; and that Laban, the brother of Rebekah, fpake a different language from the Hebrew, namely, the Chaldee ; for the fame pillar, or heap of ftones, which Jacob called גלעד galgnedh, which

---

* Bocharti Geograph. Sacra, lib. 1. cap. xv. Oper. tom. 1. p. 57. edit. 1712.
(a) Gen. xi. 27, 28.   (b) Gen. xxiv. 4.

which is a hebrew word, Laban calls in his
language יגר שהדותא jegar fahadhutha, which
is pure Chaldee (a). From whence it feems
reafonable to conclude, that Abraham's native
language was Chaldee, and that the Hebrew
was the language of the Canaanites, which
Abraham and his pofterity learnt by dwelling
among them. This Le Clerc hath endeavoured to prove *.

1ft, From the names of places, as well as
men, in the land of Canaan being pure Hebrew. Fuller indeed, in his mifcellanies †,
fuppofes, that Mofes in writing his hiftory
tranflated the canaanitifh names into Hebrew;
which, if well grounded, would entirely deftroy the argument, which he himfelf and o-
thers make ufe of, to prove, that the Hebrew
was the antediluvian language, from the names
of fome of the antient patriarchs being pure
Hebrew. But this does not feem to be the
cafe as to the names of places in Canaan; for
we find, that though the Ifraelites changed the
names of fome of them, yet their old names
were as much Hebrew as their new ones. For
inftance, Mamre, which they changed into
Hebron (b); Kirjath-fepher, which they changed into Debir (c); and Lafhem, which they
changed into Dan (d).

It is further obferved, that the names of the
cities of the Philiftines, who were a part of
the

(a) Gen. xxxi. 46, 47.
* Vid. Clerici Prolegom. 1. in Pentateuch. de Ling.
Hebr.
† Fuller. Mifcell. lib. iv. cap. iv. apud Criticos facros,
tom. ix. p. 2398.
(b) Gen. xiii. 18.   (c) Jofh. xv. 15.   (d) Jofh.
xix. 47.

the Canaanites not fubdued by the Ifraelites, were probably Hebrew; fuch as Gaza, Afhdod, Gath, Ekron, &c.

2dly, Whereas the Egyptians and other neighbouring nations are called " a people of a ftrange language" to the Jews (a), nothing like that is ever faid of the Canaanites.

3dly, If none but Jacob's family had fpoken Hebrew, where could Jofeph have found an interpreter betwixt him and his brethren, when he affected not to underftand Hebrew (b)? Probably this interpreter was fome Canaanite.

4thly, The hebrew language feems to this author, to have been originally formed by Polytheifts, and fuch as worfhipped deified heroes; particularly, from the plural name of God, Elohim; and from thofe metaphorical defcriptions of the divine attributes, which are plainly borrowed from man, as the foul, the ears, the face, the eyes, the hands of God; which metaphors, he fuppofes, would never have been ufed, if the language had been originally formed by people, who had no other notion of God but that of a pure fpirit. It feems to have been originally the language of idolaters.

5thly, He alledges the teftimony of Bochart, who fhows from fome remains of the Phœnician language, that it was originally Hebrew *. Thus the chief magiftrates of the Carthaginians, who were originally Phœnicians, or Canaanites, were called Suffites, which feems to be a corruption of the hebrew word, שפטים Shophetim, judges.

The

The moſt material objeꝗtion I can find a-
gainſt this hypotheſis, is taken from the thir-.
teenth chapter of Nehemiah (*a*), where it is ſaid,
that ſome Jews having married wives of Aſhdod, " their children ſpoke half in the ſpeech
of Aſhdod, and could not ſpeak in the jews
language." Now Aſhdod was one of the cities of the Philiſtines, who were Canaanites ;
from whence, therefore, it ſhould ſeem, that
the jews language, namely, Hebrew, and that
of the Canaanites were not the ſame. But it
may be anſwered.

1ſt, That this was after the captivity, when
the Jews had in a great meaſure loſt the Hebrew. So that by the jews language we may
here rather underſtand Chaldee, than Hebrew.

2dly, That the ſpeech of Aſhdod, perhaps,
might differ from that of the Jews only in pro-
nunciation and dialeꝗt ; as the Ephraimites (*b*)
pronounced differently from the other tribes,
while yet they all ſpoke Hebrew *.

Having thus endeavoured to trace the antiquity of the hebrew language ; we now come
to conſider the language itſelf.

It being common for people to find out pe-.
culiar excellencies in their own language, the
Hebrews have done ſo in theirs ; and many
Chriſtians have joined with them, in beſtowing
high encomiums upon it, as ſuperior to all o-
thers. But whether that be owing to its real
intrinſic excellencies, or to its advocates being
prejudiced in its favour, on account of ſo many

of

(*a*) Nehem. xiii. 24.
(*b*) Judg. xii. 6.
* For proof that the Hebrew was the language of the
Canaanites ſee alſo Joſeph. Scaliger. Epiſt 242. & 362.
Walton. Prolegom. ii. §. 13,—19. Selden. cap. 2. Pro-
legom. de Diis Syris.

of the facred books being written in it, we do not pretend to determine.

This language is faid to abound in the apteft etymologies and roots of the names both of men and things; that in it the names of brutes exprefs their nature and properties, more fignificantly and accurately than in any other known language in the world; that its words are concife, yet expreffive, derived from a fmall number of roots, yet without the ftudied and artificial compofition of the greek and roman languages; that its words follow each other in an eafy and natural order, without intricacy or tranfpofition; and above all, that it hath the happieft and richeft fecundity in its verbs, of any known tongue either antient or modern; which arifes from the variety and fufficiency of its conjugations; by means of which, as Bellarmine obferves in his hebrew grammar, all the variety of fignifications, into which it is poffible for a verb to be branched out, are expreffed, with a very fmall variation either of the points, or of a letter or two; which in any other language cannot be done without circumlocution. In a word, this language is faid to be fo concife, yet fignificant; fo pathetic, yet free from lightnefs or bombaft, as of all others to approach neareft to the language of fpirits, who need no words to convey their ideas to each other.

But whether this language deferves thefe high encomiums, in preference to all others, or not; yet, as God hath thought fit to convey to us fo great a part of his revelations thereby, it certainly concerns us to be well acquainted with it. But it is not my prefent bufinefs to teach it; nor do you need inftruction from me on this head.

All

All I shall further offer with respect to the language itself, will regard the letters in which it is written.

Concerning these there are two controversies; one about the consonants, the other about the vowels, or points.

First, Concerning the consonants. It is disputed, whether the sacred books were originally written in the present Hebrew square character, otherwise called the Assyrian or Chaldee character; or in the old Samaritan. Each side of this question is warmly maintained by different critics; though the latter opinion is now more generally received.

Joseph Scaliger, in his notes upon Eusebius's chronicon *, thinks it so evident, that the sacred books were originally written in the Samaritan character, at least those of them written before the captivity; that he saith, it is luce clarius; and with the usual politeness of a great critic, calls those of the contrary opinion, semi-docti, semi-theologi, semi-homines, and Asini.

He, with others on this side of the question, conceives, the Samaritan was the antient Phœnician character; and constantly used by the jews, till the babylonian captivity; when, learning the Chaldee character from the Babylonians, they preferred it to their own on account of its far superior beauty. So that by the time they returned from the captivity, they had in a manner, quite disused their antient character; for which reason Ezra found it requisite to have the sacred books transcribed into the Chaldee
square

---

* Scalig. Animadversiones in Euseb. Chronic. sub anno 1617. p. 111. See also his epist. 242, & 362.

fquare character, and from that time the old character hath been retained only by the Samaritans.

But there are others, who ftrenuoufly contend for the antiquity of the prefent hebrew letters, as if they, and no others, were the facred character in which the holy fcriptures were originally, and have always been, written; and that the Samaritan was never ufed for that purpofe, except among the Samaritans; who in oppofition, they fay, to the Jews, wrote the law of Mofes, which is faid to be the only part of fcripture they received, in this character, different from that which was ufed by the Jews. Some of the Talmudifts *, indeed, are quoted by father Morin, bifhop Walton † and others, as having declared for the contrary fide. Neverthelefs other talmudical writers maintain the antiquity of the prefent character ‡. And there is a remarkable paffage in the tract Megillah, wherein, on occafion of its having been faid by Mofes, that the tables of the law were written on both their fides, מזה ומזה mizzeh umizzeh, on one fide and on the other (a), we are informed, that the letters were cut through and through fo as to be feen and read on both fides. And when it is afked, how it was poffible for the middle of the ם famech and ם mem claufum, or final mem, to fupport itfelf, the anfwer is, it was fufpended by a miraculous power §.

Vol. II.   Z   Certainly

---

* Vid. Cocceii Excerpt. Gemar. cod. Sanhedr. cap. ii. §. xiii. p. 186.

† Walton. Polyglot. Prolegom. iii. §. 32, 33. p. 21.

‡ Vid Excerpt. Gemar. ubi fupra, p. 186, 187.

(a) Exod. xxxii. 15.

§ Talm. Babylon. cod. Megillah, cap. i. & de Sabbatho, fol. 104. col. 1. See Buxtorf. Differt. Philologico-theolog. Diff. iv. §. 16. p. 174, 175.

Certainly thofe talmudical rabbies, who have
advanced this ftory, did not at all dream of
the Samaritan being the antient Hebrew character; for the Samaritan Samech and Mem are
of a quite different fhape from the prefent Hebrew, and would have ftood in need of no fuch
miracle, to fupport the middle of them. Not
to add, that the Samaritans make no difference
between the final, or the medial and initial letters *.

Buxtorf † endeavours to reconcile thefe two
opinions, by producing a variety of paffages
from the rabbies ‡ to prove, that both thefe
characters were antiently ufed; the prefent
fquare character being that in which the tables
of the law, and the copy depofited in the ark
were written; and the other character being
ufed in the copies of the law which were written for private and common ufe, and in civil
affairs in general; and that after the captivity
Ezra injoined the former to be ufed by the
Jews on all occafions, leaving the latter to the
Samaritans and to apoftates. And whereas the
talmudical rabbies ftile the Hebrew fquare characters אשורית afhurith, fcriptura Affyriaca, this
is faid not to be a proper name, denoting the
country where this character was ufed and from
whence it was borrowed, but to be nomen ap-
pellativum, derived from אשר afhar, beatum
reddere, and to fignify therefore, beata fcriptura,

---

* Univerfal hiftory, book i. chap. vii. concerning the
language, writing and learning of the Jews, note (v.)
† Buxtorf. Differtat. Philolog. theologic. Differt iv. de
Literar. hebraic. genuinâ antiquitate, §. 14, 15, 17, 18,
20, 42,—44.
‡ In particular Maimon. & Bartenor. in Mifhn. tit. Ja-
daim, cap. ult. §. 5. tom. vi. p. 490.

tura, the blessed scripture. R. Gedaliah indeed
supposes, it was called the Assyrian character,
because it was appropriated to sacred, and never
employed for common purposes, before the
captivity in Babylon, from whence it was
brought by the elders, who alone had the
knowledge of it by tradition *. However, a
bare inspection of the two characters renders
the supposition, that both of them should ever
have been used at the same time, somewhat improbable; for whereas the Chaldee is one of
the most beautiful, the Samaritan, on the contrary, is one of the most uncouth, unsightly,
and puzzling characters, that ever was invented; and it can hardly, therefore, be imagined,
that if the Jews had been acquainted with one
so much superior as the Chaldee, they would
ever have used the other, unless out of a superstitious regard to it as sacred, and as deem-
ing it a prophanation to use it in common and
civil concerns. But it can scarcely be believed,
that such an idle and superstitious opinion prevailed among them in the times of Moses and
the prophets.

The chief arguments, on both sides of this
question, are as follow.

1st, Those who argue in favour of the present square character being the original, alledge

1st, The following passage of St. Matthew,
" One jot or tittle shall not pass from the law,
till all be fulfilled (a)." From hence it should
seem, that Jota or Jod, was the least of the
consonants; as indeed it is in the present Hebrew, but in the Samaritan it is one of the

largest

---

* Buxtorf. ubi supra, §. 44. p. 203.
(a) Matt. v. 18.

largeft letters. Schickard calls this argumen-
tum Palmarium *. But bifhop Walton replies,
that, fuppofing Chrift fpeaks here of the leaft
letter of the alphabet, which, however, he does
not admit, all that can be fairly inferred from
it is, that the prefent Chaldee character was
ufed in our Saviour's time; which is not de-
nied by thofe who maintain the Samaritan to be
the original †.

2dly, They alledge the following paffage of
Ifaiah, "Of the increafe, לםרבה lemarbèh, of his
government and peace, there fhall be no end,
&c (a)." where the word לםרבה lemarbèh, hath
a mem claufum in the middle of it, of which
there are only two inftances. It is imagined,
this contains a myftery, and fignifies, that
Chrift fhould come ex utero claufo. But this
myftery cannot be expreffed in the Samaritan
character, it having no mem claufum. The
prophecy of Ifaiah, therefore, it is faid, was
originally written in the prefent character. It
is anfwered, that it is only gratis dictum, there
is any myftery in this letter; and the eafieft
way of accounting for it, is by the carelefsnefs
of fome tranfcriber ‡.

3dly, They argue from the temper of the
Jews, who being an obftinate and fuperftitious
people, would never have fuffered their facred
character to be altered. But this is more than
can be proved, efpecially if it was done by the
direction of Ezra.

4thly,

---

* Vid. Schickard. in Bechinath happerufhim, Difp. v.
p. 82, 83.

† Walton. ubi fupra, §. 36, p. 23.

(a) Ifaiah ix. 7.

‡ Walton. ubi fupra.

4thly, They fay, that Ezra could not do this, if he would; nor would he, if he could. He could not do it, becaufe it was impoffible to make this alteration in all their copies. But it may be afferted as well, that the old Englifh black letter, in which bibles were formerly written and printed, could not be changed for the Roman, which we know is now univerfally ufed. It is further faid, that Ezra would not do it, had it been practicable; for fince he blamed thofe that fpake the language of Afhdod (a), he would not furely prophane the facred writings with a heathen character. But this argument fuppofes fome fanctity in the fhape of the letters, which we can hardly imagine, Ezra was fo fuperftitious as to believe.

5thly, They argue from antient coins found in Judea, with Solomon's head on the face, and the temple on the reverfe, with a legend in the Chaldee or Affyrian character. But thefe medals were probably made by fome knavifh Chriftians, in order to get money by impofing on the pilgrims to the holy land.

The fame may be faid of fome Hebrew infcriptions in the prefent character, upon the fepulchres of the patriarchs, Abraham, Ifaac, Jacob, Rachel and Leah; which R. Benjamin faith, he faw in the year 1170 *.

The arguments on the other fide, for the Samaritan character being the original, are

1ft, From the account in the fecond book of Kings (b), that when the ten tribes were carried captive, and the Samaritans put in their room, they

Z 3

(a) Nehem. xiii. 23.
* Walton ubi fupra, § 35. p. 22. See Conringii Paradoxa de Nummis Hebræorum, cap. v, vi, vii. & xi. apud Crenii Fafcicul. fecundum. (b) 2 Kings xvii. 28.

they were annoyed with lions ; upon which a jewifh prieft was fent to teach them the manner of the God of the land, or the worfhip of Jehovah ; in order to which he muft certainly teach them the law ; but we have no account of his teaching them the language or character ; from whence it is prefumed the law was then written in the character which the Samaritans ufed.

2dly, It is argued in favour of the Samaritan character from the authority of Jerom, who obferveth on occafion of the prophet Ezekiel's being ordered " to fet a mark," in the Hebrew תו tau, " upon the forehead of the men that figh and cry for the abominations done in the midft of Jerufalem (a) ;" that this mark was the fign of the crofs, there being a refemblance of that figure in the Tau of the antient alphabet ; which, faith he, is what the Samaritans now ufe. If fo, the form of this letter muft have been, as fome affert it was, different in his time from what it is at prefent, in which the refemblance is very fmall *.

3dly, The chief argument is taken from the old jewifh fhekel, which on one fide hath the pot of manna ; and on the other, Aaron's miraculous rod that budded ; with a legend on one fide, " The fhekel of Ifrael ;" on the other, " Jerufalem the holy ;" both in Samaritan

tan

(a) Ezek. ix. 4.
* Hieron. in loc. Antiquis, inquit, Hebræorum literis, quibus ufque hodie utuntur Samaritani, extrema litera 'Thau crucis habet fimilitudinem. See Dr. Kennicott's fecond differtation on the ftate of the hebrew text, p. 49, 50. and Hieron. Alexandri. Epift. Jo. Morino, apud Antiquitates Ecclefiæ Orientalis clar. virorum Card. Barbarini, &c. Differtationibus epiftolicis enucleatas, epift. vi. p. 144, 145. Londini, 1682.

tan characters. Some of the fhekels were in the poffeffion of rabbi Mofes Nachmanides, and rabbi Azarias * among the Jews ; and of Montanus †, and Villalpandus ‡, and others among the Chriftians.

Now this fhekel could not belong to the Samaritans after the captivity, whofe hatred to the Jews, would never have fuffered them to ftrike fuch an infcription on their coin, as " Jerufalem hackodefh." It muft, therefore, have belonged to the Jews before the captivity ; which confequently proves, the Samaritan character to have been then in ufe. This argument feems indeed to be demonftration. Neverthelefs, confidering the many notorious impofitions with refpect to coins and medals, we fhould be well affured of the genuinenefs of thefe fhekels §, before we are abfolutely determined by them ‖.

We

---

* Menor Enaim, p. 171. See the paffage apud Ezec. Spanhem. de ufu & præftant. Numifm Differt. 4. p. 334. edit. Amftel. 1671. or in Hottinger de Nummis Oriental. Differt. 3. ad calcem Cippor. Hebr. p. 133,—139. edit. 2. Heidelberg. 1662.

† Ariæ Montani Tubal-Cain, de Siclo, vol. iii. ab init. apud Criticos facros, tom. 8. p. 657. edit. Londin.

‡ Villalpandi Apparatus in Ezekielem.

§ Hottinger maintains the genuinenefs and great antiquity of thefe fhekels, fuppofing at the fame, that the Samaritan character was ufed only for civil and prophane purpofes, and not for writing the holy fcriptures. See his Crippi hebr. Differt. iii. de Nummis Orientalibus. On the other hand Conringius, in his Paradoxa de Nummis Hebræorum, cap. viii. ix. endeavours to prove they were ftruck after the captivity, in the times of the Afmonean princes, and of the Herods : See alfo Reland de Nummis Samaritanis, Differt. i.

‖ See concerning the hebrew letters Ludov. Capell. de Antiq. Literar. Hebraic. Morini Exercitat. in Pentateuch. Samarit. Exerc. ii. cap. iii. §. 4. & feq. Father Simon's Critical Hiftory of the Old Teftament, book i. chap. 13.

We proceed now

2dly, to confider the points, or vowels; concerning which there is likewife no little controverfy; whether they are of the fame antiquity and authority with the confonants, or of a later original. In the beginning of the fixteenth century, the famous Elias Levita, a german jew, ventured to call their antiquity in queftion, and afcribed the invention of them to the Maforites of the fchool of Tiberias, about five hundred years after Chrift. The book, which he publifhed on this fubject, foon raifed him a cloud of adverfaries, both of his own nation and among Chriftians. Of the latter were principally the two Buxtorfs; the father, in his book called Tiberias, five Commentarius Maforeticus; and the fon, in his Tractatus de Punctorum, Vocalium, & Accentuum, in libris Veteris Teftamenti hebraicis, Origine, Antiquitate & authoritate * ; which he wrote in anfwer to Ludovicus Capel, a proteftant divine, and hebrew profeffor at Saumur, who in his Arcanum Punctationis had efpoufed Levita's opinion; as did likewife Jofeph Scaliger †, Morinus ‡, Drufius §, and feveral other criticks.

This controverfy hath employed the learned for upwards of two hundred years,

I fhall

Pfeiferi Critica Sacra, cap. iv. §. 2. Leufden. Philolog. Hebræus; Prideaux's Connect. part. 1. book vi. fub A. 446. and Scaliger, and Buxtorf, and Walton, as beforequoted.
   * See Buxtorf. de Antiquitate Punctor. part. ii. cap. xi.
   † Scaliger. Epift. ad Buxtorf. 243.
   ‡ Morin. Exercitat. Biblicæ, Exercit. vi. & Epift. Buxtorfio apud Antiquitates Ecclefiæ Orientalis, &c. Differtationibus Epiftolicis enucleantas, Epift. lxx. præfertim, p. 368. ad finem.
   § Drufius ad Loca Difficil. Pentateuch. cap. 25.

I shall first give an account of the several Hypotheses, which have been advanced on this subject, and then of the arguments pro and con.

The hypotheses are

1st, That the points are coeval with the consonants, and were written along with them in the original copies of the sacred law.

The second is, that they were added by Ezra, at the time when he is supposed to have changed the old samaritan for the assyrian or chaldee character.

The third is, that they were invented and added by the Maforites of the school of Tiberias; certain jewish grammarians, who devoted themselves to the revisal of the hebrew text, and in order to prevent any future alterations, numbered the sections, words and letters in each book.

The school of Tiberias in Galilee was a very famous one, and flourished long after the destruction of the second temple. The grammarians, or criticks, of that school; commonly called Maforites, are supposed to have invented the points after the completion of the talmud. The Papists generally embrace this hypothesis, because in their opinion, it serves the cause of oral tradition, and hath a tendency to weaken the authority and sufficiency of the sacred text; and for other reasons several Protestants have received it. As for Capel, the most celebrated christian champion for this hypothesis, although he agrees with Elias Levita in ascribing the first addition of the points in the text to the Maforites of Tiberias, he nevertheless differs from him in this, that he makes the invention of them to be purely human, and so represents

reprefents them as of no authority ; whereas
Levita fuppofes the points expreffed the true
and genuine reading, which had been preferved
and handed down by tradition from the firft
writers of the facred books ; fo that in effect
they are of equal authority with the confonants.

There is yet a fourth hypothefis of Dr. Prideaux, who goes a middle way betwixt thofe
who contend for the points being coeval with
the confonants, or at leaft for their being added by Ezra under divine infpiration ; and thofe,
who allow them no higher original, than the
fchool of Tiberias. He conceives they were
added by more antient Maforites, foon after
Ezra, when the Hebrew ceafed to be a living
language ; but did not come into common ufe,
nor were taught in the divinity fchools, till after the compiling of the talmud. There were
antiently two forts of fchools among the Jews,
the fchools of the Maforites, and the fchools of
the rabbies. The former only taught the hebrew language and the reading of the fcriptures
in it ; the latter, the underftanding of the fcriptures, and the traditional interpretation of them.
Now the vowel points, Dr. Prideaux fuppofes,
were in ufe in the fchools of the Maforites feveral ages before they were introduced into the
fchools of the rabbies ; and thus he accounts
for their not being mentioned in the talmud,
nor by the antient chriftian fathers before the
time of the Maforites of Tiberias *.

We now proceed to confider the arguments
for, and againft, thefe different hypothefes.

1ft, For the antiquity and divine authority
of

* Prideaux's Connect. part i. book v. vol. i. p 5 ,—
520. edit. 10.

of the points, whether coeval with the confonants, or added by Ezra.

To prove that they were not invented by the Maforites of Tiberias, it is alledged,

1ft, That there is no mention in any jewifh writer, of fuch an alteration being made in the hebrew bible; which doubtlefs there would have been, had it been fact *.

2dly That all the annotations, or notes of the Maforites, upon the vowels relate to the irregularity of them. For inftance, in their comm. ntaries on the nineteenth chapter of Genefis, and the fecond verfe, they obferve, on the word הִנֵּה hinne, ecce, which ought regularly to have been הִנֵּה hinnè, that every הנה hinne in this fenfe is with kametz parvum, (by which they mean the vowel which we call tzeri,) except only in this place. And in the fixteenth chapter of Genefis, there being in the thirteenth verfe שֵׁם fhèm, which in the fifteenth verfe is שֵׁם fhem, they remark that every שֵׁם fhèm is with a kametz parvum, except fix. Now had the Maforites been the inventors of the points, it is not to be thought they would have made them irregular according to their own judgments ; confequently they muft have had their irregular points in the copies that were before them †. But it is obferved, that though we fhould fuppofe the Maforites of Tiberias invented the points, yet others, perhaps feveral ages afterwards, might make critical remarks upon

---

* Pfeifferi Critica Sacra, cap. iv. Sect. ii. Quæft. ii. p. 83, 84. Lipfiæ, 1712.

† Buxtorf. Tiberias, cap. ix. p. 47. & feq. edit. Bafil. 1665. & Buxtorf. fil. de Punctorum Antiquitate, part. ii, cap. vi. p. 338. & feq.

upon them.   For the Maſorah, as printed in
our preſent bibles, ſaith Dr. Prideaux, is a collection and abridgement of the chief criticiſms
made on the hebrew text from the beginning *.

3dly, There is expreſs mention of the points
or vowels, in books more antient than the
Talmud ; namely, Bahir and Zohar, the firſt
of which is ſaid to have been written a little before our Saviour's time ; and the ſecond, which
quotes and refers to it, not much above a century after †. Buxtorf the elder, quotes the
following paſſage, among others, out of Bahir,
Talia ſunt puncta cum literis legis Moſis qualis
eſt anima vitæ in corpore. But theſe two books
are rejected by Capel ‡, and others, as ſpurious and modern. Prideaux ſaith, there are
many particulars in them, which manifeſtly
prove them to be ſo, and that for above a
thouſand years after the pretended time of their
compoſure, they were never heard of, quoted
or mentioned §.

4thly, That the points were in uſe in our
Saviour's time, and therefore long before the
Maſorites of Tiberias, is argued from the following paſſage of St. Matthew, " One Jota,
or κεραια ;" which we tranſlate Tittle, " ſhall
not paſs from the law (a)." The tittles or
points therefore at that time belonged to the
law

---

* Capelli Arcanum Punctationis, lib. ii. cap. x, xi.
Prideaux's Connect. part. i. book v. vol, 2. p. 504.
edit. 10.

† Buxtorf. Tiberias, cap. ix. §. 3. p. 70. Buxtorf fil.
de Antiq Punctorum, par. i. cap. v. p. 68. & ſeq.

‡ Capell. Arcanum Punctat. lib. ii. cap. iii. & Vindiciæ
Arcani, lib. i. cap. viii. §. 13. & ſeq.

§ Prideaux's Connect. part. i. book v. vol. 2. p. 501,
502. edit. 10.

(a) Matt. v. 18.

law *. But Capel underſtands by the κεραιαι, not the points, but the Corollæ, or flouriſhes, ſometimes made about the hebrew conſonants †.

For the high antiquity of the points, and that they muſt be coeval with the conſonants, it is argued

1ſt, That as it is impoſſible to pronounce the language without vowels, ſo it would be alike impoſſible to teach it, unleſs the vowels were expreſſed ‡. And

2dly, If it be allowed, that the preſent vowel points are not of the ſame authority with the conſonants, but merely of human and late invention, it will greatly weaken the authority of the holy ſcriptures, and leave the ſacred text to an arbitrary and uncertain reading and interpretation §.

It is indeed advanced by the gentlemen on the other ſide of the queſtion, that the Aleph, He, Vau, Jod and Gnain originally ſerved for vowels ‖. To which it is replied, that there are multitudes of words, in which none of theſe letters occur **. And it is certain, they were not in all words in Jerom's time, who in his commentary on Iſaiah ſaith, that the word דבר dhabhar,

---

* Buxtorf. fil. de Punctorum Antiquitate, part ii. cap. xv. p. 435, 436.

† Capelli Arcanum Punctationis, lib. ii. cap. xiv. and Vindiciæ Arcani, lib. ii. cap. xiii. See alſo Marckii Sylloge Diſſertationum, Exercitat. iii.

‡ See Buxtorf. de Punctor. Antiq. par. ii. cap. i. p. 305. & ſeq.

§ Buxtorf. Tiberias, cap. ix. p. 86. & Buxtorf. fil. de Punctor. Antiq. par. ii. cap. xiv. p. 419. & ſeq. Carpzovii Critica Sacra, par. i. cap. v. Sect. vii. p. 243,—248.

‖ Capelli Arcanum Punctationis, lib. i. cap. xviii, xix.

** Buxtorf. de Punctorum Antiq. par. i. cap. xiv. p. 198. & par. ii. cap. viii.

dhabhar, is written with three letters *. But
Capel thinks it reasonable to suppose, that neither Moses nor Ezra would have used the A-
leph, Vau and Jod at all, if they had been the
authors of the points, which render these letters
needless.   And though all words have not these
Matres Lectionis, yet wherever they are wanting, they may easily be supplied in reading,
by those who are skilled in the tongue, as the
persons undoubtedly were, to whom it was a
native language †.   To which some have added, that these letters have been struck out of
many words, in which they were formerly written, as being of no use since the invention of
vowel points.   To this it can only be replied,
If that were the case, many " Jotas must have
perished from the law." Besides, who would
venture to expunge these letters ? Not, surely,
the Maforites ; who were so superstitiously scru-
pulous and exact, as to preserve even the irregularities of the letters.   And having counted
and set down the number of the letters contained in each book, they thereby placed a
guard against its being done by any body after
them.   But notwithstanding all their care ‡,
it is certain, the Matres Lectionis have been
sometimes omitted ; for they are more frequent
in

---

* Hieron. in Isa. iii. 8.
† Capel. Vindiciæ Arcani, lib. ii. cap. vi.
‡ Concerning the inconsistency and imperfection of the
Maforah, and its insufficiency to guard the purity of the
sacred text, see Capelli Critica Sacra, lib. v. cap. xii.
p. 373. & seq. lib. iii. cap. xvi. p. 156, 186. cap. xix.
p. 203. Dr. Kennicott's first Differt. on the hebrew text,
p. 247, 26°. & seq. 297. & seq. 348, 349, 546, 547. Second Differt. p. 245. & seq. 262,—291, 451, 468, 469,
and in some other places.

in some of the older manuscripts, than in later manuscripts, or in the printed text *.

The foregoing arguments for the antiquity of the points are produced, chiefly, by Buxtorf. We come now

2dly, To consider the arguments against the antiquity of the points, by which Capel endeavours to prove, they were added by the Maforites of Tiberias. These are drawn from grammar, from testimony and from history.

1st, The grammatical arguments are built principally upon the Keri and Chethibh. The Chethibh, from כתב chathabh, scripsit, is the reading in the text, the Keri, from קרא kara, legit, the reading in the margin. Generally the wrong one is in the text, and the true in the margin. Some of the more modern rabbies ascribe these marginal corrections, or various readings to Ezra. Abarbanel imputes the Chethibhim, the irregularities and anomalies in the text, to the original writers, who designed to comprize some mysteries in them. Or, he thinks, they might, in some instances, be owing to their inadvertency, or to their want of skill in grammar and orthography; and that Ezra not willing to insert in the text his corrections even of the mistakes of the original writers, contented himself with placing them in the margin. Elias Levita very absurdly maintains, that the various readings themselves were derived by tradition from the original writers †. The first of these opinions is the most plausible, namely that Ezra, in reviewing

the

---

* See Dr. Kennicott's first Differt. on the hebrew text, p. 303.

† Capelli Critica Sacra, lib. iii. cap. xiv.

the different copies, in order to publish a perfect edition, marked the several variations, and put one reading in the text, and the other in the margin. But it is a strong objection to Ezra's having done it, that such marginal readings, different from the text, are found in the book of Ezra itself, who cannot be supposed to have been in doubt of the true reading of his own writings; and therefore they must, at least partly, have been inserted since Ezra's time *.

Further, it should seem that these marginal corrections were not in the copies, from whence either the seventy, the chaldee paraphrast, Aquila, Symmachus, or Theodosian made their versions; since they sometimes follow the Keri, sometimes the Chethibh; whereas had these marginal corrections been in their copies, they would doubtless, ordinarily, if not always, have followed them. Neither Josephus, nor Philo, nor Origen, nor Jerom make any mention of the Keri and the Chethibh; nor does the Mishnah. The Gemara, indeed, mentions those words, which were written but not read, and those which were read but not written, as also obscene words, instead of which were read others that are more pure and chaste. But it does not take notice of the other part of the Keri and Chethibh, namely those words which are written, and read in a different manner. From all this it is concluded, that the Kerioth began to be collected a little before the completion of the Talmud, probably by the Masorites

---

* That the Kerioth were properly a collection of various readings, whoever made the collection, is well proved by Dr. Kennicott, second Differt. on the hebrew text, p. 281. & seq.

forites of Tiberias *. From hence Capel argues againſt the antiquity of the points, en-
deavouring to prove that they have no higher
an original than the Keri and the Chethibh :
and for this he offers the following reaſons,

1ſt, The Kerioth are various lections of the
conſonants only ; there are none of the vowels
or points, as doubtleſs there would have been,
had the points been in the copies from whence
the Kerioth were made †.

2dly, There are certain irregularities in the
punctuation, which ſhow that the points were
not in the copies, from whence the Keri and
the Chethibh were made. Now theſe irregularities are obſerved, both in whole words, and
in parts of words.

1ſt, In whole words ; theſe are either ſingle
words, or words combined, or divided. Thoſe
in ſingle words are when the conſonants are either redundant, or defective, or are wholly
ſuppreſſed. Of the firſt ſort, there is an inſtance in the fifty-firſt chapter of Jeremiah and
the third verſe ; where ידרך jidhroch, is written twice. And this ſuperfluous word hath no
points : which is thus accounted for ; that thoſe
who ſettled the Keri and Chethibh, finding the
word in their copies, durſt not ſtrike it out,
but perceiving it to be an erratum and ſuperfluous, they would not point it ; whereas had
it been pointed in their books, they would
doubtleſs have given it as they found it, and
no more have dared to expunge the vowels,
than the conſonants. Hence it is inferred, that
the Kerioth were more antient than the points,

---

* Capell. Critica Sacra, lib. iii. cap. xiv, xv.
† Capell. Arcanum Punctationis, lib. i. cap. vii.

and that the copies which fupplied them were unpointed.

Of the fecond fort, where the confonants are defective, we have an inftance in the thirty-firft chapter of Jeremiah, and the thirty-eighth verfe; where we have the vowels of a word in the Chethibh, without the confonants, which confonants are fupplied in the Keri; and without which fupplement the text is not fenfe. The Maforah obferves eleven inftances of this kind. Now it cannot be thought, the words were written thus originally, or by Ezra, or that any other tranfcriber through carelefsnefs fhould omit the confonants, while he fet down the vowels. Therefore it is fuppofed, that thofe who invented the points, found the word o-mitted, doubtlefs through the incuria of fome tranfcriber; yet durft not put the confonants in the text, but in the margin, and the vowels only in the text.

There are alfo inftances of the confonants being fupprefled in reading the text, by other confonants being put in their room in the margin; as, when the original word feemed to thofe who invented the vowels to be obfcene, and therefore not proper to be read, they have fubftituted another word in the margin, and put the vowels proper to that word under the word in the text. For inftance, in the eigh-teenth chapter of the fecond book of Kings and the twenty-feventh verfe; where the confonants in the text, cannot be read with the vowels annexed to them, which evidently belong to the confonants in the margin. We cannot, therefore, fuppofe, that the vowels in the text were originally affixed to the words they are now under, or that they were put to thofe words

before

before the invention of these marginal readings *.

There are observations likewise made on the
combinations of words. Thus the word
מאשתם meeſhtam, in the ſixth chapter of Jeremiah and the twenty-ninth verſe, ought to be
written in two words, as in the margin; for
the punctuation is not juſt, if the conſonants
are joined together; but agrees very well with
the conſonants, if they are divided.

Sometimes, again, we find one word broke
into two in the text, which are joined together
as they ſhould be, in the margin. In the thirty-
fourth chapter of the ſecond book of Chronicles and the ſixth verſe, בחר בתיהם bechar
bothehem, ought certainly to be one word, as
in the margin; otherwiſe the punctuation is
very irregular. Now the books of Chronicles
are generally ſuppoſed to have been written by
Ezra. But whoever wrote them, it cannot be
imagined, that this irregular punctuation was
in the original copy; but the conſonants hap-
pening to be afterwards divided through the incuria of the tranſcriber, thoſe who invented the
points, fixed them, as if it had been, what it
ought to have been, one word. Thus much
for the irregularities obſerved in whole words†.

2dly, The irregularities which are obſerved
in parts of words, or letters, are.

1ſt, A pleonaſm, when there are ſuperfluous
letters, either in the beginning, middle or end
of a word. In the beginning: as בבית for
בית beth (a): יצאו for צאו tſeu (b). In the

A a 2 middle

* Capell. Arcanum Punctat. lib. i. cap. xi. eſpecially,
§. 6,—9.
† Capell. Arcanum. ubi ſupra, §. 10.
(a) 2 Kings xxii. 5. Jer. iii. 11. (b) Jer. l. 8.

middle: as בְּרֹכֶב for ברב berobh (a): וְלַהֲלַחֶם
for והלחם vehallechem (b). In the end: as
אַשֶׁד for איש ifh (c): and בָעֵיר for לֵעֵי
langnai, and בעי bangnai (d): in all which
places the fuperfluous letter hath no vowel to
it; which fhows, that the vowels were affixed
to the text, fince thefe errors crept into it.

2dly, An ellipfis, or the omiffion of a letter,
either in the beginning of a word: as עָשֶׂה
for יעשׂה jangnafeh (e); where the vowel is in
the text, under the place of the confonant
which is omitted. So likewife לֹא for וְלֹא
velo (f): אֵין for וְאֵין veein (g): — Or in the
middle of a word: as תַּחְפַּנְם for תחפנחם tac-
caphanchem (h): אָנוּ for אנחנו anachnu (i),
where the nun and cheth are both wanting: —
Or at the end of a word: as אָמֶר for אמרו
ormu (k).

3dly, Permutation, or changing one letter
for another: as, וְדִכֶּה for ירכה jidhcha, vau
for jod (l); which error occurs in twenty-two
places: — יִשְׁאַל for ושאל vefhaal, jod for
vau (m); which error occurs feventy-five times:
— גִּרְל for גדל gedhal, refh for daleth (n): —
הָיָה for היו haju, he for vau (o): — and עָבְרִין
for עברך gnabhdhecha, vau for caph final (p).

4thly, Metathefis or tranfpofition: as, יוּמֶת
for ימות jamuth (q): — יָמֶוּת for יומת jumath (r).

5thly,

(a) 2 Kings xix. 23.   (b) 2 Sam. xvi. 2.
(c) 2 Sam. xxiii. 21.   (d) Jofh. viii. 12.   (e) 1 Sam.
xx. 2.   (f) Lam. ii. 2.   (g) Lam. v. 7.   (h) Jer.
ii. 16.   (i) Jer. xlii. 6.   (k) 1 Sam. xviii. 19.
(l) Pfal. x. 9.   (m) Prov. xx. 4.   Pfal. lxxvii. 12.
(n) Prov. xix. 19.   (o) Jofh. xv. 4.   (p) 2 Sam.
xiv. 22.   (q) Prov. xix. 15.   (r) 2 Kings xiv. 6.

5thly, Separation; when a letter is prefixed
to one word, which belongs to the next word
before it: as, הָיְתָה מוֹצִיא for הָיִית הַמּוֹצִיא
hajitha hammotfi (a): שָׁמָּ הַפְּלִשְׁתִּים for פלשתים
שָׁמָּה fhammah phelifhtim (b).

From thefe and the like inftances Capel infers, that the punctuation was regulated by,
and confequently is more modern, than the
Kerioth *; the time of collecting which, as I
have already obferved, he endeavours to fix to
about five hundred years after Chrift. We proceed now to the

2d. Clafs of arguments againft the antiquity
of the vowels; which are drawn from teftimony; and that, according to Capel, is either
tacit or exprefs.

Of the latter fort is the teftimony of Aben
Ezra, R. David Kimchi, R. Jehuda Levita,
and R. Elias Levita; who are all of this opinion †.

Tacit, or confequential, teftimony is taken
from the copies of the law, which are kept and
read in the fynagogues; or from the cabaliftic
interpretation, or from paffages of the talmud.

1ft. From the copies of the law, called
ספר תרה Sepher-torah, written on a fcroll of
parchment, and read every fabbath in the jewifh fynagogues. Thefe copies are accounted by
them the moft facred, and preferred to all
others; and they are conftantly written without points. But had the points been of equal

A a 3   authority

(a) 2 Sam. v. 2.   (b) 2 Sam. xxi. 12.
* Capell. Arcanum Punctat. lib. 1. cap. xi. §. 11. &
feq.
† Capell. Arcanum Punctat. lib. i. cap. ii, iii. Bux-
torf. de Punctor. Antiq. cap. iii. p. 11. & feq. & Capell.
Vindiciæ, lib. i. cap. i.

authority with the confonants, doubtlefs a pointed law would have been always looked upon as the moft facred *.

2dly, From the cabaliftical interpretations, which relate to the confonants, and none of them to the vowels. And hence it is inferred that the vowels were not in being, when thofe interpretations were made †.

3dly, From the talmud, which contains the " jura & decifiones magiftrorum fuorum," the determinations of the doctors concerning fome paffages of the law. It is evident, they fay, the points were not affixed to the text, when the talmud was compofed, becaufe there are feveral difputes concerning the fenfe of paffages of the law, which could not have been difputed, had there been points. Befides they never mention the vowels, though they have the faireft opportunity and occafion to mention them, had they been then in being. In the commentary on this paffage of the firft book of Kings, " After he," that is, Joab, " had fmitten every male in Edom (a)," the talmud relates, that when Joab returned from this expedition, he told David, that he had fmitten every male in Edom. David afked him, why he had left the females alive? Joab anfwers, the law fays, זכר zakar. No, faith David, we read, זכר zeker, memoria. Whereupon Joab went to afk his mafter, how he read this word? His mafter read it, zeker; and upon this Joab drew his fword with a defign to murder him. Now had there been points at this time, it would have been impoffible to have made this miftake. And had there been

* Capell. Arcanum Punctat. lib. i. cap. iv.
† Capell. ubi fupra, cap. v. §. 1,—3.
(a) 1 Kings xi. 15.

been points when the talmud was wrote, there would have been no room to have invented this story ; for the points determine it to be zakar : and besides, if the talmudists had been in pos-session of vowels-points, they would certainly have made use of them in telling this story, that so the sense might have been plain and not liable to be misunderstood ; whereas the two words are no ways distinguished, being both written with the consonants only.

Another instance of this sort occurs in the twelfth chapter of Leviticus and the fifth verse ; where the talmudists dispute about the meaning of the word שבעים. These consonants signi-fy, either two weeks, or seventy days. Now had the vowel-points been then used, they would have had the fairest opportunity of saying, it must be two weeks ; because there is a kibbutz under the beth ; and they would doubtless have written it, שְׁבֻעָיִם shebhung-naim ; whereas they put down only the conso-nants.

Again, on the fifty third chapter of Isaiah and the seventeenth verse they dispute, whether כל־בניך signifies children, or builders. The consonants may signify either, but the vowels determine it to mean children *.

We proceed now to the

3d. Sort of arguments, which Capel draws from the chaldee paraphrases of Jonathan and Onkelos, the greek versions of Aquila, Sym-machus and Theodotion, and especially that of the septuagint, by which he endeavours to prove, that the copy, from which they tran-slated, was without points. This appears with

A a 4 respect

---

* Capell. ubi supra, §. 4. & seq.

respect to them all, from their tranſlating ſeveral words in a ſenſe different from that
which the points determine them to mean. I
ſhall ſelect ſome inſtances from the ſeptuagint
only. In the fifteenth chapter of Geneſis, and
the eleventh verſe, for וַיָּשֶׁב אֹתָם vajjaſhèbh
otham, "he drove them away," the ſeventy
read וַיֵּשֶׁב אִתָּם vajjèſhèbh ittam, and accordingly render it και συνεκαθισεν αυτοις, he ſat
down by them, (that is, the carcaſes,) to watch
them, that the fowls might not devour them.
In the forty-ſeventh chapter and the thirty-firſt
verſe, for הַמִּטָּה hammitah, a bed, they read
הַמַּטֶּה hammatteh, a ſtaff; and accordingly
tranſlate it ραβδε αυτε. In the eighteenth chapter and the twelfth verſe, for עֶדְנָה gnedhnah,
pleaſure, they read עֲדֶנָּה gnadhennah, hitherto, rendering it εως τε νυν. In the thirty-ſecond
Pſalm and the fifth verſe, "I ſaid, I will con-
feſs my tranſgreſſions," or upon my tranſgreſſions; for עֲלֵי gnalèi, upon, they read
עָלַי gnalai, rendering it κατ' εμε (a). In the
forty-ſeventh Pſalm and the tenth verſe, for
עַם gnam, the people, they read עִם gnim, with;
inſtead of "the people of the God of Abraham," it is in their verſion, μετα τε Θεε Αβρααμ,
with the God of Abraham. In the thirty-
third Pſalm and the ſeventh verſe, inſtead of
כַּנֵּד cannedh, like a heap, they read כְּנֹד can-
nodh, like a bottle, rendering it ωσει ασκον.
In the ninth chapter of Hoſea and the firſt
verſe, for אֶל el, to, they read אַל al, not,
rendering it μηδε. In the firſt chapter of Joel
and the eighteenth verſe, for נָבֹכוּ nabhochu,

are

are perplexed, they read נִבְכוּ, nibhchu, wept, from בכה bachah, flevit ; and accordingly they render it εκλαυσαν. From thefe and feveral o- ther inftances it is infer'd, that the tranflators of the feptuagint had no bible with points ; or at leaft, that the copy they tranflated from, was not pointed as ours is.

The inftances of the like fort which Capel produces out of the chaldee paraphrafes, and other antient verfions, are not fo evidently to the purpofe of his argument, as thofe from the feptuagint.

Let us now fee what is replied to thefe ar- guments of Capel by Buxtorf and others, who contend for the high antiquity and authority of the hebrew points.

1ft, As to the argument drawn from the Keri and Chethibh :

Buxtorf admits the Keri and Chethibh to have been prior to the points ; and therefore, in order to maintain his opinion, that Ezra was the author of the points, he afferts, that it was Ezra, and not the Maforites of Tiberias, who firft collected the Kerioth and then regulated by them the punctuation in the text *. We have already taken notice of the reafons, which Ca- pel offers on the contrary, for allowing the Kerioth no higher antiquity than the time of the Maforites of Tiberias.

There are others, who affert, that the vari- ous lections, which are to be found in the Ma- forah, and part of which are inferted in the margin of the hebrew bible, are made upon the

---

the vowels, as well as upon the confonants *;
and they endeavour to fhow, that the various
lections upon the confonants are owing to the
irregularity of the vowels; and if fo, the
vowels muft have been prior to thefe marginal
corrections. Thus they prove the antiquity of
the points from the Keri and Chethibh; and
their argument is this : There are many inftances, where the confonants in the margin are
plainly fitted to the vowels in the text. But
had there been no vowels in the text when the
Keri were made, there would have been no occafion for thefe corrections; for the text might
have been read with other vowels, and the
fenfe of it much mended. For inftance, in the
eighth chapter of Genefis and the feventeenth
verfe, where the word in the text is הוֹצֵא
havtfè, bring forth, the Keri reads הֵיצֵא haj-
jetfè, divide; which is plainly fuited to the
punctuation in the text; for had there been no
points, they would rather have read it הוֹצֵא
hotfè, as it ought to be, and then there would
have been no occafion for this marginal cor-
rection. There is much fuch another inftance
in the fifth Pfalm and the ninth verfe, where
הַוְשַׁר havfhar, in the text is corrected by הֵישַׁר
hajfhar, in the margin; whereas it ought to be
הוֹשַׁר hofhar or הוֹשֵׁר hofhèr, in the imperative
hiphil, from יָשַׁר jafhar, rectus fuit. In the
twenty firft Pfalm and the fecond verfe, the
word יָגֵיל jageil, exultabit, is changed in the
Keri into יָגֵל jagel; but the confonants in the
text are regular in Hiphil, and fhould be pointed יָגִיל jagil. There could, therefore, be no
reafon

---

† See Whitfield's differtation on the hebrew vowel-
points, Sect. ix. p. 134. & feq. Liverpoole, 1748.

reafon for the Keri to leave out the letter Jod,
but only to make the confonants fuit to the erroneous punctuation in the text. In the fifty-
firft Pfalm and the fourth verfe, הָרְבַה, mul-
tiplica, in the text is corrected by הרב herebh
in the margin. Now had there been no points
in the text, they would doubtlefs have read
הַרְבֵּה harbèh, of which הֶרֶב herebh is nothing
but a contraction. In the fifty-ninth Pfalm and
the fixteenth verfe, יְנוּעוּן jenungnun, vagabun-
tur, is made in the Keri יְנִיעוּן, fuited to the
erroneous punctuation, יְנִיעוּן; for had there
been no points, inftead of making this correc-
tion, they would doubtlefs have read it יְנוּעוּן,
as it ought to be; for the fenfe is plainly in
Kal. In the feventy-feventh Pfalm and the
twelfth verfe, אַזְכִּיר recordabor; in the margin
it is אֶזְכּוֹר ezchor; whereas it might have been
as well read אַזְכִּיר azchir in Hiphil. In Pfalm
the eighty-ninth and eighteenth verfe, תָרִים exultabit, is changed by the Keri into תָרוּם ta-
rum, in kal; whereas תָּרִים tarim in Hiphil
better agrees with the context. See more inftances of the kind in the eighty-fifth Pfalm
and firft verfe, the hundred and fifth Pfalm
and eighteenth and twenty-eighth verfes, the
hundred and fortieth Pfalm and ninth verfe,
the hundred forty-fifth Pfalm and fixth and
eighth verfes; and efpecially the thirtieth Pfalm
and the fourth verfe, where מִיּוֹרְדִי from ירד
jaradh, defcendit, is corrected in the Keri by
leaving out the Vau, and fo making it the infinitive or gerund Kal with the affix Jod, מִירְדִי,
a defcendere me: whereas the fenfe is better, if
we retain the Vau, and point it, as the parti-
ciple

ciple מִיּוֹרְדֵי mijjoredhei ; according to the seventy, who render it απο των καταβαινοντων,
which is followed in the old englifh verfion,
" Thou fhalt keep my life from them that go
down into the pit." This inftance is faid to
have convinced Pocock above all others, of
the antiquity of the points.

However it may be obferved on this argument, that it fuppofes the Kerioth not
to have been various readings collected from
manufcripts, but corrections of the text, made
in conformity to an anomalous punctuation. Now, admitting that this erroneous
pointing was prior to the Kerioth, would it not
have been more natural to have put a Keri upon the vowels, than to have placed erroneous
confonants in the margin in conformity with
erroneous vowels in the text ? If we fuppofe
the Kerioth to have been the various readings
of different copies, all that feems neceffary to
account for their being often worfe than the
readings in the text, is to fuppofe, that thofe
who collected them were very injudicious perfons, or had a great reverence for particular copies, the readings of which they on that account preferred, though lefs eligible in themfelves than the readings in the text. Befides,
fuppofing the Kerioth were made in conformity
with the vowels in the text, we muft then fuppofe likewife, that with refpect to the inftances,
where we meet with points in the text without
confonants, the tranfcriber wrote the points,
forgetting at the fame time to write the confonants, which is very hard to conceive ; and
where we meet with confonants without points,
if the points were there when the Kerioth were

made

made, why fhould the points be omitted in the text any more than the confonants ? To the

IId, Clafs of arguments againft the antiquity of the points, which are taken from the Sepher-Torah, the Cabala and Talmud, it is replied,

1ft, As to the Sepher-Torah *, it is acknowledged, that the copies of the law, which were publickly read in the jewifh fynagogues, were always, at leaft as far back as we can trace them, without points. But to the inference, that the points are of modern invention, becaufe the Jews durft not make any alteration in their law, but would tranfcribe it juft as they found it, it is replied : that from hence it might as well be proved, that the Keri did originally belong to the law, (which is abfurd to imagine,) as that the points did not. The Jews give two reafons for the Sepher-Torah's being written without points. The one is, that it is thereby capable of more myfterious interpretations ; the other, that every one is bound to write over the law once in his life, or at leaft to get it written for him ; and it muft be written without any blunder, for one blunder profanes the whole. It is therefore proper it fhould be written without points, becaufe in fuch a vaft number of points it would be morally impoffible to avoid blunders.

Perhaps a third reafon may be added for the Sepher-Torah's being written without points, namely, that being written meerly for the ufe of fuch perfons as are well verfed in the hebrew tongue, (for it is not to be fuppofed, that any others are employed as publick readers in the fynagogue,)

---

* See Buxtorf. de Antiq. Punctor. part. i. cap. iv. and on the other hand Capell. Vindiciæ Arcani, lib. i. cap. ii.

synagogue,) there was no need to write it with the points, they being very capable of reading without them. But as M. T. C. is sufficient for one who is versed in the roman contractions, while a more unskilful person cannot read unless Marcus Tullius Cicero be wrote at length; so those copies, which were written meerly for the use of the learned in the hebrew language, being written without points, will by no means prove, that points were not necefsary for, and anciently used by, the more unlearned.

As for the assertion, that the Jews durst not make any alteration in their law, but would transcribe it just as they found it, and that therefore they would have inserted the points into the Sepher-Torah, if they had then been used originally, or had been invented by Ezra; this supposes, that the same superstitious regard was always paid to the characters and letters in, which the law was written, as hath been done since the time of the Masorites of Tiberias; and that the Jews would have scrupled to write out copies without points, for the use of their publick readers, who did not need them; which is not probable, even though they had looked on the vowel-points to be as authentic as the consonants.

Again, though the modern Sepher-Torah is written without points, yet we cannot be certain, how the fact hath always been, particularly how it was in the time of Ezra; for there are no copies of the law now extant, near so ancient as his time. As for the copy in the church of St. Dominick in Bononia pretended to be written by Ezra himself, it is in a fair character on a sort of leather, and made up in

a roll

a roll according to the ancient manner ; and it hath the vowel-points ; but the freſhneſs of the writing, which hath ſuffered no decay, prevents our believing it to be near ſo ancient as is pretended. We are not informed, whether the points in this manuſcript appear to have been written by a later hand than the conſonants ; but in many manuſcripts, examined by Dr. Kennicott, and thoſe ſome of the oldeſt and beſt, either there are no points at all, or they are evidently a late addition *. The

. 2d, Argument againſt the antiquity of the points was drawn from the Talmud, which makes no mention of them. To which it is replied †, not only that there are books ſaid by Buxtorf, to be older than the Talmud, though rejected by Capel as ſpurious, in which they are expreſsly mentioned ; but likewiſe that it is highly probable the Talmudiſts, though they make no mention of the points, nevertheleſs uſed pointed copies ; becauſe all the ſenſes they give of ſcripture, are agreeable to the preſent punctuation ; whereas if there had been no points, it can hardly be thought, they would always have given the ſame ſenſe of words, as the points determine them to mean. As to the

3d, Argument which is taken from the Cabala ; it is replied, that both antient and modern cabaliſtical writers have found myſteries in the points, as well as the conſonants. For inſtances

---

* See Dr. Kennicott's firſt Diſſert. on the hebrew text, p. 313,—342. paſſim. And Jſ. Voſſius aſſerts that in examining above two thouſand hebrew MSS. he had never met with any pointed, that were above 600 years old ; or if the books were older, the points were a late addition. Voſſ. de Sept. Interp. Tranſlat. cap. 30.

† See Buxtorf. de Antiq. Punctor. part. i. cap. vi. and in anſwer to him Capell. Vindiciæ Arcani, lib. i. cap. vii. See alſo above, p. 348.

ftances of which fee Buxtorf de Antiquitate.
punctorum *, and what Capel faith in confuta-
tion of him †.   The

IIId. Sort of arguments againft the antiquity of the points was drawn from comparing
the ancient verfions, particularly the feptuagint, with the original; by which, they fay, it
appears, that the hebrew copies, which thofe
ancient interpreters ufed, had no points.   But
thofe of the contrary opinion remark ‡,

1ft, That hereby one argument for the antiquity of the points is greatly confirmed;
namely, that without them the fenfe would be
uncertain.   It is pretended indeed, that though
there are a number of hebrew words of diffe-.
rent fignifications, whofe confonants are the
fame; yet where thefe words occur, the context will always determine the true meaning.
But we fee the contrary in thofe ancient verfions,
which are made from copies without points;
for they have frequently miftaken the fenfe by
reading with wrong vowels.

2dly, They remark that if this argument
proves any thing, it proves to much; for if the
copies we now have of the Septuagint, be juft
tranfcripts of the original verfion, we may as
eafily prove by it, that the hebrew copy, from
whence that verfion was made, had no confonants, as that it had no vowels; fince it differed as much from our copy in the former as in
the latter.   This appears in a variety of inftances, not only as to the letters, but likewife
as to words and fentences.

In

* Buxtorf. de Antiq. Punctor. part. i. cap. v.
† Capell. Vindic. Arcani. part i. cap. viii.
‡ See Buxtorf. de Antiq. Punctor. part. i. cap. ix, x.
and on the other fide Capell. Vindiciæ Arcani, lib. i. cap.
iv, v.

The hebrew points. 369

In the firſt place, as to letters: there are many inſtances

1ſt, Of the metaſtoicheioſis, or putting one letter for another. In the fifty-ſixth Pſalm and the ninth verſe, inſtead of א their copy muſt have had ג, in the word בנאדך ; for they read it בנגדך, and accordingly render it ενωπιον σε. In the ſixtieth chapter of Iſaiah and the fifteenth verſe, for ב they read ו, for עובר tranſiens, עוזר auxilians, and accordingly they render it ● βοηθων. In the thirty-fourth chapter of Ezekiel and the ſixteenth verſe, for ד they read ר, for אשמיד diſperdam, אשמיר cuſtodiam. In the eighth chapter of the firſt book of Samuel and the ſixteenth verſe, for ה they read ר ; for ועשה & faciet, they read ועשר, and render it και αποδεκατωση, & decimabit. In the ſixtieth Pſalm and ſixth verſe, for ט they read ת, for קשט veritas, קשת arcus. In the ſixth chapter of the firſt book of Samuel and the eighteenth verſe, for ל they read נ; for אבל, אבן λιθος. In the third chapter of Ezekiel and the eighth verſe, for מ they read נ; for מצחם frontem eorum, נצחם, νικος αυτων. On the contrary, in the firſt book of Samuel, the twenty third chapter and the ſeventh verſe, for נ they read מ; for נכר tradidit they read מכר vendidit. In the hundred and fourth Pſalm and the twelfth verſe, for ע they read ק; for עפאים frondes, קפאים, and tranſlate it πετροι, rupes. In the third chapter of Geneſis and the fifteenth verſe, for פ they read ר; for ישופך, conteret tibi, they doubtleſs read ישורך, which they render σε τηρησει, ſc. κεφαλην. In the eighth chapter of Iſaiah and the twentieth verſe, for ר they read ד; for שהר Aurora, שהד munus. Again, in the thirteenth chapter of Zechariah and the firſt verfe, for ר they read מ; for מקור fons, מקום locus. In the thirty-feventh chapter of Ifaiah and the twenty-fifth verfe, for ת they read ח; for ושתיתי & bibi, they read ושחיתי, as if from שחת perdidit; and accordingly they render it ηϱημωσα.

2dly, There are inftances of Epenthefis, or letters inferted in words in the copies they tranflated from, which are not in the prefent copy. In the twenty-eighth chapter of Proverbs and the twenty-eighth verfe, בקום in furgendo, they read במקום, and render it εν τοποις, in locis.

3dly, Metathefis, or changing the place of letters in a word In the twentieth Pfalm and the fixth verfe, for נהגל vexillum erigemus, they read נגרל from נרל gadhal, magnus fuit, and render it μεγαλυνϑησομεϑα (a).

4thly, Aphærefis, or leaving out letters. In Ifaiah the fourteenth and thirty fecond verfe, for מלאכי nuncii, they read מלכי reges, and render it βασιλεις εϑνων.

Thus much for a fpecimen of the difference in letters, betwixt the hebrew copy, from which the feventy tranflated, and ours.

Secondly, There appears alfo to have been a confiderable difference in whole words and fentences. In the fecond chapter of Job and the ninth verfe, there is a long fpeech of Job's wife in the feptuagint, which is not in the prefent hebrew copy. At the end of the forty fecond chapter there is a long genealogical hiftory, which is faid to be taken out of a fyriac book. There is a whole Pfalm added at the end of the book of Pfalms. Twenty verfes are left out of the firft book of Samuel about the middle

(a) Pfal. xix. 5. in the Greek.

middle of the seventeenth chapter *: In the seventeenth of Jeremiah there are four verses wanting in the beginning; and in the thirty-third chapter (a) thirteen verses at the end. There are also strange tranpositions, particularly the thirty-sixth, thirty-seventh, thirty-eighth and thirty-ninth chapters of Exodus are miserably confused.

So that upon the whole it appears, that if the septuagint version we now have be genuine, the hebrew copy it was translated from differed greatly from our present copy, as well in the consonants, as the vowels; and therefore it is said, that the argument drawn from this version against the antiquity of the points, will either prove too much, or nothing at all.

As to the hypothesis of Dr. Prideaux †, that the points were added to the hebrew text soon after Ezra's time by the ancient Masorites, and used in their schools in teaching to read the bible; yet not received into the schools of the rabbies till several hundred years afterwards: in support of the former assertion, he alledges the utter impossibility of teaching to read the hebrew without points, when it was become a dead language; which it is allowed on all hands to have been ever since the captivity.

This opinion, that the points were invented and used by the Masorites soon after the time of Ezra, who is supposed to have settled the true reading of the hebrew text, makes their authority very considerable. But if it can be proved, that they were invented a little after Ezra's time, because they were necessary to

B b 2　　　　　　　teach

---

* See Dr. Kennicott's second dissert. on the hebrew text, p 418,—431, 554,—558.　　(a) Chap. xl. in the Greek.
† Prideaux's Connect. vol. 2. part i, book v, p. 505, &c.

teach the reading of the hebrew, when it was become a dead language ; I fee not, but the fame argument will prove, they were invented in his time ; for the hebrew was a dead language then as well as after.

The latter affertion, that though they were not introduced into the fchools of the rabbies, till fome hundred years afterwards, is advanced in order to account for the filence of the Talmud, Jofephus, and Philo, with moft of the ancient chriftian fathers, concerning them. Now this filence will indeed prove, that there was no difpute about them in thofe times ; but, whatever prefumption it may be, it is no demonftration, that they were not then ufed even in the fchools of the rabbies.

Indeed it was fo natural for the inventors of the alphabet to contrive characters for the vowels as well as the confonants, that no fmall prefumption arifes from hence, that the prefent points were coeval with the confonants, unlefs the Matres Lectionis are fuppofed to have been the original vowels. To which fome add, the ufe of the points, in determining the different meanings of feveral words, which have the fame confonants ; particularly, in diftinguifhing the two conjugations of Pihel and Puhal in all the moods and tenfes except the infinitive. And this fhows, the modern points to be at leaft as ancient as the prefent ftructure of hebrew grammar. However, this controverfy not admitting of demonftration on either fide of the queftion, I fhall leave you, after confidering what hath been faid, and what Buxtorf and Capel have further offered, to judge for yourfelves, on which fide the greateft probability lies ; and

proceed

proceed next to confider the ufual divifions of the hebrew bible.

Of the general partitions and divifions of the bible.

The general title of the whole is עשרים וארבעה Nefrim vearbangnah, that is, the twenty-four, becaufe it contains twenty-four books; though, from a paffage of Jofephus in his firft book againft Appion it appears, that in his time they divided the whole bible into twenty-two books, correfponding to the number of letters in the hebrew alphabet. He faith, we have only twenty-two books, which are defervedly believed to be of divine authority, of which five are the books of Mofes. The prophets, who were the fucceffors of Mofes, have written thirteen. The remaining four books contain hymns to God, and documents of life for the ufe of men *.

At prefent the Jews make the facred books to be twenty-four; for they reckon Ezra and

Nehemiah

B b 3

---

* Jofeph. contra Appion. lib. 1. §. S. tom. 2 p. 441. edit. Haverc.

This paffage of Jofephus is much infifted on by Mr. Whifton and fome others, to difprove the divine authority of the book of Canticles. We have now, they fay, five books in our bibles, which anfwer to this title, Hymns to God and documents of life for the ufe of men; namely, Job, Pfalms, Proverbs, Ecclefiaftes and Canticles; whereas it is plain, that in Jofephus's time there were but four. Therefore the book of Canticles, they conceive, hath been added fince. See Mr. Whifton's fupplement to his Effay towards reftoring the true text of the Old Teftament proving that the Canticles is not a facred book; printed 1723, and on the other fide, a defence of the canon of the Old Teftament in anfwer to Mr. Whifton, by William Itchinger, M. A. 1723.

Nehemiah as one book, and the twelve minor
prophets as one, and the two books of Samuel,
of Kings, and of Chronicles each as one book;
which reduces the thirty-nine books according
to our division, to twenty-four. And these
twenty-four they distinguish into five of the
law, eight of the prophets, and eleven of the
hagiographa. The law, or pentateuch, which
they call חמשה חומשי תורה chamishah chu-
mishèi torah, that is, quinque quintæ legis,
contains the five books of Moses ; each of
which is called by the word, with which it begins, or the most confiderable near the beginning, as Bereshith, Shemoth, &c. The prophets, in Hebrew נביאים nebhiim, are diſtinguished into נביאים ראשונים nebhiim rishonim,
or former prophets, which are Joshua, Judges,
Samuel and Kings; and the נביאים אחרונים nib-
hiim acharonim, or the latter prophets; which
are again diſtinguished into the majores, which
are Iſaiah, Jeremiah and Ezekiel; and the
twelve minores, namely, Hoſea, Joel, &c.
which are all reckoned one book.

The hagiographa, or ספר כתובים ſepher
chetubbim, contain Pſalms, Proverbs, Job,
Canticles, Ruth, Lamentations, Ecclefiaſtes,
Eſther, Daniel, Ezra, Nehemiah and Chronicles. But in ſome books, as Athias's and
Plantin's editions, the חמש מגלת chameſh megillath, that is, the books of Canticles, Ruth,
Lamentations, Ecclefiaſtes and Eſther, are
placed juſt after the pentateuch ; and then the
hagiographa contain only Pſalms, Proverbs,
Job, Daniel, Ezra, Nehemiah and Chronicles.
The reaſon why the Jews divide them in this
manner is, that they might have no occaſion
to carry the whole bible to their ſynagogue,

but only the pentateuch and thofe five books, which are read at different feafts ; namely, Canticles at the paffover, Ruth at the pentecoft, Lamentations at the faft which is kept in July in commemoration of the burning of the temple ; Ecclefiaftes at the feaft of tabernacles, and Either at the feaft of purim. This laft book is written in a little roll by itfelf, and called מגילת אסתר me-gillah Efther, from גלל galal, volvit *.

The divifion of the bible into thefe three parts, the law, the prophets and the hagiographa, feems to be referred to in the following paffage of St. Luke, " All things muft be fulfilled, which are written in the law of Mofes, and in the prophets, and in the Pfalms concerning me (a)". As the book of Pfalms ftood firft in the hagiographa, or the third divifion, that whole divifion was commonly called the Pfalms ; as the whole book of Genefis is named by the firft word in it, and fo feveral other books. This enumeration, therefore, the law, the prophets, and the Pfalms, include the whole bible.

On the fame principle Dr. Lightfoot accounts for a fuppofed falfe citation in St. Matthew (b). " Then was fulfilled that which was fpoken by Jeremy, the prophet, faying, And they took the thirty pieces of filver, the price of him that was valued, whom they of the children of Ifrael did value ; add gave them for the potters field." The paffage here cited is not in Jeremiah, but in Zechariah. Accordingly Beza ftiles this difficulty, Nodus, qui vetuftiffimos quofque interpretes torfit. St. Auftin

B b 4   fuppofes

---

* See on this fubject Buxtorf. Tiberias, cap. xi.
(a) Luke xxiv. 44.   (b) Matt. xxvii. 9, 10.

supposes it to be αμαςτημα μνημονικον, a slip of St. Matthew's memory; which is by no means, to be admitted, if we allow that he wrote by the special guidance of the spirit of God. Dr. Wall, observing that Dr. Mill supposes it to be a lapsus calami of St. Matthew, thinks it more likely that the greek translator of his gospel should have been thus mistaken than the evangelist himself; and if so, saith he, it is pity somebody did not do here, as St. Jerom did in a similar difficulty relating to "Zacharias, the son of Barachias," who is said to have been "slain between the temple and the altar;" namely, consult the hebrew copy of St. Matthew's gospel before it was lost *. Indeed St. Jerom saith with respect to the present difficulty, that a nazarene Jew shewed him a book, accounted an apocryphal book of the prophet Jeremiah, where this passage is expressed verbatim †.

The learned Joseph Mede conceives, that these words, as well as several passages, which now stand in the book of Zechariah, were originally spoken by Jeremiah; but have been misplaced through the unskilfulness of the persons who collected their prophecies ‡.

However Dr. Lightfoot, by testimonies from the rabbies, shews us, that Jeremiah did anciently stand first in the book of the prophets. And hence he came to be mentioned before all the rest in the following passage of St. Matthew, "Some say, that thou art John the baptist,

---

* See Dr. Wall's critical notes on the New Testament, on Matt. xxiii. 35.

† See Dr. Wall on Matt. xxvii. 9, 10.

‡ Mede's works, book iv. epist. xxxi. p. 786. London. 1677.

tift, fome Elias, and others Jeremias, or one of the prophets (a)." Accordingly, as the whole hagiographa is called the Pfalms from the Pfalms being the firft book, fo the whole volume of the prophets is for the fame reafon called Jeremiah *.

There is yet another, and perhaps more probable, conjecture of bifhop Hall; who imagines, that Zechariah having been written contractedly, Ζριυ, was by fome tranfcriber miftaken for Ιριυ.

Others after all fuppofe, that the name of the prophet is an erroneous marginal addition, now crept into the text; fince the fyriac verfion only faith, " It was fpoken by the prophet," without mentioning his name.

I fhall conclude the whole with an account of the moft confiderable editions of the bible. I mean thofe which may be called pompous editions; for the plain, or the mere editions of the hebrew text, are too numerous for our attempting a detail of them. By the pompous editions, otherwife called Opera Biblica, I intend thofe, which contain not only the facred text, but likewife fome commentaries, or verfions, joined with it; and they are chiefly thefe four, the Biblia Complutenfia, Biblia Regia, Biblia Parifienfia, and Biblia Polyglotta.

The Biblia Complutenfia, fo called from Complutum in Spain, where the work was printed, is contained in one volume folio. It was publifhed under the care of cardinal Ximenes, anno 1514, containing the Old Teftament in Hebrew, the vulgar Latin; the targum of Onkelos

(a) Matt. xvi. 14.
* Lightfoot's Horæ hebraic. on Matt. xxvii. 9.

Onkelos on the pentateuch, and the feptuagint verfion, with the latin tranflation of both; alfo the New Teftament in Greek and Latin.

The Biblia Regia, fo called from Philip II. of Spain, at whofe charge the work was executed, contains eight volumes, printed at Antwerp, anno dom. 1571. with a better letter and paper than the former. Arias Montanus had the greateft fhare in this work; which contains feveral things more than the Complutenfian, namely, the chaldee paraphrafe on all the Old Teftament, with a latin verfion of it; the interlineary verfion of the New Teftament; and alfo the New Teftament in Syriac, expreffed both in hebrew and fyriac charaéters.

The Biblia Parifienfia in ten volumes, was printed at Paris, anno dom. 1645. at the charge of a private man, Michael de Jay; and therefore it is alfo called Jay's bible. It was done under the direétion and care of Dr. Gabriel Sionita, profeffor of the oriental languages at Paris, of Johannes Morinus, and Abraham Ecchellenfis.

It exceeds the Biblia Regia both in paper and in print; it hath, befides all which that contains, the pentateuch in Samaritan, all the Old Teftament in Syriac, and both Teftaments in Arabic.

The Anglicanum opus Biblicum, called the Polyglot, was printed chiefly under the care of Dr. Bryan Walton, in fix volumes at London 1657. This contains feveral things which Jay's bible hath not. It has Arias Montanus's interlineary verfion, the Septuagint from the Vatican and Alexandrian copies, which are fuppofed to be the beft; the old vulgate latin tranflation of the Septuagint, which alone, he tells
you

you, is that which the latin church ufed four
hundred years after the apoftles. It has the
perfic pentateuch in the perfic character, the
Pfalms, Canticles and New Teftament in the
Ethiopic, the jerufalem targum, the chaldee
paraphrafe of Jonathan, &c *.

Dr. Edmund Caftell, arabic profeffor at
Cambridge, publifhed a Lexicon for the ufe
of Walton's Polyglot in two volumes folio,
which generally goes with it, making in all
eight volumes.

* See the preface to the London Polyglot,

The END.

ERRATA.

INDEX of TEXTS
illuſtrated or explained.

GENESIS.

xxxv.

INDEX of TEXTS, &c.

INDEX of TEXTS, &c.

INDEX of TEXTS, &c.

A

xxxii.

INDEX of TEXTS, &c.

INDEX of TEXTS, &c.

INDEX of TEXTS, &c.

ISAIAH.

INDEX of TEXTS, &c.

ISAIAH.

Cc 3   DANIEL.

INDEX of TEXTS, &c.

INDEX of TEXTS, &c.

JOHN.

JOHN.

ACTS.

INDEX of TEXTS, &c,

xiii.

INDEX of TEXTS, &c.

x.

INDEX.

INDEX of HEBREW Words
and Phrafes explained.

בצאת

חדש

INDEX of HEBREW Words, &c.

לסרבה

קהל

INDEX of HEBREW Words, &c.

INDEX of HEBREW Words, &c.

INDEX of GREEK Words.

D d 2

γενεων

INDEX of GREEK Words.

INDEX of GREEK Words.

INDEX of GREEK Words.

INDEX of GREEK Words.

D d 4   Φορος

INDEX

TO THE

TWO VOLUMES.

NOTE, The Letters i. ii. denote the VOLUMES, the Figures the PAGES.

A

AARON, the high-priesthood alloted to him and his family, i. 194, 195. the manner in which it was limited to them, i. 198.

ABARBANEL, his opinion about the antiquity of the hebrew language, ii. 318.

ABEL, what his sacrifice consisted of, i. 148.

ABRAHAM, the Chaldee language was that of his country, ii. 331. He afterwards learnt the Hebrew by dwelling among the Canaanites, ii. 332.

ABSALOM, whether he was a Nazarite or not? i. 417. the prodigious weight of his hair considered, i. 418.

ADAM, the father of all mankind, i. 3. Special honours paid to him, i. 4.

AHASUERUS, king of Persia, the Jews dispersed in his reign, ii. 306. A question among the learned who this king Ahasuerus was, ii. 307. his kindness to the Jews owing to queen Esther, ii. 307. this name a common appellation of the kings of Persia, ii. 308.

AHAZ,

INDEX.

INDEX.

I N D E X.

INDEX.

H.

I N D E X.

a name

I.

INDEX.

I.

INDEX.

INDEX.

I N D E X.

E e 4   i. 401.

INDEX.

INDEX.

tabernacle,

notion

I N D E X.

I. **OBSERVATIONS** on divers Paſſages of Scripture, placing many of them in a Light *altogether new*, aſcertaining the Meaning of ſeveral, *not determinable* by the Methods commonly made uſe of by the Learned, and propoſing to Conſideration *probable Conjectures* on others, different from what have hitherto been recommended to the Attention of the Curious; grounded on Circumſtances *incidentally* mentioned in Books of

VOYAGES and TRAVELS into the EAST.

1. Relating to the *Weather* of JUDÆA. 2. Their *living* in *Tents* there. 3. Its *Houſes* and *Cities*. 4. The *Diet* of its Inhabitants, &c. 5. Their Manner of *Travelling*. 6. The Eaſtern Method of doing Perſons *honour*. 7. Their *Books*. 8. The *natural, civil* and *military* State of JUDÆA. 9. EGYPT. 10. *Miſcellaneous* Matters. 6 *s.*

II. A careful and ſtrict Enquiry into the *modern* prevailing Notions of that FREEDOM of WILL which is ſuppoſed to be eſſential to *Moral Agency, Virtue* and *Vice, Rewards* and *Puniſhment, Praiſe* and *Blame*. By the late Rev. Jonathan Edwards, A. M. and Preſident of the College of *New-Jerſey*. 5 *s.*

III. A Treatiſe on Religious Affections, by Jonathan Edwards, abridged by the Rev. Mr. Gordon. 2 *s.* 6 *d.*

Likewiſe in the Preſs, and ſpeedily will be Publiſhed.

I. A Treatiſe on ORIGINAL SIN, in Anſwer to Dr. Taylor. By Jonathan Edwards.

II. The ſecond Part of the Life of JOHN BUNCLE, Eſq;

III. The Chriſtian in compleat Armour. By W. Gurnall. A new and correct Edition, being the *ſeventh*.

A short Account of a

CHART of BIOGRAPHY.

By JOSEPH PRIESTLEY, L.L.D.

The Second Edition.

THE Chart of Biography, of which the Plate annexed exhibits a Specimen, is about three Feet in Length, and two in Breadth. It reprefents the Interval of Time between the Year 1200 before Chrift, and 1800 after Chrift, divided, by an equal Scale, into Centuries. It contains above two thoufand Names of Perfons the moft diftinguifhed in the Annals of Fame; and the Length of their Lives is reprefented in it by Lines drawn in Proportion to their real Duration, and placed fo as to fhew, by Infpection, how long any Number of Perfons were cotemporary, and how long one Life began before, or extended beyond another, with every other Circumftance which depends upon the Length of Lives, and the Relation they bear, both to one another, and to univerfal Time; Certainty being always reprefented by full Lines, and Uncertainty by Dots, or broken Lines. The Names are, moreover, diftributed into feveral Claffes by Lines running the whole Length of the Chart, and the Chronology is noted in one Margin by the Year before and after Chrift, and in the other by Succeffions of Kings.

As an Example of the Ufe of the Chart, let any Perfon but attend to the black Line which reprefents the Life of Sir ISAAC NEWTON; he will fee, by the Length and Situation of it, that that great Man was born before the Middle of the feventeenth Century, and lived till near the Middle of the eighteenth. He was born a few Years after the Death of Lord BACON, and about as many Years before that of DESCARTES. He was a younger Man than BOYLE, whom he outlived many Years; and Sir HANS SLOAN, MONTFAUCON, ROLLIN, BENTLEY, and LE CLERC, lived to about his Age, and were his Cotemporaries the greateft Part of his Life. Almoft any Number of Lives may be compared with the fame Eafe, to the fame Perfection, and in the fame fhort Space of Time.

The Price of the Chart, together with a Book, containing a DESCRIPTION of it, a CONTINUATION on a fmaller Scale, as high as the Creation, and a CATALOGUE of all the Names inferted in it, with the Dates annexed to them, is HALF A GUINEA.

It is printed for the Author, and fold by himfelf in Warrington; by Mr. J. BOWLES, in Cornhill; C. BOWLES, in St. Paul's Church-Yard; T. JEFFERYES, at Charing-Crofs; and R. SAYER, in Fleet-Street, London; where Specimens may be had gratis.

Paracelsus   Harvey   Beerhaave

Copernicus   L.^dBacon   Newton

Cardan   Descartes   Hans Sloan

C. Agrippa   T. Brahe   Boyle   Maclaurin

Calvin   Pascal   Shaftesbury

Luther   Grotius   Le Clerc

Erasmus   Arminius   Tillotson

Beza   Locke

Francis 1.st   Cromwel   Peter Gr

Columbus   Philip 2.^d   Turenne   Charles 12.th

Albuquerque   Henry 4.th   Lewis 14.th

Charles 5.th   Richlieu   Marlborough

50 · · · 1500 · · · 50 · · · 1600 · · · 50 · · · 1700 · · · 50

J. Priestley L.L.D. invet delin.^t   J. Mynde

www.ingramcontent.com/pod-product-compliance
Lightning Source LLC
Chambersburg PA
CBHW030941110726
47900CB00004B/1086